# A CHRONOLOGICAL                                              F

**1944**
**(cont.)**
National Building Regulations revised : Compulsory Annual Revision Act.
Introduction of Balbo (sliding) shuttering.
Completion of first of National Urban Birth Control Clinics, by H.M.O.W.

**1945**
Construction of floating platforms begun for revival of transatlantic air service : Sir Owen Williams appointed engineer.
Assassination of Adolf Hitler : tension in central Europe : industrial boom in northern European countries.
National aerial transport system initiated : construction of aerodromes.
State Control of Burial Act.
First long-distance heating station built in conjunction with new power station to serve N.W. London.
Cantilever Court, Hammersmith, completed.

**1946**
European chaos : second cultural immigration into England.
Compulsory inclusion of " craft " in secondary schools' curriculum.
Amalgamation of R.A., R.S.A. and D.I.A. to form new Art organization, the R.S.N.I.A.
First of the National Housing Estates completed at the White City.
Completion of the fourth Soviet five-year Plan.
Passing of Density Laws.
Appointment of National Committee to report on pre-fabrication and standardization of building.
Completion of first State Crematorium and Cemetery at Hindhead (The Devil's Punchbowl).

**1947**
Fascist Central European *bloc* : further cultural immigration.
Quinquennial Census shows first year of decline in English population.
Plans published for New B.B.C., which include State Auditoria for opera and symphonic concerts, light musical productions and ballets, and drama.
Professor Toyo Matakuro in London : lecture on Japanese sectional fabrication, arranged by MARS.

**1948**
Great International Architectural Congress held in the Zoological Gardens, Regent's Park.
New B.C.C. building completed : old B.B.C. building (owing to fort-like interior) acquired by British Union of Fascists.
Furnishing first represented on Housing, Pre-fabrication and Standard Committees.
Homer T. Franklin President of United States of America : 14th " New Deal " : National Recovery Act.
Completion of first English sky-scraper : 24 storeys in height.

### THE PRE-FABRICATION PERIOD
**1949**
Establishment of first factories for pre-fabricated, standardized units.
Appointment of specialists for research into high building problems : American engineers.
New plan for centralization of industry.
Experiments in stratosphere air travel.
Street advertisements limited to central urban zones : street signal colours illegal for illuminated signs.

Secon
F

**1950**
First l
Su
Presentation of National Planning Report.

**1951**
Central European War.
First Atlantic platform for heavier-than-air machines : new transatlantic air service
Pan-Asiatic Union.
*Duchess of Kent* launched : panel of architects appointed for " shipline " interiors.

**1952**
France and Germany involved in European War : war general throughout Europe.
D.I.A. secedes from R.S.N.I.A. (under old title of Design and Industries Association) as a protest against interior of the *Duchess of Kent*, demanding restitution of applied ornament : D.I.A. motto, " Fitness for purpose," altered to " Honi soit qui mal y pense."
First National Transport factory opened : standard cars, lorries and motor cycles.
Abolition of steel riveting by National Building Commission : the welding code.

**1954**
Housing accommodation catches up with requirements, aided by population decline.
Economic rustless steel production.
Formation of Psycho-phantasmagorical Group in Art : Exhibition at the Burlington Galleries.
Rival Art Group formed : the Neo-Somnambulists.
L.P.T.B. takes over goods distribution in central London zone.
Architect appointed chairman of Planning and Housing Commissioners.

**1955**
Mono-rail tracks for short-distance transport services.
Bernard Shaw's new play, *Enough Ado About Everything* : propaganda against Utopian housing.
Hire purchase becomes illegal.

**1956**
European Peace Treaty : brought about by exhaustion of economic resources.
Perfection of light-metal alloys : making possible (among other advances) stratosphere air travel.
Zoning extended to all large towns.
Private cars prohibited in central London zone.
Parking station programme in outer zone begun.

**1957**
Electric power and heat available for all urban services : fuel-burning prohibited in urban areas.
The great period of urban reconstruction : demolition of obsolete building to provide open spaces under the Zoning Act : the beginning of tower town architecture new central boulevards begun.
Charing Cross scheme suspended for reconsideration.
First auto-gyro garage.
Birth of Otto Arkwright.
Flat roofs made compulsory for play and landing grounds on all buildings of over 200,000 cubic meters.

# Serge Chermayeff: Designer, Architect, Teacher

## Alan Powers

RIBA Publications

© Alan Powers 2001

Published by RIBA Companies Ltd, which trades under the name of 'RIBA Publications', Construction House, 56-64 Leonard Street, London, EC2A 4LT

ISBN 1 85946 075 5

Product Code 20335

Publisher: Mark Lane

Commissioning Editor: Matthew Thompson

Editor: Ramona Lamport

Design Consultant: Ivan Chermayeff

Design: Bettina Hovgaard-Petersen

Printed and bound by Godfrey Lang Ltd, London

To Susanna

# Acknowledgements

In addition to those mentioned in the Introduction, I would like to acknowledge the following:

Harvard University Archives and Yale University Archives for permission to quote from documents in their collection; The Art Institute of Chicago for permission to quote from the interview with Chermayeff compiled by the Department of Architecture, Chicago Architects Oral History Project, 1986.

The staff of the British Library, London Library, National Art Library, National Monuments Record, RIBA Library and Drawings Collection, University of East Anglia Archives (Pritchard Papers), Tate Gallery Archive (Ben Nicholson papers), and Museum of Modern Art, New York.

John Allan, Alison Auckett, Amanda Baillieu, Charlotte Benton, Thomas Boss, Dr Sophie Bowness, Sarah Butterfield, Jim and Betty Cadbury-Brown, Nicholas Callow, Robert and Virginia Chapman, Maro Chermayeff, Olive Cook, Mary Daniels (Graduate School of Design, Harvard University), Nick Dawe, Howard Duckworth, James Dunnett, Alvin Eisenman, Rita Gibbs (Archivist, Harrow School), Patrick Goode, Michael Grice, Patrick Gwynne, Lady Hamlyn, Professor Bernard Hanson, Elain Harwood, Birkin Haward Jr., Robert Hornung, Richard Ivey, Ted Korth, Professor Diane Lewis, Timothy and Jane Lingard of Gallery Lingard, Nicholas Long, John McAslan, Max Marmor, Andrew Mead, Esther Mendelsohn-Joseph, Hattula Moholy-Nagy, Professor Gillian Naylor, Mrs Pompi Parry (Archivist, The Wilton Carpet Factory), Michael Payson, James Peto, Monica Pidgeon, the late Myfanwy Piper, Michael Rich, Margaret Richardson, Hedwig Saam, Deirdre Sharp (Pritchard Papers, University of East Anglia), Aileen Smith (Architectural Association Library), Gavin Stamp, Joanna Sutherland, Jill Theis, Professor Marc Treib, Barbara Tilson, Dennis Wardleworth, Brian Webb, Christopher Wilk, Caroline Wunderlich.

# Contents

# Introduction

I met Serge Chermayeff over the course of two days at the end of April 1994, when he was 93 years old. It was a memorable visit. I drove almost the whole length of Cape Cod before taking my hired car down a bumpy dirt track and pulling up in front of the colourfully painted house, set among trees which were just coming into leaf, masking the view of the pond on the other side. When I went in, Barbara, his wife, then aged 88, was sitting at the dining table while Serge was asleep in their bedroom. Barbara and I talked as the sun started to set over the pond, flooding the room with light, while the yellow winter jasmine growing outside the window deepened in colour against the blue of the sky and water. Barbara had clear memories of her own life before meeting Serge in 1927, and told me the legends of his own family in Russia. When it was completely dark, there were stirrings in the passageway and Serge came in, wearing a red checked dressing gown, bent over a walking frame. I assumed that he had been told of my visit but his first words, spoken with equal weight and great deliberateness, were 'Who are you?' Since he was completely deaf, it was hard to answer. We drank Martinis and had dinner, and the atmosphere loosened a a bit. I was able to show him photographs of 1930s modern buildings and textiles in two of my books which I had brought with me. Before we went to bed, Serge gave me one of the many felt-pen drawings which he made every morning, seated in his Thonet rocking chair.

The next morning we were able to talk more, about his old friends Raymond McGrath and Wells Coates, and about his sons, Peter and Ivan, whose work he often felt was more important and interesting than his own. He also talked about his own career as a tango dancer in the 1920s, before he became an architect, 'When I was young, we were all crazy about jazz … I was one of the best two or three dancers in the world.' Conversation as such was difficult, and required writing words on a slate for him to read. I explored the bookshelves in the studio, finding pre-war books with his bookplate, reading 'It cannot be too widely known that this book is the pleasure and property of Serge Chermayeff, please return, address in

1

London telephone book.' After lunch, I walked in the spring sun, paddled in the Atlantic, and departed, feeling that I had visited a different and largely forgotten world, but a vivid one which I had experienced fragmentarily through meeting other architects and artists of his generation. This world needed explaining and Chermayeff's life and work could offer a way into it.

In February 1992 I had given a lecture on Chermayeff in London, partly out of a personal curiosity to know more about this figure who was still living, but remote in time and space from England; and partly to test my own intuition that modernism - which many of my contemporaries in architectural history had decisively rejected - was redeemable if understood in greater depth. In researching and presenting the lecture, I had become fascinated by the diversity of Chermayeff's life and work, but also felt that there was an underlying unity. A book about Chermayeff, *Design and the Public Good*, edited and introduced by Richard Plunz, had been published in 1983, but had failed to create the revival of interest that was beginning to be enjoyed by colourful and significant figures of 1930s modernism in England such as Ernö Goldfinger and Berthold Lubetkin. Consciously or not, I had probably absorbed the admiration felt by my father, Michael Powers, an architect trained in the 1930s, for Chermayeff's unshowy, commonsense architecture and its demonstration of an almost Epicurean pleasure in simple living. The house my father built for us in Heath Side, Hampstead in 1959 seemed to echo in several respects both Chermayeff's Bentley Wood and his later house at New Haven. My father died in 1994 and I regret not having been able to share the development of this project with him.

Chermayeff had virtually withdrawn from contact with the world over the course of the previous fifteen years, and was further cut off by deafness. He had a reputation for not answering letters. Having sent him the text of my lecture, I received a reply, after several months' delay, which began, 'Am most grateful for your thorough research + clear account', and signed off, 'an old frail, forgetful + confused old man, Serge Chermayeff'. This was enough to make me feel that I should make the journey to Cape Cod, even though it had to be delayed for over a year. I cannot say that I knew Chermayeff on the basis of one meeting, although I was able to return to the Cape and talk again to Barbara and look at more of the documents in the house after his death on 8 May 1996. Barbara herself died in June 2000.

She was a great person and I could not have understood Serge without having met her too, but if I was too late to get Chermayeff's story at first hand from him, I have been very fortunate in the generosity of those who have preceded me in researching his life and work, most notably Professor Richard Plunz of the University of Columbia.

Professor Plunz allowed me to read the transcripts of taped interviews he made with Chermayeff between 1975 and 1980, as part of a project also involving the cataloguing of Chermayeff's papers and their deposit in the Archives of the Avery Architectural Library at Columbia, and the compilation *Design and the Public Good*, which is composed largely of Chermayeff's lectures and occasional writings. This book has been of special value to me because of its comprehensive lists of Chermayeff's architectural projects and their places of publication, as well as lists of his published writings and unpublished manuscripts. Few other architects have been so thoroughly and accurately documented. *Design and the Public Good* is not, however, a complete monograph on Chermayeff, through no fault of Richard Plunz, but rather because Chermayeff himself did not want one. Nonetheless, Professor Plunz's introduction to the book, with his comprehensive bibliography and list of buildings and their publication, has made the task of writing my own book infinitely easier. Anyone seriously interested in Chermayeff should make a point of using his book in conjunction with mine.

Another valuable text is the unpublished *Never Trivial* by Victoria Milne, based on interviews with Chermayeff and his friends and colleagues in the early 1990s, and commissioned by Ivan and Peter Chermayeff. A further interview text, available to the public, is one from 1985 carried out by Betty Blum for the Chicago Architects Oral History Project in the Department of Architecture at the Art Institute, Chicago.

Research for this book has mainly been carried out at the Avery Library of Columbia University, where the Librarian is Angela Giral. I am especially grateful to Janet Parks, the Keeper of the Archives and Drawings Collection, and her assistants at different times, Dan Kany, Anne-Sophie Laure and Jim Epstein, for keeping me supplied with documents in the course of a number of intense annual research visits, making large numbers of photocopies, and arranging photography for this book.

Ivan and Peter Chermayeff, the two sons of Serge and Barbara, have been generous, in the course of extremely busy professional lives, in their encouragement, loan of documents, hospitality and advice.

In the economics of contemporary architectural culture, a book and an exhibition become mutually dependent, and one cannot happen without the other. A retrospective exhibition of Serge Chermayeff is taking place in March 2001 at Kettles Yard, Cambridge, with a further, most appropriate, showing at the De La Warr Pavilion, Bexhill-on-Sea. The idea for the exhibition came from Michael Harrison, the curator of Kettles Yard, and was developed in collaboration with Caroline Collier at Bexhill, and her successor, Alan Haydon. Michael's support, and the research and travel funding from the Arts Council of England Architecture Unit which has resulted from it, have made a substantial contribution towards the book as well as the exhibition, the major funding for which has come from the Arts Council Lottery.

The family of Raymond McGrath, the Australian-born architect who was one of Chermayeff's friends in the 1930s, and the subject of an earlier research interest of mine, have also played an important role in bringing this book to fruition. His son-in-law Donal O'Donovan, who visited and interviewed Chermayeff in the course of preparing his monograph on McGrath, *God's Architect*, excited my curiosity about him at an early stage, and Norman McGrath, Raymond's son, one of the best architectural photographers in the world, has been particularly generous in making available photographs he has taken of Chermayeff buildings over a number of years, as well as undertaking a special shoot of the Payson House in Maine in the summer of 2000.

I have been able to talk to two assistants from the 1930s London office of Mendelsohn and Chermayeff, H.J. Whitfield Lewis and Birkin Haward, and his teaching colleagues in America, Gerhard Kallmann, Professor Eduard Sekler, Professor Jerzy Soltan and Professor Albert Szabo, all of whom have provided valuable first-hand reminiscences. I had an enjoyable meeting with the architectural writer Peter Blake, who knew Chermayeff from 1938 onwards and at one time began to assemble material for a book on him. I have also had valuable contact with the co-authors of Chermayeff's two books, Professor Christopher Alexander and Professor Alexander Tzonis.

Research for this book has involved many visits to the USA, and I am specially grateful to my hosts in New York on different visits, Elaine Hirschl Ellis and John Ellis, Ben Pentreath, and Rebecca More in Providence, from whose house I set out on my first visit to Cape Cod.

Financial assistance towards the cost of photographs and reproduction payments has been contributed by the Marc Fitch Fund, the Paul Mellon Centre for the Study of British Art, and Robert and Virginia Chapman, and I am most grateful for their support.

Finally, thanks to Mark Lane, Matthew Thompson and Ramona Lamport at RIBA Publications for their patience and understanding.

Alan Powers
London
November 2000

# The Education of an Outsider 1900-30

'My Russia is in a haze of small remembrances and large hearsays', wrote Serge Chermayeff to the Russian-born author Paul Grabbe, many years after his birth as Sergius Ivan Sergeyev Issakovitch, near Grozny on 8 October 1900.[1] His ancestors, according to family legend, had arrived in the Caucasus from further north in Russia. They were Sephardic Jews who had driven their cattle across Europe from Spain in the aftermath of the Napoleonic wars. It is uncertain whether their arrival in Russia, via the Black Sea and Poland, was deliberate or accidental but they became attached to Prince Kropotkin for whom Serge's grandfather bred bulls while his grandmother became a dancer in the corps de ballet of Kropotkin's ballet.[2]

The city of Grozny was built by the Cossacks sent to subdue the Chechen tribes in Daghestan in 1818. The area remained unstable until the final suppression of the legendary religious leader, Imam Shamil, in the 1870s when Cossacks were granted property rights and started to develop their land as estates - as did some of the Chechen who had cooperated with Russian rule. Somewhere in this pattern of development Chermayeff's grandfather, Akim Issakovitch moved into the area, opening an inn as a relay station on the way, before settling to breed bulls and horses among the Chechen and Ossetin tribesmen. He met Tolstoy when the writer was 'on his last romantic visit to the Caucasus'[3] and became a Tolstoyan, believing in a humanistic progress of all people. Serge remembered making a plasticene head of Tolstoy at the age of six for his grandfather as a birthday present. Prior to this, in Serge's words:

**Akim Issakovitch, Serge Chermayeff's grandfather.**

> Grandpa made everyone's life miserable around Grozny by getting a school established for the 'Mountain Jews' who spoke ancient Hebrew between themselves and spoke to nobody else in any language, were illiterate and even more prickly/tribal than the Chechen, with whom my family (most unorthodox) mixed in the deepest Moslem and General Caucasian sense.[4]

Akim Issakovitch was one of the constituents of a composite character, the engineer Ilya Isakovitch in Alexander Solzhenitsyn's novel *August 1914*. He and his family became fully assimilated with the Chechen, making pacts of blood-brotherhood with them, and also contracting the important relationship of milk-brother, the result of being placed with the same wet-nurse as another boy. The surname Issakovitch, derived from Serge's great grandfather, Issak, was only two generations old, since surnames were only introduced when the Russians conquered the northern Caucasus in the second half of the nineteenth century.

Through the connections of Serge's 'milk-uncle', Topa Chermoyoff or Chermoyev, who was an officer in the Imperial Guard and a friend of Grand Duke Nicolaivich, the governor-general of the Northern Caucasus, the Issakovitchs supplied horses to the Russian Imperial cavalry. It was from him that Serge took his adopted surname in 1924, a name apparently based on a village in Chechnya called Chermoy. He explained that Topa, who died in London in 1924, encouraged him to adopt the name, as did his own aunt, Judith Issakovitch, on the grounds that it would be less likely to provoke anti-semitism. He changed the spelling slightly, apparently because Topa Chermoyoff was seriously in debt and Serge did not wish to become liable for his debts.[5] His first name was sometimes used in the original form of Sergius on official documents.

About ten years before Serge's birth the oil in the Grozny area was first extracted from shallow pits, and in 1893 an English engineer, Alfred Stuart, struck the first two 'gushers' of a rich underground deposit, part of the Baku oil field extending into Persia.[6] The Issakovitch family's land lay over oil, and together with other local landowners, they became unexpectedly wealthy. As Chermayeff remembered the story, 'The valley was suddenly tapped by wildcatters who came out of Texas.'[7] One of them was appointed manager by Serge's father and grandfather but was murdered by bandits. A proper infrastructure was needed, and this was developed by a German, G. Spies, who came into the area in 1897 and had two partners in London, one being the young Calouste Gulbenkian, later famous as an art collector and benefactor. The Issakovitch family must have put their assets in Spies's hands, and even played a part in the company, for Chermayeff mentioned him several times in his reminiscences. The Grozny oil field was rich in gasoline, and Charles van der Leeuw, the historian of oil in the Caucasus, writes that with the advance in motoring, 'the position of the Grozny-based producers in the European market for gasoline had become seemingly invincible by 1910'.[8] In that year, Henry Deterding, the extremely skilful head of Royal Dutch, which had recently taken over the English Shell company, moved into the region and took over Spies and all the other producers without reducing their income.

Issakovitch family servants.

Left: the Issakovitch family at home in Grozny. Serge seated at front, c.1910.

Serge's father, Ivan, went to school in Odessa, where he worked as a banker and met his future wife, Rose Sonnschein. With their oil wealth, they were cosmopolitan and kept an apartment in Moscow, where Serge's mother liked to hold whist parties with much gambling that lasted for days on end, while his father, who hated parties, courted ballerinas. In fact, Serge's unmarried aunt, Judith, born in 1870, played an important role in running the oil company. One of his uncles, Constantine, was a doctor who ran a clinic near Grozny, later emigrating to Argentina and, among other achievements, breeding a cross between an apple and a pear. The family employed German, French and English governesses for their two children, Serge and his sister, Nina, so that they learnt several languages. One of Serge's earliest memories was of being woken up in the night and driven swiftly in a troika with his sister, away from the sound of gunfire, probably an anti-Jewish pogrom in the year 1906.[9] His time was divided between Moscow and the family home near Grozny, which stood in a broad valley. He remembered the great natural beauty of the landscape. Many members of his family were outstanding horsemen, and Serge became a good rider, naturally gifted in communicating with animals.[10]

There are surviving family photographs showing Serge's grandfather, a bearded figure in a dressing gown, and the family servants. Serge himself appears as a bright-eyed small boy who later grew to a height of 6ft 1in, and probably gave an impression of greater size because of his large head and hands. Chermayeff's early life was undoubtedly influential, although he never lived properly in Russia after the age of ten. Among a generation which carried forward the experience of the more spacious and hopeful world before the Great War, he had seen places where modern life had hardly begun to have an impact. This may have helped him, much later in life, to see architecture as one aspect of a worldwide problem of protecting the environment against the adverse effects of development. Amidst Moslems and the Russian Orthodox, his family were completely secular. Chermayeff liked what he knew of the Chechen, and the description of them in 1887 by a French traveller, Ernest Chautre, would have fitted his idea of a good society: 'They live as people unaware of class distinctions … They all possess the same rights and enjoy the same position. Chechen are gay and witty. Russian officers nicknamed them the French of the Caucasus.'[11] For most of Chermayeff's life, the world heard little of Grozny and Chechnya, after Communism suppressed the culture and language of the local people. As events of the 1990s have shown, the oil fields still play an important strategic role and local independence was far from being extinguished.

In the autumn of 1910, Serge was brought to London by his father to enter a preparatory school, Peterborough Lodge, in Netherhall Gardens, Hampstead, of which the headmaster was Harold Linford. The English involvement in the Grozny oil field may account for this choice, for Chermayeff explained in 1940, 'my father had always had a great respect for the institutions of England and had, further, a great attachment to that country.'[12] One would imagine that, for that time, it was a strange experience both for him and for the school, even though the prestige of English boarding education attracted many privileged pupils from other countries. He made friends among the English boys and claimed to have attended practically every theatre performance in London. One of his friends and a member of the theatre-going group, Bernard Linford (who must, presumably, have been related to the headmaster), later went into advertising and undertook the publicity for the PLAN Ltd. company which Chermayeff helped to establish in 1932. The only other significant information about these years of Chermayeff's life is his own account that he was entered for many competitions of the Royal Drawing Society and won a number of prizes.

This is the earliest evidence of his artistic leanings and is of some interest. The Royal Drawing Society was founded by T.R. Ablett in 1888, under the inspiration of John Ruskin, transmitted through Ruskin's editor and biographer, E.T. Cooke, in opposition to the prevailing dry art-teaching methods of the time which were imposed as a national system from the Department of Science and Art in South Kensington. Ablett encouraged children between the ages of four and 16 to paint and draw directly from life and from imagination.[13] The Society saw art as an activity for everyone and as a means of communication as good as words. It owned a cinematograph at its London headquarters in order to show films that would inspire children.

In 1912, the Society's reasons for the activity of learning drawing in school were described by Richard Whiteing, as 'not primarily to enable children to produce great works of creative art – these must ever come as they may – but simply to enable them to receive impressions of things and to record them in the only universal language in actual use to this date, the language of the brush'.[14] This essentially Ruskinian view of the value of art was given an up-to-date interpretation, in this, the year of the Second Post-Impressionist exhibition and the outbreak of modern art in London, in Whiteing's further comment that 'the very heresies of modern Art, charitably judged, are often but attempts to recover by violent means that contact with life and truth which ought never to have been lost from the very beginning of the course'.[15] Although not quite a precursor of the Bauhaus and its pedagogy of 'basic design', the philosophy of the Royal Drawing Society provides an independent statement of the use of art as an everyday practice and as a form of investigation with a moral element to it, seemingly disconnected from the other art teaching institutions of its time. It was a lucky beginning for Chermayeff, who intermittently did a lot of painting during his life and liked to think of this as his original vocation, coming before architecture. Can one even catch an echo of Whiteing's words in Chermayeff's comment on his daily drawing activity in his extreme old age, 'I do this to keep myself alive'?[16]

When he moved to Harrow School in 1915, Chermayeff was able to benefit from the art teaching of Egerton Hine, one of the best public-school art masters of the period, who included Victor Pasmore and Cecil Beaton among his later pupils.[17] Chermayeff recounted that there was a suggestion that instead of being a member of an ordinary school house, he should live in Egerton Hine's house, presumably in order to imbibe his artistic influence but this was not carried through. On two occasions, in 1916 and 1918, he won the Henry Yates-Thompson prize for Design and Colour. In 1917, the prize went to the Hon. John Seely, later a partner of the successful architectural firm, Seely and Paget. Chermayeff recalled in 1930 that Hine was 'a great friend throughout his school days'.[18] He also mentioned that 'I spent my war years at Harrow, between drawing rude pictures … of naked girls wearing silk stockings or very rude caricatures of people that everybody hated.'[19]

There is no known reason why Harrow was chosen for Chermayeff but being near London it may have been a school to which Peterborough Lodge sent a number of its pupils. Although perhaps less exclusive than Eton, it offered a good social start in life, and Chermayeff made several useful contacts for his future professional life, sometimes while on Officer Training Corps camps. His house was The Knoll. Chermayeff claimed, 'I swept through Harrow. I got three double removes, I think, and was in the sixth form at the end of three years instead of five.'[20] This is an exaggeration but he did well in exams nonetheless. In the summer of 1916, Chermayeff's father asked him to travel back to Russia, to see his grandfather who was dying. Despite the war and the presence of U-boats in the North Sea, Chermayeff made a visit via Archangel and a train journey to the Caucasus.[21]

In 1917 the outbreak of the October Revolution in Russia changed everything in his life. Chermayeff reputedly threw handfuls of worthless banknotes out of the window of his Harrow room. Although he was accepted for entry to Trinity College, Cambridge, he was unable to attend as his family suddenly lost all their money. As a matter of principle, his father had refused to move money out of the country, and his Aunt Judith hastened to hand over the oil fields to the Bolsheviks. According to Chermayeff, she was delivering the payroll to the work force and found that the local bandits had cut the throats of the manager and his family. She had come with an escort of two Cossacks and left immediately. Apparently, she surrendered the company with such good grace that she was offered a job in Paris in AMTORG, the Russian trade bureau, and thus escaped from Russia. Chermayeff's mother was having an affair with a man high up in the Bolshevik hierarchy which enabled her to retain the family home until she escaped with her jewels in the false bottom of a suitcase. His father, for whom an escape was planned with the British fleet which was supposed to rescue the Russian Imperial family, was generally in favour of the Revolution and refused to leave Russia until 1921 when both parents were reunited in Berlin, where Chermayeff spent three or four months with them. Serge's sister, Nina, escaped through Istanbul and married Douglas Williams, an English correspondent with Reuters. Having had a daughter, she separated from her husband and committed suicide in Paris in 1931, during an unhappy love affair with a Pole. Chermayeff's mother refused to come to England, but following her death his father was placed in an old people's home in West London where he died.[22]

In the various later interviews and written accounts, Chermayeff gave enough information of his life in the early 1920s for an outline story of his activities but it is hard to corroborate these from other sources. He left Harrow shortly before the Armistice and was apparently gazetted 'for about ten minutes' to the British Army as an interpreter to General Maynard who was conducting a war of intervention at Murmansk, but was almost immediately dismissed because of his conflict of interest as a Russian.[23]

Needing to earn a living, Chermayeff, through his brother-in-law, became an employee of the Amalgamated Press, an arm of Harmsworth Bros. Ltd. developed with personal attention from Lord Northcliffe, which produced popular magazines, educational part works and children's annuals.[24] He worked as an illustrator and reporter, which, as he remarked, was 'nicer than trying to be a bank-clerk'. The Amalgamated Press prided itself on the intellectual calibre of its staff and in 1925 declared that 'on the staff of the *Children's Newspaper* are some of the best known writers and scientists of today'.[25]

Chermayeff left Amalgamated Press after a year or two to take up dancing in London full-time. 'These were the days, 1919, 1920, 1921 – the finest American jazz began to make its appearance', he recalled, 'small bands . . . in all kinds of night clubs, and, you know, what is a young man with expensive taste to do after dinner, so to speak? … I taught people dancing and won a lot of competitions for the champion fox trot, waltz, tango, for several years.'[26] Chermayeff frequented a club called Rector's, and the more upstage Savoy and Berkeley hotels, where his perfectly tailored clothes and dancing were admired. As he said in an interview in 1994, 'I was a dandy. The Savile Row tailors used to give me suits, tail coats and evening stuff simply because I was such a classy dancer. I won enough international competitions so that I was quite in demand as a showman.'[27] He was not only in demand as a dancing partner but also as a lover, and in the liberated climate of post-Armistice London, girls would often invite him home. Sometimes, the band would stop when he entered the room and his dancing career culminated in his winning the International Tango Competition at the London Palladium in 1927, shortly before his marriage. Barbara was not a dancer and he put this life behind him. Rumours of this exotic early career circulated in the architectural world of the 1930s when Chermayeff may have preferred to forget it, but later in life he was justifiably proud of his achievement.

As a result of his dancing fame, an older friend, who was a judge, proposed that he should start his own magazine about dancing and offered to back the venture. This project came to fruition in the magazine *The Dancing World*, for which Chermayeff 'illustrated, reported and did everything'.[28] In 1922, however, he left London for Argentina, to work on the estancia of an English friend, Larry Thornhill. He described this in one interview as the result of a sudden disillusionment with ballroom dancing. Most of two years in Argentina were spent almost alone on a ranch but he claimed to have been a partner in a dance-hall enterprise in Buenos

Aires, and he also learnt the tango in its place of origin. He recounted: 'I learned the real tango without any sort of fancy steps. Really it was a slow walk with a slight wobble. Your feet moved, but your shoulders just swung, as if you were on skates.'[29] At the end of the two years, Chermayeff decided to return to London, working his passage back by accompanying a racehorse on board ship. The horse became ill on the voyage and nearly died, while Chermayeff had to clean up its quarters, but it perked up on sensing the approach of the Canary Islands a day before they actually reached them, and recovered.[30]

It was on his return to London in 1924 that Chermayeff's career in art and design began to take shape, coinciding with his change of name. While still at Harrow, he had produced paintings and sold them privately. As he described it, 'I was absolutely mad at painting imaginary submarine scenes, great lobsters and wonderful things floating around – I just loved drawing lobsters.'[31] He did not paint much in the early 1920s, although he recalled exchanging paintings with other artists such as Paul and John Nash, as well as buying a Modigliani for £20 before his marriage. When he visited his parents in Berlin in 1921, he could have seen interiors of theatres and other buildings, representing modern design. If the information on his RIBA Fellowship form, repeated with variations on later CVs, is reliable, he was also in Paris for some time in the period 1921-2, studying at the Ecole des Beaux Arts. The same form states that in the Argentine he worked with Nordiska Buenos-Aires, a branch of the Swedish department store, under a Mr Wirt, although no other evidence corroborates this. During 1924, Chermayeff also stated that he attended lectures and studios in Germany, and put in the word 'Bauhaus', before crossing it out. He certainly seems to have travelled to these places, and also to Holland, but the sparse and sometimes contradictory information makes it difficult to establish how these activities contributed to his education as a designer. His involvement with any teaching institutions was probably brief and informal but his knowledge of languages and quick intelligence would have meant that it did not take him long to find out what was going on.

On returning to London Chermayeff was given his first real design job in a decorating firm in Mayfair, Ernest Williams Ltd., at 27 Davies Street, of which an old Harrovian friend, Ronald Trew was a partner. Williams himself was a specialist in period interiors, and Chermayeff seems to have been recruited partly to respond to the emerging demand for something more novel, although historical reconstructions provided the majority of the work. Trew had contacts which brought in the commissions, including a redecoration of suites at Claridges Hotel for the manager, Mr Mambrino. Chermayeff relates that he 'did all the important suites, painting fish myself in the bathrooms'.[32]

The Ernest Williams phase of Chermayeff's career lasted until 1928. It would have given him a background in dealing with craftsmen and clients, the essentials of running a job which became the basis for his later career as an architect for which he received no other formal training. One job listed on his RIBA Fellowship nomination form for this period was alterations and decoration at Hedsor Park, near Cookham in Buckinghamshire, a Victorian house which was Georgianised in 1925 for Darcy Baker, including classical interiors and a marble bathroom.[33] He also developed contacts in the theatrical world in London, becoming a friend of the actor-producer Gerald du Maurier, another old Harrovian who maintained his links with the school. Chermayeff designed sets for drawing-room comedies, in which he claimed that he was able to be more experimental in design than with private clients. One of these was *The Last of Mrs Cheyney* by Frederick Lonsdale, in which Du Maurier appeared with Gladys Cooper who played a high-society lady jewel thief. The production opened in September 1925 at the St. James's Theatre and ran on well into the following year. Chermayeff's sets were relatively conventional, although there was in the regular square panelling of the drawing room set (misleadingly described in *The Times* as 'ultra-modern') a feeling of architectural discipline which went beyond the conventional.[34] Chermayeff also mentioned having made the acquaintance of George Bernard Shaw in this theatrical milieu.

Barbara and Serge Chermayeff, c.1928.

Left: stage set for The Last of Mrs Cheyney by Frederick Lonsdale, starring Gladys Cooper (centre stage), St James's Theatre, London, 1925-6.

The most significant event of this period, however, was Chermayeff's meeting with his future wife, Barbara Maitland May, born in 1904, the elder of two daughters of Frank May – a director of the high-quality London building firm, Holland, Hannen and Cubitts – and his wife Sibyl. Barbara had been educated at Heathfield School and excelled in all sports, including sailing on the River Alde at Aldeburgh, Suffolk in the summer holidays. She was not an intellectual girl but modern in spirit and impatient of convention. She had already visited America, staying with a school friend in New York, but had come back to live with her family at their country house, Abbot's Wood, at Puttenham, Surrey. One weekend in July 1927, she accepted an invitation to play tennis with neighbours and there met Chermayeff, who was immediately attracted by her beauty and personality. He did not know that she had recently had her horoscope cast by 'a French colonel in white gloves' whom she had met at a London party, who had predicted that on this weekend she would meet her future husband. On account of this she had originally intended to cheat fate by staying at home while her mother and sister went away for the weekend, but she got bored by Saturday afternoon, not knowing what lay in store on the tennis court.[35] Her younger sister, Jocelyn, had recently married a

Belgian painter, Georges LeBrun, and Barbara's mother apparently initially resisted having another foreign son-in-law. The marriage took place, nonetheless, early in 1928, coinciding with Serge's naturalisation.[36] Very soon, Serge and his mother-in-law, who left her husband and flouted convention by having a long-running and deeply-felt love affair with a married man, became close friends and allies, and at the end of her 103 year life she lived with Serge and Barbara in New Haven and Cape Cod.

On Chermayeff's behalf, the Chairman of Holland, Hannen and Cubitts, J.B. Stevenson, approached Lord Waring, the chairman of Waring and Gillow, one of the leading firms for furniture and interiors in London, based on an amalgamation with the distinguished Lancaster firm of Gillow, with a history going back to the late eighteenth century. The firm provided complete interiors for houses, hotels and ocean liners and, although it did not operate as an architectural practice, could also provide architectural designs for the houses themselves. Through this connection, Chermayeff was appointed Director of the Modern Art Studio and Department at Waring and Gillow, a firm described by the design writer Noel Carrington as 'favoured equally by maharajahs and shipping companies'.[37]

This new venture was a response to the increasing publicity afforded to modern design in England.[38] As Chermayeff described it in 1979, 'the Modern Art Department was something sold by SC to Lord Waring with the full backing of J.B. Stevenson, a Director and Chairman of Holland, Hannen and Cubitt … I had been to Germany and France with my eyes wide open before I got the Waring job.'[39] The established French designer Paul Follot (1877-1941) had already been engaged to bring the new style of design and decoration popularised by the Paris Exhibition of 1925 to the Parisian branch of Waring and Gillow, and Chermayeff was engaged to supervise the London end. Much later, he acknowledged the value of going into an established firm, writing that 'My designs, developed with a talented group of younger men as my assistants, were produced by the Gillow factory. This was staffed by a remarkable group of elderly cabinet makers of great knowledge and skill. These, to my surprise, welcomed the change from a tradition going back to the eighteenth century and became enthusiastic collaborators.'[40] Follot referred to his junior collaborator as 'Mon cher Mayeff'.

The Department was launched with a large exhibition, Modern Art in French and English Furniture and Decoration, on the fourth and fifth floors of Waring and Gillow's premises at 164-180 Oxford Street, with 68 room arrangements, which opened in November 1928 and carried on into the following January. The mood of the moment seemed right. The Ideal Home Exhibition in March that year had featured 'The House of the Future', designed by the architects R.A. Duncan and S. Rowland Pierce, which attracted attention as one of the first home-grown manifestations of modernism, including 'futuristic' labour-saving devices.[41] As the historian Barbara Tilson notes in her account of the Waring and Gillow Modern Art Department, the London firm of James Shoolbred & Co. held an exhibition with a modern flavour slightly earlier than Waring and Gillow,[42] although this included mostly bedroom furniture and was gathered together from existing designs by various manufacturers.[43] Exhibitions of design attracted publicity, something which Chermayeff, with his early background in journalism, understood and succeeded in developing. Lord Waring's speech at the opening was printed in full in *The Times*, only discreetly acknowledged as an advertisement, while also receiving editorial coverage.[44]

Follot also spoke at the opening, celebrating the strength of the design revival in post-war France (including not only furniture and interiors but posters and graphics) and its effect in changing production techniques and driving out teaching based solely on past precedent. While supporting the idea of a new style for the age, he also advocated a style of practical comfort in the home:

> The seats will be lower, deeper, softer, because our hurrying life demands more repose, and our clothes and our less decorous customs permit of freer attitudes. Living and working more and more in the evening, we require at the time more light, and light which does not hurt the eyes. Again all the incandescent points of the lamps will be hidden, and the lighting effect will be greatly increased by improved methods of diffusion, refraction or reflection.[45]

One of the most enthusiastic reviews came from Christopher Hussey, in *Country Life*, who believed that the intention to be moderate had been successfully realised, 'There is a delightful feeling of comfort and intimacy about their rooms, without the weight of conscious antiquity that is often oppressive in the twentieth century home. They have, in fact, done what the great English designers of the past did: met changing requirements by clear thinking, superlative workmanship, and forms in harmony with the taste of their age.'[46] An editorial, the following week, asserted that the new style 'has outgrown cubist forms, jazz decoration and general lawlessness and now comes before us with a striking air of dignity and repose'.[47] Ralph Edwards, a noted furniture historian, wrote to the magazine to express the hope that the development of worthwhile new forms would save craftsmen from their present role largely as makers of reproduction antiques.

The choice of the word 'Art' in the title of the department, rather than design or decoration, was unusual and slightly provocative. Apart from the activities of an avant-garde fringe such as Roger Fry's Omega Workshops 1913–19, interiors had not generally been seen as an aspect of 'art' in England since around 1900, when the Arts and Crafts movement was largely replaced by a conservative neo-Georgianism, alternating with neo-Tudor. The word seems to have been used quite loosely in the context of Waring and Gillow and, unlike the Omega workshop, they made no promises to employ artists as designers. The 'art' must have been implied in the refinement of the designs on offer and in the attention given to the complete ensemble of the room, something which England was only learning slowly from France, where interior designers like Follot were often known as 'ensembliers'. Chermayeff spoke more briefly at the exhibition opening, showing slides of buildings which demonstrate how he was already extending his concern to architectural problems.[48]

The word 'Modern' had only recently begun to acquire a special meaning in England, and although current by the late 1920s, had no clear definition.[49] During the 1920s there was a mounting frustration among designers and the small number of interested amateurs, represented by the Design and Industries Association (DIA), founded in 1915 with the slogan 'Fitness for Purpose', who looked abroad to France, Germany and Holland without necessarily approving of all that they saw. A prominent DIA member, W.J. Bassett-Lowke, commissioned a house, 'New Ways' outside Northampton from Peter Behrens in 1925, and this attracted attention with its white walls and cubic shape. The *Architectural Review* began to publish articles on the work of architects such as Walter Gropius and Hans Poelzig in 1925. Le Corbusier's *Vers une Architecture* with its appearance of iconoclasm, became a minor sensation when published in English translation in 1927. These events created a lot of excitement around the idea of modernism, but also a tendency to view it as irredeemably foreign, and as something that appealed only to a minority. While the Waring and Gillow exhibition was well-publicised, Chermayeff appears to have considered it only a qualified success, at least to judge from the brief biographical text (which he presumably supplied himself) appearing beside his photograph in *Country Life* in 1932 and describing it as a 'courageous but unsuccessful attempt to popularise modern furniture and decoration in this country to the same extent as it enjoys abroad'.[50]

In an interview in *The Cabinet Maker and Complete House Furnisher*, a journal which responded enthusiastically to the Waring and Gillow exhibition, Chermayeff quoted the views of 'an old and delightful gentleman, an architect by profession, that he was proud to have spent his life carrying out the work which was the most intimate and human among the arts. He went on to qualify this statement by saying that he had tried to do everything from the designing of the house itself down to the finishing touches in the detail of the knives and forks, so that each component of the whole bore a direct relation to the others.'[51] This survivor was probably C.F.A. Voysey, who was then living in chambers in St. James's, frequenting the Arts Club in Dover Street, and beginning to enjoy a revival among a younger generation. The identification is strengthened by Chermayeff's direct mention of Voysey in a broadcast of 1932, where he said 'Mr Annesley Voysey, the father of contemporary architecture, said that he found it as important to design the pepper-pot for the dining room as to design the house in which it was to be used'.[52] Voysey had a compelling message, and gave Chermayeff a link to the ideology of the Arts and Crafts movement of the 1890s with its view of architecture as an activity intimately linked to the art of the room, one which in turn was to be governed by a sense of fitness which was both functional and moral. The artistic culture of the previous century had to a large extent gone underground in England, even though it provided the inspiration for modernism in Europe, but through Voysey and the Royal Drawing Society Chermayeff had direct links to it. Voysey's doctrine accords with Follot's message of harmony as the basis of psychological comfort, both being at odds with the sensationalist character of some of the few modern rooms in London of this date, and the more numerous examples across the channel. There is more than a hint of scorn in the contrast made by Chermayeff between Voysey's approach and that of 'a very young architect, no doubt conscious of his own superiority over mere mortals who were not entitled to a degree from an august body', who had stated that the interior was not the architect's responsibility.

Chermayeff's early published statements, including an article 'Modernism' in the *Cabinet Maker* in June 1930, show his concern with the historical background of the new movement, and a pleasure in using it as the basis for discussion, which soon led to him becoming one of the principal spokesmen for it, in print, on radio and on the lecture platform. Speaking on 'Modern Furniture' at the Victoria and Albert Museum Chermayeff gave a straightforwardly Corbusian definition of 'modern', based on 'a new spirit and ideals' produced by contemporary conditions, as those 'works ... and their creators ... who have contributed to the expression of this spirit and those ideals which are peculiarly of our time'. He expressed a suspicion of self-conscious modernism or 'functionalism' and like Le Corbusier, he was far from condemning the work of the past. Even though Chermayeff was probably as well informed about continental modernism as most designers working in London, he explained the Waring and Gillow exhibition as an attempt to adapt French and German modernism to English taste by eschewing its more dramatic qualities in favour of a quieter style. As he wrote, 'The somewhat hackneyed phrase about the "Englishman's home" contains too much truth, not to bear repetition. It is in direct relation to this basic characteristic of the nation that the new English style is being constructed.'[53] Perhaps it was easier for an Englishman by adoption, who had grown up among the kind of wealthy but liberal-minded middle-class people who were the likely patrons of new furniture and decoration, to have this outsider's perception of Englishness, although some critics felt that his version was still excessively foreign. The intention was more significant than its realisation, since it indicated a faith in the combination of commonsense and good craftsmanship that Chermayeff recognised as underlying past achievements in England. Some commentators made reassuring parallels between what was on show at Waring and Gillow and the revered works of the English past, one of them, John C. Rogers, writing that the designs were 'as truly fitting for the everyday use of any modern town dweller as the fashionable creations of Chippendale in the eighteenth century'.[54]

Chermayeff wanted to make modern furniture and other items which would have sufficient integrity to work with the best of the older design. He also introduced the theme of comfort, which in different forms was to run throughout his career, writing that 'The modern school of designers who know their mediums, and the demands of today, have created interiors which are noteworthy for their combination of Art and Comfort, the last being the natural requirement of the age from the former.'[55] At the same time, Chermayeff introduced some tubular steel furniture into the Waring and Gillow exhibition which demonstrated a much more modern outlook. The upright chair which was illustrated alongside a round table on steel strap legs, is a rather hesitant piece, but still appears to have been one of the first of its kind made in England.[56]

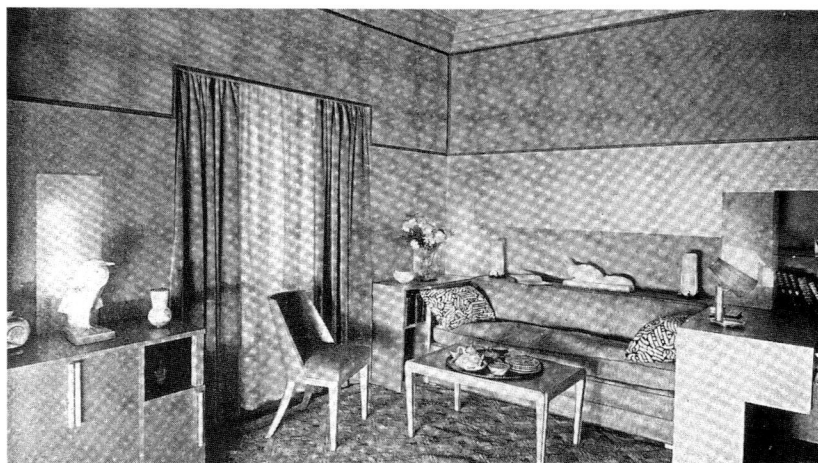

Paul Follot and Serge Chermayeff, metal chair and table for Waring and Gillow, 1929.

Right: 'Young girl's boudoir', Modern Art in French and English Furniture and Decoration, Waring and Gillow, 1928. 'An amusingly decorative scheme on very geometric lines in both the decoration and the furniture is carried out in panelling of ash and oak cellulosed silver. The upholstery and frieze are in a grey and green fabric in the same spirit as the carpet. An unusual feature of the room is the mantelpiece composed entirely of mirrors with a very modern clock.' (Text from exhibition catalogue.)

Colour was an important aspect of Chermayeff's work from the beginning. He had a preference for light and cheerful colours, using a lot of pale yellow and setting it off against pale blue. This combination remained constant through many phases of his work, appearing in the paintings he did in the last decades of his life. Strong colour was a feature of many rooms in the 1920s, often being the most daring aspect of an otherwise traditional looking room. Amateur decorators found it an easy way of creating an 'amusing' effect. Chermayeff wanted to find a more solid rationale for the use of colour, and he also related it to the clothes of the women who would be in the rooms, writing that 'as she dresses so frequently in what we may describe as pastel shades it becomes necessary to employ in furnishing tints which will not decoratively kill her stone dead'.[57] At this early stage he began using broad drum-shaped lamp shades, wrapped in pleated silk, as his preferred form of standard lamp. He went on using them throughout the 1930s, when other styles had become more fashionable, explaining in 1937, 'I still think that light through silk is the most becoming to women.'[58]

The Waring and Gillow exhibition rooms offered a range of modern styles, responding to the different anticipated tastes of men and women, and to preferences for English or French styles, consisting of a 'French apartment', mostly by Follot, and an 'English flat', mostly by Chermayeff, each with its suite of rooms. Chermayeff's role was as a design director, coordinating the work of others as well as contributing his own. His own attributable pieces included furniture and flat patterns on rugs and furnishing fabrics, the latter not differing greatly from similar work being produced in France and England at the time. The rugs, which were handmade by Royal Wilton with large geometric motifs, were often very similar to the paintings of Robert Delaunay, signed with the initials S.C. One, with a radial pattern, appeared in the 'Entrance Hall in Oak'.[59] In the 'Drawing Room in Mahogany', Chermayeff designed a carpet with a repeat pattern of tartan-like squares, set on the diagonal, with a curtain fabric of similar design.

Serge Chermayeff and Denham McLaren, 'Man's bathroom', Modern Art in French and English Furniture and Decoration, Waring and Gillow, 1928. 'The Bathroom is designed to amuse as well to provide utilitarian application of modern materials. The scheme of black, white, red and metal shelves, rubber flooring and oilcloth curtains leaving a clean untarnished surface, no matter how full of steam the room may be. The furniture in metal by Denham McLaren, exercisers and a punch ball, give a combination of the decoratively amusing and hygienic.' (Text from exhibition catalogue).

Left: Serge Chermayeff, 'Dining room', Modern Art in French and English Furniture and Decoration, Waring and Gillow, 1928, with sideboard veneered in macassar ebony in background (pair to 'buffet' now in collection of Royal Pavilion, Museum and Art Gallery, Brighton), painting of Adam and Eve by Edmund Dulac, 'the colour note of the room is black and yellow'.

The furniture is typically veneered on to cubic-looking shapes, mostly symmetrical, although the 'reading table' from 'A Young Girl's Sitting Room' has a desk surface cantilevered from a plinth with a bookstand and a standard lamp arching over it. Some pieces were given canted corners so that they could be assembled into groups. The cocktail cabinet in the dining room was designed as a 'counterchange' of the sideboard, one with side wings in coromandel ebony and a walnut centre, the other externally identical but with the materials reversed.[60] The Department was supported by the skilled craftsmen in the Waring and Gillow workshops whose skills in veneering had been developed in making reproduction Georgian furniture and could now be turned to international fashion of the period, displayed in the work of Eric Ruhlmann and many other French Art Deco designers.

The designer Hamilton T. Smith of Heal's, speaking at the Architectural Association in March 1929, complained that the furniture in the Waring and Gillow exhibition was 'really designed by an architect accustomed to working in marble rather than by a furniture designer accustomed to working in wood',[61] although it conformed to the widespread 'look' of the period. His assumption was unintentionally ironic, given that Chermayeff was still to become an architect. A 'Lady's Bedroom' in the English flat, in macassar ebony, illustrated in colour in the *Studio* (see page 155), has smooth curved corners and a contrasting band of lighter walnut veneer dividing the main surface from a recessed base. Hamilton Smith saw this as being entirely French in character, rather than English as claimed. Perhaps these distinctions were a hostage to such critics. They certainly did not project Englishness as it was currently understood, for in a reply to Hamilton Smith's paper, the architect Grey Wornum said that although the bedroom 'has been a tremendous favourite with the entire public', it only showed that Chermayeff had proved that 'the Englishman's home is a secret of the Englishman, and must be more or less created by the Englishman with an English tradition behind him all through'.[62]

'Living room', Waring and Gillow Ltd., London, c.1929. 'A centre group in Australian walnut . . . the settees can be moved to sides of fireplace without disturbing unity. The centre of the tea table rises, containing a complete cocktail cabinet.'

Some of the room sets were designed by Follot, and some by other designers, notably the exceptional young English designer Denham Maclaren (1903–89), whose pieces Chermayeff included in a number of his rooms.[63] Maclaren designed the 'Man's Bathroom', with a black glass lining to the bath recess and a lightweight chrome-framed chair and what appear to be geometric abstractions of coloured rectangles on a glass inner door and a wall panel.[64] This looks the most 'modern' of the interiors to later eyes. In some rooms, the work of several designers was mixed together, including an iron fire screen by the well-known French metalwork designer Edgar Brandt in the 'Drawing Room'.

The work of the Modern Art Studio stands on the cusp of Art Deco and Modernism, insofar as either of these terms has a well-defined edge. Follot's work was more inclined to floral decoration, while geometric 'Jazz' patterns appear in some of Chermayeff's rooms, but never subsequently in his independent commissions. Many designers in England who later became well-known as modernists entered via this route, including Joseph Emberton and Wells

Coates. Denham Maclaren's round glass table of 1930, published in a puzzling sideways photograph in the *Architectural Review*, and his chair of the same year, with glass sides and a zebra-skin padded seat, were representative of the latest Parisian style, altogether more adventurous than any of Chermayeff's early pieces.[65] He was also travelling in Europe at this time to buy accessories for Waring and Gillow stock and commissions, and early in 1931 reviewed a furniture exhibition in Leipzig.[66]

The studio had a design staff of twelve under Chermayeff's direction, including three French designers, one woman designer and one Hungarian designer, as well as the Italian designer Rancati, and John Eastland Fortey (1900–76), who trained at Westminster School of Art and was selected by Chermayeff to work at Waring and Gillow, staying with him as his chief design assistant until 1939. Fortey was joined by his wife who had studied at the Central School of Arts and Crafts.[67] An important aspect of their work was the production of coloured renderings of projected rooms. One of the gouache originals, for the foyer of the Cambridge Theatre, is in the V&A Museum, bearing Chermayeff's signature but also an illegible name, possibly Hungarian, which may represent the artist of the rendering. While Chermayeff's drawing ability was not in doubt, these specialised skills were no doubt available from several of the office staff. Two similar coloured renderings were published in the German magazine, *Moderne Bauformen* and one in *Decorative Art*, 1930. No graphic work by Chermayeff himself in this manner remains to offer a comparison.[68] Framed drawings of rooms appear on the walls of Chermayeff's office, as illustrated in 1930, in a manner familiar from German and French design journals of the 1920s.[69]

Serge Chermayeff in his office at 73 Oxford Street, 1930.

The Modern Art Department began its outside commissions with a drawing room at Claridges Hotel, designed by Paul Follot and completed in November 1929. Work in the hotel continued with the dining room, sub-contracted by the designer Basil Ionides who was working at the same time on the interiors of the Savoy Theatre for the same client, Rupert D'Oyly Carte. It is difficult to attribute the various contributions. As Barbara Tilson writes, the carpet, the first item to be installed, is in a floral Art Deco manner associated with Follot. Existing dining chairs were altered, with back rails straightened and new 'Jazz' style upholstery. The lighting was reorganised to provide a more even light from panels recessed in the broad beams spanning between the columns, which had previously carried the light fittings, as well as evenly spaced light fittings like triglyphs on the beam downstands.[70] The Department also contributed the dining room for the French ocean liner *L'Atlantique* in 1929.[71]

Chermayeff's other commissions in London included the redecoration of a morning room at Bath House, Piccadilly, for the twice-widowed Lady Ludlow, née Alice Mankiewitz (1862–1945).[72] Bath House, at the corner of Bolton Street, was built in 1821 and remodelled internally for Lady Ludlow's first husband, Sir Julius Wernher, in a 'French Dixhuitième' style.[73] Chermayeff recalled that his room 'was rather simply done ... the furniture was macassar ebony and walnut with golden silk'. Chermayeff persuaded his client to make a rug, about 16ft square, from an extensive collection of fur coats which one of her husbands had given to her by way of an apology whenever he had an affair. This appears in photographs of the room as a 'throw' over a sofa, while the room itself was panelled in richly grained wood veneer on a canvas backing with metal fillets, treated as alternating bands of vertical and horizontal grain pattern. One published picture shows the same room with a patterned wallcovering of the same large-scale Art Deco character that was previously used for upholstery on the furniture, the identical pieces then appearing in plain upholstery to contrast with the decorated walls.[74] Perhaps this whimsicality was to be expected from a patron who decided around this period that everything in her life should be mauve, including the footmen's uniforms. The room was a setting for the painting *Quai du Port, Marseilles* (1924) by Edward Wadsworth (now in the Government Art Collection) and two works by Paul Nash, *A Wood on the Downs* (now in Aberdeen Art Gallery) and *Opening* (private collection), both of 1931, which Chermayeff may have persuaded Lady Ludlow to buy for the room from another of his design clients of this period, Nash's dealer, Dudley Tooth.[75] The modern paintings and furniture were combined with small 18th-century French bronzes from the Werner collection. Chermayeff also redecorated the Gallery at Luton Hoo, Lady Ludlow's country seat. For Dudley Tooth he converted a flat out of two houses at 41 Gloucester Square, Hyde Park, a rich setting with walls fully panelled in 'exotic woods' on which hung paintings by Nash, Cedric Morris, Augustus John and others.[76]

**Morning room for Lady Ludlow at Bath House, Piccadilly, with paintings, *A Wood on the Downs*, and *Opening*, both 1931, by Paul Nash.**

Office for C. Derry at
Ambrose Wilson Ltd, 1930.

Opposite: Chermayeff
House, 52 Abbey Road,
1930, view from dining
room to living room.

In one of his more widely illustrated schemes of this period, Chermayeff designed offices for
C. Derry at Ambrose Wilson Ltd. in Vauxhall Bridge Road, in 1930, with a decorative theme
based on triangles in the carpets and ventilation grilles. This was similar in some respects to
the designs of Frank Lloyd Wright, with Chermayeff perhaps inspired by the coverage of the
Hollyhock house, Los Angeles, in *Wendingen* magazine in 1926. Chermayeff's room shares
with Wright's Kaufmann office of 1935–7 an acoustic and visual separation from the outside
world, with 'warm coloured glass' in the double-glazed window and a curtain of 'string colour
decorated with designs in brown and orange'.[77] The whole colour scheme was in the tones of

the oak and walnut veneer of the wall panelling, with rugs and upholstery in pale yellows and brick reds. The desk, built against the window wall, had a black glass top, and was equipped with machinery for opening the door automatically.

While none of the Waring and Gillow rooms appears to survive as a complete entity, there are often individual pieces of furniture in circulation in the antique trade, some to the same models as those included in the original exhibition, but recognisably different in their veneer patterns.[78] These, ironically, are easier to locate and identify than the supposed 'mass-production' pieces that he later designed or marketed through PLAN Ltd. (see Chapter 2). Not all modern style pieces from Waring and Gillow are necessarily by Chermayeff, however. The Modern Art Department survived his departure early in 1931 and the liquidation of Waring and Gillow Ltd. in 1932, following which it was reconstituted as Waring and Gillow (1932) Ltd., a mark which appears on later pieces of furniture.[79]

Far left: bookcase and cocktail cabinet in living room, 52 Abbey Road. Head of Barbara Chermayeff by Jocelyn May LeBrun.

Middle: dining room sideboard and mural, Gourmandise by John Eastland Fortey, 52 Abbey Road, 1930.

Living room, 52 Abbey Road, with double doors closed.

Belonging to the end of this period in Chermayeff's career was the dual purpose studio-flat for Anthony Gibbons Grinling in Swan Court, Chelsea (see page 155). Grinling, a Harrovian friend of Chermayeff's, came from one of three families who, through several generations, had shared the ownership of W.A. Gilbey, the distillers and wine and spirit merchants.[80] He was a director of the company, responsible for providing Chermayeff with his first office premises, immediately opposite Waring and Gillow, on the top floor of the Pantheon at 173 Oxford Street, which was used by Gilbeys as a warehouse before it was redeveloped as Marks and Spencer in 1937.[81] Grinling's flat had a corner window curtained in 'putty-coloured jute', and panelling in Australian walnut with a strong vertical stripe figure. An electric fire was built in with flanking bookshelves and a recessed mirror over it. The flat was furnished with tubular steel upright chairs and a wooden-armed chair covered in zebra hide. The interiors of the bookshelves and the radiator recess beneath a broad shelf under the window were painted in a deep rose pink.

Opposite: Dining room, 52 Abbey Road. Chairs by Mies van der Rohe for Thonet, Curtains by Eric Bagge.

Two projects designed by Chermayeff during his period as Design Director of the Waring and Gillow Modern Art Department stand out in their significance for his future direction and the publicity which they attracted on completion in the later part of 1930.

In June 1929, Chermayeff took a lease from the Eyre Estate on a house at 52 Abbey Road, St John's Wood, an early Victorian semi-detached villa. The presence of something unorthodox was announced by angular lettering on the street gate, and again by the double doors and horizontal glazing bars in the rectangular fanlight. [82] Chermayeff made substantial changes to the interior, using Waring and Gillow craftsmen, which were published in many illustrated books and magazines.[83] Existing architraves and mouldings were removed. The main living room, to the right of the entrance, was divided in two halves, the opening between them fitted with sliding doors horizontally veneered, an effect continued on the flanking walls. On the living room side, the corner next to the fireplace was built out with a two-tiered box, which concealed the food lift, opening onto the other side of the wall. By the doorway opposite, a low-level bull-nosed pedestal, fitted as a bookshelf and cocktail bar with a cantilevered top, contributed further to the architectural quality of the room, providing a kind of projecting jetty for the settee. On this stood a fine bronze head of Barbara Chermayeff by her sister Jocelyn, who had studied sculpture with the Romanian, Osip Zadkine. A small round table in the window had a standard lamp built into the centre on a curved stem. The three deep armchairs had chromium-plated steel bands acting as floor runners and extending up the front of the arms. The fire was replaced by a chromed gas fire in a dado of veneered panelling, above which was a quasi-Vorticist mural of skyscrapers painted by Alexander Bayes, a young artist, the son of the distinguished painter and teacher Walter Bayes, the head of Westminster School of Art, who worked occasionally with Chermayeff at this time.

The back half of the room was furnished as a dining room, in which the chief novelty was the dining table, which extended out in flexible jointed sections from the chimney-breast, like a tambour front on a desk, complete with its chrome legs, allowing adjustment to the size of the party. The chimney-breast was formed into a mirrored recess, to give the illusion that the table continued beyond the glass. A dining table with only one end seating position became a feature of all Chermayeff's houses thereafter. The dining chairs were imported from Thonet in Austria, being a design by Mies van der Rohe in chrome with leather seats. This must have been one of the first occasions when this pattern was seen in England, and Chermayeff used them to convince sceptics of the value of modern design, explaining in a broadcast in 1932, 'shy at first, they sat down and enjoyed its comforts, and many of them have bought similar chairs for themselves'.[84] There was a discrepancy between styles involved here, which was noticed by the literary critic Raymond Mortimer in reviewing the book *Modern English Furniture* by John Rogers, in which the Abbey Road interiors were illustrated, remarking that 'Mr Chermayeff often deserts the Operating Theatre for the Cocotte', mixing functionalism and Art Deco.[85]

Opposite the table was a sideboard, specially designed to fit in a recess with a double break front and horizontal banding, with a painting of *Gourmandise* above it by John Eastland Fortey, featuring a hanging pheasant and other food and drink, on a stylised set of shelves. The pheasant fitted the colour scheme, which was described in an approving article in *Country Life* as 'quiet; russet browns and fawns being used, with relieving touches such as cushions of artificial silk in rainbow colours, and a rich orange yellow vase filled with artificial leaves'.[86] Three rugs with patterns of segmented and overlapping circles were a feature of the linked rooms. Chermayeff wished it to be known that they related to the placing of the furniture, with the largest rug centred on the legs of the extended dining table, the smallest complemented by a four-legged round side table, and the middle-sized one describing the main seating circle. A rug in the V&A Museum (see page 156), acquired in 1978 from a dealer, loosely resembles the smallest of the actual rugs from the living room at 52 Abbey Road.[87] Although other designers such as Marion Dorn and Marion Pepler were producing site-specific rugs from the early 1930s onwards, Chermayeff seems to have developed a particularly architectural interest in their function in controlling space and directing movement. The curtains in the front room at Abbey Road were credited to the designer Eric Bagge, whose rugs of this period quite closely resemble Chermayeff's. No rugs after this date are directly attributed to Chermayeff, although he continued to use rugs in most of his domestic schemes, with rather more subdued patterning.

**Box office foyer, Cambridge Theatre, Seven Dials, London 1930, with bas relief by Anthony Gibbons Grinling.**

The entrance hall and stairs were also recast, with an abstract rug in blues, greys and blacks by Alexander Bayes and a plywood casing to the original stair rail. More or less every corner of the house was photographed and published in journals and books at this time, including the German magazine *Innen Dekoration* and the book *Die Neue Raumkunst* of 1930, in which it appeared inevitably somewhat conservative beside its continental contemporaries.

The major project of Chermayeff's Waring and Gillow period, and the only one to survive substantially intact, was the Cambridge Theatre at Seven Dials in London. The project was a development by Bertie Mayer and financed by Sir Harold Werner of Luton Hoo, the son of Chermayeff's client Lady Ludlow. However, Chermayeff's connections in the theatre world from the mid 1920s may also have helped him to get the job. The architects for the exterior were the mainstream commercial practice of Wimperis Simpson and Guthrie, who provided Portland stone elevations similar to designs by Charles Holden. At this pivotal point in the arrival of modernism in London, it was not uncommon for the more daring effects to be reserved for the interior of an otherwise conventional building, as happened in 1929 with Oliver Bernard's foyer for the Strand Palace Hotel. The Cambridge Theatre's entrance is in the wedge-shaped corner, beneath a semi-circular door fitted by Chermayeff with a simple grille of concentric semi-circles, a foretaste of the visual theme of the interior. Beyond a short hallway, the wide door opening had a sculptural relief by Anthony Gibbons Grinling, already mentioned as Chermayeff's client for a flat around this time. There were three pieces by Grinling in the theatre, this lunette over the door into the inner foyer, and silvered panels in the space beyond, one being of a nude female in different poses of awakening against a background of a musical stave, with a contemporary clothed dancing couple in the centre. The foyer in which it appears originally had a floor decorated with circles, similar to the rugs at 52 Abbey Road, and a ceiling with tiers of inset recessed panels, lit along their edges, an effect similar to several illustrated in the *Architectural Review* in 1930, mostly from photographs of Berlin theatres collected by Chermayeff's friend, the architectural critic P. Morton Shand.

Lighting was one of the principal themes of the Cambridge Theatre. The auditorium had concentric arcs of gilded plaster, with continuous lighting troughs concealed from the view of the audience, so that light could be thrown onto the surfaces and controlled in a dimming process focusing down towards the stage. Small low-level lights were placed on the end seats of the rows to help latecomers find their way, and lights were also placed along the rows of seats for reading the programme. The floor patterns were colour coded, with the idea that the audience could follow a particular colour, matching their tickets, and arriving in the right place. A fine cocktail bar was installed in the upper foyer, where the carpet has a 'C' device (see page 156). The lavish brochure for the opening on 8 September 1930 explained (presumably in Chermayeff's own words):

The consistent modern treatment of an interior wherein to present the advanced technique of the stage of today is unquestionably logical . . . S. Chermayeff has been ruled by the principle of functionalism and has endeavoured to let fitness for purpose decide the final forms and colours in the various areas of the building . . . there is no useless ornament to distract from form and cut up its long sweeping lines of construction.[88]

The truth of this depends on the definition of 'useful ornament', for there were many ornamented surfaces, which other critics found restless.[89]

Even so, Chermayeff's desire to create unity in a decorative scheme, and to relate the fashionable Art Deco style to functional purpose was recognised by the German critic Herbert Hoffmann, who compared its design to the more purely ornamental modern work at the recently opened Whitehall Theatre, declaring that the Cambridge Theatre 'can be regarded as modern in the functionalist sense, therefore modern in a sense which stands extremely close to our German artistic sensibility'.[90] Chermayeff belied this in an article in 1933 in which, with self-critical hindsight, he declared that the theatre was typical of its period, containing 'some interesting mistakes . . . all of which have been copiously plagiarised and wrapped in specious argument. A complete theory has been evolved which experience has since shown to be based on false premises.'[91] Hoffman also stressed the 'extraordinary sense of unity', even while admitting that a German viewer would 'prefer more peaceful effects in one carpet or another, or in the decorative finishes on and over doors, galleries'.[92] Whether effective or not, Chermayeff's declared intention of creating an effect of unity rather than excitement is consistent with his expressed aims at Waring and Gillow, and offers an important clue to his future development.

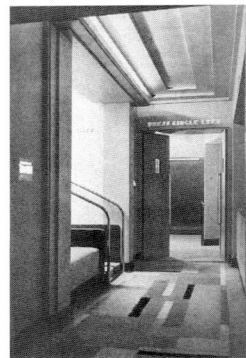

**Dress circle entrance, Cambridge Theatre.**

The Cambridge Theatre was built as a variety and revue theatre, and Chermayeff designed several sets and some costumes for the opening performance of *Charlot's Masquerade*. It has never been one of London's most successful theatres but following a repair of the surviving original features in the 1980s, it has staged a series of musicals, including a première of Ben Elton and Andrew Lloyd-Webber's *The Beautiful Game*, in the autumn of 2000.

As the conditions of economic recession worsened following the New York stock market crash of October 1929, Waring and Gillow suffered too, partly owing to Lord Waring's extravagance. Chermayeff had been able to use Waring and Gillow as a springboard for his career, having become one of the best-known young designers in London in the course of two years, and left to become freelance at the end of 1930.

## Notes

1 Quote from undated letter to Paul Grabbe, Avery Library. Chermayeff's passport dating from the 1930s gives his date and place of birth as 5 December, Odessa. The form of his original name is taken from the records of Harrow School. In a letter to J.M. Richards, of 25 January 1980, he wrote: 'When I came to England, I was indeed Sergei Ivanovitch Issakovitch. Some bureaucrat along the way made the patronimic into Ivan. I dropped this when I changed my name by deed poll in 1927.' [The date for his name change was in fact 1924.] Copy of letter in collection of Richard Plunz.

2 This account is based principally on transcripts of interviews between Chermayeff and Richard Plunz, conducted in 1975. I am particularly grateful to Professor Plunz for giving me access to these papers and permission to paraphrase and quote from them. The transcripts have no unified numbering system, so that it is impossible to reference them effectively. A summary of the events in Chermayeff's life, based on the interviews, was printed as 'Chronology', in *Design and the Public Good*, pp.307-21. Further information is derived from conversation with members of the Chermayeff family, notably a conversation with Barbara Chermayeff in April 1994. Some additional details are taken from the text 'Nothing Trivial' by Victoria Milne, 1994-6, based on interviews with Chermayeff commissioned by his sons and made available through them. Chermayeff's accounts of his past are not always reliable in detail and occasionally admit discrepancies.

3 Letter from Chermayeff to Clare Robinson and Molly Panter-Downes, n.d. (c.1970), Avery Library. This visit may be datable to 1895.

4 ibid.

5 Letter from Chermayeff to J.M. Richards, 25 January 1980, providing information for an advance obituary for *The Times*. Copy of letter in papers held by Richard Plunz. Topa Chermoyoff was 'a great horseman' and became a General at the end of the First World War in command of the Caucasian Brigades. He was elected to represent the Chechen, Ossetin and Lecquin tribes at the Versailles Congress but could not get a hearing. He stayed on in Paris where he was rescued financially by Henry Deterding and brought to London.

6 See Charles van der Leeuw (2000), *Oil and Gas in the Caucasus and Caspian. A History*, Richmond, Surrey, Curzon Caucasus World, p.74ff.

7 Richard Plunz interviews.

8 van der Leeuw, 2000, p.80.

9 Milne, 1996, p.4.

10 This gift with animals prevailed in the family. In 1912, one of Serge's cousins was appearing at Olympia in London as a rider. He went to watch the performance. The horse was frightened by the sudden turning on of the lights as it was approaching a jump but the rider spoke to it and it took the jump from a standing position, achieving a great round of applause.

11 Quoted in Vanora Bennett (1998), *Crying Wolf, the Return of War to Chechnya*, London, Picador.

12 Serge Chermayeff, 'Biographical Note - Written 1940', Avery Library, SC Box 5 (40-44).

13 See Richard Carline (1968), *Draw they Must, a History of the Teaching and Examining of Art*, London, Edward Arnold, Ch.11: 'Ruskin A New Approach to Art Teaching - Ruskin, Cooke and Ablett'.

14 Richard Whiteing, *Drawing from Delight, introduction to 23rd annual exhibition of the Royal Drawing Society*, 1912, p.19 . Copy in National Art Library, London.

15 ibid, p.28.

16 In conversation with the author, April 1994.

17 Chermayeff usually gave his attendance dates at Harrow as 1914-17, which would have been correct for his age, but the school records show that he entered in the autumn of 1915 and left in the summer of 1918. I am grateful to Rita M. Gibbs, the Harrow School Archivist, for making this information available to me, together with Chermayeff's academic grades.

18 'A London Furnishing Studio', *The Cabinet Maker and Complete House Furnisher*, 25 January 1930, p.158.

19 Richard Plunz interviews.

20 ibid.

21 Conversation with Barbara Chermayeff, April 1994. Not mentioned in Chermayeff's own interviews.

22 The chronology is confusing. In several statements, Chermayeff gave his father's date of death as 1924 but in an interview tape stated that his father met and approved of his future wife, Barbara, whom he only met in 1927.

23 Evidence for this comes from Chermayeff's interviews with Richard Plunz. There was no General Maynard serving in the British Army at this date, according to the Army List. This incident therefore remains mysterious.

24 See George Dilnot, compiler (1925), *The Romance of the Amalgamated Press*, London, The Amalgamated Press (1922) Ltd.

25 ibid., p.38.

26 Richard Plunz interviews.

27 Milne 1996, p.6.

28 Only one issue of the magazine has survived in the collection of the British Library in London. Dated October 1920, being the sixth monthly issue of the first volume, it was edited by Byron Davies.

29 Milne, 1996, p.6.

30 Barbara Chermayeff in conversation with the author, April 1994.

31 Richard Plunz interviews.

32 ibid.

33 See Nikolaus Pevsner and Elizabeth Williamson (1994), *Buildings of England: Buckinghamshire*, London, Penguin Books, p.381.

34 See *Illustrated London News*, 31 October 1925, p.853.

35 Conversation with Barbara Chermayeff, April 1994.

36 Naturalisation Imperial Certificate No.5794, dated London 2 March 1928. Information from Chermayeff's passport.

37 Noel Carrington (1976), *Industrial Design in Britain*, London, George Allen & Unwin Ltd., p.87.

38 The title appears in variant forms, as Modern Art Studios, Modern Art Studio and Department, Modern Art Department.

39 Serge Chermayeff, 'Notes on self for Richard Plunz' 1979, kindly communicated by Professor Plunz.

40 Serge Chermayeff, 'An Explosive Revolution', *Architectural Review*, CLXVI, Nov 1979, p.309.

41 See Deborah S. Ryan (1997), *The Ideal Home through the 20th Century*, London, Hazar, pp.56-7.

42 Barbara Tilson, 'The Modern Art Department Waring and Gillow 1928-1931', *Journal of the Decorative Arts Society 1890-1940*, No. 8, p.41.

43 See Chermayeff's paper 'Modern Decoration', Avery Archive, c.1930.

44 *The Times*, 28 November 1928, pp.10 & 15.

45 Paul Follot (1928), 'The Evolution of Decorative Art: its motives, its history and its present tendencies', MS in Avery Library, p.7.

46 Christopher Hussey, 'The Modern Home', *Country Life*, 8 December 1928, pp.840-3 (p.840).

47 *Country Life*, 15 December 1928, p.856.

48 MS notes attached to Follot's speech.

49 An unsigned editorial 'Modernism' in *Builder*, 9 July 1915, seems to be the first instance in the English architectural press.

50 'The Makers of Broadcasting House', *Country Life*, 28 May 1932, p.603.

51 'A London Furnishing Studio', *The Cabinet Maker and Complete House Furnisher*, 25 January 1930, p.159.

52 Serge Chermayeff, 'Away with Snobbery, Sentiment and Stupidity', *Listener*, VIII, 21 September 1932, p.393.

53 Serge Chermayeff, 'Modern Decoration' MS Avery Archive, p.2. The same wording appears in the *Cabinet Maker* article of January 1930.

54 John C. Rogers, 'Modern Decoration at Warings', *Design and Industries Quarterly Journal*, December 1928, pp.4-6.

55 ibid.

56 See Barbie Campbell-Cole, 'The Arrival of Tubular Steel Furniture in Britain', in Campbell-Cole and Tim Benton, eds., *Tubular Steel Conference Papers*, London, The Art Book Company, 1979, pp.52-67.

57 Serge Chermayeff, 'Modernism', *The Cabinet Maker*, 28 June 1930, p.734.

58 *Architectural Review*, December 1937, p.265.

59 Illustrated in the *Studio*, p.135.

60 The sideboard in the collection of the Royal Pavilion, Art Gallery and Museum, Brighton, appears to be the same piece as the one exhibited in 1928, judging by a comparison of the figuring of the woodgrain on the veneers with original photographs.

61 Hamilton T. Smith, 'Modern Furniture', *Architectural Association Journal*, April 1929, p.372.

62 ibid., p.377.

63 On Maclaren, see obituary by Paul Greenhalgh in the *Independent,* London, 22 November 1989.

64 The room was attributed to Maclaren in a review by the architect Howard Robertson, *Architect & Building News*, 30 November 1928, p.695, where he described it as 'the sensation of the exhibition'.

65 Chermayeff included one of Maclaren's tables in the interior of the house Shrub's Wood, Chalfont St Giles, in 1935, designed in partnership with Eric Mendelsohn, It remains in the house.

66 'German Furniture. Notes on the Exhibition in Leipzig', *The Cabinet Maker*, 28 March 1931, p.789.

67 See Tilson 1984, p.40 and note 5, citing a letter from Fortey to Peter Wilcockson, 6.10.75. The identification of Rancati is conjectural, based on a rug illustrated in *Studio Yearbook, Decorative Art, 1931*, p.93.

68 See *Decorative Art 1930 Yearbook of the Studio*, 'showroom design by S. Chermayeff for a firm of dressmakers', colour plate facing p.88, also plate on page 33, Serge Chermayeff, 'Design for a Study' 1928/29, in Torsten Brohan and Thomas Berg (1994), *Avantgarde Design 1880-1930*, Cologne, Taschen. I have not been able to trace the source of this drawing. In style, it appears more likely to be a work by Chermayeff from c.1931-2. Two original designs by

Chermayeff from this period were sold in 2000 by the book dealer Thomas Boss of Boston. One of these was for the Cambridge Theatre.

69 *Architectural Review*, July 1930, p.36.

70 In interview tapes, Chermayeff said that the Claridge's dining room was carried out during his time at Ernest Williams Ltd, but other evidence contradicts this. He also mentions that Ronald Trew was a friend of Mambrino, the manager of Claridge's, which may have been Chermayeff's initial contact.

71 Barbara Tilson attributes this to Follot, while Chermayeff's claim in interview to have designed it is the basis for its mention in Plunz, 1983, p.308.

72 See Raleigh Trevelyan (1991), *Grand Dukes and Diamonds, The Wernhers of Luton Hoo*, London, Secker & Warburg.

73 Nikolaus Pevsner (1957/73), *Buildings of England, London I: The Cities of London and Westminster*, Harmondsworth, Penguin Books, p.627. Bath House was demolished c.1960.

74 Richard Plunz interview, 20 September 1980. For wood veneer scheme, see *Architect and Building News*, 1 January 1932, pp.2-3, and *Architectural Review*, February 1932, p.76. For patterned wall scheme, see *Decorative Art Yearbook 1932*, London, The Studio, 1932, p.32, described in caption as 'Corner of a study in a London house. The walls are covered with patterned silk in pale-grey and buff tones; settee upholstered in buff repp, with a bearskin rug; furniture in macassar ebony with almond tops; rug in deep browns, grey and rust-reds'.

75 For Nash's reference to Chermayeff's modern room, see Andrew Causey (1980), *Paul Nash*, Clarendon Press, Oxford, p.237.

76 Chermayeff interview with Richard Plunz. See 'Pictures in the Modern House', the newest phase in interior decorating' *Studio*, July 1932, pp.48-9.

77 Caption to photo in *Architectural Review*, July 1930, p.40.

78 A bedroom suite, to the same design as that from the 'Lady's Bedroom' at the 1928-9 exhibition, but not the same pieces, was kindly shown me by Mr Michael Rich.

79 For an example of a piece thus stamped, see James Peto and Donna Loveday (1999), eds., *Modern Britain 1929-39*, London, Design Museum, p.86.

80 Grinling's dates are 1896-1982. He could not, therefore, have been a close contemporary of Chermayeff at Harrow. See Benedict Read and Peyton Skipwith (1986), *Sculpture in Britain between the Wars*, London, Fine Art Society, pp.86-7.

81 For the history of the Pantheon, designed by James Wyatt, 1772, see *Survey of London, vol.XXXI, The Parish of St. James's, North of Piccadilly, Part 1*, London, Athlone Press, 1963, pp.268-83.

82 The lettering is shown in a photograph in Avery Library, not apparently published. The front door and other details illustrated in Noel Carrington (1933), *Design in the Home*, London, Country Life Ltd., p.87.

83 I made a visit to the house in 1992, at which time the double sliding doors and food lift fitting survived, together with the stair-rail casing and other small details. The house has changed hands since. Chermayeff assigned the remainder of his 21-year term to Wilfred Gilchrist on 8 May 1937 (information privately communicated).

84 The chairs, model MR10, 1927, were made and imported by Thonet, who opened a London showroom at 52 Great Eastern Street in 1929. A single chair of this pattern was ordered for the Headmaster's house at Dartington School in 1931. Chermayeff eventually presented his set of chairs to the Museum of Modern Art in New York, in a much worn condition. Quote from Chermayeff, 'Away with Snobbery, Sentiment and Stupidity', *Listener*, 21 September 1932, p.394.

85 Raymond Mortimer, 'Modern Furniture and Decoration', *Architectural Review*, December 1930, p.253.

86 Randal Phillips, 'In Modern Manner: furniture and decoration at No.52 Abbey Road, St John's Wood', *Country Life*, 21 June 1930.

87 Another rug of this period is in the collection of Ivan Chermayeff, bought from a dealer. Its pattern of coloured segments of circles and bands, struck from a common centre, in browns and pinks, is similar to the other two rugs in the Abbey Road living room and dining room.

88 Cambridge Theatre souvenir programme, 1930. Copy in Theatre Museum, London.

89 See Madge Garland (1968), *The Indecisive Decade*, London, Macdonald, p.131: 'The Cambridge revealed an interior designed by Serge Chermayeff which illustrated many of the newest building techniques, but presented a singularly unattractive version of the taste of the time.'

90 Herbert Hoffmann, 'Das Neue Cambridge-Theatre in London', *Moderne Bauformen*, XXX, May 1931, pp.217-24. Translation kindly contributed by Patrick Goode.

91 Serge Chermayeff, 'A Grammar of Groundwork', *Architectural Review*, October 1933, p.147.

92 ibid.

# Theory and Design in the early 1930s

If there was a modernist 'establishment' in England at the end of the 1920s, it was centred on the house 'Finella' at Cambridge, the home of Mansfield Forbes (1889–1936), a fellow of Clare College, who in 1927 commissioned a young and unknown Australian architect, Raymond McGrath (1903–76), visiting England on a scholarship, to transform the interiors using a great deal of glass and other modern materials such as copper-faced plywood, 'Plymax'. The effect was novel and theatrical, raised to fantasy by Finella's mythical iconography of a Celtic Queen who invented glass and died by falling into a waterfall. The interiors were published in 1929 but equally important was Forbes's role as a catalyst among people, mixing architects, Cambridge students, scientists and businessmen in chaotic and eccentric parties, fired by a poetic reforming zeal and fuelled by plentiful liquor.[1] Barbara Chermayeff remembered 'Manny' performing a fake black mass in the mirrored hall, turning off all the lights and making it up as he went along.[2]

Nina Chermayeff was working in the showrooms at Waring and Gillow (as 'Madame Roni'), and met McGrath and Forbes when they visited the exhibition.[3] Thus Chermayeff entered the

Finella circle. Through Jack Pritchard (1899–1992), a Cambridge graduate then working as a plywood salesman, he also met Wells Coates (1895–1958), a Canadian with a background in engineering, who became another close friend. Like Chermayeff, he was virtually self-educated in design and had what Chermayeff so far lacked, a restless desire to use design to change the world.

Another important friendship was with Hubert de Cronin Hastings (1896–1986), part-proprietor by inheritance of the *Architectural Review*, Britain's leading monthly architectural magazine, founded in 1896, and also owner of the sister paper, the weekly *Architects' Journal*. Hastings, who studied for a while at the Slade School of Art and the Bartlett School of Architecture, joined the Architectural Press, publisher of the two magazines, in 1921 and became responsible for layouts of the *Architectural Review* in 1927, transforming it into a rich and often quirky display of his wide-ranging interests. Modern architecture was certainly one of them but Hastings encouraged an irreverent and questioning attitude towards it, anxious that its social and philosophical liberation should not be foreclosed by formalism.[4] Both papers reviewed the Waring and Gillow exhibition, and throughout the 1930s Hastings gave special support to McGrath, Coates and Chermayeff, whom he called 'The Three Musketeers', giving prominence even to quite minor works by them, often with colour plates, rare at the time, and commissioning them to write articles and reviews.

The Architectural Press, in its early Georgian premises at 9 Queen Anne's Gate, London, was a meeting point for many of the same people who would be found at Finella. Most of them came from outside the architectural profession but were fired by an interest in the subject. P. Morton Shand (1890–1960) probably the best-informed commentator on modern architecture and its immediate antecedents, at least before the arrival of Nikolaus Pevsner in England in 1933, was one of these. Shand's series of articles, 'Scenario for a Human Drama', 1933–4, traced the history of modernism, moving backwards chronologically, and giving emphasis to Britain's role in providing the theoretical and ethical background for modernism in the form of the Gothic Revival and the Arts and Crafts Movement.

In 1930, Hastings employed the poet John Betjeman (1906–84) as Deputy Editor, a surprising decision given the latter's lack of experience but an inspired one in terms of enriching the magazine's culture with visual and verbal jokes, and giving Betjeman space for his pioneering reassessment of the Arts and Crafts movement, partly based on his meetings with survivors such as Voysey, Baillie-Scott and George Walton. Betjeman became a close friend of Chermayeff's in the early 30s, when Betjeman and he would go about, Betjeman preaching parody sermons while standing on the bar in a pub, or silencing the restaurant at the Army and Navy Stores by suddenly shouting 'Darjeeling!'[5] Chermayeff called him 'Jaggers' in a version of Harrow schoolboy slang. Fundamentally, they may have had little in common and Betjeman was capable of using Chermayeff as an object of jokes, as he did with most of his friends, but in 1980 he wrote, 'Serge was much the most amiable of the MARS Group, except of course Etchells.'[6]

Frederick Etchells (1886–1962) was another interesting and anomalous figure in the world of modern architecture at the beginning of the 1930s. Formerly a Vorticist painter, he had run a private press in the early 1920s and translated the writings of Le Corbusier and Amedée Ozenfant for publication by John Rodker. He later became a specialist in liturgical planning and Anglican church architecture, so that he conformed to the type of interested and well-informed onlooker to Modernism. In 1924, Etchells had mooted the creation of a group called the 'Vers' group after the title of Le Corbusier's newly-published book, with the *Country Life* writer Christopher Hussey (1899–1970), to discuss and promote modern architecture.[7] Nothing came of this but it provided the seed for another evanescent association with which Chermayeff became involved in 1930, based around some of the key members of the Finella and *Architectural Review* circles. This was the Twentieth Century Group, which made its sole public announcement to the world in the *Architects' Journal* in July 1930, proposing to use the Ideal Home Exhibition in 1933 as a platform for the promotion of modern design. Chermayeff was one of a group, with Joseph Emberton (1889–1956), Howard Robertson (1888–1963) and Maxwell Fry (1899–1987), who met at Finella that year to discuss the wider possible implications of the group. This led to a further meeting at the Travellers' Club in London (Mansfield Forbes's club), with Chermayeff, Coates, Robertson and Jack Pritchard. Of the other architects involved, Emberton was beginning to design authentically modern buildings, drawing on the skills of his architectural assistants, while Robertson was more of an establishment figure, the Principal of the Architectural Association School who believed that the compositional systems of the past and modernism were more or less interchangeable. Maxwell Fry, the youngest of these three, made his name as a modern architect after 1934 but hitherto had worked only in a Neo-Georgian style.

A meeting in January 1931 elected a committee, of which Chermayeff was one of seven executive members, with his friend Anthony Grinling as secretary. By this time, Noel Carrington, the Secretary of the Design and Industries Association, was also involved. At a large meeting of 80 people held over lunch at the Savoy on 26 February 1931, Wells Coates delivered a complex and emotional paper, 'Sketch Plan for a New Aesthetic', a text which has never been published, but which reveals much about Coates's wide ranging hopes for the transformation which modern design might achieve in English society.[8] He was a reader of books by Wyndham Lewis, and shared Lewis's belief in the artist's role as the originator of dynamic change in society. Chermayeff quoted occasionally from *The Caliph's Design*, 1919 in which Lewis dismissed almost all the architecture of the time, except for W.R. Lethaby's book of 1912, *Architecture*, which was sufficiently radical for his approval, asking, 'Architects, where is your vortex?'.

There was a danger of factional splits and Chermayeff, Coates and Forbes seem to have seen themselves as the guardians of ideological purity. Forbes wrote to McGrath after the first meeting, 'I hear there was no end of time wasted by absurd disputes re arbitrage of "modernism" – as tho' the whole point of summoning so select a number of individuals, in the first place, was not on the tacit understanding and premise that the least modernistic thing the dud-est of the Group could do would pass the minimum, pessimum Criterion for exhibition.'[9] Coates's paper was ill-adapted to act as a rallying point, but an exhibition sub-committee of the group met on 3 December to try to engage with the exhibition idea. By this time, Frederick Etchells was also involved, together with Chermayeff and Coates. This was probably the occasion following which Chermayeff wrote to Etchells an undated letter, a copy of which survives among his papers, to which is attached a 'Brief Statement and skeleton of the Twentieth Century Group idea and exhibition'.[10] In this letter, Chermayeff expressed impatience with Etchells's tolerance of 'the tepid waters of discretion' provided by unnamed members. Chermayeff evidently had plenty to say himself at committee meetings, which gave 'a talking opportunity to extraverts like myself' but declared that McGrath and Emberton were too reticent to get the hearing they deserved, and declared that 'agreeable as I find our meetings and sherry, I would rather employ my spare time in work than talk'.

The stress of the manifesto text is on industrial design rather than architecture. This was a topical subject in the Depression, since the decline of British industry was attributed by many to the lack of investment and technical development. Most products looked out of date. There had been mounting pressure for government action since the critical self-appraisal of the British Pavilion at the Paris Exhibition of 1925, but the Board of Trade, the responsible agency, was slow to act, waiting until 1931 to appoint a committee of enquiry under Lord Gorrell which reported the following year. Exhibitions and semi-permanent and travelling displays were seen by all parties as the proper medium for achieving change, educating consumers, trade buyers and manufacturers alike and creating a sense of excitement that would break through the deadlock of mediocrity and superficial styling. The success of the Waring and Gillow exhibition, in pre-depression conditions, was evidence of the didactic and publicity value of exhibitions while the success of the Stockholm exhibition of 1930, in which that country's respected decorative arts and architecture seemed to have 'gone modern' in a single leap, was in people's minds. The sixth point of the manifesto reads, 'That after the foreign precedent of exhibitions in France, Sweden and Germany the time is now ripe for a similar exhibition of rational modern art in England.' The text also stressed the difference between modernism as a fashion and as a true expression of contemporary life, and the need to suppress individualism in the design contributions in favour of a 'rational character'.

Chermayeff's views on the difficulty of defining and explaining functionalism are stated in a long unpublished letter to the editor of the *Architect and Building News*, dated 31 October 1930, following a discussion at an Architectural Association dinner. Chermayeff had come to the conclusion that 'paradoxically enough the very people who were unable to define functionalism were the architects, who were in most cases completely irrelevant on the subject of the matter in hand'.[11] Chermayeff was in no doubt that there was an essential aesthetic component to functionalism, produced through social causes, to which material causes were secondary. Thus he argued:

> Broadly speaking, the functions of any structure or components of that structure are made by the demands of the times and not by available materials. What I mean is that the demands of the designer, having no precedent, stimulate the discovery of new materials in the first place and demand a new technique and form in the second place. The demands of any given structure and its components should be satisfying both from the material and aesthetic point of view. Thus Mr [D'Arcy] Braddell's complaint about function, as he understands it, is a purely material one and 'too bare to live with' is an inadequate understanding of the meaning of the word function. That idea seems to me to be the very contradiction of functionalism. [12]

Chermayeff's position was based on a broad sense of the national condition, rather than a narrow stylistic preference, and he concluded his letter by saying that 'England seems to me in particular danger of not fulfilling its economic function in the world today by virtue of its achievements in the past, of which it should be justly proud but not to the lengths of falling into a retrospective stupor.'[13]

Meetings of the Twentieth Century Group continued in the subsequent years, up to 1933, by which time another group had an exhibition proposal in hand, which resulted in the 'Exhibition of British Industrial Art in Relation to the Home' at the Dorland Hall, Regent Street, in June and July, in which both Coates and Chermayeff were involved in creating the kind of model furnished interiors which were suggested in Chermayeff's earlier document. This, and the formation of the MARS Group in the course of 1933, in which Coates was closely involved, were reasons why the Twentieth Century Group faded away. It represented hopes for modernism only partially realised in Britain in the 1930s, notably the paradigmatic position of industrial design between architecture and art, and the intimate relationship between design and the whole moral and economic culture – issues perhaps too vast to be encompassed by a voluntary organisation.

Chermayeff joined the MARS Group in 1935, a year after its launch, becoming its representative on the RIBA Foreign Relations Committee.[14] At the first meeting he attended, Morton Shand and he pressed for the representation of structural engineering and services engineering within the group, and the minutes record 'point referred for future action, not without opposition'. For the exhibition which MARS began planning in 1936, but which did not take place until the beginning of 1938, Chermayeff was allocated to work on the section on childhood and school, although he did not pursue this brief.

Like the Twentieth Century Group, MARS was always prey to factional in-fighting, and at a meeting on 5 October 1936, Chermayeff suggested finding general issues rather than pursuing a personal controversy, in this case about the assessment of a competition in Birmingham. He allied himself with Shand and other members in a motion of censure against the Central Executive Committee of MARS in January 1936, including the accusation that 'they allowed what meetings there were to be wasted on impractical dissertations, as for example, general statements on aesthetics which have been repeatedly and more competently stated by the more experienced pioneers of the very movement which MARS professes to represent'.[15] As a result of such misplaced energy, the group had failed to carry out the practical research which it had announced as its aim, particularly in the editing of technical data, researching building case law and in housing research. Writing a satirical commentary in 1934, for publication at the beginning of the following year, as if from a hundred years ahead, Chermayeff and J.M. Richards saw the frustration which lay behind the inability to make these groups more effective. 'Unable to make buildings and other things, they made and unmade groups and circles, and had fights among themselves, and made their feeble forces even feebler.'[16]

Chermayeff's involvement with the Twentieth Century Group, particularly his contact with Wells Coates, must have been the impulse which purged his style of any lingering traces of Art Deco visible at Abbey Road and the Cambridge Theatre. Coates's life story was as exotic as Chermayeff's. He was raised in Japan as the son of Canadian missionaries, joined the Royal Flying Corps in the First World War and studied in London for a doctorate in engineering, as well as being a journalist for the *Daily Express*. By the end of 1930 he had created a number of shop interiors and fascias for Cresta Silks, a successful producer of hand-blocked dress fabrics and made-up garments, as well as their offices in Welwyn Garden City, which were starkly elegant. Coates had a challenging manner which often attracted converts to modernism, although he had difficulty translating talk into action. As well as showing Chermayeff a more radical architectural style, Coates would have shown the way that it was based on a critical ideology, more challenging than the comfortable middle-of-the-road sentiments expressed by Chermayeff in association with Waring and Gillow. Chermayeff called him 'the most gifted intellectually and artistically of his generation with the possible exception of Lubetkin'.[17] Coates's ideas were often tantalisingly suggestive of some resolution beyond his reach, while Chermayeff was usually more pragmatic and less visionary.

Wells Coates and Jack Pritchard formed a close bond (cemented rather than otherwise by Coates's affair with Pritchard's wife Molly), and when Pritchard awarded the design of the 1930 Venesta plywood stand at the Building Trades Exhibition to Le Corbusier and Charlotte Perriand following a competition, Chermayeff was invited to meet Perriand during her stay in London in September. In October, Coates and Chermayeff were in contact about a house that Chermayeff intended to build in the country, an ambitious affair including a garage, a swimming pool and a badminton court, which Coates envisaged as a demonstration project linked to the two houses he was then planning to build for Pritchard at Lawn Road, Hampstead.[18]

In a repeat competition for a Venesta Stand in 1931, Coates's design won the prize while Chermayeff was a 'commended' runner-up, his design surprisingly blocky and 'moderne' rather than 'modern'.[19] The two architects travelled together to Germany with Pritchard in the summer of 1931, reputedly visiting the Bauhaus, although this was not among the buildings recorded by Chermayeff in 'Film Shots in Germany' in the *Architectural Review*, November 1931.[20] This was an article in the form of an avant-garde graphic travel diary, covering Stuttgart, Frankfurt and Berlin, with particular prominence given to buildings by Mendelsohn, whom they visited at his new house on the Rupenhorn in Berlin. The tone of Chermayeff's commentary is brisk and ironic, emphasising the range and quality of modern architecture, spanning a wide range of building types and whole housing districts, with which England had scarcely anything to compare.

The 'Three Musketeers' were working together during 1931 on interiors for the BBC Broadcasting House, opened in 1932, which helped further to promote Chermayeff's name and show his work in the context of his closest associates. McGrath, the youngest of the three, was given the role of Decoration Consultant for the interiors in the course of 1930, through contacts of Mansfield Forbes, and set up his practice on the same floor of offices as Chermayeff at 173 Oxford Street, with both their names on the door and some overlapping of staff. Coates and Chermayeff were, however, selected by the BBC directly, the latter on the strength of the Cambridge Theatre, rather than by McGrath himself.

Broadcasting House, still standing in Portland Place, was designed by the architect G. Val Myer, who effectively inherited with the site when a hotel scheme collapsed in the depression. He made a reasonably skilful use of the restricted bull-nosed site with a stone-clad steel-frame building, but with its Art Deco ornaments it was only half modern in character. Although several other designers, such as the architect Edward Maufe, were involved in the interiors, the modern work in the building - now all completely destroyed - was designed exclusively by the three friends. Val Goldsmith, the Assistant Controller of the BBC wrote at the time that it was 'an opportunity of modern decorative design on a more extensive scale than is common, and was perhaps, up to this moment, the greatest opportunity in this country'.[21] McGrath said in a lecture in 1972, 'The designs for the BBC gave the first real fillip to industrial design in England and Wells Coates, Chermayeff and myself were three of the first architects to work in that field in London.'[22] As the designs were coming to completion, Paul Nash wrote that

'Serge Chermayeff working in partnership with Raymond McGrath, has probably done more to bring about a change of taste than any other designer in England to-day.'[23]

McGrath's work is the most strongly coloured and purely decorative, while Coates was allocated areas like the Sound Effects studio which called for a more scientific approach. Chermayeff contributed a distinctly different flavour to the suite on the eighth floor which included the Military Band Studio (Orchestral Studio 8A), the only studio in the building to have natural light (see page 157). He kept to the natural brown tones he had used before, adding pieces of tubular steel furniture, such as the lemon yellow desk of composition resin board (called 'Beatl') in the eighth floor waiting room, with its desk chair of cellulosed scarlet leather adding the highlight to a reddish brown seating fabric (see page 157).

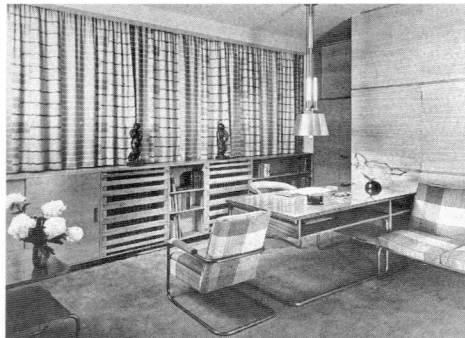

The Studio itself was decorated in bands of untreated building board with aluminium fixing strips. The ceiling had six large pale green discs, mounted to cover the air intake vents, with a lighting trough of straw coloured flashed glass on each disk, projecting dynamically over its edge, supposedly like a banjo. An enlarged pattern of one of these assemblies was formed in the different toned cork floor tiles. Seating, with broad orange and red striped fabric, lined the walls. F.R.S. Yorke, a young architect who was another of De Cronin Hastings's protégés, wrote in the *Architectural Review*, 'The work of Mr Chermayeff is robust; he uses materials boldly and has an interesting sense of colour.'[24] He also commented on the 'brilliant blue-green' of the cellulose painted doors. Chermayeff designed various other rooms at Broadcasting House which were widely illustrated, furnished with newly-designed or adapted chairs and tables.

The tubular steel pieces were provided as a mixture of specials and stock designs from the Pel (Practical Equipment Ltd.) Company which acquired its name in March 1932 having existed since 1930 as a department of the metal tube manufacturers Accles and Pollock of Birmingham, continuing as the largest maker of tubular steel furniture in England. The upholstered furniture selected by Chermayeff for the Waiting Room was probably supplied by Walter Knoll of Stuttgart but since it had become a matter of pride, as well as economics, to

**Broadcasting House, Debating Table for Talks Studio, 1932.**

**Middle: Broadcasting House, Director of Talks office, 1932.**

**Far left: Broadcasting House, Talks Studio, 1932.**

find as many components as possible for Broadcasting House from British manufacturers, the publications are silent on the subject. Chermayeff's name was attached, in 1934, to the tubular steel nesting chairs (Model R.P.7) used throughout Broadcasting House, which in the *Architectural Review* survey of the building in 1932 are attributed to Joseph E. Leopold Quittner of Vienna.[25] Chermayeff also designed interiors for Broadcasting House in Birmingham in a similar style in 1933–4. Although the Twentieth Century Group was never visible to the public, the Broadcasting House project did much to further its programme of design reform, specially in encouraging British manufacturers to produce synthetic building boards, surface finishes and fittings to match those made in Germany.

Eric Gill (1882–1940), who contributed sculpture and reliefs to Broadcasting House, was a visitor to Finella in June 1929 and became one thinker whose influence Chermayeff consistently acknowledged. Although considerably younger than Voysey, Gill was a survivor of the pre-1914 artistic avant-garde in London who had chosen his own pathway of lifestyle, religion and philosophy out of that short-lived ferment. As much concerned as Wyndham Lewis with changing the world, Gill was more ready to connect modernism with distant antecedents, and argue for it in the language of St Thomas Aquinas. Against the mechanistic orthodoxy of the 1930s, he was a defender of hand craftsmanship as the basis for any proper society, but Chermayeff's differing views on this subject did not appear to create a barrier between them. His direct references to Gill, occurring at intervals through his writings, usually consist of quoting the phrase 'Beauty looks after herself', the title of one of Gill's collections of essays. In his own copy of Gill's *Art*, Chermayeff noted, for the benefit of his son Ivan, 'Read this from end to end again & again. EG was my friend and mentor. Pop 1951.'[26]

'Beauty looks after herself' is a deceptively simple phrase, sometimes seen as an abdication of responsibility on the part of the designer. Given Chermayeff's immense attention to detail in design, this cannot literally be the case, and the meaning may be understood rather as a question of intentionality. Beauty is desired but will not come by being worked at directly, rather by allowing the other aspects of the design process to lead to it. As Gill discovered from his friend Ananda Coomaraswamy, this was a universal belief among the traditional art cultures of the world, which was only challenged with the advent of the renaissance in Europe. In common with many modernists, Chermayeff believed that the changes he was advocating should produce contact with an underlying reality, in which material and spiritual factors were not separated. In England, this belief was seldom put into words but it formed a theme in Chermayeff's writing and lecturing around 1933, when he wrote this passage:

Whims and modes, unrelated to realities, are irrelevant to design. They have no background. They are not 'real'. We have seen around us forms resulting from copyism and adaptation: things created gratuitously to be 'different', or to express some irrational individual ingenuity: forms which are a mockery, belonging to other things disguising the real.[27]

**45**

Delivering a formal lecture at the RIBA in December 1933, on 'New Materials and New Methods', Chermayeff avoided the temptation to bang a drum for everything modern in what he may still have seen as the enemy camp, but gave instead a clear and humorous overview of the relationships between technique, society and building form which was even critical of the more sensational aspects of modernism which his audience had probably come to mock. As he stated elsewhere, the designer's task was not so much to invent as to select.[28] Intelligence and judgment were needed, above all.

> If we were to employ immediately and intelligently the materials and methods of our machine age, to supply the economic and physical needs of humanity, we would release a society of sane individuals.[29]

Chermayeff's emerging architectural ideology contained scientific and social aspects which he believed were as important as the aesthetic. These views were widely shared among modern architects but Chermayeff seems to have gone into these areas with a particularly strong sense of intellectual curiosity which may be attributable to his missed opportunity of studying for a degree at Cambridge, combined with having avoided the sometimes narrowing cultural formation of a standard architectural course and career. The artistic culture of 1930s England was much in awe of science, hoping to find a universal methodology within it that would assist in solving problems in other fields, an alternative way of reaching the bedrock of reality. Chermayeff's contact with the scientific world came through Albert Bacarach, working in baby foods but also a writer on classical music, who introduced him to the well-known scientists J.D. Bernal, the brilliant crystallographer and uncritical admirer of Soviet Russia, Hyman Levy – an Edinburgh Jew from a background of extreme poverty – Lancelot Hogben, Bertrand Russell and A.N. Whitehead.[30] Some of these were members of the 17 October Club, a left wing political forum in which Chermayeff took part, which was also attended by Wells Coates and the young RIBA Librarian, E.J. ('Bobby') Carter, a close friend of the Russian architect Berthold Lubetkin (1901–90) whom Chermayeff knew from soon after his arrival in London.[31] Chermayeff, Lubetkin and Ernö Goldfinger (1902–87) were all significant figures in the London architectural world, all over life-size personalities and all married to English wives, which differentiated them from some of the later émigrés. The three knew each other but each had a markedly different approach to architecture. Unlike the 'Three Musketeers', they never became close friends.

A less predictable influence on Chermayeff's thinking was Andrew Messer, Chief Medical Officer of Health for Newburn District Council in Northumberland from 1893, whom Chermayeff met in the 1920s through Messer's son, the editor of *Farmer's Weekly*, or possibly through Lord De La Warr, one of Messer's circle of friends which included the scientist J.B.S. Haldane, Ramsay MacDonald and the politician Arthur Henderson.[32] As H.C.T. Smith wrote in 1972, 'his interests were by no means confined to medicine. Astronomy, economics, philosophy and above all literature were his favourite subjects. He acted as adviser to one publishing house and lexicographers would ask for his advice on the definition of words'.[33] From Chermayeff's point of view, Messer was important for introducing him to the books and ideas of Patrick Geddes (1854–1932). 'He was very kind to this then young architect, interested more in why, what, where to construct rather than in how and which "shape". I never knew Patrick Geddes but we spoke much of him.'[34]

Geddes had diminished in prominence in the inter-war period but his synoptic view of environment and knowledge stands as one of the continuously challenging exemplars in the English speaking world of planning and architecture. Chermayeff visited Messer in 1939, shortly before leaving for America, and was given an introduction to Geddes's American disciple, Lewis Mumford who developed the idea of the integral environmental region, rather than the city or any other sub-division, as the proper unit for study and action. Jaqueline Tyrwhitt (1905–83), Chermayeff's English teaching colleague at Harvard in the 1950s, was a student of Geddes, and words from Geddes are quoted as epigraphs in the two books written by Chermayeff after the war.

In his speech at the RIBA in December 1933, Chermayeff declared that the ideological battle for modernism had been as good as won during the previous twelve months. His speech indicates a sense of continuing national crisis, nonetheless, and his own activities during the period represent a series of rapid strides. In the first years of his independent practice, he announced himself on his letterhead as an 'Interior Architect'. Perhaps with intentional reference to Chermayeff, Eric Gill commented on this:

> There are a few architects who have really escaped from the play-acting obsession of the period of the Commercial Fulfilment, men who actually see building for what it primarily is; the covering of a space and for whom, therefore, the interior is not an accident. Such is the irony of the situation that they have to call themselves 'interior architects'; but they are the only real architects we have had since the Middle Ages.[35]

In October 1932, Chermayeff applied for a Fellowship of the RIBA, with a form signed by the architects G. Grey Wornum and Edward Maufe, and the architect-writer Christian Barman, the editor of the *Architects' Journal*. In his statement of recommendation, Wornum made some special pleading to cover Chermayeff's lack of architectural training and experience of building, stating that 'He has succeeded in many of his decorative works by a considerable exercise of his architectural ability – in the widest sense of the word.' Wornum was a sympathetic onlooker to modernism rather than an active participant but may have been one of those intended by Chermayeff when he said that he and his group ' found a great number of middle-aged architects who did not quite understand what we were trying to do but were very sympathetic to the effort.'[36] Maufe was one of the older designers working on

Broadcasting House and later supported Chermayeff in his planning appeal over Bentley Wood. The Fellowship application was successful, being passed shortly before the provisions of the Architects' Registration Act of 1931 made it more difficult to acquire professional status solely by peer-group acclamation.

Chermayeff's activity accordingly progressed from 'interior architecture' to encompass the outer frame for the interiors. He designed a project for his own country house at Puttenham, presumably intended to be built on part of Barbara's parents' estate. This exists only in the form of a single published drawing in the *Architectural Review*, November 1932, but the drawing is an elaborate cut-away axonometric in colour, by Chermayeff's early assistant, Colin Crickmay, showing the interior furnishings in detail, with furniture placed to suggest different areas of activity (see page 158). The main bedroom is on the ground floor, with an upper floor to the rear of the house which appears to be a self-contained guest suite with its own kitchen. There is no evidence of a nursery, although the birth of the Chermayeffs' first son, Ivan, on 6 June 1932 might have prompted these ideas of expansion. The text accompanying the publication states that two houses were intended to be built. This house project, presumably a successor to the one discussed in 1930 with Wells Coates, was probably suspended for economic reasons but can be seen in many ways as the germ of Bentley Wood, the weekend house which Chermayeff completed in 1938.

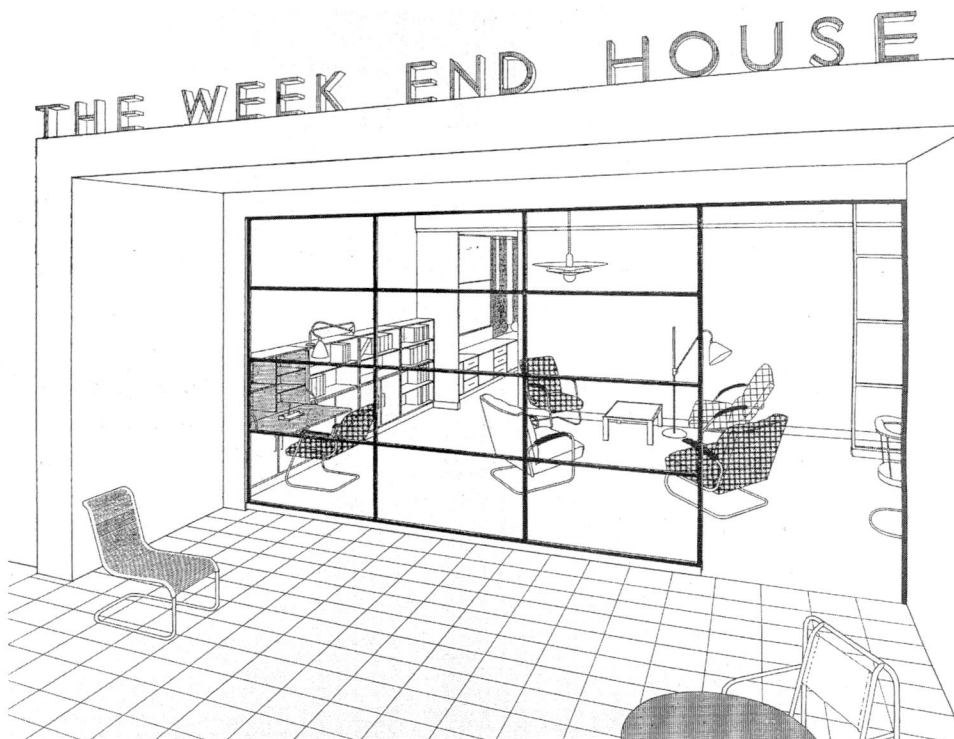

'Week End House', display for Exhibition of British Industrial Art in Relation to the Home, Dorland Hall, 1933.

Chermayeff was interested in the concept of a specific 'weekend house' in the early 1930s. The habit of leaving the city from Friday to Sunday night or Monday was almost universal among the London professional classes who did not already commute in from the Home Counties. In a time of agricultural depression, it was easy to rent a country cottage and still relatively easy to find building land. Both Chermayeffs enjoyed being in the country with dogs, games and weekend guests. They also seem to have liked nude sunbathing, in common with many of their progressive contemporaries, following the fashion begun in Germany after the First World War.[37]

**'Week End House', at Dorland Hall, 1933, showing two PLAN chairs.**

**'Week End House' with PLAN chairs and unit furniture, with wall-mounted 'Bestlite'.**

The cumbersomely-titled Exhibition of British Industrial Art in Relation to the Home, at which Chermayeff exhibited his 'Week End House', was devised by a committee, in which the leading figures were Christopher Hussey and the architect Oliver Hill (1887–1968). Chermayeff and his group viewed them with some suspicion as carpetbaggers in the modernist territory but they succeeded, partly through Hill's amazing powers of persuasion and his contacts in the building trades, in raising backing for the exhibition where the DIA and Twentieth Century Group had failed in their similar ventures.[38] The whole national mood had changed since Waring and Gillow's exhibition five years before, but Chermayeff had moved faster than many other designers. In the minds of purists, Hill's theatrical demonstrations of materials, such as his stone dining room and glass boudoir, which were intended more to catch the attention of the press than as models for modern living, were an unwelcome distraction from their didactic purpose. Hill and Hussey's agenda was primarily aesthetic and sensual but it succeeded in attracting a wide public for modern design, bringing publicity to Chermayeff, Coates and McGrath in the process, among other architects and designers.

At the exhibition, usually referred to as 'Dorland Hall', after the building in Lower Regent Street where it was held, Coates exhibited 'The Minimum Flat', a prototype for the flats at Lawn Road which were just commencing construction in Hampstead for Jack Pritchard's new business enterprise, Isokon. Chermayeff's Week End House was the counterpart to this in the exhibition, exhibited by the company 'PLAN Ltd.' with which Chermayeff was closely associated. PLAN was formed in December 1932 and operated from Chermayeff's offices at the Pantheon, 173 Oxford Street. The publisher Dennis Cohen, later a client for a house by Mendelsohn and Chermayeff, was one of the directors.[39] As Barbara Tilson describes it, 'PLAN Ltd. was solely a selling company for interior furnishings which were manufactured for it by other firms.'[40] It issued catalogues containing a range of products selected or specified by Chermayeff, some of which were adaptations of existing designs, such as the wall-mounted version of the 'Bestlite', first produced by Best & Lloyd of Smethwick in 1931 and still in production today. The range was deliberately small, distinguished by its chairs with sprung upholstery and removable covers.

As Barbara Tilson has discovered, these were based almost without variant on designs by Walter Knoll of Stuttgart. This derivation was not publicly declared in the 1930s and Chermayeff seems to have been happy for them to be published as his own designs, for example in Herbert Read's *Art and Industry*, 1934, which made a prominent feature of PLAN items. The licensing of German designs for manufacture in Britain was one way of circumventing the high import duties introduced in 1931 but while Chermayeff was anxious to give credit to the Austrian-born designer Franz Schuster for his authorship of PLAN's unit furniture, the source of the chair designs was never publicly revealed.

The unit chests of drawers and shelves were designs developed by Schuster in connection with the Frankfurt housing programme under Ernst May in 1930–31, and would probably have been seen by Chermayeff on his visit to these projects with Coates and Pritchard in 1931, given Pritchard's interest in the use of plywood in furniture. Coates himself was also developing very similar unit furniture at this time. As Chermayeff wrote, 'Professor Schuster's furniture is so rational and unmannered as to be inevitable, and in my opinion is the best solution of economic yet good class furniture which has yet been produced in this country at any time.'[41]

In preparing these designs for manufacture by Henry Stone and Co. of Banbury, Chermayeff adjusted the dimensions from metric to imperial, based on a module of 1ft 8ins, with 4ins increments.[42] The architect Birkin Haward, who was an assistant with Mendelsohn and Chermayeff, believes that John Fortey contributed his 'craft backing' to the making of the pieces in England. Cheap furniture in England was built with thin plywood facings and panels on a solid frame, imitating – however remotely – a more traditional frame and panel construction, while Schuster's designs used a thicker plywood, reducing the bulk of the piece and removing the distinction between carcass and facing, with no nail holes or other visible construction on the outside. For the English market, PLAN furniture was available in 'All Oak' (in fact a veneered plywood), as well as with figured birch doors or drawer fronts. Further colours were 'coral, shagreen, sky blue, primrose or ivory'.[43] There was, indeed, a sense of analogy between this furniture – which was intended to offer a degree of individuation in the assembly of units with modular dimensions, rather than in the individual units themselves, and the concept of the unit house which Coates and Chermayeff were both working on at this time. Chermayeff believed that its lessons had been incorporated in the wartime Utility Furniture scheme in Britain.[44]

PLAN Chairs, catalogue cover, 1934, with photograph from Walter Knoll Co. catalogue.

Right: PLAN Chairs, catalogue, 1934. 'M' series chairs with metal frames.

Bottom: PLAN Chairs, catalogue, 1934. 'W' series chairs, with wooden frames.

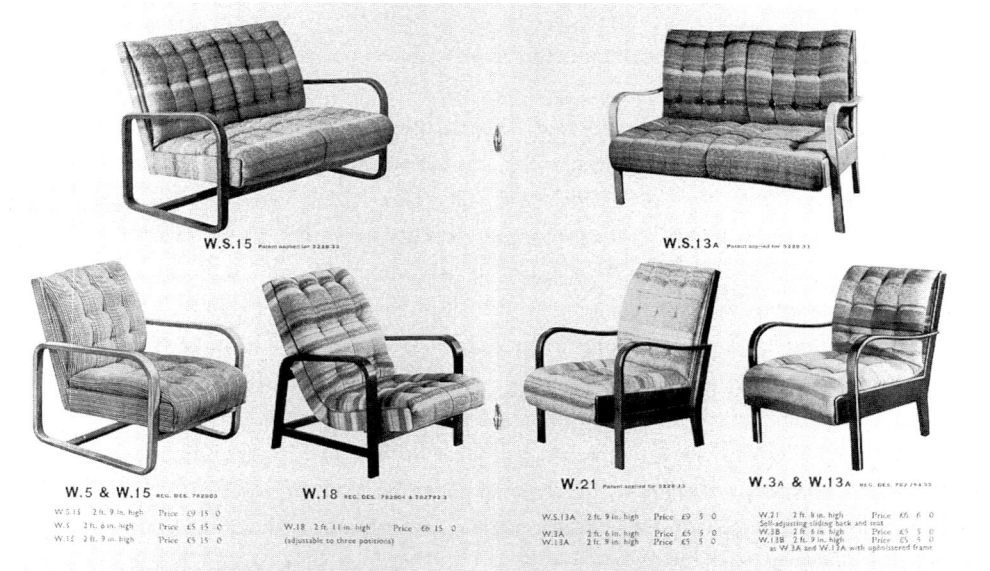

The original chairs by Knoll seen and admired by Chermayeff were in the station hotel at Stuttgart, a design by Paul Bonatz whose adjacent railway station of 1914 was a key work of German proto-modernism. The distinctiveness of these chairs lay in the flat steel springing, in place of a conventional bulk-creating coiled spring. This acted more like a webbing in the seat and back of the chair. Over this was buttoned a feather-filled cushion spanning seat and back together, providing the comfort of an upholstered, sprung chair with much less visual or physical weight, and also a covering that could be removed for cleaning. Knoll's catalogue *Polstermöbel: Stahlrohrmöbel* of 1932 shows a range of variants on this principle, including tubular steel arm and leg frames cantilevered in the manner already conventional in steel-frame furniture. The seat and back frames were always in timber. A larger number of models had wooden arm and leg frames, sometimes in a continuous loop, sometimes an inverted U, and sometimes with separately articulated joints with the back or the arm supports. There were some two-seater models, and some with adjustable backs. On the steel framed models, the arms always had an added piece of polished wood, or in one case, an upholstered arm-piece, to avoid the cold sensation of the steel.

Chermayeff patented these designs in England under the name of PLAN in May 1933, some including minor modifications of the Knoll originals. He patented Knolls springing method under his own name for use in England. There was nothing underhand about this and Chermayeff remained on good terms with Walter Knoll, whose son Hans came over to London in the later 1930s when the Knolls were trying to find more capital to rescue PLAN. Even so, Chermayeff seems to have enlarged his original role as entrepreneur and adaptor of these designs to claim an unjustifiable degree of authorship, and was defensive when challenged about this in later life. We may extend the philosophy behind his statement to the *Architects' Journal* about Schuster's designs to a general principle that where a good design exists, there is no need to invent another for its own sake, for the conflict raises a broader paradox about the relationship between modernism's search for the ideal type of anonymous generic product on one hand, and the simultaneous growth in the prestige of attributing designs to individuals as a means of marketing on the other. Design history stands uncomfortably between collectors' and museums' desires for identifiable authors and the knowledge that most products are the outcome of a collaborative process.

It is most unlikely that Chermayeff was able to make much money out of PLAN Ltd. Joan Ridge, who was employed in 1934 as a young secretary for PLAN business, found that 'there was no organisation behind this … and there were very few orders anyway', so that she was diverted to general work for the architectural practice.[45] The most popular model of chair was the W5, with a continuous wooden arm/leg, made of solid jointed wood rather than bent ply, unlike the chairs by Alvar Aalto which were introduced to London with an exhibition at Fortnum and Mason organised by Morton Shand in 1933 and which probably cut into PLAN's potential market. A sample of W5 was purchased by Manchester City Art Gallery following its tour with a reduced version of the Dorland Hall exhibition, as a specimen of good modern design. Three to four thousand of these chairs were produced per year.[46] Nikolaus Pevsner remarked that 'in proportion and detail both the single units and the complete wardrobes, chests of drawers, etc. are equally perfect. The prices are high, owing partly to the difficulties in advertising furniture under a brand name.'[47] The sales were accordingly disappointing and Chermayeff relinquished his interest in the company in 1936 to

Walter Trier, a German émigré, while Henry Stone & Son withdrew from their involvement in sales and manufacture at the same time. Stone's sales manager, Frank Dancer, told Barbara Tilson that the tubular steel models sold least well.[48]

Chermayeff liked to be identified with these pieces and had them in his home. They exemplify his design philosophy of physical and psychological comfort, already evident in his Waring and Gillow period, as well as his feeling that modern design in England should avoid extremes. The catalogue for PLAN chairs introduces the concept of 'the NEW laziness', explaining 'it is the laziness of modern people (like you) who do a hard day's work and have, perhaps, a flat or a small house and no servant. Such people demand and deserve an easy chair of sublime comfort, that takes up very little room, can easily be pushed about and needs no effort at all to keep clean.'[49] The PLAN furniture catalogue announced that 'PLAN is modern furniture, but it is not extreme.'[50]

The Week End House at the Dorland Hall was a way of launching the PLAN range as well as being an end in itself. To put the nature of this project in context requires some understanding of the high hopes that were held about standardisation and prefabrication in the building industry at the beginning of the 1930s. In Frankfurt, where Schuster developed his furniture, conventional attitudes to construction and equipment had been completely transformed. The municipally-sponsored programmes of research and development, like Grete Schutte-Lihotsky's work on kitchens, were guided by technology and social science, resulting in a 'scientific' analysis of human ergonomics. The results not only looked better but worked better and were cheaper. Design reform in England was still at the stage of improving the individual product, rather than being able to grasp the totality of the environment, except in special conditions like the London Underground, where Chermayeff's sponsor for his RIBA Fellowship, Christian Barman, was working under the direction of Frank Pick to create a unified visual identity.

The design reform lobby was given a wider hearing in the early 1930s than in the previous decade, on radio and in the general press, including the *Listener* and the *Weekend Review*, a paper founded by Gerald Barry in 1930. The lobby hoped that given the profundity of economic crisis, the government might act, and Jack Pritchard became involved in the group, 'Political and Economic Planning' (PEP for short) which worked to provide a plan for action on a range of social and cultural issues. In fact, the political situation in Britain never became so bad that the laws of liberal economics were suspended by state intervention – as they were to a large extent by Franklin Roosevelt in the USA – and as the economy began to improve during 1933, it was left to private enterprise to make at least symbolic gestures towards the creation of standardised prototypes, with the hope that these would become commercially successful. With Pritchard's backing, Wells Coates made designs for concrete 'Isotype' houses in 1931. At the Ideal Home Exhibition of 1933, his concept for the 'Sunspan House' was promoted by the contractors E.L. Berg, who imagined large suburban estates of them instead of the twenty or so examples that were ever actually constructed.

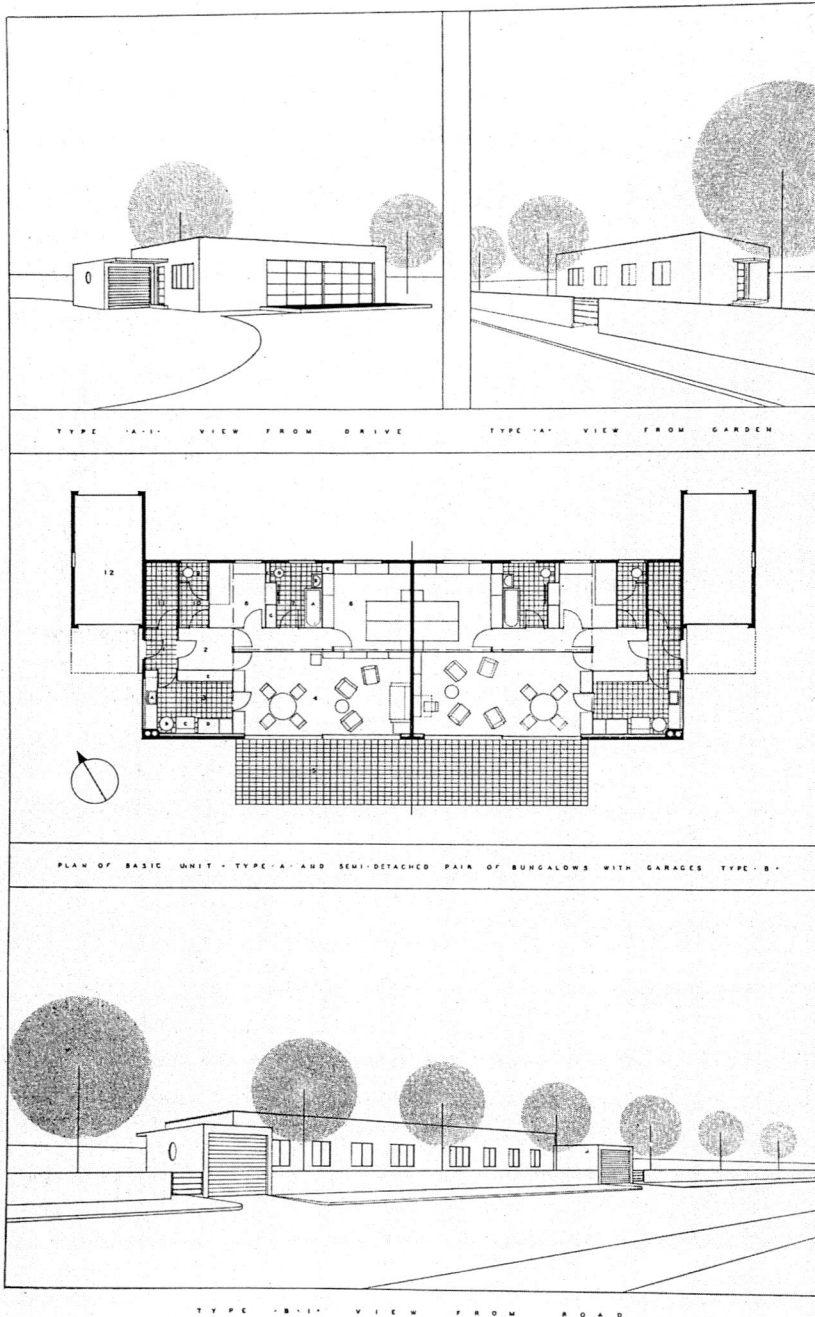

TYPE ·A·I· VIEW FROM DRIVE    TYPE ·A· VIEW FROM GARDEN

PLAN OF BASIC UNIT · TYPE ·A· AND SEMI-DETACHED PAIR OF BUNGALOWS WITH GARAGES TYPE ·B·

TYPE ·B·I· VIEW FROM ROAD

Chermayeff's Week End House was a representative of a comparable system called the 'Kernal House' devised for PLAN Ltd., to be built of concrete. Both presented the architect in the role of product designer, and the house as an industrial product, which it was hoped would at last benefit from the design research and rationalised production associated with industry, as already demonstrated in the big German housing programmes. The example at the Dorland Hall omitted the kitchen and entrance hall but included the rest of the plan, its presentation being sponsored by Whiteley's, the department store in Bayswater. Visitors could enter the house, with its plywood-lined walls, through the large living room window and experience rooms furnished with PLAN products and other selected items, including Best & Lloyd lights.[51] 'Housewives should not miss the solution of bed making in the Chermayeff bed,' wrote Joseph Peter Thorp in the *Architectural Review*. The bed had a tubular steel frame but other details of this device were not recorded.[52]

Published information on these Kernal houses is scarce, consisting chiefly of a double page of 'Unit Houses' in the DIA magazine, *Design for Today*, which discusses the plan but gives no technical information. Among Chermayeff's papers in the Avery Library at Columbia University, there are photographs of other combinations in similar graphic style. Five main types were available, with one- and two-storey versions, the latter being designed either as a family house or as a block of flats. The houses were conceived as freestanding or as semi-detached pairs, with mirrored plans, on a wide frontage. The published plan of Type 'A' shows Chermayeff already considering the separation of different domestic functions that grew as a theme through his work. Thus the kitchen is placed next to the front door (there being no 'tradesman's entrance'). The main entry route bypasses the kitchen and leads into a relatively generous lobby – such as Chermayeff might later have termed a 'lock'. This acts as the only link between living-dining room, representing the daytime use, and the bedrooms and bathroom. This room has large sliding windows coming right down to the ground, and access to a terrace on the same level. On the 'night' side there is one single and one double bedroom, with a shared bathroom between them giving an acoustic separation. The rear windows are square and relatively small. The houses mostly have attached garages which offer the only relief to their cubic austerity.

It is hard to imagine a more reductive design than the Kernal House, which has none of the jauntiness of Coates's Sunspan houses. It seems to have fitted Chermayeff's mood of 'tabula rasa' however. In his letter to Eric Bird of the *Architect and Building News* he wrote that 'prophets and pioneers must, I think, be fanatics and purists, exaggerating their cause in order to successfully propagate their gospel'.[53] A typescript for an after-dinner talk to the Architecture Club on 'Unit Building' survives among Chermayeff's papers. This group was founded in 1923 to air architectural issues in a friendly atmosphere, mixing professionals and outsiders. The talk does not refer to Chermayeff's own projects but shows his underlying interest in standardisation of dimensions. As he concluded, 'The intelligent use of these units may give us "units of intelligence". We may thus achieve culture.'[54]

Barbara Tilson has drawn attention to the similarities between the Kernal House and a series of designs for 'Kernhaüser', published in *Moderne Bauformen* in June 1932.[55] Some of these are in timber, some in concrete, mostly single-storey, plain like Chermayeff's design but tighter in plan and less lavishly windowed. Some are shown with exemplary modern furniture. These were presumably a response to the decline in construction of public housing in Germany after 1929, and are a mixture of paper projects and built examples. 'Kern', as in English, means the centre, nucleus or kernel, and some of these examples were designed for the addition of rooms at a later date. Chermayeff offered a range of models but they were not accretive 'wachsende haüser' in this way. Still, it is highly likely that Chermayeff knew of these German examples.

The promotion of the Kernal House (the name was quickly dropped) and PLAN were taken still further in the exhibition which Chermayeff arranged at Whiteley's store in Bayswater in the winter of 1933-4, as an 'Exhibition of Modern Living', constructing another version of the Week End House, complete with all its rooms, and showing it in a setting purged of the more playful elements of the Dorland Hall, with samples of a whole range of house furnishings. This exhibition has never been given the same level of attention as the 1933 Dorland Hall show. It was to some extent a repeat of the Waring and Gillow formula of an exemplary demonstration within a department store, having a commercial umbrella to avoid the need either to find sponsors or rent out space, but was very different in actual content, showing the distance travelled not only by Chermayeff but by the whole modernist design faction in England. It also had more the character of a building products exhibition, bringing to a potentially wider public the kind of display that had been inaugurated in the Building Centre, opened in 1931 in New Bond Street. As such, it showed a kind of equivalence between furniture and other components. Although PLAN furniture was given prominence, there were also samples of a wide range of Thonet chairs and tables, and fabrics, rugs, paintings, wood engravings and books. An advertisement, presumably written by Chermayeff, in *Design for Today* magazine, announced that 'a great theme runs through this exhibition. The theme is the UNITY of a home that is equipped honestly for modern living', revealing some of Chermayeff's underlying outlook in relation to design and life.[56]

Advertisement for Exhibition of Modern Living, Whiteley's.

The architect F.R.S. Yorke wrote enthusiastically in his 'Trade Notes' column in the *Architects' Journal*, that it was 'the best organised and most intelligently selected collection of materials and equipment for the modern home I have ever seen assembled. Architects should visit this exhibition and get to know it by heart.'[57] The writer 'R.P.' in the DIA magazine, *Design for Today* even referred to it as 'Mr Chermayeff's Platonic heaven', since it was set up as a showroom rather than as a place to buy the things on show. Whiteley's was a solidly middle-class store, and this writer felt that the modernist aim of reaching lower down the social scale had once more been missed because of the prices and the nature of the location, even though many of the objects themselves were 'in their sphere, the first artistic fruits of a hundred years of industrial development, the response to the growth of an urban proletariat'.[58] The inadequate publicity meant that fewer people heard about the exhibition than it deserved. By 1936, advertisements show that it was still running but that the purity of the initial conception had been diluted.[59]

**Exhibition of Modern Living, Whiteley's.**

If the Kernal House, with a score of zero, was commercially even less successful than the Sunspan House, it was the evolutionary precursor of the first house that Chermayeff built, at 116 Dunchurch Road, Rugby, 1933–4, discussed in the next chapter. The ideal of the standard house type, more or less industrially produced, a commonplace of modernism, stayed with Chermayeff for the rest of his career and grew in importance in his mind, although he became increasingly interested in the organisation of the plan form and its broader planning implications, the latter an aspect not consciously considered in the 1930s.

After Whiteleys, the initiative in design polemics passed back to Oliver Hill, when he coordinated a successor exhibition at Dorland Hall in 1934, the Exhibition of Contemporary Industrial Design in the Home. This displayed a mock-up of a flat from Lubetkin and Tecton's Highpoint 1, which was shown with PLAN chairs and unit furniture, mixed with some Aalto pieces, a combination transferred almost without alteration to the flat at Highpoint occupied personally by Berthold Lubetkin.[60] In other respects, Hill allowed his showmanship to carry him away, with items like a piano covered in shagreen (snake skin). PLAN Ltd. exhibited a living room in a prominent position near the beginning of the exhibition, with 'W' series wooden chairs and unit furniture, Canadian birch plywood wall panelling, a plain brown rug from Royal Wilton and an 'Ekco' radio by Wells Coates. This was one of several purely modern room sets, including a 'Plastic Bathroom' by Connell, Ward & Lucas, perhaps the most extreme modern architects of the decade.

While Oliver Hill was clearly friendly towards Chermayeff, the feeling was not mutual. The latter was one of 14 signatories of a letter to the *Architects' Journal* of 1 November 1934, supporting an editorial in the magazine critical of the exhibition because of its concentration on luxury goods. Coates had actually withdrawn from the exhibition. In a lecture of 1935 to the Publicity Club, Chermayeff said, 'Unfortunately, decorative mountains have been made out of Oliver Hills, which loom large in the public eye but do not represent the industrial machine age at all.'[61] By this time, modernism was in danger of becoming a fashion, for Chermayeff's talk coincided with the Royal Academy's Winter Exhibition of British Art in Industry. This could have represented a takeover by the modernists of the citadel of convention but the task of reconciling a modern style to values of class and nationhood represented by the Royal Academy and its partner, the Royal Society of Arts, meant the sacrifice of those characteristics that Chermayeff recognised as modern. His talk recalls the real nature of design; in his words, 'Design is far more [than] the application of technique to materials. It stands for the application of technique to thinking.'[62] Chermayeff proposed that insularity should be abandoned and that figures of the stature of Walter Gropius, László Moholy-Nagy (both resident in England by this date) and Mies van der Rohe should remind the 'fashionmongers' how far behind the times they actually were.

The most successful product of Chermayeff's career as an industrial designer was the first of the two radios he designed for the firm of E.K. Cole & Co. of Southend, a predecessor to the Coates version exhibited at the Dorland Hall in 1934. In 1932, the company invested in heat-forming equipment for the production of Bakelite in order to avoid the import duties on German Bakelite cases which they had previously used. Chermayeff and McGrath were invited to submit designs. Chermayeff's Ekco 74, an upright rectangle on a recessed base, with rounded edges and two metal-covered strip handles on the sides to help in lifting the heavy object, was chosen for production in 1933. It was the first plastic radio made in Britain, competing with the popular Murphy cases, designed in wood by the architect-designer, R.D. Russell. The face is symmetrical, with a circular loudspeaker fret in the upper part, a double tuning band below, and three knobs at the bottom. Its formal quality derives from appearing like a sliced-off section of an extrusion. It was made in black, of which Chermayeff approved, and a mottled finish resembling walnut, which he deplored, but which the company hoped would appeal to 'the market'.

A tubular steel stand was available for it, wrapping around three sides of the base. A writer in *Design for Today* questioned whether this was an appropriate material, and was firmly squashed

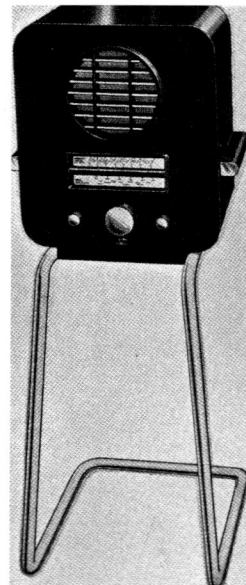

Ekco 74 radio on tubular steel stand, for E.K. Cole & Co, 1933.

by Chermayeff's reply to the magazine that 'Highly proficient engineers of both the British Broadcasting Corporation and the makers themselves have no qualms with regard to it. As for the rest, it is surely less questionable as a support to a wireless set than straw, plasticene or marmalade.'[63] Nonetheless, a more conventional wooden stand was available for the faint-hearted. At 13 guineas in 'walnut' and 14 in black, with an extra 35 shillings for the stand, the Ekco 74 radio was not cheap, and a different version was marketed as the Model 64 which was probably cheaper to make, for its handles grow out of the sides as an integral moulding, presumably requiring less assembly time.[64]

Nikolaus Pevsner wrote, 'the shape of it was something completely new, nothing comparable existed, either in England or abroad. It was the result of a careful study of function and a genuinely artistic imagination.' [65] In fact, McGrath's design for a standard loudspeaker cabinet for Broadcasting House was not dissimilar in overall form, with its rounded edges and inset base, although made of laminated timber.[66] It was a commercial risk for the company because of the high cost of tooling up for production but it paid for itself in sales, giving them confidence to add Coates's circular AD 65 to the range in 1934, together with another of his designs. The AD 65, one of the best-known industrial designs of the 1930s, took the shape of the loudspeaker as the basis for its circular form.

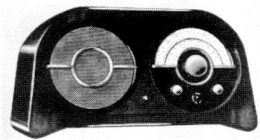

**Ekco AC86 radio for E.K. Cole & Co, 1935.**

In 1935, Chermayeff designed a further radio for Ekco, the AC 86, with a speaker and dial in matching circles at each end of a low-lying case with a rounded top, coming down to fin-like legs at each end which raised the main body off its surface. This model advertised the new 'clear-cut reality' receiver. Pevsner related the story of these commissions as a parable about the commercial advantages to be derived from good modern design, although in another context he also saw them as the innocent origin of applied streamlining in radio design.[67] Chermayeff's catalogue of industrial designs was extended by two clocks for Garrard of London, shown in the Royal Academy Exhibition of 1935, and an adaptation of a Steinway piano, with white tapered legs, made by Whiteley's and featured in some of Chermayeff's interiors. He appears to have continued designing rugs at least until 1935, but his designs were no longer signed or identified in published photos of his interiors.

Notes
1 See Raymond McGrath, 'Mansfield D. Forbes, an intimate appreciation', *Architectural Review*, April, 1936, pp.173-6; Hugh Carey (1984), *Mansfield Forbes and his Cambridge*, Cambridge University Press.
2 Conversation with author, April 1994.
3 See Donal O'Donovan (1995), *God's Architect, a life of Raymond McGrath*, Dublin, Kilbride Books, p.110.
4 See Susan Lasdun, 'H. de C. reviewed', *Architectural Review*, September 1996, pp.68-72 and Alan Powers, 'Function and Propriety at the Architectural Review', *Matrix*, 19, 1999, pp.22-9.
5 O'Donovan, 1995, p.134.

6 See Betjeman's letter to George, Anne and Anthony Barnes, 8 January 1946, in Candida Lycett-Green, ed. (1994) *John Betjeman Letters, Volume One: 1926 to 1951*, London, Methuen, p.382. Quote from letter of Betjeman to Gavin Stamp, 14 January 1980, kindly communicated by Gavin Stamp.

7 Reference from 'Chronology of the MARS Group 1927-39', by Kenji Watanabe, as part of MA thesis at the Architectural Association. See also John Cornforth (1988), *The Search for a Style*, London, André Deutsch, p.77.

8 A complete text appears as an appendix in F. Elgohary (1965), 'Wells Coates and his position at the beginning of the modern movement in England', PhD, University College, London.

9 McGrath, 1936, p.175.

10 Letter to Etchells in Avery Library. Points 1-15 reprinted in Plunz, 1983, pp.109-10, where the text is dated 1930.

11 Chermayeff to Eric Bird, 31 October 1930, Avery Library.

12 ibid. Some punctuation added.

13 ibid.

14 This and subsequent information comes from MARS papers in the RIBA Library, Ove Arup MSS, ArO 1/5/1.

15 ibid. ArO1/4/2. The motion was seconded by J.M. Richards, F.R.S. Yorke, Francis Skinner, Frederick Gibberd and H. de C. Hastings. Chermayeff is recorded as having made an additional amendment but it is unclear what it was. 'I was too busy and involved to be in on the foundation of MARS but joined soon after the Athens Charter period,' Chermayeff to Anthony Jackson, 13 December 1963, Avery Library.

16 Chermayeff and Richards, 'A Hundred Years Ahead', *Architects' Journal*, 10 January 1935, p.80.

17 Chermayeff to Anthony Jackson, 13 December 1963, Avery Library.

18 See letters from Wells Coates to Jack Pritchard of 21.10.30 and 27.10.30, in Pritchard Archive, University of East Anglia, PP/23/2/26 and 34.

19 See *Architect and Building News*, 13 March 1931, p.376.

20 When asked by Richard Plunz, in interview, when he had visited the Bauhaus, Chermayeff replied that it was in 1931.

21 V. H. Goldsmith 'The Studio Interiors', *Architectural Review*, July 1932, p.53.

22 Raymond McGrath, 'Recalling the Twenties and Thirties', 8 February 1972. Text in McGrath biography file in RIBA Library.

23 Paul Nash (1932), *Room and Book*, London, Soncino Press, p.32.

24 F.R.S. Yorke, 'Details', *Architectural Review*, July 1932, p.68.

25 See *Architectural Review*, July 1932, p.65, plate 64, and Herbert Read (1934), *Art and Industry*, p.79. For other publication listing, see Plunz, 1983, p.378.

26 Copy at the Chermayeff house, Cape Cod.

27 'Design Demonstrated', *Design for Today*, July 1933, p.92.

28 e.g. 'The Modern Approach to Architecture and its Equipment', lecture at Leeds, published as 'The Modernist in Leeds', *Architects' Journal*, 8 March 1933, p.339.

29 'New Materials and New Methods', *RIBA Journal*, 23 December 1933, p.173.

30 On these scientists, see Gary Werskey (1978), *The Visible College*, New York, Reinhold and Winston.

31 Information on scientists from Chermayeff interview with Richard Plunz, 20 September 1980. Chermayeff seems to have been present when Lubetkin spoke on Modern Soviet Architecture to the Art Workers Guild in 1932, when George Bernard Shaw was also in the audience.

32 See letter from Chermayeff to Roy Gazzard, FRIBA, University of Durham, 20 December 1973. Avery Library. Chermayeff mentioned Messer's importance to him when lecturing at Newcastle-upon-Tyne in 1969.

33 H.C.T. Smith, Historical Note, Newburn Urban District council, Part of Annual Report of the Medical Officer of Health for 1972, December 1973. Cyclostyled document in Avery Library.

34 Chermayeff letter to Gazzard, 20 December 1973.

35 Eric Gill (1934), *Art*, p.104.

36 Chermayeff interview with Richard Plunz, 20 September 1980.

37 Photographs of Barbara in the nude are in family albums. She described to me how in Cape Cod in the 1940s she and Serge would walk nude along miles of beach in the company of Jack Phillips and his beautiful wife.

38 See Alan Powers 'Oliver Hill as exhibition designer', *Thirties Society Journal*, 7, 1991, pp.28-39.

39 In interview with Richard Plunz, Chermayeff said that Cohen first introduced him to Henry Stone & Son of Banbury, the English manufacturers of PLAN furniture.

40 Barbara Tilson, 'Plan Furniture 1932-1938: The German Connection', *Journal of Design History*, Vol.3, Nos. 2-3, 1990, pp.145-55.

41 *Architects' Journal*, 6 July 1935, p.7.

42 See Nikolaus Pevsner (1937), *An Inquiry into Industrial Art in England*, Cambridge, p.37. 'The designs are derived from the German architect Schuster in 1930. His patent on the constructional system was taken over by a distinguished architect in England who had to alter several of the sizes and proportions.'

43 1934 catalogue, author's collection. In a letter to Harry Ward of Crosby, Liverpool, 12 May 1938, inserted in the catalogue, PLAN Ltd. announce that 'as a later development we are making the unit furniture in waxed stripy walnut, birch, at the same prices as catalogued for oak'.

44 Chermayeff to Daniel Wildenstein, 12 November 1946, Avery Library. Referring to the recent acceptance of unit furniture in the USA, 'The original equivalents were developed in Germany in 1929-31 and went into mass production then - were followed by development on similar lines in England some four years later where they became consolidated in government sponsored utility furniture during the war.'

45 Joan Ridge, letter to Jill Theis, 13 August 1995. See also Miss Ridge's reminiscences in 'Trust traces living links with architects', *Pavilion Trust Newsletter*, Bexhill, July 1998, p.2.

46 Pevsner, 1937, p.34.

47 ibid.

48 Tilson, 1990, fn 35.

49 PLAN chairs catalogue, n.d. Author's collection. This is probably a post-1936 version of the catalogue.

50 PLAN furniture catalogue, 1934. Author's collection.

51 Catalogue, *Exhibition of British Industrial Art in Relation to the Home*, 1933, pp.22-5. The original 'Bestlite', a desk light with a circular base and an articulated curved arm to hold the lamp fitting, was designed by R.D. Best for the Birmingham firm, Best & Lloyd, c.1930. This was apparently adapted on Chermayeff's instructions to become a standard lamp, on a longer upright support with a wider base, and called the 'Bestplan' light, (Model 29893). A wall-mounted version of the Bestlite (Model 29532) was developed on a similar basis. Both have remained almost continuously in production and can currently be found in English stores. See Plunz, 1983, p.379 and Kate Child, 'Best & Lloyd Ltd., 1868-1989' in Barbara Tilson, ed. (1989), *Made in Birmingham, Design and Industry 1889 to 1989*, Studley, Brewin Books.

52 Joseph Peter Thorp, 'Scenario for a National Exhibition', Architectural Review, July 1933, p.23. Pointing out the congruity of the Minimum Flat and Week End House, Thorp wrote, 'One supposes that the modern young man, having moved from a Coates single flat with his charming wife into a double flat in the Isokon block, has now graduated (and collected the modest means necessary) for the possession of the Chermayeff retreat, and clearly a new race will obviously be evolved in this stimulating environment.'

53 Chermayeff to Eric Bird, 31 October 1930.

54 Chermayeff 'Unit Building', Avery Library, p.10. Dated by Chermayeff to 1929/30 but possibly later. The records of the Architecture Club were destroyed in the war. Information provided by the secretary, Peter Murray.

55 *Moderne Bauformen*, XXXI, June 1932, pp.297-308. Reference in Tilson, 1984.

56 *Design for Today*, January 1934, p.iii.

57 F.R.S. Yorke, 'Trade Notes', *Architects' Journal*, 7 December 1933, p.741.

58 'Revolution in Bayswater' by 'R.P.', *Design for Today*, January 1934, pp.32-3.

59 See advertisement in *Design for Today*, April 1936.

60 See *Design for Today*, December 1934, pp.454-5 and *Architectural Review*, January 1936, p.16 and plate ii.

61 Chermayeff MS 'Publicity Club', 21 January 1935, Avery Library.

62 ibid. I have altered the word order in first sentence and added a word, assuming it to have been wrongly typed. The original reads 'Design is far more the technique of application of materials.'

63 Serge Chermayeff, 'Ekco Radio Cabinet', *Design for Today*, November 1933, responding to comment in issue of October 1933.

64 The two stands are illustrated side by side in Raymond McGrath, 'Modern Radio Design', *Commercial Art*, August 1935, p.42. McGrath's article gives the following technical details: 'The Bakelite case is in two pieces, the case proper and the loudspeaker fret. The average thickness of the case is less than three-sixteenths of an inch, with internal stiffening ribs at intervals to which, in some cases, are attached the brass screw threads, moulded firmly into place, to which fixings for the chassis are arranged. The handles are moulded hollow. The loudspeaker fret has stainless metal strips moulded in position. Die and mould for such a cabinet weigh nearly fifteen tons. A 1,500 ton hydraulic press at the "Ekco" Bakelite factory produces two such cabinets simultaneously. The colour possibilities with the material are unlimited.' The Model 64 is illustrated in *Decorative Art Yearbook* 1934, p.126.

65 Pevsner, 1937, p.105.

66 See McGrath, 1935, p.43.

67 Nikolaus Pevsner, 'Broadcasting comes of age', *Architectural Review*, May 1940, p.190.

# The Mendelsohn and Chermayeff Partnership

Chermayeff's house in Rugby for Dr and Mrs Shann was a modest beginning to his career as an architect. Mrs Shann, whose husband was the biology master at Rugby School, was the protagonist, having apparently attended a lecture by Chermayeff at the School in which he claimed, in what sounds like propaganda for the Kernal House, that he could build a labour-saving detached house for a middle-class family for £1,000. Mrs Shann found a plot on the west side of the long Dunchurch Road, one of the southern approaches to the Midlands town, with a fairly steep gradient and open views to the rear. The house was built with her money, and although it went over budget, she kept Chermayeff to his cost limit.[1]

CANTILEVERED BALCONY and GROUND and FIRST FLOOR PLANS. Garage, heating chamber and storeroom are in a semi-basement.

**House for Mr & Mrs Shann, 108 Dunchurch Road, Rugby, 1933-34.**

**Right: Shann House, Rugby, plans.**

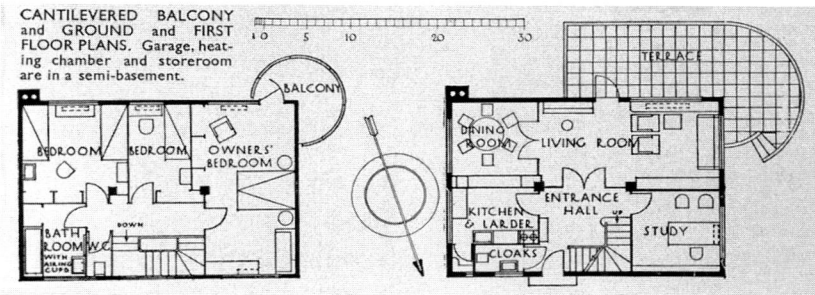

Planned as a two-by-three rectangle, on a module of just over ten feet, the house has a part-basement with store and boiler room, with an attached garage, its roof forming a terrace to the living room above.[2] The ground floor shares with the Type A Kernal House the lengthwise division of the plan into two equal zones. In this case, living and dining extend from end to end of the southern sector, with a four-leafed glazed screen in timber dividing the two parts. A Regency dining chair – of a type recognised by English modernists as being a valid precursor of modern design – is visible through the screen in one of the published photographs. The northern half of the plan is divided into three equal squares, the centre one being a generous hallway, with stairs winding up to the right of the door, a study beyond this, with maximum acoustic separation (something Dr Shann apparently took care to secure), and a kitchen to the left of the door, serving the dining room through a partition wall. The span across the middle of the plan, between the hall and the living room, was glazed across its whole width, matching the dining room partition, creating a degree of transparency without open planning as such, with double doors in the centre. The living room has a glazed door onto the terrace which is finished with a rounded retaining wall. Part of the space of the

63

kitchen is taken by a cloakroom immediately next to the front door, which is approached either from a street gate on the upper part of the site, or up stairs from the sunken driveway. The upper storey contained three bedrooms (double, twin and single) and a bathroom, with access from the master bedroom to the house's moment of expressionist exuberance, a round balcony of thin projecting concrete, describing a three-quarter circle about the centre point of the house corner, echoing the curve of the terrace below. The three bars of the balcony railing sail round the curve, and a tubular ladder ascends to the flat roof above. The ground floor windows are concentrated on this corner for the best view.

Shann House, Rugby, living room with view into dining room.

In a letter to an Open University student in 1975, Chermayeff explained, somewhat elliptically, that 'the "shape" must have come from something seen, "crisp Mediterranean" balcony of course, obvious potential with reinforced concrete, homogeneous structure design'.[3] As one of the earlier examples of a modern movement house in England, and one of the first in the Midlands, the Shann House attracted much local attention but no overt hostility. In some respects, it seems conservative in relation to the asymmetrical concrete cantilevers of the early work of Connell, Ward and Lucas. Rather than emphasising the horizontality of the glazing bars, Chermayeff treated them as pure vertical rectangles. Apart from the projecting balcony, the concrete is used no differently from a masonry wall. It may have been a coincidence - or perhaps the product of people thinking alike in the culture of modernism in England - that the publication of the house in the *Architectural Review* in March 1935 came after an article by P. Morton Shand extolling the model of the standardised Georgian house as a precursor of modernism. Shand also believed that reticence and the preservation of a solid wall surface were England's potential aesthetic contribution to the modern movement. The Shann House, a product of a latter-day revival of standardisation, seems almost a programmatic demonstration of these points.

The structure is monolithic four-inch reinforced concrete, the use of which during the early years of modernism in England was almost a religious principle, despite its very poor insulation. There was a further two inches of cork insulation, with a lining of timber in the rooms, similar in effect to the Week End House, as exhibited. The builders, Foster & Dicksee Ltd., were joinery specialists and selected for their ability to make good shuttering, 'when no small builder could undertake the experiment'.[4] They were able to construct the ample fitted furniture and cupboards that Chermayeff designed, and which were commented on as the main feature of the house in McGrath's account of it in his book, *Twentieth Century Houses*, 1934.[5]

During the construction of the Shann House, Chermayeff went into partnership with Erich Mendelsohn and his architectural career made a dramatic leap forward.[6] The two men had met more than once in Berlin, where Mendelsohn completed his house on the Rupenhorn, a western hilltop suburb overlooking the Wannsee, in 1929. In his letter to Eric Bird of October

1930, Chermayeff made somewhat scathing remarks about 'the monster booths of Mendelsohn with their horizontalism … which seem to plough their way through the city like some monster battleships in as much as they draw attention to themselves and the commercial interest they represent'.[7] He seems to have changed his views radically after meeting Mendelsohn and seeing the actual buildings on his German trip in 1931. His published account of it was dominated by images of Mendelsohn's work and he praised the Metalworkers' Union Building in Berlin as 'a real breath of sea air in this city of stuffy architectural horrors of the nineteenth century'.[8] Chermayeff made a further visit in 1932, and urged Mendelsohn to leave before the Nazis took over completely.

Mendelsohn's work was known in England and admired by a few progressives, from as early as 1925. With its striking imagery, it was often taken to be representative of modern architecture as a whole. His effects of streamlining, easily seen by visitors to Berlin at the Universum cinema in the Kurfurstendam, completed in 1928, were copied, cautiously at the outset and then with increasing confidence from 1930 onwards in projects such as the remodelling of the Olympia exhibition building by Joseph Emberton. Mendelsohn visited London in May 1930, when an exhibition of his work was held at the Architectural Association where he delivered a lecture and met Chermayeff for the first time.[9] Mendelsohn's status was such that not only did the Principal of the AA, Howard Robertson, gave a radio broadcast relaying his impressions of London, but he was also made an honorary member of the Arts Club.

In 1932, Mendelsohn joined the Dutch architect, planner and editor Hendricus Theodorus Wijdeveld (1885–1987) in launching a scheme for the 'Academie Européenne Mediterranée', in which the third leading participant was the French painter Amedée Ozenfant. Wijdeveld, a man of ideas and visions, had begun lecturing on his plans for 'An International Guild' in 1927–8, and the Academy was an attempt to carry out the scheme. He had known Mendelsohn since 1918, and published his work in his magazine *Wendingen*, with a special issue in October 1920. Ozenfant, after his collaboration with Le Corbusier in the Purist movement, had got to know Mendelsohn and painted three murals for his house on the Rupenhorn, persuading him that in view of the deteriorating political situation in 1930, it would be wiser to paint them on canvas than directly on the wall, so that they could be removed. Ozenfant was commissioned because Mendelsohn sensed his sympathy with the contrapuntal music of Bach, on which he had based the design of the house. One of the murals was titled, Music and the Plastic Arts.[10] In the words of Ita Heinze-Greenberg, Ozenfant and Wijdeveld were not always in accord, and Mendelsohn 'played the role of mediator between two strongly diverging artistic personalities'.[11]

Mendelsohn started travelling on the Academy's business from 1931, visiting Paris, Marseilles, the Côte d'Azur and Corsica. He and Wijdeveld found the property they wanted in the summer of 1932, at Cavalière, inland from Le Lavandou, with views of the sea. Mendelsohn wrote to his wife, 'up here, the academy we are planning would be an attraction and a mystical workplace'.[12] The Academy's prospectus, issued in Dutch in 1933, described it as sufficiently far from the 'mondain centre of the Riviera', while still being on the main through routes.[13] Designs were made for buildings to house a year-round community of students and resident artists. Mendelsohn left Germany at the end of March 1933, the last possible moment before Hitler took power, wishing to enjoy his house for as long as he could. According to Heinze-Greenberg, who has written the most comprehensive account so far on the Academy, Mendelsohn 'single-mindedly pursued his plans for the site in Cavalière, developing the financial and administrative basis for the academy and the content of its curriculum, as well as initial attempts at an architectural layout'.[14] He initially went to stay in Amsterdam with Wijdeveld, whom he had known since 1918, and in June 1933 came to London to look for funding for the Académie, of which Mendelsohn was Company Director, when it was floated in Paris on 27 June 1933. In its prospectus the company claimed a capital of 680,000 French Francs but needed FF3,000,000.[15]

Left: Erich Mendelsohn and H.T. Wijdeveld in the garden at 52 Abbey Road, July 1933.

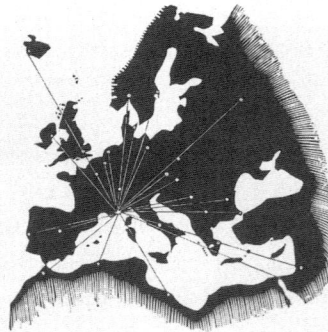

Eric Gill, engraved map for European Academy of the Mediterranean, 1933.

Chermayeff and Eric Gill were recruited as teachers for interior design and typography, respectively.[16] Chermayeff's knowledge of many languages, combined with his good contacts in London, were no doubt helpful. Gill's diary records meetings with Chermayeff from January 1933 onwards, although these may have been independent of the Academy scheme. Gill often stayed overnight with his agent at the Goupil Gallery, Cecily Marchant, in Abbey Road, the street where Chermayeff also lived, recording on 21 February, 'Dinner with Chermayeffs and party after. Slept at Abbey Road.' A note of a meeting with Chermayeff about the 'A.E.M.' occurs on 28 June 1933, followed by a meeting with Mendelsohn, his wife and Wijdeveld the next day. On 1 July, Gill went with Wijdeveld to meet Lord Howard de Walden, a friend and patron of Gill's, presumably in the hope of raising funds, after which Wijdeveld departed by aeroplane from Croydon, leaving Gill to engrave a map for the prospectus. A map of the world, placing the Mediterranean in the centre, was used for an English-language leaflet, although different maps were used for the Dutch versions.[17] Wijdeveld soon returned and

Chermayeff and the Mendelsohns visited Gill at his country home at Piggots, near Aylesbury in Buckinghamshire, on 15 July. The last meeting he recorded about the scheme was on 17 November, when the Chermayeffs hosted a dinner for Wijdeveld and the Mendelsohns, in order that Gill could meet Ozenfant.[18]

The prospectus announced that the Academy would steer a course between the stultifying effects of normal academic teaching and the freedom of independent study which, it claimed, could lead to personal eccentricity. It was also to be a geographical middle point, where artists of every nationality could come and work together. The European identity was emphasised in the maps which were used to promote the Academy, pulling together North Africa, Israel, Chermayeff's native Caucasus, Iceland and Scandinavia into a cultural unity which contradicted the existing or emerging political divisions of the time with a brave idealism. The Academy considered 'the social, economic and technical conditions of these modern times to be the basis for our work' but it also had traditional aspects.[19] Fiona MacCarthy describes the Academy as 'a sort of seaside Bauhaus', but it might also be described as a Cranbrook or Dartington, if these names evoke a more distant attitude to industrial modernity.[20] The choice of location implied a detachment from the world, and a search for modern equivalents of deep-rooted traditions, with a lifestyle which was to be simple and communal. As Heinze-Greenberg writes:

> Rather than radically breaking with conventional teaching methods, the programme of study was built on traditional ideas, above all in the field of engineering, but also in the basic principles of aesthetics such as the theory of proportion…If it had been realised according to the programme described in the brochure, the Mediterranean academy would doubtless have developed into the centre of the collected experiences of the modern movement – in contrast to the Bauhaus, which became the focus of the collected experiments of modernism.[21]

Gill was fundamentally hostile to industrial civilisation and there was to be a strong workshop element, including ceramics, to be taught by the French potter Paul Bonifas, to which textiles were hoped to be added, along with photography, film and dance. Since Mendelsohn was to be the teacher of architecture, Wijdeveld placed himself in charge of theatre design, a field in which he had gained distinction in the early 1920s, somewhat in the manner of Edward Gordon Craig. Unlike the Bauhaus, there was to be teaching of music, under Paul Hindemith. Sculpture was to be taught by the Catalan, Pablo Gargallo.[22]

The musical emphasis was perhaps implicit in the presence of theatre, and would have attracted Mendelsohn's strong support. His wife was a professional cellist, and claimed that Mendelsohn would have become a musician had he not been an architect. The craft aspect was part of Wijdeveld's background. At the age of 19, in 1903, he came to London to 'study

**67**

the works of William Morris and Ruskin, Voysey and Baillie-Scott', remaining for two years.[23] Wijdeveld's work had been celebrated with an exhibition and lecture at the Architectural Association in 1931. Chermayeff was the youngest of this group of teachers and was hardly an international name in 1933, but it is not difficult to imagine his enthusiasm and his usefulness in providing a London base. His office address was used for Academy business, and Mendelsohn imagined London becoming one of the centres for an extended academy. Mendelsohn was by 1933 becoming, of necessity as well as by inclination, very conscious of his Jewish identity and might have considered Chermayeff's Jewish origins reassuring, even if he had never made much of a point of them himself.[24]

The prospectus text under Chermayeff's own section, which is entitled *Interieur*, even in the Dutch-language pamphlet, is not greatly revealing of the intended activity:

> [The section] will study old and new materials – their origins, technical potential and practical application. The relationship of overall plan to space, and of space to furniture will be explained, developing towards the goal of space planning. The fundamentals of each project will be learnt through the techniques and conditions of this age. Drawing and photography will be applied to specific problems, using models and standard forms in the workshops serving this section.[25]

All three principals shared a romantic view of the Mediterranean as the cradle of western culture, and contrasted its timeless values with the shortcomings of the industrialised west. Attitudes of this kind were not uncommon in the 1930s, even among modernists, many of whom made an abrupt break with their earlier separation from the past and the celebration of machinery.[26] In Mendelsohn's case, this impulse was channelled into his work in Palestine between 1935 and 1940, for the Mediterranean Academy was not to be. Apparently there were difficulties and disagreements between Mendelsohn, Wijdeveld and Ozenfant, not surprising in view of the precarious financial and political situation in France.[27] There was a disastrous fire in the district of Cavalière in 1934, which put an end to the scheme, and Wijdeveld concentrated his energies instead on the 'Elckerlyc' or 'Everyman' school in the country outside Amsterdam, which he ran from 1935 to the beginning of the war.[28] Here he lectured students on how 'architecture must rise superior to technique, it must become the interpretation of a conception of life, of a new unity, it must be a resurgence of faith'.[29]

Chermayeff never discussed the Académie in such a way as to show what he might have learnt from the experience. It was his first involvement in teaching, even if he never actually had any students, and thus provides an early indication of the career he chose to follow in the second half of his working life. As such, it shows him in a wide interdisciplinary context, which he always sought in academic situations. The immediate outcome was his partnership in London with Mendelsohn, which was established in the autumn of 1933 when the latter decided that he could not concentrate exclusively on the Academy, and acquired a 55% stake in Chermayeff's architectural practice.[30] The reasons for Chermayeff's desire for a partner can only be guessed. In 1931 or 32, he had asked Raymond McGrath to join him in partnership but the offer was declined.[31] Presumably at that moment Chermayeff felt his own lack of expertise more than a lack of capital, since McGrath would not have had funds to put into the practice. Mendelsohn, on the other hand, needed to have an English partner in order to practice in the country that he believed would make him welcome. Louise Mendelsohn wrote that 'Chermayeff had become very attached to my husband. Eric had never been in partnership and was not the type to have a partner and I believe he had rather [have] had a young partner who admired Eric Mendelsohn's work as a partner than enter into partnership with an architect of his generation.'[32]

Mendelsohn was one of the first major émigré architects to accommodate himself thus in England, for it was over a year before the arrival of Walter Gropius, who became Maxwell Fry's partner in October 1934, while Marcel Breuer joined F.R.S. Yorke only in 1935. The firm of Mendelsohn and Chermayeff was formally established at 173 Oxford Street, and McGrath moved out to offices in Conduit Street. With strong backing from inside and outside the profession, Mendelsohn subsequently acquired a residence permit and in 1934 was able to bring over his chief assistant, Hannes Schreiner, from Germany, a man whom Mendelsohn described as 'almost essential to my work'.[33] He was given British nationality in 1938, although he spent more time in Palestine than in England before he eventually went to the USA in 1941.

The partnership undoubtedly made a big difference to Chermayeff's professional development. He wrote in 1979, 'My brief partnership with Erich Mendelsohn after he fled from Nazism was invaluable to me. I learnt architectural organisation and design of some complexity including both schematic presentation and meticulous detailing.'[34] After Schreiner arrived, he imposed on the English assistants a discipline more typical of German than of English work practices. Freshly-laundered overalls were provided by the firm and the staff were taught to draw in pencil to a standard suitable for reproduction. In the words of one of the assistants, Colin Crickmay, Schreiner 'was a brilliant draughtsman and had a very clear idea as to how everything on any building on which he was working should be constructed'.[35] He could also terrorise people, as he did an AA student, David Gladstone, on a holiday job in 1936, who drew some elevations in a slightly fanciful manner.[36] Even so, Schreiner had sufficient humour to draw a caricature of 'Sergius Burst of Charm-ayeff', a muffled and hatted figure with unbelievably long legs, taking a photograph with one hand, the other in his coat pocket, and Joan Ridge remembered Schreiner as 'a jolly Austrian'. Another AA student, Michael Grice, a contemporary of Gladstone's, was impressed by the ethos of the office whereby much time was spent in researching and refining: 'They would worry away at a detail beyond the point where most people would give it up.'[37]

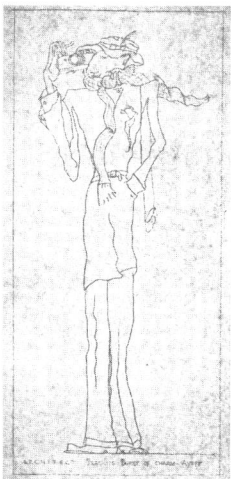

**Hannes Schreiner, caricature of 'Sergius Burst of Charm-ayeff', c.1935.**

Colin Crickmay, a graduate of the Architectural Association, was Chermayeff's chief architectural assistant from 1931–4, having been advised by his Principal, Howard Robertson, to apply to Chermayeff. He was joined in May 1933 by Geoffrey Bazeley, who had studied at Cambridge and the AA and formerly worked with Chermayeff's friend and ally, Grey Wornum. They were both already in the office at the point when Mendelsohn came into the practice, joined for about a year by Colin Penn, a graduate of Birmingham School of Architecture and a committed Communist, between 1934 and 1935.[38] Birkin Haward, a Bartlett School student, joined the office aged 22 after seeing the Bexhill competition designs, initially unpaid for four weeks, going up eventually to £4 per week. He became particularly attached to Mendelsohn, going with him to Palestine in the early spring of 1935 for an extended period.

There were moments of tension and comedy. Mendelsohn liked to work up schemes with a background of music – usually Bach – and Haward was given the job of putting the 78rpm record on again and again. Chermayeff shared the same office and, as Haward recalls, 'it got right under Serge's shirt in no time at all. He said "Stop that bloody row, how am I going to think? Stop playing the same one all the time".'[39] Herbert John Whitfield Lewis, a graduate of the Welsh School of Architecture in Cardiff who had attracted attention with his winning project for the RIBA Victory scholarship in 1933, used to circulate photographs of his girlfriend in the nude, taken on weekend trips to the country, constituting 'about the only fun we ever had', as Michael Grice comments. Chermayeff's assistant from Waring and Gillow, John Fortey, remained with the practice. Other assistants included a shaven-headed Australian, known as 'Wacko', and John Earley is remembered as making an important contribution to the office, particularly to the Gilbey building in Camden Town.

Staff in the later thirties included two Irish architects, Noel Moffatt and John Cunningham, and Derrick Oxley, another graduate of the Bartlett School, who also worked for Raymond McGrath before the war. During 1938, they were joined by the 18 year old German refugee, Peter Bloch, better known as the American architectural writer and editor, Peter Blake, who had been recommended to Chermayeff by Walter Gropius, a friend of his father's in Berlin. Acting as office boy without salary, Blake recalls that, although he found Chermayeff, with his appearance of upper-class elegance, 'like an impossible fraud on first, and possibly second, sight; he turned out to be one of the most brilliant teachers I, or anyone else, could possibly have encountered at the beginning of an architectural career.' Blake also received knowledge and encouragement from Whitfield Lewis and John Fortey.[40]

Given that Chermayeff was largely self-educated in architecture, it is natural to ask whether he displayed all the knowledge and skill of a fully-trained professional. Birkin Haward writes, 'I hardly saw any drawing from his hand in the office – it was all in words' while insisting that 'Serge was always helpful, straight and friendly, and had a committed point of view'.[41] When

Haward was working on the detailed drawings for the ICI Research Laboratories at Blackley, he made some alterations to the scheme in good faith, and was challenged by Chermayeff. He responded that he was fully qualified and probably had more experience than his boss, after which he was treated with additional respect.[42] Derrick Oxley recalls that 'Serge had NO drawing board – and I never saw him sketch – he just came round each day – making notes or scribbles on others' drawings – but he was THE BOSS and we worshipped him.'[43] Michael Grice tells how, when working as a student, he accompanied Chermayeff on a visit to Sussex in the summer of 1936, to survey the site of his future home, Bentley Wood, in order to learn the art of levelling. Chermayeff started to use the 'dumpy level', asking Grice to come closer and closer, until it became clear that he was looking through the wrong end of it and had never used one himself. Whitfield Lewis remembers that Chermayeff always knew exactly what he wanted to achieve, even though he needed his assistants in order to achieve it.

He was thus not unlike most principals of large firms who develop the creative abilities of their staff rather than keeping most of the designing to themselves, only he had not risen up the conventional ladder. The collaborative nature of the work was more than just an expedient, however, but a fundamental aspect of Chermayeff's design philosophy. To Joan Ridge, working as a secretary, the impression was that 'Mr Chermayeff was a socialite. He knew all the grand and theatrical people and was always out a lot during the day. It seemed it was Mr Mendelsohn who did the solid work on the Pavilion. Nevertheless, Mr Chermayeff was mainly responsible for the interior decoration, as great an attraction as the building itself.'[44]

Within the first months of the partnership, Mendelsohn and Chermayeff entered the competition for a new seaside pavilion at Bexhill-on-Sea, East Sussex, which was announced on 7 September, with a closing date of 4 December (extended to 29th). 'Buck' De La Warr (1900–76), after whose family the pavilion was named on completion, succeeded his father in 1905, as the owner of a large part of the land and property in the town. When he was elected mayor without opposition in 1932, the Town Corporation had already spent £28,000 on a sea front site for a new pavilion building, of a genre that was considered essential to the success of any seaside town.[45] De La Warr, although the inheritor of an ancient title, was a follower of the first Labour Prime Minister, Ramsay MacDonald and in 1931 became chairman of the newly-formed National Labour Party. The enterprise reflected the feeling current in progressive circles at the beginning of the decade that Britain needed inward investment in high quality infrastructure, both for economic and less clearly definable political reasons. This did not necessarily lead to modern design but there had been enough public statements to this effect to raise the awareness even of unartistic people.[46]

De La Warr resisted attempts to make this a private commercial venture, seeing recreation as an essential aspect of local and national regeneration.[47] Succeeding in retaining the project as a

**Erich Mendelsohn.**

**Serge Chermayeff.**

71

demonstration of municipal socialism, he outlined a brief, with the help of the planning consultants Adams Thompson and Fry, for a building combining entertainment with community functions. The assessor was Thomas Tait (1882–1954), a progressive-minded architect with a strong sense of changing conditions in construction, chosen as 'a man who is in touch with modern ideas of architectural development, in order that the younger generation of architects would feel that their plans would receive sympathetic and understanding treatment at his hands'.[48] The timing and character of the competition were such as to attract a large number of entries at a time when work of all kinds was still slack from the effects of the slump.

The conditions indicated:

> It is the intention of the promoters that the building should be simple in design, and suitable for a Holiday Resort in the South of England. Character in design can be obtained by the use of large window spaces, terraces and canopies. No restrictions as to style of architecture will be imposed but buildings must be simple, light in appearance and attractive, suitable for a Holiday Resort. Heavy stonework is not desirable.[49]

Reinforced concrete or steel-frame construction would both be permitted but competitors were required to find a finish that would not crack or craze, and pay attention to the effects of weathering.

Mendelsohn and Chermayeff, De La Warr Pavilion, Bexhill-on-Sea, perspective of sea front.

De La Warr Pavilion, Bexhill-on-Sea, perspective of north front.

De La Warr Pavilion, first
floor plans, competition
entry and executed
scheme.

Right: De La Warr Pavilion,
ground floor plan as
executed

PLAN CHANGES:
On this page is shown the first floor plan of the building as erected; below is the competition design. Few changes have been made; the more important being:—
1. The provision of a north and south corridor at the side of the conference hall, linking up the two staircases and simplifying access to the entertainments hall gallery; this suggestion was made by Mr. Tait in his assessor's report on the competition.
2. The larger stage demanded by the council has produced a squarer auditorium and a deeper gallery.
3. The reading room, originally intended for newspapers and periodicals is now to be used for books as well, and extra bays of shelving have, therefore, been provided.

First Floor as Executed

First Floor: Competition Plan

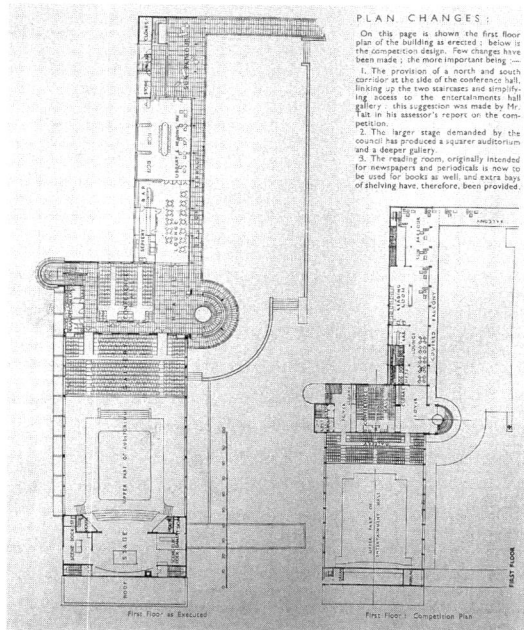

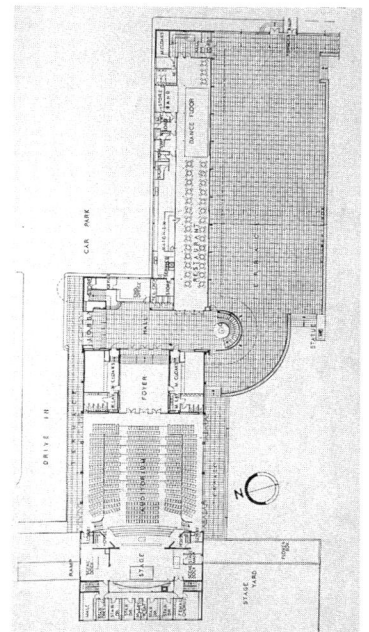

When the results were announced at the beginning of February 1934, Mendelsohn and Chermayeff were declared the winners. Tait's report recognised the 'masterly handling of architectural treatment' in their design, and although the other 'placed' designs from the total submission of 230 were modern in character, none had the conviction and coherence of Mendelsohn's scheme. In a sense, it was more than one scheme. A sequence of classical colonnaded walkways and pavilions had been constructed on the seaward side before the First World War and still remain, despite the intention of all the competitors to replace them. Mendelsohn and Chermayeff proposed a circular bathing pool in this position, with a covered walkway extending from the eastern end of the pavilion, as can be seen in detail in the fine model of the scheme, still at Bexhill, which was built in order to convince sceptics at a Public Inquiry.

Mendelsohn's early sketches, which are typically impressionistic, tend to show a grander version of the building, although the contrast of a blank-walled theatre and a fully-glazed restaurant wing, placed slightly further back on plan with the staircase at the junction, is a consistent feature.[50] The staircase forms part of a lateral volume, expressed on the entrance (north) front by a smaller bull-nosed stair tower, fully glazed, cantilevered above ground floor level, and matched by a zone of blank wall over the entrance, intended for advertising shows in the theatre. In the competition scheme, the stair tower rises one storey above its adjacent wings but the dimensions generally are much smaller than in the finished building. The 'entertainment hall' has no stage equipment and is lit from bands of high clerestorey windows.

73

In the executed scheme, a further 40ft in length was added to accommodate the stage. The restaurant wing and the entrance hall grew proportionally. In the most fully-developed scheme, published in the *Architectural Review* in 1936, soon after the building's opening, a cinema was attached to the west end of the complex, balancing the hotel, replacing an existing Victorian hotel building hard up against the back wall of the theatre. In the '1936' scheme (which would necessarily have been prepared some months earlier), and in certain of Mendelsohn's sketches, the convex face of a quadrant hotel building in this position towers over the theatre end of the pavilion. It is not clear if all these elements were in mind at the outset, so that there are in effect four alternative versions of the scheme to be considered.

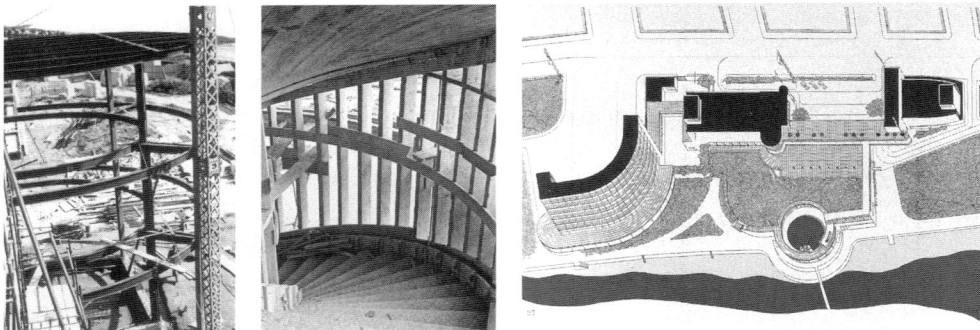

Far left: De La Warr Pavilion, steel frame structure of north stair, photo by Serge Chermayeff.

Middle: De La Warr Pavilion, reinforced concrete structure of main stair, photo by Serge Chermayeff.

De La Warr Pavilion, axonometric of complete intended scheme, with hotel to left, bathing pool and enclosure to front, and cinema to right.

The budget was set at £50,000 and Mendelsohn probably did not have an English architect's instinctive sense of how much building this sum would buy. The young quantity surveyor, Cyril Sweett, an enthusiast for modern architecture, was one member of the team who played an important role in making the concept buildable. The competition design was conceived in reinforced concrete, but the brilliant young structural engineer, Felix Samuely (1902–59), himself a refugee from Germany, via Russia and China, changed this into a welded steel frame structure – the first on this scale in Britain – producing a considerable cost saving over a rivetted frame.[51]

There was still local concern about the cost of the building, which led to the public inquiry held in April 1934 on the need to obtain a government sanction to raise a loan for the building. The addition of stage equipment had raised the price to £60,000, and other revisions to the original scheme produced a total estimate of £80,000. There was also local opposition both to the principle of financing the building in this way and to the nature of the selected design. Money became a recurrent issue. Chermayeff appeared as a witness, given Mendelsohn's inadequate English, supported by Cyril Sweett, who recalled:

> Mendelsohn took no part in the enquiry which I think he thoroughly enjoyed, leaving it to
> Chermayeff to answer the questions related to alleged extravagance which I corrected until

cross-examining Counsel protested and requested that the Inspector ask me to keep quiet. The Inspector, however, replied that I seemed to know more about the detail of the building than Mr Chermayeff and it would probably be helpful if I joined him in the witness box, which I then did.[52]

Ministerial permission was later given for a loan, but only of £70,000, so that the seaward colonnade and pool were omitted from the scheme.[53]

Mendelsohn visiting the De La Warr Pavilion site, photo by Serge Chermayeff.

Middle: Edward Wadsworth (design), Charles Howard (executant artist), mural for restaurant, De La Warr Pavilion, 1935-6.

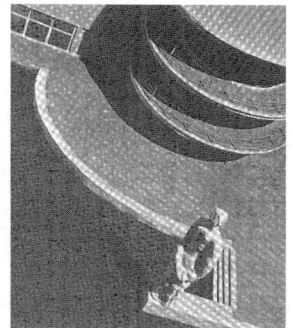

Right: Frank Dobson, model for Persephone, De La Warr Pavilion.

At the time of the competition success, there was a rash of correspondence in the *Architects' Journal*, instigated by members of the British Union of Fascists, objecting to the selection of 'foreign' architects, which reinforced the project's symbolic political dimension as a statement of international social democratic values. Chermayeff experienced similar objections to the article 'A Hundred Years Ahead', written jointly with J.M. Richards, when this was published at the beginning of 1935, because it associated Fascism with militarism, something the Blackshirts wished to deny.

Construction began at Bexhill in January 1935 and parts of the building seem to have been ready for use during the summer. It was formally opened by the Duke and Duchess of York (soon to become King George VI and Queen Elizabeth), on 12 December of that year. At the end of 1934, Mendelsohn went to Palestine and began a series of projects there which were not only more substantial buildings than his other English commissions but also of extreme emotional significance to him. He was absent during the early construction period of the Pavilion, returning to see the building at the end of March and writing to his wife:

Bexhill on Friday was a great joy. The iron [steel] frame is finished and also already a part of the walls. The situation is first-class: seen from the sea, the building looks like a horizontal skyscraper which starts its development from the auditorium. Seen from the street, it is a festive invitation. The interior is truly music. Lord De la Warr told me so: he was quite excited.[54]

75

Chermayeff was directly involved with the commissioning of two major works of art for the Pavilion. He was already friendly with the painter Edward Wadsworth (1889–1949), a survivor of the Vorticist movement who had joined a mostly younger generation in the avant-garde group 'Unit One' in 1933. The Chermayeffs often stayed for weekends with the Wadsworths at their house at Maresfield, Sussex, not far from Bexhill. Wadsworth designed a mural for the end wall of the restaurant, a typical design of emblematic, mildly surrealist character, incorporating shells and other nautical paraphernalia, with a scrolled chart of the coastline. The execution was left to a young American artist, Charles Howard, proposed by Chermayeff for the job, and Wadsworth covered the costs, making a presentation of the whole work to Bexhill.[55]

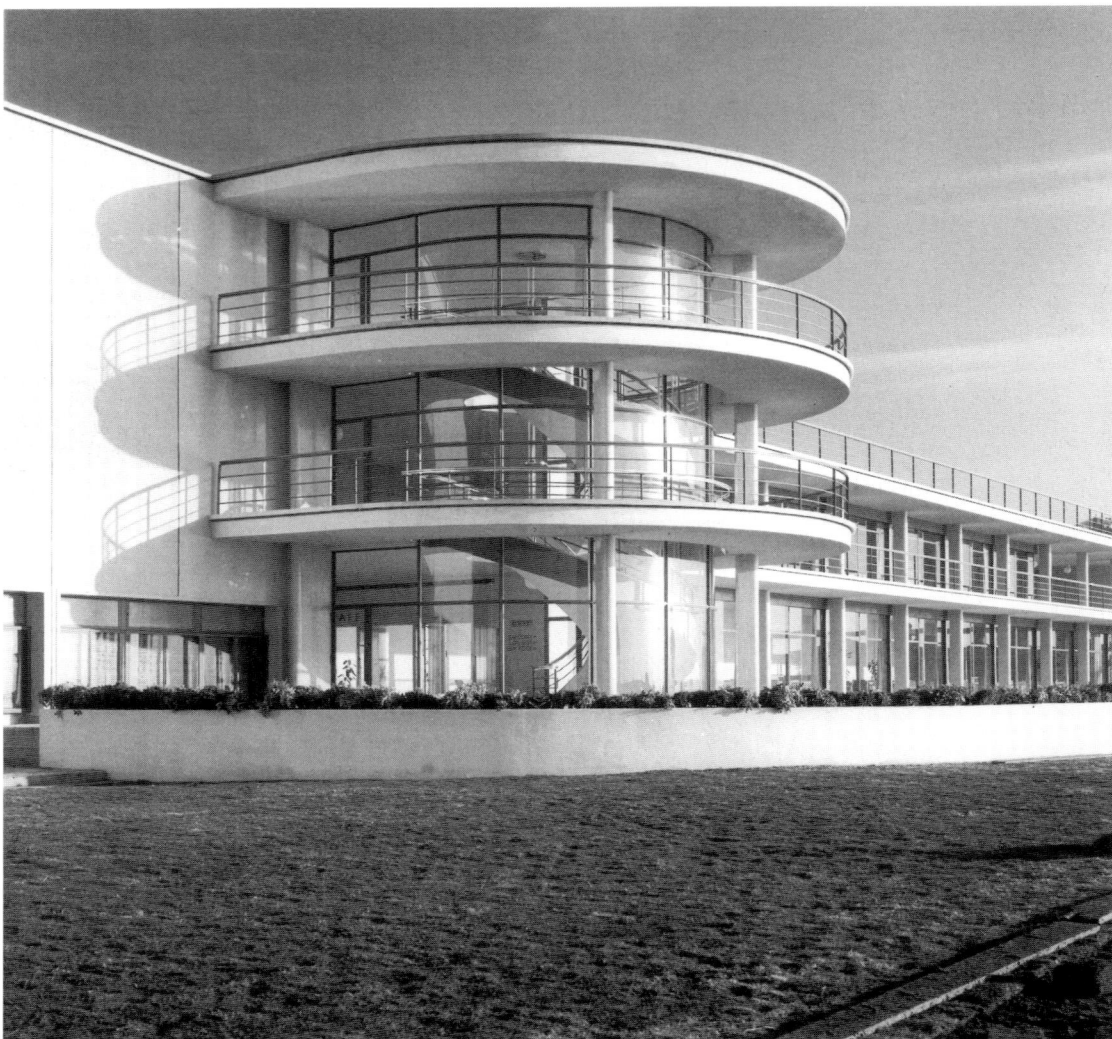

A sculpture of Persephone, the goddess of the Spring, was commissioned from Frank Dobson (1888–1963), a sculptor of Eric Gill's generation, known for his interest in architectural commissions. His freestanding figure, to be situated at a pivotal point at the corner of the terrace near the main stair, was sketched in a number of different versions, one of which was included on the large model of the scheme. Another was photographed against a part-model of a rougher kind. The iconography was an appropriate recognition of the awakening of the senses that the pavilion intended to bring, as well, perhaps, as a token of the goddess's longing gaze in the direction of the Mediterranean. The full-size figure was to have been made of reconstituted stone and Dobson was working on a clay model during the war when it was destroyed. The pavilion still needs it, or something of its kind, to complete the architectural effect.[56]

De La Warr Pavilion, south front by night, photo by Herbert Felton.

Right: De La Warr Pavilion, library interior, photo by Herbert Felton.

Opposite: De La Warr Pavilion, south front, photo by Herbert Felton.

The building was extremely well received by the critics. The unsigned article in the *Architect and Building News* was written by the weekly magazine's staff reporter, John Summerson, already becoming a distinguished historian of the Regency period to which the Pavilion was sometimes compared. He praised the directness of the building and thought that its special character was owed to two qualities, 'One is the sense of "open-ness" of the building; one has the sense of walking within enclosed space rather than in a structure. The other is the exquisite finish of the design, so far as structural details are concerned.'[57]

Arnold Whittick, a friend of Mendelsohn and author of a study of his work in 1940, wrote enthusiastically about the staircase, which above all is Mendelsohn's signature on the building, but also noted the colour scheme in the theatre, something owing to Chermayeff, 'Powder blue seats are seen against a background of dark brown carpet, walnut woodwork, and similarly

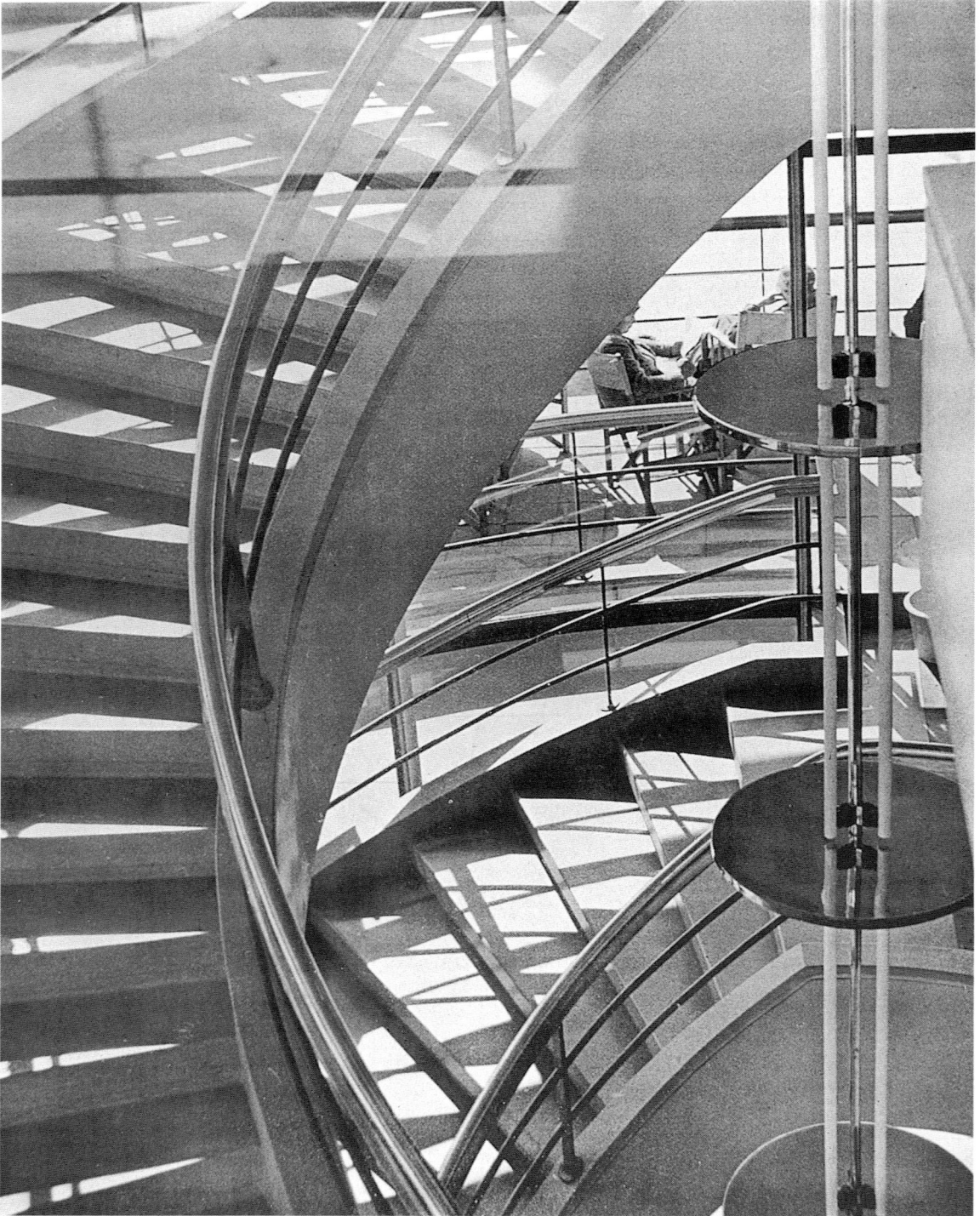

Opposite: De La Warr
Pavilion, main stair, photo
by László Moholy-Nagy.

brown curtains. Higher up is the cream of the acoustic boarding and the white of the plaster ceiling.'[58] (See page 159.) The restaurant was equipped with bent plywood chairs by Alvar Aalto, with birch frames and vermilion red seats, which, combined with the mural by Wadsworth, made it 'exceptionally bright'.[59] In the library above there were PLAN chairs upholstered in blue, and library shelves detailed in red and black. The library interior has long disappeared but in photographs it seems a model of modernist repose and calm, overlooking the ocean through the continuous band of windows which allowed the winter sun to shine in to the back of the room but shaded from the high sun of summer by the projection of the external balconies.

De La Warr Pavilion,
staircase interior, photo by
Herbert Felton.

A lecture room (also described as a Conference Hall) was provided in the space over the entrance hall, opening with folding doors to the south and thus connecting directly with the staircase. This was equipped with 200 PEL stacking chairs with canvas seats.

In October 1935 Chermayeff took the painter Percy Horton (1897–1970) to see it, who wrote to his friend Walter Strachan:

> Last weekend I went down to Sussex with the Chermayeffs. We stayed at a mutual friend's for the weekend. On the Saturday, Chermayeff motored me over to see the Bexhill building. I found it was an enormous place of concrete, steel and glass, completely functionalist in design. The staircases – huge concrete spirals encaged in delicate glass and steel cylinders – hang from the roof on a cantilever system. I thought the design was very fine indeed and was most impressed with the finish of all the appurtenances. The concert hall was being lined with a very beautiful unstained walnut veneer. The ceiling was magnificent, an enormous expanse of receding, hollow semi-spheres – these being conditioned by the science of acoustics which is apparently not an exact science.[60]

For its publication of the Pavilion in July 1936, the *Architectural Review* employed the Bauhaus teacher László Moholy-Nagy (1895–1946), who had taken up residence in London earlier in 1935, to take photographs instead of Dell and Wainwright. He made play with the spiral stair, showing it full of people with a sense of motion, perhaps rather too many for the magazine's usual taste for unpeopled views. One of his best shots, not published at the time, was described by Terence Senter in 1980 as 'a remarkable example of one of his space-time symbols'.[61] The text in the *Architectural Review* did not so much present a record of the building, as a discussion of its meaning and significance. This was not unusual for the magazine and, since the *Review* was full of pseudonymous contributors – H. de C. Hastings prominent among them – it was perhaps normal for Chermayeff to be one of the writers, using the name 'Peter Maitland' (a combination of his second son's first name, and his wife's second name). Quoting from Lewis Carroll's 'The Walrus and the Carpenter' about the difficulty of clearing up the seaside, he declared that 'the architect … must seize the mop himself'. More specifically, he quoted from a report on the 'Entertainment Hall' (or theatre) by Frank Birch, which must reflect directly his own feelings on the specific design problem involved:

> We were asked to advise on and equip a modern theatre, suitable for all purposes, conventional and otherwise, and to keep in mind the fact that the hall, which was the theatre, could also be used for other than theatrical entertainments. It is true that expenses were cut down and our scheme had to be considerably modified, but it is none the less true that the Bexhill stage can be conveniently used for every type of drama and for every technique of production and presentation. And to that extent it is unique.[62]

**De La Warr Pavilion, theatre interior, photo by Herbert Felton.**

The article proceeds to cover the management style for the theatre, the tragedy of English food and the way that the beach should be used for bathing, a wide-ranging conspectus of social issues typical of Chermayeff's breadth of thinking.

The theatre ceiling, with its continuous grid of miniature saucer-domes scooped out of a flat soffit, was carefully studied on acoustic grounds, assisted by a hard sounding board over the stage. Some of the saucers have small holes for air extraction, as part of an air conditioning system in the roof void above. The theatre interior is a skilful and enjoyable space but one which deliberately does not intrude itself between the audience and the performance. Chermayeff acknowledged the influence of Alvar Aalto's recently completed library at Viipuri in Finland, where there is a similar looking ceiling with round skylights over the main library area.[63] Combined with the use of Aalto's chairs in the restaurant, this is an influence compatible with Mendelsohn's form of romantic modernism, but tending to even more lightness. As Barbara Tilson has written:

> in the Mendelsohn/Chermayeff partnership the individual concerns of the two architects brought perhaps the ideal balance between formalism and function, and Bexhill Pavilion is the greatest realisation of this harmony between expression and utility.[64]

Cyril Sweett recorded that a local quantity surveyor decided to make trouble with accusations of corruption, having felt himself entitled to the job. The result was a further Ministry Enquiry into the costs of the building, which vindicated the professional team but declared that the gallery seating did not provide good enough sight lines. It was insisted that the matter should be rectified at the architects' expense, even though there was barely enough headroom to make the changes demanded.[65]

Mendelsohn's letter of 30 March 1935, quoted earlier, includes 'beginning the final agreement with Serge', almost the only published reference to a dispute between the partners. The fullest account comes from Chermayeff's side, in an interview in 1980, which relates that Chermayeff was initially glad to 'contribute certain things that he [Mendelsohn] wasn't really thinking about' to the development of the Bexhill scheme but became frustrated by Mendelsohn's formalistic approach to architecture, 'making aesthetic shapes'. Mendelsohn, on his part, was apparently angered by Chermayeff's changes to details during his absence.[66] It was not just an aesthetic argument, for having received a warm reception on his first visit to Palestine, Mendelsohn apparently declared that he wished to undertake his future work there outside the terms of the partnership, solely on his own account, while retaining his share in the profits of work from the London office. As Chermayeff put it, 'We really quarrelled. I thought he was being greedy and that immediately finished it.'[67] Neither man had a conciliatory temperament. Mendelsohn was fully aware of his own stature as an architect, while Chermayeff had a lifelong capacity to take against people suddenly and violently if he suspected they were in some way trying to undermine him. The financial prospects for a modern architect anywhere in the world in 1935 were uncertain, and Mendelsohn's position insecure, so money was an emotional issue. Mendelsohn's letter of 30 March 1935 continues, 'We parted fully reconciled and in the awareness that each had found his mark and his sphere of activity.'[68] Mendelsohn wrote to Oskar Beyer, the art historian in Berlin who promoted his work and edited his letters, 'I have retained my partnership in London and bought myself free for one and a half years in order to make a start in Palestine.'[69] Mendelsohn consolidated his presence in Israel by renting an old windmill outside Jerusalem. The partnership carried on until the end of 1936, perhaps in fulfilment of this 18-month period.[70]

The attribution of both executed work and projects between the partners remains difficult to determine. Chermayeff's 'sphere of activity', in the form of domestic and commercial interiors, had begun to take shape before Mendelsohn's arrival but it is clear that he did not consider himself limited to these matters. Mendelsohn was particularly interested in mass, line and space in architecture but not particularly in construction and technical issues. Chermayeff claimed that 'beauty looks after herself' but, like many modern architects, he made sure that the right conditions were established for this to happen. This distinction does not go all the way to determining who did what – a question that is difficult to answer in most architectural partnerships – but it is clear from Mendelsohn's sketches that he worked up the overall mass of the buildings, in which the plan form was implied, while Chermayeff took over with the detailing of the interiors. Mendelsohn's long periods of absence in Palestine made this working arrangement almost a necessity. Chermayeff claimed to have had more impact on the plans of their buildings than this arrangement might suggest. A note by him, inserted in a copy of a book on the modern house of the 1930s, reads 'Arnold Whittick tends to attribute anything in my association to M 'long horizontal character' or curved forms, never of course speaking of clarity of plan which is the basic contribution.'[71]

Apart from the De La Warr Pavilion, the only two built projects by the partnership were houses. Shrub's Wood in Chalfont St Giles, was built for Mr R.J.Nimmo, an oil company executive, who was a Cambridge friend of Chermayeff's assistant, Geoffrey Bazeley. Nimmo's wife was an American from Texas. The commission had begun before Mendelsohn's arrival, but he took over the design of the house, which has one of the best sites for a modern house of the 1930s in England, approached down a long woodland drive, with distant views over park-like grounds and no other houses in sight. Mendelsohn's perspective sketches, with their viewpoint right down on the ground, exaggerate the effect of contours on the site but the house has a very controlled form of dynamism, gathering its forces in a squarish mass at the western end, from which a narrow wing extends, the upper storey over-sailing at the eastern end where it forms a sheltered outdoor space with access to the broad garden terrace. The construction was in reinforced concrete and the exterior was finished in a white render.

The staircase is a prominent feature of the interior, producing a curved wall, mostly glazed, by the entrance door. The ground floor circulation spaces are varied and generous in scale, as one moves from a lobby to the stair hall, and then into a section of passageway that leads to the living room, with a continuous run of windows facing onto the garden. A ground floor study faces the driveway. There is a square dining room, with a discreet servery behind connecting with the kitchen. The master bedroom suite is in the main block of the house, with two dressing rooms fully equipped with fitted wardrobes and dressing tables, giving it something of the character of an ocean liner. Guest rooms and the nursery suite are in the long arm of the

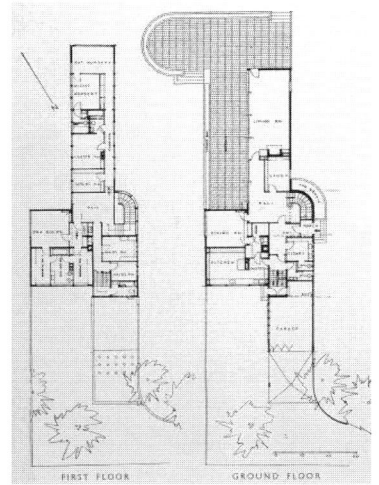

Erich Mendelsohn, perspective study of Shrub's Wood, Chalfont St Giles, Buckinghamshire, c.1933.

Top right: Mendelsohn and Chermayeff, Shrub's Wood, plans.

Shrub's Wood, staircase.

Far right: Shrub's Wood, hall.

house, accessed from a corridor. Chermayeff kept a close hand on the fittings and furniture, with a glass-topped table by his former associate, Denham Maclaren in the living room, and a patterned rug by Marion Dorn, one of several in the house. This room contained an Aalto chair and a PLAN chair, a settee which was probably specially made for the house, and two low tables in veneered wood, part of a suite which included the dining table, made by Parker Knoll, a London branch of the Stuttgart company, with simple upholstered dining chairs. The Maclaren table and most of the other original pieces have fortunately remained in the house through two subsequent ownerships. In the recess over the fitted sideboard in the dining room, lined with copper-faced plywood, there was a decorative painting by John Skeaping, showing two cowboys among cacti, an allusion to Mrs Nimmo and the Lone Star State.

Skeaping, the first husband of Barbara Hepworth, was best known as a sculptor, specialising in horses. According to Birkin Haward, Mrs Nimmo removed the mural very early on.[72]

In the house there still hangs a drawing for the garden and landscape, from the Mendelsohn and Chermayeff office, with no landscape consultant named, which is interesting in the way that it creates a more formal sense of enclosure with hedges around the house, and an orchard planted in a regular grid alongside the approach drive, which may have been a continuation of an existing orchard on the site. However, none of this scheme was carried out, and it seems that the house was set, as were many of its kind, among lawns and surviving older trees.

Shrub's Wood was included in most of the illustrated surveys of modern English architecture in the later 1930s, such as Henry-Russell Hitchcock's selection for the Museum of Modern Art in 1937, in conjunction with which Berthold Lubetkin wrote an article in *American Architect*

Shrub's Wood, dining room, with mural by John Skeaping. Photo by Dell & Wainwright.

Left: Shrub's Wood, living room. Photo by Dell & Wainwright.

Opposite: Mendelsohn and Chermayeff, Shrub's Wood. Photo by Dell & Wainwright.

*and Architecture* magazine. Like many other authors and editors, Lubetkin chose a photograph of the entrance lobby with its continuous fitted cupboards, backed by a complete wall of mirror, commenting, 'the mirror enlarges the apparent size of the narrow passage, reflects the outdoor view and establishes the architects' feeling for suavity'.[73]

One of the most interesting comments on Shrub's Wood comes from Sir John Summerson, from an article, 'Romance and Realities' in *Country Life* in February 1937. Rather than looking at the technical efficiency of a modern house, in which, in a truth seldom admitted at the time, it had only slight advantage over more conventional styles and some corresponding drawbacks, Summerson sees its function as primarily expressive:

> Here is a tremendously long living-room with one side all glass, and nothing of the drawing-room convention about it. The well-lit staircase hall might justly be called

extravagant, and the large amount of external wall might also be criticised as defying tradition for no useful purpose. Yet the whole design has something about it which seems to make the extravagance worth while. What is it? I think it can be stated in one word – romance. Our contemporary way of living is here objectified, not as continuation of old ways, but as something really new, with a charm and adventure all of its own. To live in a room with ordinary sash windows would seem rather tame after living behind a glass wall which lets in all the beauty of the park beyond it. And that is not all. The sweep of the Chalfont plan, its generous terrace and dramatic asymmetry, all have a tremendous psychological appeal. Here is a 'space-consciousness' very like what the Elizabethans must have felt when they added long-windowed galleries to their old halls and opened out their houses to the light and the newly-discovered pleasures of the English landscape and Italian garden. The modern movement, like the Elizabethan renaissance, is essentially a romantic movement. However closely it adheres to scientific standards and however rigidly it excludes ornamentalism, its mainspring is all the time romantic and irrational. That, to my mind, is its real claim to our affection and respect.[74]

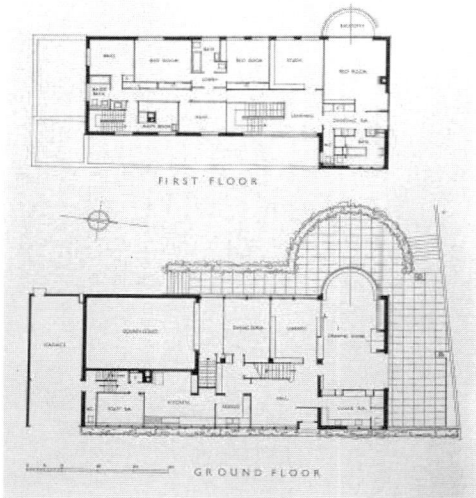

Summerson's comment was far-sighted and accurate, inasmuch as both Mendelsohn and Chermayeff were romantic by temperament, although it was manifested in each in different ways, these differences being fundamental to their problems with working together.

Their second house was 64 Old Church Street, Chelsea, part of a large site divided into four building plots, facing out onto different streets, each with a broad frontage. The eastern half was filled with a pair of houses by Oliver Hill in Neo-Georgian style, although rendered white in the modern manner. On the western side, two cousins took adjacent building plots and

Mendelsohn and Chermayeff, 64 Old Church Street, Chelsea, 1935-6. Photo by Dell & Wainwright.

Left: Mendelsohn and Chermayeff, 64 Old Church Street, Chelsea, 1935-6, plan.

agreed to build modern houses that would complement each other. The playwright Ben Levy, married to the actress Constance Cummings, commissioned Walter Gropius and Maxwell Fry to design a house which fills the northern quadrant, with its narrow side towards the road and a south-facing main elevation, leaving the remainder of the plot to Dennis Cohen, a publisher whose company, the Cresset Press, produced high quality books for the mass market. Cohen was one of the three directors of PLAN Ltd. when it was set up in 1932 and was active in work on behalf of Jewish refugees. It was therefore natural for him to choose Mendelsohn and Chermayeff to design his house in 1935.

**64 Old Church Street, garden view. Photo by Dell & Wainwright.**

One of Cohen's requirements was for a squash court and Mendelsohn struggled to place it on the site, resolving finally to incorporate it in the body of the house, partly below ground level. The main rooms all overlook the garden, including a characteristic Mendelsohnian semi-circular glazed bow to the drawing-room, from which an enfilade, assisted by sliding doors and passing through the library, makes a processional route to the dining room, which doubles as the balcony for the squash court, creating a sense of rather solemn mystery. This produces an elevation anchored by a blank wall at one end and accelerating through the rhythm of the windows to the bow at the other, with a Mendelsohnian sense of movement.[75] The staircase rises to the left of the front door, majestically contained by walls on either side but emerging into light on a broad upper landing. Like Shrub's Wood, 64 Old Church Street is distinguished by fine fitted furniture in most of the rooms and sycamore and pearwood panelling in pale yellow tones. The construction was not as pure as it looked, consisting of brick with steel beams, holding hollow slab tiles to make the roof and main floor plate, all covered with a white render that deteriorated during the war.[76]

Few photographs were published to show how it was furnished at the beginning, but a memory of the house comes from the scientist Lancelot Law White, later a personal friend of Chermayeff, who was given a bed for the night by Cohen during a war-time air raid:

In Old Church Street we reached a door in the blackout, Cohen opened it, switched on the lights, and there was the most brilliant interior I have yet seen in London. It was a Mendelsohn house, marvelously clean and bright, with Chinese pottery decorating the living-room. Soon I was in a silken bedroom. There was a large pile of books on the table beside the bed …[77]

64 Old Church Street, bay window in living room. Photo by Dell & Wainwright.

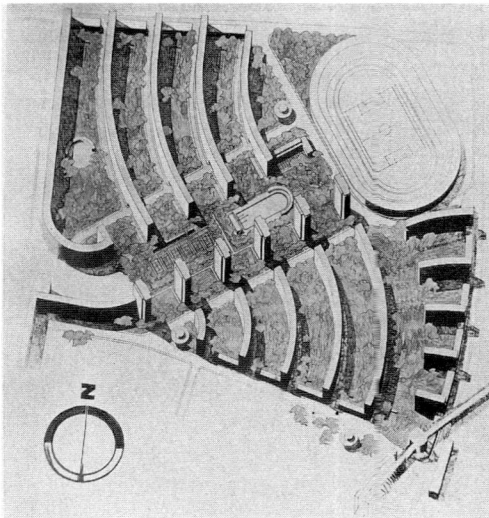

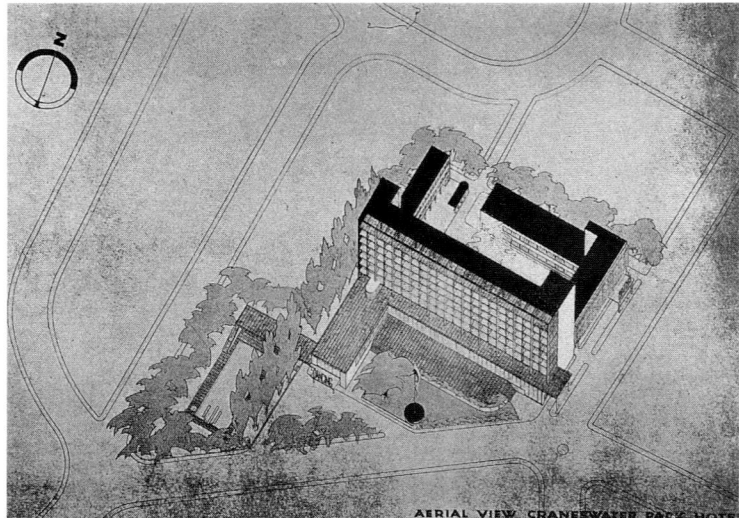

Mendelsohn and Chermayeff, scheme for hotel at Craneswater Park, Southsea, 1934.

Left: Mendelsohn and Chermayeff, White City Project, 1934-5.

The Cohen House was the focus of a televised discussion between Chermayeff and the writer John Gloag in December 1936, one of three pre-war television programmes that Chermayeff made. The two were filmed live at Alexandra Palace discussing a model of the house. Chermayeff defended the danger of weathering to the white rendered finish by explaining that the owner could afford to keep it up. 'It is one of the pleasures of living in a white house, that has to be paid for', he explained, adding that the client had wanted this finish. The discussion, in which Gloag played devil's advocate, allowed Chermayeff to shift attention away from the individual house to the value of obtaining an architect's services when building, but it also contains an interesting aside from Chermayeff about his concept of the architect's form-making role, which he defines as a need to be critical before being creative. Chermayeff and Gloag made the customary comparison between modern and Regency architecture, with its sense of civic order, although Chermayeff later thought that the house 'leaned over backwards to meet Georgian neighbours half way'.[78] Chermayeff enlarged on Gloag's formulation of this as 'tidying up everything and simplifying' by adding that 'against that simple background the particular individual arts of architecture, and painting, and sculpture can flourish like flowers cleared of weeds, if you like to find a very easy comparison'.[79]

The unbuilt projects of Mendelsohn and Chermayeff were mostly on a grander scale. The White City project, 1935, involved the whole of the former exhibition and Olympic Games site in West London, with a mixture of housing, commercial and leisure activities. Little is known of the business background to this scheme, which seems to have begun as a speculative venture but was developed and published by the architects as 'A Scheme of National Importance'.[80] The text makes it clear that this form of publication was an attempt to stimulate a public sector involvement.[81] The text, almost certainly drafted by Chermayeff, describes it as 'probably, the only remaining land so near the centre of London … situated as it is directly connected with the main road and railway transport, of such scale as to make possible a comprehensive example of social service in planning and construction; a self-contained new city which can be developed ideally under the existing political and economic conditions for dwellings of the artisan type, rather than adding to the mass of speculative buildings for the lower middle class. The following year, fifty acres of the site were indeed bought by the London County Council and developed for housing of mediocre design and layout in 1938–9.

Three versions of the Mendelsohn and Chermayeff plan were presented (although only 'A' and 'C' were illustrated), their common feature being long housing blocks in parallel curving lines. A line of tower blocks, described on Mendelsohn's sketch as 'Bachelor Towers', flanked the diagonal main axis through the site in both schemes, which barricaded itself against the Western Avenue to the north and led its traffic down the western boundary to a gateway-like entry. Scheme 'A' had an exhibition centre on part of the site, while Scheme 'C' had more housing, picking up the curves in an opposite direction to produce a serpentine effect across the site. In a later interview, Chermayeff dissociated himself from this aspect of the design, saying 'when [Mendelsohn] was doing the housing, he put a quite artificial curve into it which would give it more interest, except that there were too many parallels which was a bore, at that enormous scale, and I was against it.'[82] The scale of the scheme was beyond anything else proposed for actual sites, comparable only to the Quarry Hill flats in Leeds by R. A. H. Livett, begun in 1935. The recreational aspects, including the Olympic Stadium, a restaurant, tennis courts, a cinema and a swimming pool, were distributed around the site, together with a generous number of trees, so that the scheme would not necessarily have been oppressive, despite its size.

For the private sector, Chermayeff and Mendelsohn prepared designs in 1934 for a hotel at Craneswater Park, Southsea, the genteel resort suburb adjoining Portsmouth, attempting perhaps to catch the momentary popularity of seaside modernism engendered by Bexhill. This was an interesting and unusual design, with an open grid of balconies across the slab block that rose seven storeys above a podium formed by a long glazed public area, extending 22 bays in length. The site, an area of land later developed as suburban housing, was divided from the sea by an open green. To the rear was a therapy wing and extending forwards, a swimming pool and a ballroom with its own porte cochère and a drum-shaped elevated building, probably a café. This project was more like a building of the 1950s than the 1930s, with no obvious connection to other Mendelsohn designs apart from the general dynamism of the way the different masses were organised. It was certainly overambitious in scale for its time. The written report accompanying the project described it as:

> an architectural unity which, while imposing in scale, has a lightness and gaiety suited to both the purpose and the position of the building. This is aided by the natural colours of the pergolas, flower boxes and gardens, and the light bright colours and interplay of light and shadow of the structure itself with its balconies, terraces and coloured sun blinds.[83]

In 1937, Mendelsohn worked on a comparable proposal for Blackpool.[84] The other major unbuilt project which he undertook from his London office after the end of the partnership was for the rebuilding of St George's Hospital at Hyde Park Corner, undertaken with Hannes Schreiner, who had stayed with him. This was not reckoned among Mendelsohn's major projects.[85]

Erich Mendelsohn, a study for offices of W.A. Gilbey & Sons, c.1933.

At the end of the partnership two jobs had been started which present problems of attribution. A number of sketches exist by Mendelsohn associated with the design for the offices for W.A. Gilbey & Sons offices in Oval Road, Camden Town, one of which has the name Gilbey on the side of the building. Some of these, as identified by Bruno Zevi in 1970, are utterly unlike the building as executed. The closest in character is the one illustrated here which nonetheless suggests a different site to that finally selected.[86] Although there may have been stages in the evolution of the design in Mendelsohn's hands that have been lost, Mendelsohn's characteristic horizontal emphasis gave way in the built version to a less emphatic design, with an effect more like a classical elevation, particularly in the way that the whole facade system has a single-storey dark tiled base at pavement level, a practical measure since the white rendering would have been vulnerable here, while the six storey building is capped by an overhanging roof slab. The concave facade towards Jamestown Road as built is certainly Mendelsohnian in broad terms but the way it resolves the oblique street junction with a little 'kick' in the curve is unlike Mendelsohn's sketches or any other design of his, although Whitfield Lewis nonetheless thinks it 'really a Mendelsohn building'.[87] The executed building will be discussed in the next chapter.

Mendelsohn's involvement in the ICI Dyestuffs Laboratory at Blackley, Manchester, seems more remote, although he is remembered to have worked on the initial designs, which were ready in October 1936. Bruno Zevi published a number of drawings which he associated with

ICI's project to build in Huddersfield.[88] These show a structure more like a power station, with multiple chimneys, which can have had no relationship to the programme of the Blackley Labs. Some other drawings in this group do, however, bear a closer resemblance to the Labs. Barbara Tilson compares the layout as planned under Chermayeff's name to Mendelsohn's entry for the German Nitrogen Syndicate's administration building of 1929, and Birkin Haward suggests that it 'has the stamp of Mendelsohn-Schreiner with Serge in attendance, making as much contribution as he was allowed'.[89] Chermayeff would have contested these attributions, since he felt that both buildings were his own creation but it is a matter in which precise adjudication is impossible.

Henry-Russell Hitchcock, writing in 1937 in anticipation of his exhibition of Modern English Architecture at the Museum of Modern Art in New York, contradicted the usual assumption that Mendelsohn's English work was inferior to other periods of his output on account of its reticence. This is so rare as a piece of critical appraisal of new work of this period by a major writer that it is worth quoting at length:

> The English work of Mendelsohn in partnership with Chermayeff … is distinctly superior aesthetically to most of his German work. His houses avoid entirely the heaviness which lingers even in his own house at Spandau and his pavilion at Bexhill is generally and correctly recognised as about the most conspicuous and successful modern building in England. There is possibly an excess of drama in the cantilevered glass staircase toward the street, but on the whole, criticism of the building proves on analysis to be rather of Bexhill as a seaside resort than of the Pavilion itself. The Pavilion is, on the other hand, amazingly finished in execution and full of minor elegances of detail. It demands chiefly more wall painting and sculpture inside and a more developed setting outside to be a contemporary building of the first order.[90] In Mendelsohn's case, a certain understatement, a determined restraint, was a desirable corrective of the earlier tendencies of his personal style. Whether this change in manner represented by his English work is due to the influence of his partner, hitherto known chiefly as a decorator, is not clear.[91]

Mendelsohn and Chermayeff, proposed house on Frinton Park Estate, Essex, 1936.

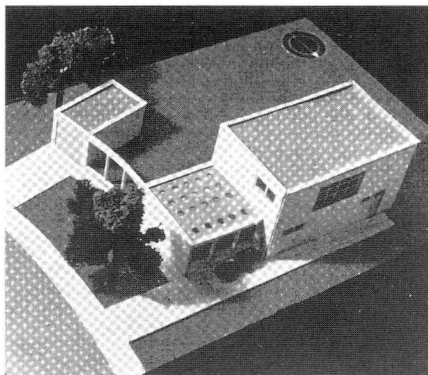

Right: House at Frinton Park, plans.

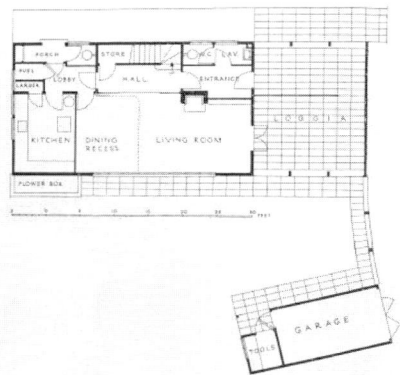

The wide popularity and appeal of the Mendelsohn–Chermayeff buildings may indicate that in some way they touched a chord with a public normally sceptical about modern architecture. Chermayeff was more strongly attracted by the quality of restraint, less typical of Mendelsohn's earlier work than of German modernism in general. Perhaps he would have felt more ideologically at ease with Walter Gropius as his partner had the occasion arisen, although they might have been too similar in their self-imposed distance from the work of the drawing board. Still, an enduring legacy of Mendelsohn's influence can be found in Chermayeff's manner of drawing buildings freehand in perspective from a very low viewpoint, with an enclosing arc overhead, to emphasise their character as three-dimensional objects in space.

A project for a house at Frinton Park Estate, Essex, was published as a product of the Mendelsohn–Chermayeff partnership. This estate, master-planned by Oliver Hill in 1933–4, was intended to become a showpiece for modern architecture. A number of modern architects were invited to design houses, although several refused when told that they would only be permitted to build in rendered brick rather than concrete, the material specified for the Mendelsohn–Chermayeff project, since this material made houses more difficult to sell. Their proposed house is sited end-on to the road, and takes much of its character from the way that a garage set apart from it – so that a curving screened outdoor enclosure, following the line of one of Oliver Hill's curving roads – is formed between it and the house, which is approached through a single storey loggia with circular roof lights. The larger part of this connects with the living room through French doors, and is partly divided by an internal wall from the entrance porch area beneath the same roof. Thus the cubic solidity of the single villa with its integral garage is rejected for a scheme which uses the garage and the space between the road and the house as a positive aspect of the site planning, an embryonic form of courtyard house, displaying some aspects of the concern about private open space that Chermayeff developed in the 1950s and 60s in his book, *Community and Privacy*. Surprisingly, only two examples of courtyard houses were built by modern movement architects in the 1930s, so Chermayeff – if we can assume his responsibility for the design – distantly anticipated his own later contribution to the theory of modern domestic planning.

Notes

1 Information in letter from Neville Shann (son) to Charlotte Benton, 8 July 1977, kindly communicated by Charlotte Benton. Cost with built-in furniture given as £1,400 in *Architectural Review*, March 1935, p.106.
2 Shann, well known for his exotic menagerie, kept a pair of slow loris, called Chermayeff and Mendelsohn, in the boiler room by day. They had a trap door into the kitchen at night. Information from Tilson 1984.
3 Chermayeff to Patricia Collingham, 6 August 1975, Avery Library.
4 ibid.
5 Raymond McGrath (1934), *Twentieth Century Houses*, London, Faber & Faber Ltd., pp.102-3.

6 Mendelsohn anglicised his first name to Eric when he took American citizenship in 1940.

7 Chermayeff to Eric Bird, 31 October 1930, Avery Archive. Chermayeff claimed in several places that he first met Mendelsohn in 1930 when travelling for Waring and Gillow.

8 Serge Chermayeff, 'Film Shots in Germany', *Architectural Review*, November 1931, p.133.

9 According to Louise Mendelsohn, letter to Charlotte Benton, 3 July 1976, kindly communicated by Charlotte Benton.

10 See Susan L. Ball (1981), *Ozenfant and Purism, Evolution of a style 1915-30*, Ann Arbor, UMI Research Press, p.147.

11 Ita Heinze-Greenberg, 'The Mediterranean Academy Project and Mendelsohn's Emigration' in Regina Stephan, ed. (1998), *Erich Mendelsohn 1887-1953*, New York, Monacelli Press, p.184. See also Louise Mendelsohn in Bruno Zevi (1970), *Erich Mendelsohn*, Milan, Etas Kompass, p.26: 'Also a certain discord between his co-directors, Wijdeveld and Ozenfant began seriously to annoy him.'

12 Mendelsohn to Louise Mendelsohn, August 18 1932, quoted in Heinze-Greenberg, 1998, p.185.

13 One version of the prospectus has many photographs of the site. Copy in British Library.

14 Heinze-Greenberg, 1998, p.185.

15 Charlotte Benton (1995), *A Different World, Emigré architects in Britain 1928-1958*, London, RIBA Heinz Gallery, p.188, and Prospectus for the Academie Européenne Mediterranée, n.d., Avery Library.

16 Chermayeff thought he had first met Wijdeveld when visiting the Van Nelle Factory in Rotterdam (by Brinckmann and Van der Vlugt, begun in 1928 and finished in 1931). Interview with Richard Plunz, 20 September 1980.

17 Gill's map is reproduced in Christopher Skelton (1983), *The Engravings of Eric Gill*, Wellingborough, Skelton's Press, No.P851 and in Fiona MacCarthy (1989), *Eric Gill*, London, Faber & Faber, p.252. A page from the prospectus, taken from a copy in the Mendelsohn archive in Berlin, is reproduced in Heinze-Greenberg, 1998, p.186.

18 Eric Gill diaries. MSS in William Andrews Clark Library, Los Angeles.

19 From an English text of the first part of the prospectus printed in *Design for Today*, September 1933, p.202.

20 MacCarthy, 1989, p.253.

21 Heinze-Greenberg, 1998, p.187.

22 Also known as Pau Gargallo I Catalán, 1881-1934, who lived in Paris 1923-34.

23 H.J. Wijdeveld (1947), *Time and Art*, Hilversum, Rotting's Printing Works, p.35.

24 Sir John Summerson told me that he once witnessed Chermayeff having a fist-fight in the street with a motorist who had made an anti-semitic insult, and getting the best of it. Conversation in July 1992.

25 Author's translation.

26 See Romy Golan (1995), *Modernity and Nostalgia, art and politics in France between the wars*, New Haven and London, Yale University Press.

27 See Charlotte Benton, 'Mendelsohn in England' in Regina Stephan, ed. (1998), *Erich Mendelsohn 1887-1953*.

28 It is uncertain whether students actually went to the Academy. *Time and Art*, 1947, says that 'young men from all countries were trained' at the Academy (p.30), but this may be an indicative wrongly replacing a subjunctive. Wijdeveld wrote to Chermayeff on 12 May 1948 to renew his acquaintance while on a visit to America as a guest of Frank Lloyd Wright: 'Next to me is laying the illustrated prospectus of the "Académie Européenne Mediterranée" which we began to construct in 1932 - with such a promising start, but which ended a year later so suddenly (and sadly) with that disastrous fire around Cavalière. I have often wondered what became of our group.' Avery Library. Ozenfant was a near neighbour of the Chermayeffs in New York City in the 1940s.

29 Wijdeveld, 1947, p.29. Ozenfant was sailing past the coast en route for Greece and saw the fire. He wrote 'Au retour j'appris que nos bois étaient en cendres et qu'il fallait renoncer a construire dans ce lugubre paysage carbonisé. Ainsi finit en fumée un beau projet; d'autres, quelque jour le reprendront et construiront un relais de l'optimisme et de la beauté en cette nouvelle Attique potentielle, la Côte d'Azur, vieille colonie grecque.' A. Ozenfant (1968), *Mémoires*, Paris, Seghers, p.299. [Author's translation: 'On my return I learnt that our woods were in ashes and that we had to give up the idea of building in this lugubrious burnt-out landscape. So a fine project went up in smoke; one day others will take it up again and will build a staging post of optimism and beauty in the Côte d'Azure, an old Greek colony and potentially a new Attica']

30 Information from Benton, 1998

31 Donal O'Donovan (1995), *God's Architect, a life of Raymond McGrath*, Dublin, Kilbride Books, p.137.

32 Louise Mendelsohn to Charlotte Benton, 3 July 1976, quoted in Benton, 1998, p.192.

33 Benton, 1995, pp.48-9.

34 Serge Chermayeff, 'An explosive revolution', *Architectural Review*, November 1979, p.309.

35 Quoted in Benton, 1998, p.194, original source Barbara Tilson, 1984.

36 Author interview with Michael Grice, March 1999 for Architects' Lives project, National Sound Archive.

37 ibid.

38 Information from Tilson, 1984.

39 Conversation with author, December 1997. See also Birkin Haward 'Recollections' in Brook et al., eds. (1984), *Erich Mendelsohn 1887-1953*, London, Modern British Architecture, p.71.

40 Peter Blake (1993), *No Place Like Utopia*, New York, p.10.

41 Birkin Haward to author, 15 June 1992.

42 Conversation with author, December 1997.

43 Derrick Oxley to Gavin Stamp, 19 May 1985, kindly communicated by Gavin Stamp.

44 Joan Ridge, 'Trust traces living links with architects', *Pavilion Trust Newsletter*, Bexhill, July 1998, p.2.

45 Comparable examples are the White Rock Pavilion, Hastings, by the architect C. Cowles-Voysey, 1923 and The Pavilion, Worthing, by S.D. Adshead, 1926, both of which were effectively theatre/concert halls.

46 See Russell Stevens and Peter Willis, 'Earl De La Warr and the competition for the Bexhill Pavilion, 1933-34', *Architectural History*, XXXIII, 1990, pp.135-51 and 'Bucking the Trend: a portrait of the Ninth Earl De La Warr 1900-1976' by Jill Theis and Alistair Fairley in *Pavilion Trust Newsletter*, Bexhill, July 2000, pp.2-3.

47 'Holiday resorts … have a key place in the economy of the country and … the public should never confuse enterprise with extravagance in promoting them.' *Times* report. In a comparable venture in 1932, Sir Ralph Glyn, the Parliamentary Private Secretary to Ramsay MacDonald, was instrumental in gaining the commission for the rebuilding in modern style of the Midland Hotel, Morecambe, by Oliver Hill. See Alan Powers, 'The Stone and the Shell - Eric Gill and the Midland Hotel, Morecambe', *Book Collector*, XLIV, Spring 1998.

48 *Bexhill-on-Sea Observer*, 24 February 1934, p.4, quoted in Stevens and Willis, 1990.

49 Competition conditions in Oliver Hill papers, RIBA Library, HiO/79/3, quoted in Stevens and Willis.

50 Five sketches and a plan are in the Mendelsohn Archive, Berlin (Staatliche Museen Preussischer Kulturbesitz). One of these is illustrated in Sigrid Achenbach (1987), *Erich Mendelsohn 1887-1953 Ideen Bauten Projekte*, Berlin, p.87, (Cat.257). One internal and one external perspective were presented to the RIBA Drawings Collection, London, by Louise Mendelsohn.

51 'This method of construction has enabled important savings to be made in cost, and has given a framework of exceptional lightness and elegance.' *Builder*, 20 December, 1935, p.1100. The cartel of steel producers in Britain priced reinforcing bars for concrete at an artificially high level, to encourage the use of structural steel (information from Professor Adrian Forty).

52 Cyril Sweett 'Recollections' in Brook et al. eds., 1987, p.69.

53 See Jeremy Brook, 'The Story of the De La Warr Pavilion' in Brook et al. eds., 1987, pp.23-33.

54 Letter of 30 March, 1935, in Oskar Beyer, ed. (1967), *Eric Mendelsohn, letters of an architect*, London, p.140.

55 See Barbara Wadsworth (1989), *Edward Wadsworth, a painter's life*, Wilton, Michael Russell, p.217. The painting is still in the Pavilion, although not in its original position. The Pavilion Trust also owns Wadsworth's original design in oil on canvas.

56 See Neville Jason and Lisa Thompson-Pharoah (1994), *The Sculpture of Frank Dobson*, London, Lund Humphries

57 'The De La Warr Pavilion, Bexhill-1', *Architect and Building News*, 20 December 1935, p.343. Attribution to Summerson based on his own list of anonymous articles in Summerson papers, RIBA Library.

58 A.W. [Arnold Whittick], 'The De La Warr Pavilion, Bexhill', *Building*, January 1936, p.10.

59 ibid., p.12.

60 Percy Horton to Walter Strachan, 22 October 1935, in Hewett, Christopher, ed. (1984), *The Living Curve, Letters to W. J. Strachan, 1929-1979*, London, Taranman Ltd., pp.10-11.

61 Moholy's photos in *Architectural Review*, July 1936, include contextual shots of Bexhill, some taken from the upper windows of houses opposite the Pavilion. Further photos are in Andreas Haus (1980), *Moholy-Nagy*, Photographs and Photograms, London, Thames and Hudson, plates 27 and 28 (the image referred to by Senter). A photograph of Moholy at work at Bexhill is in Arts Council of Great Britain (1980), *Moholy-Nagy*, London, p.4, quote from Senter, ibid., p.49.

62 'Peter Maitland, IV: The Architect', *Architectural Review*, July 1936, p.23.

63 Chermayeff interview with Richard Plunz, 20 September 1980.

64 Barbara Tilson, 'Form and Function', *Building Design*, 4 December, 1987, p.15.

65 See Cyril Sweett 'Recollections' in Jeremy Brook et al., eds., 1987, p.69.

66 See Louise Mendelsohn's comment in Bruno Zevi (1970), *Erich Mendelsohn, Opera Completa: Architetture e Immagine Architettoniche*, Milan, Etas Kompass, p.208: 'When he returned [in March 1935],

many reasons for disagreement came to light on account of the details of the buildings as they were carried out. It appeared clear that the partnership could not continue.' [Author's translation]

67 Richard Plunz interview, 20 September 1980.

68 Beyer, 1967, p.140.

69 ibid., p.142.

70 A printed circular letter, dated December 1936, announced that 'Erich Mendelsohn and Serge Chermayeff want their friends to know that they are dissolving their partnership by mutual consent.... They further take this opportunity to send their best wishes for 1937.' Proof copy from Shenval Press archive, collection Brian Webb.

71 Inserted in Jeremy Gould (1997), *Modern Houses in Britain 1919-1939*, Society of Architectural Historians of Great Britain, at the Chermayeff House, Cape Cod.

72 Recorded in Tilson, 1984.

73 Berthold Lubetkin, 'Modern Architecture in England', *American Architect and Architecture*, February 1937, p.39.

74 John Summerson, 'Romance and Realities', Supplement to *Country Life*, 13 February 1937, pp.ii-iii.

75 In 1993, Norman Foster and Partners made alterations including the creation of windows in the squash court and a two-storey conservatory at the south end, replacing an earlier smaller conservatory added by Dennis Cohen in the 1960s. These changes were the subject of considerable controversy at the time and have not been comprehensively published.

76 See photo in Lionel Brett (1947), *The Things We See: Houses*, Harmondsworth, Penguin Books, p.37.

77 Lancelot Law White (1963), *Focus and Diversions*, London, Cresset Press, p.158.

78 Chermayeff letter to Susan Mayhew, n.d. (c.1971), Avery Library.

79 'Television talk between Mr John Gloag and Mr Serge Chermayeff', Avery Archive.

80 See 'A Scheme of National Importance', *Architectural Design and Construction*, April 1935, pp.192-9.

81 In 'A Hundred Years Ahead', 1935, Chermayeff and J. M. Richards forecast for 1943, Housing Bill: L.C.C. exercises compulsory powers and acquires White City and other sites for slum decanting.' p.83.

82 Richard Plunz interview, 20 September 1980.

83 Craneswater Park, General Report, 18 July 1934, Avery Library.

84 See perspective repr. in Achenbach, 1987, no.269, p.89 and Benton, 1998, p.203.

85 Achenbach, 1987 pp.90-92.

86 Zevi, 1970, p.216, nos.1, 2 & 6.

87 Conversation with author, 1992.

88 Zevi, 1970, p.217, nos.10-16.

89 Tilson, 1987, p.62 and Haward interview with Charlotte Benton, April 1998, in Benton, 1999, p.199.

90 Footnote to original text: 'The plans, of course, provide for the eventual addition of terraces, pergolas, pools, etc, towards the sea, which shoud answer this objection.'

91 Henry-Russell Hitchcock, 'An American in England', *Architect and Building News*, 15 January 1937, p.69.

# A Philosophy of Modern Architecture in Action 1934–9

During his most intense decade of practice, the 1930s, Chermayeff was also active as a writer and lecturer. Most architects in the modern movement in England took part in some form of activity beyond the designing and erecting of buildings. Wells Coates, like Chermayeff, had a background in journalism prior to taking up architecture which gave both men a disposition towards publicity and Chermayeff's activity gains additional significance in view of his later career as a teacher and theorist. Given that discussion of architectural theory in relation to English modernism of the 1930s is still at a relatively undeveloped stage, it is interesting to see what his distinctive contribution to the decade might have been, and how his buildings and projects relate to his ideas.

Chermayeff's work with Mendelsohn gave him the opportunity to develop a way of working in his office through research and collaboration. This was an ideal widely shared at the time, which conferred on architecture the virtues of scientific objectivity and a sense of liberation from individualism. The best-known example was the Tecton partnership, set up by Berthold Lubetkin in 1932, which made a public and didactic statement of its research for Highpoint I flats when they were published in 1935.

Finding the MARS group inadequate in respect both of research and political engagement, members and friends of the Tecton office were instrumental in setting up the Architects and Technicians Organisation (ATO) in 1934.[1] Chermayeff lectured to the students' section of the ATO in March 1935, explaining:

> new planning and new design of structures is not merely a variation in aesthetic principles, a consequence of new discoveries in structural materials. It is infinitely more. It is the expression of an earnest desire of intelligent and highly trained people to change the living conditions in proportion to the immense strides made in general education, medicine and applied technique.[2]

The profession of architecture, on which Chermayeff had the perspective of a newly-recruited outsider, was due to change, and the ATO was committed to raising the importance of salaried architects in public service. The present was a time of crisis, requiring a temporary abdication from individualism on the part of architects in order to allow these new factors to take effect. Chermayeff also took the chair at an ATO meeting at Conway Hall in the autumn of 1935 to introduce John Strachey, the Labour politician, as the speaker.[3] Lubetkin recognised the difficulties of making effective connections with the working class constituency to which the ATO had dedicated itself, which 'suggested that it was our role to guide and not wait to be guided. Indeed it soon became very clear that our proper task was not so much to collect opinions as to gain the confidence and trust of the community by demonstrating that we were on their side, and were willing to prove it by participating in direct action.'[4]

Chermayeff typified the contradictions of left-wing intellectuals in the 1930s, with his privileged background and good social and business contacts from Harrow, his agreeable lifestyle and marriage to an Englishwoman with money and social standing. He was far from alone in this paradoxical state, nor was it exclusively limited to modernists. Chermayeff's circle of professional friends included the architect Clough Williams-Ellis (John Strachey's brother-in-law), who was not a modernist but one who proclaimed that socialism would bring the pleasures of life to more people. Writing to him in 1972 to congratulate him on his knighthood, Chermayeff asked: 'Do you recall those happy pioneering days when we flung ourselves into battle for the "Modern" (now obsolescing)?'[5]

During the first half of the 1930s, Chermayeff was a prominent campaigner for design, taking part in the network of activists – including John Gloag and Noel Carrington – all speaking a similar message while hoping to reach a non-specialist audience. This writing is usually tedious to revisit but Chermayeff's often has a verbal edge to it which lasts. His radio broadcast of 1932, characteristically titled 'Away with Snobbery, Sentiment and Stupidity' was printed in the *Listener*, making it his first appearance before a general audience. Much of it is devoted to criticising the 'sham modern' promoted by furnishing stores in the wake of the Waring and Gillow exhibition.

The nature of Chermayeff's political commitment was scrutinised by an intense young woman art student, Leonora Carrington (b.1915), who came to London from Lancashire in 1937 to study with Amédée Ozenfant. She was placed under Chermayeff's guardianship by her parents but met the surrealist Max Ernst at a dinner party with his old Parisian friend, Ernö Goldfinger, and defied Chermayeff's orders by eloping with him. In her novella, *Down Below*, published many years later, she portrayed him as 'Egres Lepereff', writing a perceptive physical description of 'the great architect', who 'paused on the top of the steps so that everyone could get a good look. He was dressed as a Cossack. He carried his head between his shoulders in such a way as to intensify the immense length of his curved though elegant nose. He descended the stairs gracefully, twitching his nostrils like a racehorse.'[6] Carrington exposed the gap between Chermayeff's desire for a purified architecture and the inability of ordinary people to appreciate it. The nervous hero, Francis, says, 'But if you build abstract houses, the more abstract you make them the less there'll be there, and if you get abstraction itself there won't be anything there at all', to which Lepereff replies, 'It takes a certain time to grasp; these things are not included in elementary education ... An intellectual aristocracy ... on a purely abstract basis with a smattering of Marx's social system, is the only way I can find of rendering the world less uninhabitable for intelligent human beings.' In the story, the 'great architect' has expressed his contempt for common humanity by designing a perfectly functional device for executions, which he describes as 'a symphony of pure form'.[7]

The frigid intellectualism of Carrington's fictional portrait is belied by Chermayeff's major piece of 'political' writing. 'A Hundred Years Ahead: Forecasting the Coming Century' was written jointly with J.M. Richards (1907-92) and published in the *Architects' Journal* in 1935, rather in the manner of a New Year entertainment, with a teasing form of humour. It has the character of one of Mansfield Forbes's elaborate academic in-jokes and is the sort of thing that is best undertaken collaboratively, although Richards declared that the article was almost all Chermayeff's work.[8] It is written in 'Basic English', the simplified vocabulary promoted by the Cambridge English scholar C.K. Ogden and adopted by Raymond McGrath for his book, *Twentieth Century House*s. It was a sequel to Richards's chronology of the period 1834–1934, starting from the foundation of the RIBA, published two months earlier. This centenary, coinciding with the RIBA's occupation of its new headquarters building in Portland Place, had stimulated a number of similar retrospects but only Richards and Chermayeff did a forward projection, making some surprisingly accurate predictions of architectural matters among items from a fantasy world reminiscent of H.G. Wells. 1997, for example, is marked by a Mackintosh centenary celebration in Glasgow, an event which actually took place in 1996, while in 2000 Japan was to build the world's highest structure. Neither of these events would have seemed at all obvious at the time.

The text is also a serious commentary on current conditions, noting that modernism in the 1930s was only a beginning on a future path, still conditioned by several centuries of confusion. The authors explained that 'our article, if lighthearted in detail, was serious as an attempt to relate cause to effect'.[9] With imaginary hindsight, modernism is equated with Gothic in a sort of symmetry with the view of 1835 from the vantage point of 1935:

> Science was being put to such a great number of new uses, and so much new knowledge was being tested in the years when the first work was done in steel and concrete that the buildings of this time are less clear in design than those produced in earlier times when the process of change was slower ... A little of the Gothic feeling may be seen in the records and the small number of examples of building in the early thirties which are still in existence. Designed by men with a new outlook and a given form in new materials, they had at least a certain quality of true structure common with the earlier Gothic buildings.[10]

Perhaps only in the guise of fiction could the authors blame 'the self-interested and foolish outlook of the masses' for lack of progress in their own time, together with the ideological splits among architects themselves. The solution lay round the corner, with the 'Second Socialist Government' in 1936, whose measures may be taken as a true statement of Chermayeff and Richards's desires:

> it straightaway made use of the ideas of serious experts and was responsible for the first system of organisation and necessary building named 'Planning'. Faced with the crying need for those fruits of early discoveries which made it possible for men to be healthier, happier, and to have a higher level of comfort, but which had been used till now only for the well-off, the new government got to work to give these fruits to everyone and a new society was produced.[11]

These changes were to be imposed by a rigorous aesthetic control on buildings but this restriction of architecture to technical development is seen as the necessary purgation preliminary to the flourishing of a new art of architecture. This was due to arise after 'the destruction and general waste of the second European war and the fight which overcame the Fascist government'.[12]

'A Hundred Years Ahead' indicates the sense of continuing crisis, felt not only by architects but by painters and sculptors who wished their own practices to make a difference to the world. Not many actually joined the Communist Party, finding it too doctrinaire, but many of those in the artistic world gave support to the left-wing Artists' International Association, including Chermayeff's new friend Percy Horton, whose actual paintings were conservative in character.[13] Chermayeff himself gave a lecture at the Karl Marx House in Clerkenwell on 3 February 1935. The AIA demonstrated its support for republican Spain as the Spanish Civil War worsened in the course of 1935, an event on the world stage which allowed for direct action, as Nazi Germany and Fascist Italy as yet did not. Events in Spain contributed to the sense, from 1935 onwards, that there was a mounting crisis and that time was running out.

**Working Men's Flats competition entry, Cement Marketing Company, 1935.**

Chermayeff's most direct engagement with the ATO and its concerns was his entry for the competition in 1935 for Working Men's Flats, promoted, in a cross-over with capitalist interests which was entirely typical of the period, by the Cement Marketing Company. The issue of mass housing was on the minds of public and politicians at this time. The private housing market, building almost exclusively semi-detached suburban houses, was booming, but at the expense of civic cohesion. Government funds for building accommodation for those unable to make a deposit and payments on a house were limited, and usually channelled through the conservative Borough Surveyor's office of a local council. The competition was therefore an attempt to consolidate the few private sector attempts at modern flat-building, such as Wells Coates's Lawn Road Flats (opened in the summer of 1934) by Thelma Cazalet, the Labour Minister of Housing, and Lubetkin and Tecton's Highpoint, completed in 1935, and to demonstrate the alliance of concrete and modernism in the service of political change. Architects tended to pick up German 'Zeilenbau' housing of the post-1929 period, with its parallel rows of walk-up flats calculated for the most economical return on land with strict daylighting standards.

Chermayeff's design was made in collaboration with the engineering and technical team who were working on the De La Warr Pavilion at the same time, Helsby and Hamann with Felix Samuely as Structural Engineer, Cyril Sweett as Quantity Surveyor and J. Stinton Jones as Mechanical Engineer. The winners were Tecton and Lubetkin but Chermayeff's scheme was among those commended. This was a much more austere design than White City, with no sign of Mendelsohn's involvement. The structure was to have been precast concrete with box girders making a continuous floor plate, removing any need for downstand beams. This was an unusual development, more sophisticated in many ways than the monolithic structure of Lubetkin's Highpoint I, with scope for flexibility in the internal layout, since the precast structure allowed plenty of servicing through voids, with additional vertical ducting for waste disposal. It was a practical demonstration of the ideas expounded by Chermayeff in 'New Methods and New Materials' at the end of 1933, combining economy of material with speed of assembly and modular standardisation. The plans were evolved on a 4ft module, allowing for different sizes. The housing consultant Elizabeth Denby, collaborator with Maxwell Fry on Kensal House, the most significant pre-war housing project from within the inner circle of the modern movement in England, reported favourably on the scheme in the *Architects' Journal*, dealing mainly with the plan form:

> The large living room and the relative sizes of the bedrooms, each with separate access to each, is admirable. A back-to-back range between living room and kitchen, a gas copper and gas fires in bedrooms are provided … It is essential, I think, to have one open fireplace in a dwelling, however [this was a requirement of the competition]. The large balconies, bounded by a flower box in concrete as part of the structure, are surmounted above a 6-in gap by wire mesh in tubular surround. I have used this method myself and know of nothing better![14]

Members of Tecton flew to Paris for a weekend outing on their £300 premium but there were few opportunities for modern architects to put their claims of high standard environments at low costs to the test.[15] Chermayeff and Mendelsohn made a speculative scheme for flats and a boathouse at Chiswick Mall, on a riverside site beside the Old Church, begun in 1935 and developed into a final scheme by Chermayeff alone in 1937. These were luxury flats for the private sector.[16] Mendelsohn's sketches for the scheme were, predictably, a more formally adventurous scheme than the version developed by Chermayeff, in which the plan form was a series of connected T-shaped blocks, linked on a straight spine, with a uniform canopied roof line, similar to the Working Men's Flats in the extreme simplicity of the design. The balconies on the forward-projecting blocks face upriver towards the south-west.

Group photo at opening of MARS Group exhibition, January 1938, left to right: Godfrey Samuel, Le Corbusier, Wells Coates, J.M. Richards, Serge Chermayeff, Maxwell Fry.

Chermayeff was widely known in most of the circles of London modernism in the mid-1930s. He made friends with artists whose links can be traced through J.M. Richards's wife, Peggy Angus (1904–93), who was a fellow student at the Royal College of Art with Percy Horton. Jim Richards himself knew Myfanwy Evans (1911–97), who started the magazine *Axis* for the promotion of abstract and other progressive art in the spring of 1935, with help from the painter John Piper (1903–92) whom she married in 1937.[17] In later life, Myfanwy Piper remembered Chermayeff as 'a great swaggerer'.[18] Angus was also a close friend of the painter Eric Ravilious (1903–42), another Royal College student whose wife, Tirzah (1908–51), was a friend of Richards before he met Eric. Ravilious often stayed with Angus at Furlongs, her cottage on the South Downs in Sussex, not far from Bexhill and the other places where Chermayeff liked to spend weekends. Chermayeff counted Ravilious among his friends.[19]
At Furlongs, in a primitive outdoor lavatory, there was a souvenir, in the form of a hand-shaped wire holder for a roll of toilet paper, of a visit from the American sculptor Alexander Calder (1898–1976) who became a friend of the Pipers around 1936 when he was dividing his time between London, Paris and Normandy. With performances of his toy circus, which he carried in a suitcase and manipulated to a background of gramophone records, Calder

inspired a sense of fun about abstract art which helped to win support for the movement in England.

Chermayeff also got to know Ben Nicholson (1894–1982), the painter who considered himself the main strategist of abstract art in England and who, from 1932 onwards was living in Hampstead with Barbara Hepworth (1903–75). Indeed, a flower painting by Nicholson and a street scene by his friend Christopher Wood (1901–30) hung in the 'Entrance Lounge' in the Waring and Gillow exhibition in 1928. The sculptor Henry Moore (1898–1986) lived and worked alongside Nicholson and Hepworth, and belonged to the same social group, as did the critic Herbert Read (1893-1968). Chermayeff had associated mainly with an older generation at the beginning of his career. Now he was among his comtemporaries and showed an openness to new friendships and influences. All felt that their fight against convention in art was part of the fight against Fascism, by whose running-dogs Chermayeff had been pursued after the Bexhill competition success. In this company, he also met the émigré architects and designers who followed Mendelsohn in flight from Hitler to Hampstead, notably the Bauhaus colleagues, Walter Gropius (1883–1969), Marcel Breuer (1902–81) and László Moholy-Nagy, whose lives intertwined with his own in various ways in America in the 1940s and later, and whose presence gave English modernists a greater sense of their own significance, while showing how in many ways they were still lagging behind the continental movement. They were later joined, for varying periods of time, by Piet Mondrian (1872–1944) and Naum Gabo (1890–1977), about whom Chermayeff wrote articles in American journals in the 1940s.

The excitement of the period came from the sense of shared political and artistic endeavour across many specialisms. The discussion of Chermayeff's work which follows therefore tries to combine influences and friendships from many directions which can be related to his buildings and his other activities in what was his richest period of productivity as an architect.

From the beginning of his design career, Chermayeff had displayed an interest in the use of colour. This developed in 1935 to the publication of a large-format booklet, *The Application of Colour in Modern Buildings*, a publication so rare that no library appears to hold a copy. Knowledge of its content is therefore restricted to two leaves from it that were presented by Chermayeff to the RIBA Drawings Collection, and a report on it in the *Architects' Journal*. The booklet was probably commissioned by Cecil Cronshaw of ICI, Chermayeff's client in 1936-8 for the Blackley Dyestuffs Laboratory, since he was from 1935 on the Board of Management of the British Colour Council, and the booklet was produced by an ICI subsidiary, Nobel Chemical Industries. The available pages show the colour scheme of the theatre in the De La Warr Pavilion. The text sets out some basic principles for the use of colour in domestic interiors, the area with which Chermayeff was most familiar, but with a pleasing lack of dogma:

First, the private, the domestic, requiring discretion, a background for personal preferences of colour, restfulness. Colours seen during prolonged periods of contemplation. Secondly, the public, the effective, stimulating, gay, startling, propagandist, permissible exaggerations for transitory contemplation.

A great many effects of colour are too easily overlooked.

The use of too heavy colour and the consequent lack of light reflection. Too many rooms are robbed, in this relatively dull climate, with its lack of brilliant sunshine, of the light that they might possess.

The sense of refuge in a positive colour or texture in an internal partition or wall against which one sits.

The compensating glare of yellows when light itself is cold. The ideally orientated kitchen to the north is a more pleasant room if it has a warmth in its wall colour.

The principle 'from the ground up' light walls and ceilings, weight of colour on the floor in carpet or rug, in low upholstered furniture provides a natural balance and a completely satisfactory distribution for nearly every purpose.

Different colours to satisfy individual preferences within one room, for example a Living Room with one discreet wall and a deep-toned chair, beside a light wall and a bright chair.

Simplicity in colour. Avoidance of experiment in too obviously 'arty' colours and tones, far removed from natural colours – of earth and of the primaries.

The fortunate possessor of a good modern painting cannot do better than to build up a whole room in terms of the artist's canvas harmonies, if he can arrange them within the structural and functional plan which it has been attempted to describe here.

In the booklet, Chermayeff offered practical advice in the development of a 'colour card' system, which would be made in every office with poster colours, working from the three primaries down through three modifications of each, which are then mixed with white to produce a series of tones, so that equally matched tones of differing hues are arrived at. Evidently speaking from experience, Chermayeff advocated the use of some ready-mixed tertiary colours such as burnt umber, because 'this most useful colour with ultramarine blue and white produces a range of beiges which are not easily obtainable from any other mixture'.[20]

Opposite: Elmhirst apartment, 42 Upper Brook Street, London, 1934.

W.B. Corset Showroom, Regent Street, London, 1934, entrance.

Chermayeff's controlled use of colour can be imagined in the W.B. Corset Showroom in Maddox House, Regent Street, 1934, within one of the dreary Portland-stone-clad office buildings that replaced John Nash's stuccoed Regency buildings, amidst much protest in the 1920s. The outside world was kept at bay with floor-to-ceiling curtaining in the main showroom, with light filtered through an internal window of obscured glass, reflecting in the mirrored partition that divided the showroom from the 'sample room'. Mannequins would emerge through a mirrored door when the showroom was in use for fashion parades. A porthole opening in the mirror glass provided not only a peephole but also an opportunity for dramatic photography, and was one of a series of circles in a greater design, including the hanging globe lights. PLAN chairs in red, blue and brown provided accents of colour in Chermayeff's favourite hues against a background described as 'a rather dead yellow in the main showroom and what might be called "corset pink" in many of the other rooms, two colours which have to be very carefully used to avoid either dullness or vulgarity'.[21] A mural by the young graphic designer Milner Gray, later to become one of the leaders of post-war industrial design, illustrated the slogan 'we girdle the world', with sprightly female figures imposed over a simplified world map. Milner Gray set up the Society of Industrial Artists in 1930, holding some of the early meetings in Chermayeff's office. The showroom was also distinguished for its use of Marcel Breuer's Thonet B64 upright armchair of 1928 with a cane seat and back panels, possibly the first sighting of this model in England.[22]

The apartment which Chermayeff designed for Dorothy Elmhirst at 42 Upper Brook Street in Mayfair, in 1934, shows the gradual emergence of a new character in his work, not radically

different from what went before, but lighter and brighter. The apartment was a conversion within a Neo-Georgian block of 1928–9 by T.P. Bennett and Son.[23] These were service flats without a kitchen and were planned with a long journey between the service hatch and the dining room which wasted space in corridors. Chermayeff rationalised the plan by providing a dining space for eight (four on each side of the table, no places at the ends), in a bay off the main living room, divided by a curtain but forming part of the way in from the hall. An inconvenient structural column had to be left in place but the wall between the living room and dining room was turned into a partition with a floor-to-ceiling finish of sycamore veneered plywood, with recessed shelving and cupboards inset. The flat was well served with built-in storage, including a unit running below the five windows in the living room, incorporating radiators, with a wall mounted 'Bestlite', one of Chermayeff's adaptations of the standard design, a sideboard unit in the dining room with a white rubber top, on which a propped-up painting was casually displayed, and twin dressing table units on either side of the bedroom.

Over the electric hearth in the living room was a major painting, Fishermen Dancing by Christopher Wood, painted in 1930 in the last summer of his life, and now in Leicester City Art Gallery (see page 160). Dorothy Elmhirst and her husband Leonard had other paintings by Wood which remain at Dartington Hall in Devon, their main residence from 1926 onwards and the seat of their remarkable experiment in education, agriculture and the arts, financed by her inherited Whitney fortune and shaped by the couple's shared idealism.[24] In 1930, Dartington commissioned its first modern building, the Headmaster's House, High Cross, by the Swiss-American architect W.E. Lescaze, who continued to work on the Estate for some years. Chermayeff never worked in Devon but the quiet warmth of the flat in London may be more indicative of Dorothy Elmhirst's personal taste than Lescaze's more dramatised compositions. The furniture was mainly a mixture of pieces by PLAN and by Aalto, with severe geometrically patterned rugs whose authorship was not revealed in the publications.[25]

A third significant London interior, designed three years later in 1937, should be considered in conjunction with the Elmhirst flat. This was within a converted Victorian house in Connaught Place, with views southwards over Hyde Park, for Commander Teddy Heywood-Lonsdale, a Royal Navy officer who was a close friend of Lord Mountbatten and a mentor in the early life of the Duke of Edinburgh. It is not clear how he met Chermayeff but the latter explained in an interview published in the *Architectural Review*:

My clients' willingness to place faith in the expert they had employed resulted in the possibility of increasing the available floor space by 25 per cent, by constructing a mezzanine floor. By being permitted to please myself therefore, free from the usual cramping compromise, I have in the finished scheme been able to please my clients.[26]

The mezzanine was possible because of the floor-to-ceiling height, creating something like a duplex apartment with a grand L shaped double-height general purpose living room, from which a staircase led up to a balcony dining room, served from a kitchen unconventionally placed on the upper level. There was generous accommodation for a maid which was fitted on two levels, and although the segregation of 'upstairs' and 'downstairs' was sacrificed, the space was economically used. The flouting of convention may have come naturally to a Naval officer, used to the close proximity of ship's quarters. The fitted wardrobes were in the living room to save space in the small bedroom and dressing room, and Chermayeff explained that the owners had their clothes brought to them by the servants. The nautical feeling was increased by the bunks in the guest bedroom.

Drawing Room, Heywood-Lonsdale apartment.

The placing of the furniture, once more consisting largely of PLAN chairs grouped in pairs, helped to articulate the big space which also contained one of Chermayeff's grand pianos, designed in 1936 for a piano exhibition at Dorland Hall. The legs were painted white to give a floating effect, as was the inside of the lid, in order to emphasise the harp shape and reflect the pattern of the metal strings on red felt. In the generally reticent colour scheme of the room, an accent was provided by the strong coral colour panel on which the radio controls were mounted, concealed behind a tambour front as part of a bookshelf and cupboard unit. The room was dominated by a large Picasso painting, bought by Chermayeff on behalf of his client, in which a sleeping woman (his young lover Marie-Thérèse Walter) is overlooked by a head on a pedestal, with a strong viridian green background.[27] This choice was meaningful in 1937, the year in which Picasso's *Guernica* was exhibited in the Spanish republican pavilion at the International Exhibition in Paris and later in London. Picasso's reputation was in eclipse in England during the height of enthusiasm for abstraction in the first half of the 1930s but Myfanwy Evans and John Piper made his rehabilitation part of their programme for *Axis* magazine, as a deliberate criticism of the narrowness of abstraction, showing how, without joining the Surrealist movement, it was possible for modern art to be expressive of ordinary human emotion.

Other aspects of the Heywood-Lonsdale apartment are indicators of Chermayeff's alliance with this viewpoint. He chose a glass-topped table by Denham Maclaren – of the same 1930 design he had used at Shrub's Wood – and partially masked the hanging globe light in the centre of the room with a silvered metal shade, partly to focus the light on the Picasso but also because 'the sphere seemed to float better than any other shape in the volume of the room'.[28] More significant of a change of mood was the almost Georgian treatment of the staircase with its plain upright wooden balusters and polished wood handrail descending to a 'wreathed' curling termination. It looks appropriate in its place, and Chermayeff explained that 'I played about with various flowing and streamlined patterns, but eventually decided that this simple verticality and reticence would serve best to form a contrast.' It closely resembles the treatment of the staircase at Bentley Wood. The dining balcony has a double curve on plan, partly explained in structural and functional terms but undoubtedly an expression of formal pleasure for its own sake.

**Guest Bedroom, Heywood-Lonsdale apartment.**

Of special interest is Chermayeff's revealing response to the final interview question, 'What is your conception of the next step in interior design?', which is quoted here in full, being a self-criticism of some of his earlier works and evidence of a more general change of mood at this time among modernists of all kinds in England:

> Elimination of complication with a view to eliminating chances of making mistakes: less meticulous planning for function, which results in interior paralysis: greater freedom of disposition: an attempt to escape from the fetish of possession and the too easy satisfaction with ingenious detail. I agree with you when you say that modern architecture of today is different both in kind and in possibilities from the modern architecture of even five years ago. I think appreciation of form, texture and colour, and humanism, will increase beyond the mere preoccupation with the fulfilment of function.[29]

This statement acknowledges Chermayeff's earlier over-dependence on functional justification, not in order to promote in its place any anti-functional aestheticism but in recognition of the reality that life is more fluid than any architect can predict. It is not clear exactly what Chermayeff meant by humanism but easy enough to imagine it as a mutual exchange between

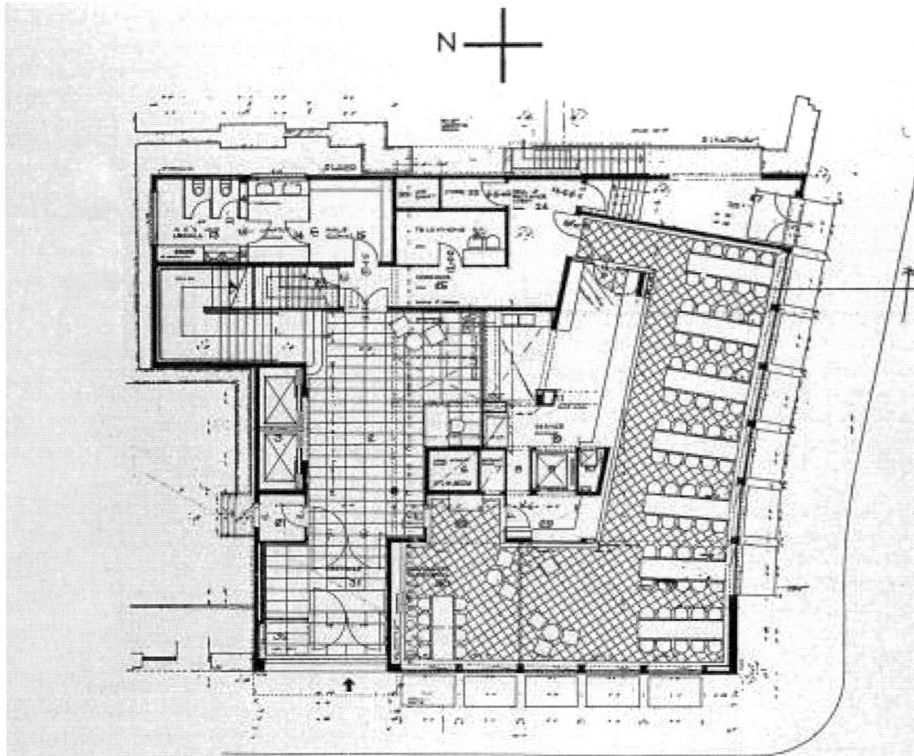

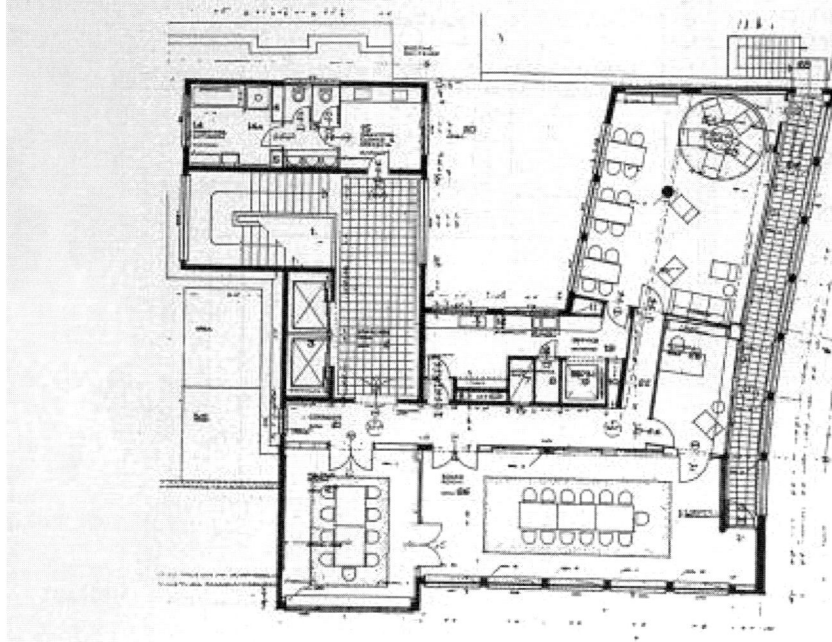

110

professional skill and imagination and the needs of society, from the individual client outwards to the world in general. Perhaps Chermayeff was influenced by the title, at least, of Geoffrey Scott's book, *The Architecture of Humanism*, 1914, for in 1963, his own first major book, *Community and Privacy* was sub-titled *Towards a new architecture of humanism*, an equivalent to the old, which Scott defined as the classicism of the Renaissance.

Chermayeff's sense of an almost classical equipoise in architecture, evident in the Heywood-Lonsdale apartment, is carried through his two major commercial buildings of the late 1930s which were inaugurated during his partnership with Mendelsohn, which have already been mentioned. The W.A. Gilbey building, on the corner of Oval Road and Jamestown Road (then James Street) in Camden Town was a redevelopment of part of a site already occupied by the company, and accessible by rail and by the Regent's Canal which runs behind the site. The new building was the result of their relocation from the Pantheon but Camden Town was not then the natural site for a company headquarters, complete with board room and directors' suite. The special problems of the site included the noise from the railway to the rear which is the main line to Euston Station, and from the iron-wheeled carts which were still in use over the granite setts of the roadway in front. These factors determined Chermayeff to produce a completely air-conditioned building, and to prevent the transmission of noise through the ground by mounting the reinforced concrete frame on four-inch pads of cork as sound insulation. In this he acknowledged the assistance of 'a German engineer … named Levy, who was a little man we used to call "The Penguin".'[30]

W. & A. Gilbey building, model, Oval Road, Camden Town, 1937.

Opposite: W. & A. Gilbey building, plan

The character of design is mildly patrician without any of the obvious trappings of a company headquarters. The curve on plan of the longer elevation has already been noted as a feature of the building, also its quasi-Georgian hierarchy of a 'rusticated' tiled basement, which was finished at the top with an early example of a 'flashgap' detail, a recessed channel with an aluminium beading, giving a feeling of lightness. Lubetkin was developing various versions of the flashgap at this time, and it became a valuable and almost universal aspect of modern architecture, typical of the 1950s, offering a modern alternative to classical mouldings as a way of making transitions between different materials on a single plane. The 'cornice' is in the form of an overhanging roof slab, a detail used by Mendelsohn in several of his urban buildings, and a commonsense answer to the problem of weathering, albeit one which many modern architects resisted. This willingness to accept the commonality of classicism and modernism, even unconsciously, is indicative in a change in Chermayeff's own design idiom already discussed as an aspect of the Heywood-Lonsdale apartment. According to one story, the directors, who were introduced to Chermayeff by Anthony Gibbons Grinling, were suspicious of him as a modernist until they learnt that he had been to Harrow, so he may also have made a slight accommodation to their conservative instincts. The Italianate quality of the building is emphasised by the loggia at rooftop level, where the director's suite, with clubroom, restaurant and boardroom was placed. The theory was that as this was high above the noise, it would be possible to open the windows and stand on a terrace, with light coming through the circular skylights, to enjoy the view over London.

The rooms at this level included old company portraits and an antique tapestry which covered one wall of the boardroom, with an uncompetitive alliance of past and present of a kind seldom attempted at this period. There were PLAN chairs for relaxation, and comfortable leather boardroom chairs for business. In the same spirit as the Heywood-Lonsdale apartment, this was a masculine modernism that could appeal to the non-aesthetic English gentleman, with its sense of quietly-spoken quality and technical perfection, like a good yacht or car, while at the same time unencumbered by the fading symbols of class and nation. The air-conditioning system which protected the building from outside noise was not unique or revolutionary but it was relatively unusual among modern architects to give greater attention to services engineering than to the more glamorous area of structural engineering.

Left: W. & A. Gilbey building, directors' dining room.

W. & A. Gilbey building, exterior.

The Jamestown Road façade carried the name 'GILBEY' in huge red italic sanserif three-dimensional lettering, ranged vertically on the white margin to the left of the windows, but the original intention was to place this more modestly over the tiled ground floor round the corner in Oval Road, to mark the entrance. This was the only fault found by the young architect Hugh Casson, who described Gilbey's as an 'example of sound vernacular design'.[31] The original building was extended to the north in 1960–2. Chermayeff was invited by Anthony Grinling's son, Jasper Grinling, to make a scheme but the work was carried out by the London firm of Richard Siefert and Partners.[32]

The ICI (Imperial Chemical Industries) Dyestuffs Division Laboratories at Blackley, near Manchester, were, like Gilbey's, concerned with the exercise of precision in the industrial production of liquids, but in a rather different setting. The commission came through a personal friendship of Chermayeff's – not through a Harrow contact but through a coalminer's son, Percy Crosland, who had risen from a poor background through study at Manchester University. His ingenuity as an industrial chemist while still a student enabled him to solve the problem of making an unfading black dye. He was a man of whom Chermayeff spoke with consistent and unreserved admiration. How he met Crosland is not recorded but he made alterations to a house in Manchester for him, including a mural in the bathroom. Crosland was not in ICI but must have recommended Chermayeff to Cecil Cronshaw (1889-1961), Managing Director of the Dyestuffs Group, one of the many semi-autonomous subsidiaries of ICI.

Due in part to Cronshaw's pioneering work, the application of dyestuffs went far beyond the textile industry to cover a variety of industrial products, food colouring and medical uses. Such a building would normally have been built to a single storey height, with industrial north-facing roof lights, giving 'a depressing atmosphere in which to work'.[33] The text in the opening brochure describing old conditions betrays Chermayeff's rhetorical manner, 'In the early days of chemistry any spare basement or room was used as a laboratory where inspiration and high-thinking rubbed shoulders with alchemy and charlatanry in an atmosphere of dirt and desolation.'[34] The purpose of the building reawakened the almost mystical feeling about the value of research that characterised English modernism at the beginning of the decade. Unwillingness to invest in research was being propounded by the 'Cambridge Scientists' as one of the chief causes of national malaise.[35] Chermayeff wanted to have views from the laboratories to humanise the working environment, and introduced fume cupboards into the laboratories in his three-storey building as part of a complete scheme of services engineering. The individual laboratories were given the devoted attention of his office staff, so that every detail could be thought through and serve as a prototype.

**Block model of intended complete scheme for ICI Dyestuffs Group, Blackley, Manchester.**

**Right: ICI Dyestuffs Group, Blackley, 1938, typical section through laboratory showing air circulation and fume cupboard outlet.**

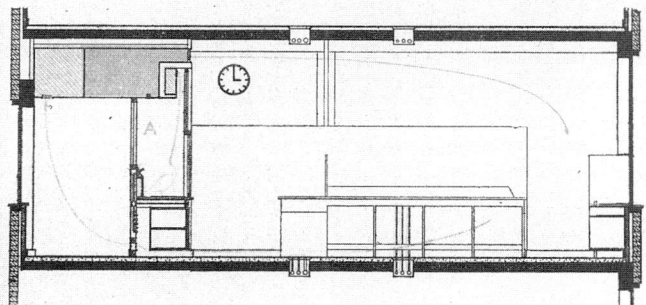

The site was already occupied by the ICI Dyestuffs Group and one purpose of the project was to rationalise the existing buildings by replanning. What was built was therefore a fragment of a much larger intended complex of buildings, all of similar character, branching off a central stem. This was clearly explained in diagrams in the accompanying publication. The executed building is a T-shape in plan, with a 400ft long stem of laboratories linked by corridors to one side, accessed from the cross-bar which contained some private laboratories. This section was slightly curved on plan, so that when extended to support other stems, they would be angled inwards to fit the tapering site, with spaces for gardens in between. On all the laboratory floors the corridor and the laboratories were divided by a thickened-out partition containing fume cupboards and sinks, feeding into an air-extract duct running overhead in the corridor. The labs themselves were fully air-conditioned from the same ducting, which was something Chermayeff suggested to the clients, assuring not only that pollution generated internally was quickly dispersed but that external pollution did not enter. The attention to mechanical servicing carried forward the high standards set at Gilbey's. This vital aspect of modern building was often neglected by modern architects in the 1930s, or otherwise subjected to unrealistic if ingenious inventions. After 1935, certain architects, such as Berthold Lubetkin at the Finsbury Health Centre and William Crabtree at the department store, Peter Jones, paid attention to the issue, but in Chermayeff's mind it loomed larger than in most others.[36]

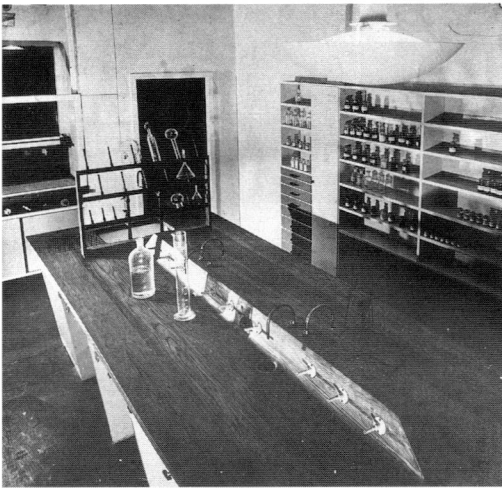

Left: ICI Dyestuffs Group, laboratory.

ICI Dyestuffs Group, research laboratories, exterior from the south.

The east-facing laboratories received good daylight, seldom shining in directly. Flexibility of layout was intended, with regular servicing points in the floor void between the concrete beams of the frame. The frame itself was provided with two sets of expansion joints, an unusual provision at this time and for many years to come. It was proclaimed that 'as much as $1\frac{1}{2}$ inches total movement has been measured in the building without cracking'.[37] Externally, the walls were built in reinforced brick, allowing a thinner skin of brickwork, whose harsh colour pleased even Chermayeff's ally, Professor Charles Reilly (1874–1947) when he reviewed the building as part of his annual roundup in the *Architects' Journal* in 1939. As he wrote, 'Externally the walls are of alternate layers of shiny Accrington red bricks, which I personally always have disliked, and large sheets of plate glass in metal frames. Here, however the glass and the surface of the brickwork are practically in the same plane, with the result that their hard glittering surfaces have a new and happy relationship to one another. These bricks seemed to me for the first time a fine material as well as the right one for this sort of building.'[38] The bricks gave local character and a smoothness of finish appropriate to a building characterised by mechanisation in all parts. The great extended unstressed elevations are terminated by a staircase with solid walling, sufficient to act as a compositional stop. Aesthetically, the neatness of the laboratories, with their teak-topped benches, was inherent in their efficiency. A touch of fantasy came in the scarlet paint of the lift cage.

The Blackley Laboratories were the building Chermayeff liked to claim as his best. They exemplified the scientific aspirations that he and many other architects shared, which in Chermayeff's mind were inseparable from his aesthetic aims. Local papers reported that at the opening visitors were introduced to world-shaping products such as Perspex and Neoprene, as part of a comprehensive exhibition of the history of organic chemistry and its industrial applications.[39] The *Daily Dispatch* reported, probably from Cecil Cronshaw's speech at the opening, the sentiment that would have appealed to Chermayeff, that there was 'an amazing similarity between the trend of architecture in bricks and mortar and the trend of "architecture" in the invisible atoms and molecules that are the chemist's "building materials".'[40]

The building showed how, even in unpromising conditions, beauty might be trusted to look after herself, with some helpful encouragement. The original no longer survives, so it is hard to judge. The extended scheme was developed after the war, with additional buildings following Chermayeff's original designs but the first wing was demolished, followed in recent years by the remainder of the complex. Its success was such as to attract the doubtful compliment of a copy, built in Argentina during the war, that was so blatant that Chermayeff started a lawsuit against it.[41]

While the Blackley scheme was under construction, Chermayeff was also employed to design a building for ICI, in Huddersfield, a large project into which he put much office time and enthusiasm, including a model made in the office by Derrick Oxley. The scheme was sadly cancelled after only a sports pavilion had been built on the site, probably in the autumn of 1938, with dire results for Chermayeff's finances. His other unexecuted scientific project, in 1936, was for laboratories at Gordonstoun School in Morayshire, Scotland, a school of German origin replanted in Britain by its anti-Nazi founder-headmaster, Kurt Hahn, and famous for its Spartan regime. The commission may have come through Heywood-Lonsdale's connection to Lord Mountbatten, as his nephew Prince Philip was a pupil at the school between 1935 and 1939. This was a modest single-storey timber building on rough stone footings with a pitched roof, attached to an existing building whose design it matched.

## Notes

1 See John Allan (1992), *Berthold Lubetkin, architecture and the tradition of progress*, London, RIBA Publications, pp.322ff.

2 Chermayeff, 'The Future for Students', report of lecture 'The Architect and the World Today', 18 March, *Architects' Journal*, 21 March 1935, pp.435-6.

3 See letter from Percy Horton to Walter Strachan, 22 October 1935, in Christopher Hewett ed. (1984), *The Living Curve, Letters to W.J. Strachan, 1929-1979*, London, Taranman Ltd., p.11.

4 Allan, 1992, p.323.

5 Chermayeff. to Clough Williams-Ellis, 9 January 1972. Avery Library

6 Leonora Carrington, 'Down Below' in *The House of Fear*, edited and introduced by Marina Warner (1989), London, Virago Press, p.134. I owe my knowledge of this passage to a reference in Anthony Vidler (1992), *The Architectural Uncanny*, Cambridge MA and London, MIT Press, p.150.

7 ibid., pp.134-5.

8 J.M. Richards in conversation with author. For a discussion of the article, see Hélène Lipstadt, 'Polemic and Parody in the battle for British modernism', *AA Files*, 3 1983, pp.68-76.

9 Chermayeff and Richards, letter to *Architects' Journal*, LXXXI 1935, p.189.

10 Richards and Chermayeff, 'A Hundred Years Ahead', *Architects' Journal*, 10 January 1935, p.79.

11 ibid., p.80.

12 ibid., p.81.

13 Francis Skinner of Tecton was a CP member 'Bobby' Carter was closely associated with the party. See Allan, 1992, p.323.

14 *Architects' Journal*, 28 March 1935, p.484.

15 Allan, 1992, p.285.

16 Bruno Zevi (1970), *Erich Mendelsohn, Opera Completa: Architetture e Immagine Architettoniche*, Milan, Etas Compas, p.227. A scheme for the same site, dated 1935, was made by the architect John Campbell (1878-1947), for a developer H. Mendelsohn, who seems to have been the same H. Mendelsohn who commissioned a house from Campbell in Berlin in the 1920s. See Alan Powers (1997), *John Campbell, Rediscovery of an Arts and Crafts Architect*, London, Prince of Wales's Institute of Architecture. There is no evidence that he was related to Erich Mendelsohn, and it is likely that several developers might have produced schemes for this site at the same time. The date of 1937 for Chermayeff's scheme comes from a print of a perspective drawing in the RIBA Drawings Collection, captioned and dated by Chermayeff at a later date for presentation to the collection. An original print of the same image is in the Avery Library, University of Columbia. A block plan exists among Chermayeff family records.

17 Anthony West (1979), *John Piper*, London, Secker & Warburg, p.67 records Piper's memory that 'the nearest thing I had to a sale in those days came after '33 when the architect Serge Chermayeff swapped a picture of mine for a table of his - a table he'd designed and had made for some project that didn't come off.'

18 Telephone conversation, February 1992.

19 The writer Olive Cook remembers meeting Chermayeff at Furlongs when he was on one of his post-war visits to England. In 1940, when Chermayeff was proposing an exhibition of contemporary British art in Oregon, he wanted to include Ravilious and his friend Edward Bawden. (Chermayeff letter to John Piper, 14 November 1940, kindly communicated by the late Myfanwy Piper.)

20 Philip Scholberg, 'Trade Notes', *Architects' Journal*, 23 January 1936, p.175-6.

21 'R.P.', 'A Wholesale Showroom', *Design for Today*, April 1934, p.136.

22 For the complicated legal story of the attribution and patenting of this chair, see Christopher Wilk (1981), *Marcel Breuer, Furniture and Interiors*, New York, Museum of Modern Art, pp.75-7.

23 See Survey of London (1980), vol.XL, *The Grosvenor Estate in Mayfair, Part II, The Buildings*, London, Athlone Press, pp.217-8.

24 See Michael Young (1982), *The Elmhirsts of Dartington, The Creation of an Utopian Community*, London, Routledge & Kegan Paul.

25 In two of the main published accounts of the flat (*Studio*, May 1935 and *Architectural Review*, May 1935), one of the photographs of the living room, showing the windows, is 'flipped' or mirror-imaged, making it difficult to understand the organisation of the space.

26 'A Remodelled interior in Connaught Place', *Architectural Review*, December 1937, p.262.

27 It is possible that the painting could have been bought direct from Picasso's studio when Chermayeff was in Paris in June 1937 for the International Exhibition. He owned another related Picasso, seen in photographs of Bentley Wood, see Chapter 5, note 12.

28 ibid.

29 ibid., p.268.

30 Victoria Milne, 'Nothing Trivial', p.18.

31 Hugh Casson, 'Good and Bad Theatre Building', *Night and Day*, 9 September 1937, p.118.

32 Chermayeff's drawings are in the RIBA Drawings Collection (one drawing) and Avery Library.

33 W.A. Cordingley, 'Research Laboratories, Manchester', *RIBA Journal*, 7 March 1938, p.441.

34 *The New Research Laboratories of Imperial Chemical Industries Limited Dyestuffs Group, Blackley, Manchester*, 1938, p.5. Photocopy kindly supplied by ICI Archives in 1992.

35 See for example J.D. Bernal (1939), *The Social Function of Science*, London, G. Routledge.

36 The laboratories did not satisfy the clients in all respects. An internal report of November 1943, 'Research in the Dyestuffs Group', by J.D. Rose, criticises the lack of storage space and space for writing up reports and using calculating machines. Information courtesy of Dennis Wardleworth.

37 *RIBA Journal*, 1938, p.443.

38 *Architects' Journal*, 19 January 1939, p.143.

39 See *Description of the Exhibits which are to be housed in the new Research Laboratories of the Dyestuffs Group of Imperial Chemical Industries Ltd on the occasion of the opening ceremony January 11th*, printed by Curwen Press. Copy kindly loaned by Dennis Wardleworth.

40 *Daily Dispatch*, Manchester, 11 January 1938, photocopy kindly supplied by I.C.I. Archives.

41 Laboratorio Investigaciones 'YPF' en Florencio Varella, architects Jorge de la Maria Prins, Hugo M. Rosso, Jorge M. Verbrugghe and Jorge Ros Martin. Illustrated in *Revista de Arquitectura*, March 1943, pp.85-100.

## 'Beloved Bentley'

In the course of 1935 or 1936, Chermayeff found a site to build himself and his family a country house. He bought 84 acres of land from the Bentley Farm estate, surveyed the site with Michael Grice as already described, and made a design which was submitted for planning permission by November 1936. Sussex was a natural choice of location for the Chermayeffs, since it was near Edward Wadsworth's house at Maresfield and not far from Peggy Angus's Furlongs at Glynde, nestled beneath the South Downs which closed the view from Bentley. A large part of the site consisted of Bentley Wood itself, from which the house took its name, after originally being called New Bentley, The Knoll and Halland.

**Model of Bentley Wood, original design scheme.**

The initial scheme, known only from two published photographs of a lost model, was larger than the house as built. The south elevation of the main block of the house already had its open frame, but no open loggia on the upper floor. There was a substantial single-storey cross-wing at the west end, running back to form an entrance courtyard, and the drive reached the house behind a long garden wall extending the main frontage line of the house. Along the whole length of the house and garden wall was a terrace, raised above the surrounding park-like grassed landscape, and extended to curve around an existing tree at its farthest end, as seen in one of the two photographs of the model, but apparently removed from the version here.

It appears from the model that the house was designed from the first to be built of timber, both as structure and cladding. In part, this reflected the local vernacular but it was also a material increasingly considered appropriate for modern architecture. This tendency probably began in Germany, where Chermayeff's future colleague, Konrad Wachsmann, published *Holzhausbau* in 1930, showing the pitched roof house he had designed for Albert Einstein

**119**

near Potsdam, and his more modern-looking Earth Sciences Institute at Ratibor, with windows set flush into tongue and groove siding.[1] Timber was being strongly promoted for all kinds of building in England, so that in February 1936 the *Architectural Review* was devoted to the subject, showing £800 country houses by young architects from the competition organised by the Timber Development Association in the previous year. The second prize design, by William Tatton-Brown, a member of Tecton, is interesting in relation to the Bentley Wood design for its use of a projecting pergola on a raised terrace, although the resemblance ends there. Some of the competition designs were reprinted in the book, *The Romance of the Timber House*, 1936, with an introduction by Robert Furneaux Jordan, a young architect then teaching at the AA.

Timber houses by modern architects were probably completed too late for inclusion in these publications, included 'Avalon' (1935) at Churt, in Surrey, by Anthony Chitty, a former Tecton partner, which was not published at the time, although his timber gardener's cottage nearby appeared in the *Architect and Building News* in June 1935. The Wood House, Shipbourne, Kent, by Walter Gropius and Maxwell Fry, 1937, is a house Chermayeff might well have heard about while it was on the drawing board, given the close connections between his office and Gropius and Fry's during the construction of the houses in Old Church Street, Chelsea. The client was the lawyer Jack Donaldson and his wife Frances, whom Chermayeff remembered as a schoolgirl in 1925, attending the rehearsals of *The Last of Mrs Cheyney*, written by her father, Frederick Lonsdale. Neither of these examples can have affected the design of Bentley Wood directly, only in the general sense that 1935-6 was almost 'the year of the timber house', with a special emphasis on the suitability of this material for modernist use.

It is not surprising to find Chermayeff using timber. It forms part of a romantic turn in English modernism, already outlined in John Summerson's interpretation of Shrub's Wood, and discussed more fully at the end of this chapter. Concrete may even have seemed *vieux jeu* by this time, and supplies became increasingly difficult as it was diverted into defence construction. On a technical and practical level, Wachsmann and Jordan's texts both emphasised the suitability of timber for prefabricated construction, something that interested Chermayeff in common with most modernists, and which had been demonstrated in small house building in Germany and Sweden. The Jarrah-wood frame for Bentley Wood was prefabricated, at the Holland, Hannen and Cubitts workshops in Gray's Inn Road, where Chermayeff could depend on top quality workmanship and may even have had favourable financial terms. It is also likely that Felix Samuely, who carried out the engineering for Bentley Wood using some novel jointing techniques, would have had experience of recent German practice in timber.

Sometimes timber was an expedient to help a modern design pass the Planning Committees which had taken the limited powers of aesthetic control contained in the Town and Country

Planning Act of 1932, originally intended to prevent ribbon development, and increasingly applied them to exercise a prejudice against modern architecture. The Bentley Wood scheme was rejected by Uckfield Rural District Council at a meeting on 19 November 1936, when Chermayeff was present, on the grounds that the elevation and general design were in severe contrast to the usual type of development in the area and would seriously injure the amenities of the immediate locality. Chermayeff began appeal proceedings, which led to the Public Inquiry, held on 26 January 1937 under the Ministry of Health.[2] Chermayeff rallied his supporters and succeeded in getting a leader placed in the *Listener*, the BBC's magazine, for 10 March, recording the success of his appeal as an object lesson in misdirected local zeal.[3] Some aspects of his defence, comparing his own design to various historical precedents, including the flat roof of Crowborough District Council's Neo-Georgian offices, where the appeal was heard, appeared as a prelude to the *Architectural Review*'s account of the house in January 1939.

**Bentley Wood, the approach to the house.**

It is not clear exactly when and why the design of Bentley Wood was changed subsequent to the appeal. The revised working drawings are dated September 1937, when a resubmission was made for planning permission, after Serge and Barbara had rented a nearby cottage at Blackboys, from the painter Richard Wyndham for the summer. They spent a lot of time working on the garden at Bentley Wood, planting bulbs and thinning trees, also adding new planting. Growing familiarity with the site may have been an important motive and the position of the house may have been changed slightly in relation to the existing trees. The new scheme was probably cheaper, although the cost differences cannot have been as great as the changes in character, judging from the repositioning of the main elements that can be read from the model. The cross-wing, containing a garage and other outdoor offices, was transferred to the eastern end of the house, making a low entrance gateway spanning the drive, now entering from the opposite of the house. The sense of passing into an enclosed space was enhanced by the addition of a long low wall extending southwards to screen the garden terrace, and northwards to mask the garages. A single storey link separated the wall from the main body of the house. With these adjustments in place, the previous extent of the terrace was curtailed to act as a more precise base for the house, which appears thereby more clearly as an object in the landscape, enclosing a more compact set of spaces and more effectively framing the distant views. All these changes served to reduce resemblances to Mendelsohn, so that Chermayeff began to appear increasingly as his own man. The new formation of the terrace led to the idea of commissioning a sculpture, and a plinth was designed at the far end, where the brick-paved surface of the terrace enclosed a flight of six steps leading up from the lawn. Chermayeff showed this to Henry Moore, who felt it was a suitable challenge and began work in the summer of 1937 on his Recumbent Figure, carved directly in Hornton Stone. If, as suggested earlier, the Chermayeffs enjoyed nude sunbathing, the solid wall to the new terrace was a practical precaution, making an area protected against wind and onlookers, while the sculpture was, in its way, a sunbather in all weathers.

Another clue comes from an unexecuted design for a house for 'a single artist' at Dorney, Buckinghamshire, which Chermayeff published in October 1937 in the form of a photograph of a model with plans. This was to be a brick house, linked by a pergola to another existing house. The main elevation had a recessed upper balcony with the principal joists expressed as pergola timbers, which was its main resemblance to Bentley Wood. Its flat front also recalled houses in the Berlin suburbs by the Brothers Luckhardt which Chermayeff noted on his visit in 1931.[4] The pergola of the Dorney house extended at right angles from the house, resembling the executed design of Bentley Wood more than the first model.

Timber construction lends itself to modular repetition, and Bentley Wood is based on a unit of 2ft 9ins, which was found to be the most economical in terms of standard dimensions of materials. This was also the standard adopted by Ernö Goldfinger, one of the visitors to the house in the summer of 1938.[5] Each bay is four units, making 11ft, the whole frontage being 66ft long. The main body of the house is 33ft in depth, a double square slightly extended at the northwest corner. The main elevation towards the garden also forms three squares, each two bays wide, with the upper storey naturally slightly lower than the ground floor. When Frank Lloyd Wright visited in the summer of 1939, he complained that the bedrooms were seven inches too high, to which Chermayeff replied that he wanted to lower them by precisely that amount, but since this would have been a contravention of the bye laws, he chose to avoid further trouble with the Council.

Internally, the planning of Bentley Wood has formal characteristics recognisable from other Chermayeff designs, going back to the 1932 scheme for a house at Puttenham. Compared to this effort of only four years earlier, Bentley Wood has a much more sophisticated plan. The house is L shaped, although the projection on the north side, making an internal angle for the front door, is relatively shallow. The enclosure thus formed is roofed with a covered way linking across to the garage, making a long entry route to the far end of the house, away from the single storey service quarters which overlook the entrance like a kind of lodge joined onto the house. These were occupied by a married couple. The plan is divided longitudinally by a spine wall of cupboards, facing southwards into the living room and dining room, and doubled northwards into the kitchen, intended not only to act as storage but as an acoustic barrier. They also housed paintings and sculptures that could be opened to view or closed off as desired. There is a change of floor level along this line, stepping down three steps to the living room from the stairhall, a graceful transition although one that irritated Arnold Whittick, who explained it as a result of Chermayeff's desire to look down over the landscape from the raised dais of his study.[6] The ground floor windows, in their heavy wood frames, slid in noise-proof felt-lined tracks to make an interior more open to the outside than any other modern house. One section, opposite the door and the three steps, was made with fixed glazing in bronze and opening lights.

Project for house for an
artist at Dorney,
Buckinghamshire, 1937.

Opposite: Bentley Wood,
garden front.

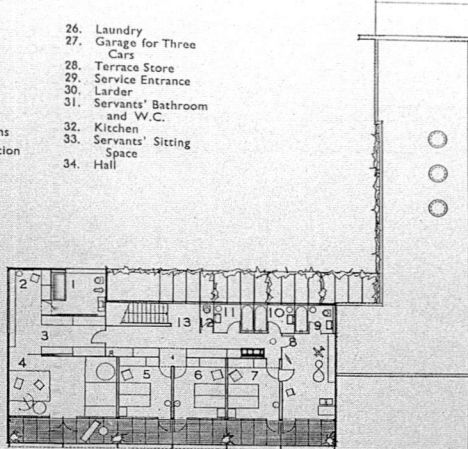

FIRST FLOOR PLAN

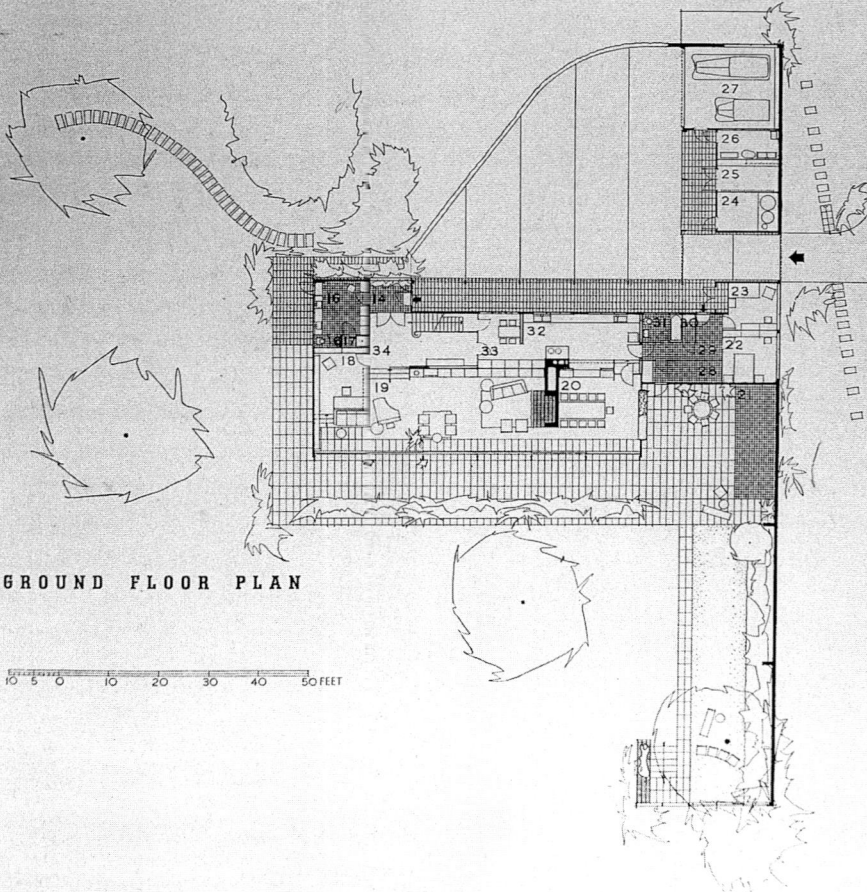

GROUND FLOOR PLAN

10 5 0   10   20   30   40   50 FEET

Bentley Wood, living area, 1939, with John Piper, Forms on Dark Blue, 1936 behind the piano designed by Chermayeff.

Right: Bentley Wood, living area, view towards fireplace, with painting by Jean Hélion.

Opposite: Bentley Wood, plan.

The main living accommodation ranges along the garden front, with the living room occupying over three structural bays, entered at the western end, with a fireplace in a brick spur wall separating it from the dining room beyond, which has a boxed-out window on the end wall overlooking the angle of the terrace with its pool of water. The fireplace makes a core of flues for the kitchen and for the boiler located in a small basement area below. On the model, the stack appearing on the roof lies along the direction of the house, indicating some significant change in the internal plan in relation to the fireplace. The range of three rooms linked along a wall of windows occured at 64 Old Church Street and was a fairly common modern planning device. Whittick and other commentators have noticed the resemblance to the interconnected living room and music room in Mendelsohn's house on the Rupenhorn, where the right-angled walls were used for the display of large paintings and reliefs. Chermayeff's version of this plan at Bentley Wood is different, however, because the windows come right down to the ground and slide open to make large openings. The connection with outdoors is emphasised by the way that the paving of the terrace is brought inside where it forms a junction with the polished wood floor. The study, in the end bay of the house, can be reached from the living room through a sliding partition, or through a door in the hall, allowing for privacy, while at the other end of the living room, behind the fireplace, there is a dining room with a characteristic Chermayeff dining table, end-on to the back of the chimneybreast. There is a generous-sized cloakroom off the outer hall, making a tiled 'wet area' also accessible from a glazed garden door.

Bentley Wood, study.

Right: Bentley Wood, cloakroom with poster of Dazzle Camouflage by Edward Wadsworth.

The staircase is Georgian in character, a straight flight with a timber handrail and balustrade similar to those in the Heywood-Lonsdale flat. Whitfield Lewis, who made the working drawings and carried the house through to completion, recalls that he succeeded in deflecting Chermayeff from his original idea of the staircase being 'something much more fruity', by persuading him that it would become out of date. The upper floor carries through the line of cupboards, dividing the bedrooms from the corridor, each occupying a single structural bay of 11ft. The master bedroom suite, with its own bathroom and dressing room, is at the western end of the house. Here, some feminine luxury becomes apparent, with a white fur rug and a Bruno Mathsson recliner with his typical woven canvas webbing. The low bed is the same simple tubular steel model as that shown in the Week End House of 1933. The cheval glass is held between floor and ceiling by metal supports welded off-centre to its own frame, and supporting a projecting circular mirror to one side. Two guest bedrooms are entered through an inset lobby with a veneered column of oval section on the centre line of the house. An identical twin bedroom serves as a night nursery for Ivan and Peter (born in May 1935), connected to the day nursery with its own bathroom at the eastern end.

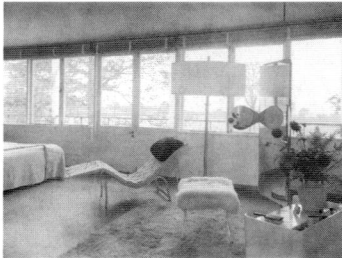

Left: Bentley Wood, bedroom.

Middle: Bentley Wood, dressing room.

Bentley Wood, upper balcony.

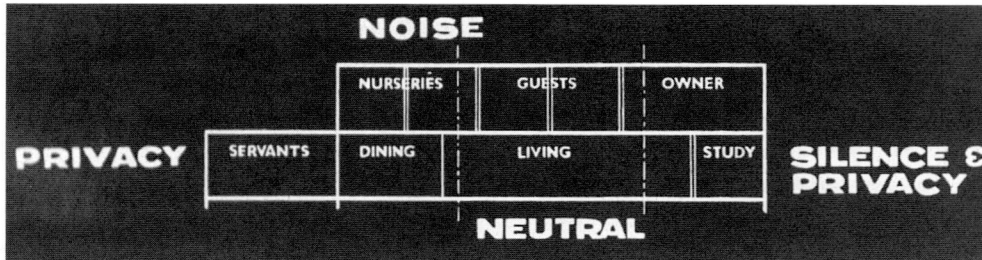

Diagram of zones of noise and privacy, drawn for Architectural Review, January 1939.

All these rooms have access onto the upper balcony. The acoustic dynamics of this plan were explained by Chermayeff in a diagram published in the *Architectural Review*, which emphasises his concern to organise space for protection from noise. Thus the study and owner's suite at one end of the house ('Silence and Privacy') is separated by a 'Neutral' zone of living room with guests over, from the 'Noise' zone of nurseries and dining, adjoining the privacy of the servants' accommodation. The water tanks next to the guest bedrooms were fitted with silent filling devices. It is not a very sophisticated schema and doubtless other architects thought in similar terms. What is interesting, though, is that Chermayeff thought it worth explaining, so that the appreciation of the house should not be purely visual.

The living room contained one of Chermayeff's white-legged pianos, and also an early version of a hi-fi system, with radio and gramophone wired to different parts of the house from equipment housed in the wall of cupboards, with a tambour front for the turntable, and drop-down fronts for the records. The drop-down front of the drinks cabinet, an important element of any Chermayeff home, was fitted with a white lino surface. Apart from the fireplace – which had a symbolic as much as a calorific role – heating was provided from electric wall panels upstairs and underfloor elements beneath the paving under the sliding windows below, so that everything was invisible. The house was serviced to an equivalent degree of sophistication in other respects, with circuit breakers instead of fuses in case of overload, and a 'dashboard' panel with switches, bell-pushes and electric sockets beside every bed.

Bentley Wood, wall of cupboards in living room, with paintings by Edward Wadsworth (left) and John Piper (right), sculpture by Barbara Hepworth (centre).

Right: Bentley Wood with Henry Moore's Recumbent Figure, 1938 in foreground.

The technical achievements of the house need to be placed in context with its cultural meaning. Of the modern houses of the later 1930s, Bentley Wood was the one that attracted the most universal attention and praise, remaining fresh in the minds of architects even in the 1950s, when most of the other pre-war modern houses seemed impossibly dated. In this respect, it counts as the most important work of Chermayeff's whole career. Since Bentley Wood was a frame for a number of art works representing Chermayeff's friendships and enthusiasms, these in turn help in interpreting its architectural form. Its setting was also a notable example of landscape design, involving the collaboration of Christopher Tunnard (1910–79), whose small body of work has attracted considerable attention. It offers an opportunity to look across the disciplinary boundaries at the unity of modernist culture in England. For this reason, I am treating it as the linking thread among a number of events and movements in the period 1937–9 which help to emphasise the importance of the house as a gathering point and to explain its enduring influence.

Of the works of art, Henry Moore's Recumbent Figure is the most nationally significant. Since 1939, it has been in the collection of the Tate Gallery, where it is frequently on display. During the 1930s, Moore's work frequently expressed the sense of anxiety and insecurity which most people felt during the decade. Moore developed the formal devices of constructivism, opening holes through his stone carvings, and introducing string threaded through holes, but used them to move closer to the rival alternative school of Surrealism in evoking sinister presence and various possibilities of harm. The Recumbent Figure was the first of his sculptures to revert to an almost classical sense of calm, after Moore had spent most of his career deliberately avoiding Mediterranean influence. The rounded female figure is indeed pierced with a large opening in the area of the stomach, but this emphasises its balance and serenity. The lower part of the figure is massive and maternally reassuring. As small children, Ivan and Peter Chermayeff used to climb over it and sit in its recesses. Much of the stone is cut away from the base, so that the figure has several points of transparency. Moore described it later as 'the first of the figures in stone to be substantially opened out'.[7]

Moore resisted architectural commissions in the earlier part of his career because he wanted to give his work independence in an architectural setting. Chermayeff already owned at least two other Moore works, one of which, Figure, 1933, in travertine marble, appears in photographs in the deep box frame of the dining room window at Bentley Wood. He offered Moore the kind of freedom he wanted from an architect, although it seems from his account that Chermayeff initially envisaged a vertical figure, more like Dobson's Persephone at Bexhill. 'He wanted me to say whether I could visualise one of my figures standing at the intersection of terrace and garden', Moore explained.

It was a long, low-lying building and there was an open view of the long sinuous line of the Downs. There seemed no point in opposing all these horizontals, and it was then that I became aware of the necessity of giving outdoor sculpture a far-seeing gaze. My figure looked out across the great sweep of the Downs, and her gaze gathered in the horizon. The sculpture had no specific relationship to the architecture. It had its own identity and did not need to be on Chermayeff's terrace but it, so to speak enjoyed being there, and I think introduced a humanising element; it became a mediator between modern house and ageless land.[8]

The Hornton stone, a rich yellow-brown limestone, had to be laminated in three layers, with dowel fixings, to make a block of sufficient size, which was carved by Moore and his assistant Bernard Meadows, and delivered in September 1938. Chermayeff commissioned the sculpture for £300, paying a deposit of £50. The balance was never paid, owing to Chermayeff's financial crisis in 1939, when Moore was keen to return the deposit so that the figure could be bought by the Contemporary Art Society. This charity collected subscriptions so that new works could be bought, which were usually passed on to public collections too impoverished or conservative to be able to buy them directly. Each year, a different expert chose what to buy, and during 1939 it was the turn of Sir Kenneth Clark, Director of the National Gallery and a powerful establishment figure who had recently become one of Moore's greatest supporters. He initially suggested it to the Museum of Modern Art in New York but through the CAS purchase it passed to the Tate Gallery in London instead, still at the cost of £300. This was a significant moment since the new Director, John Rothenstein, had only in 1938 succeeded an implacable hater of Moore's work and all modern art. Chermayeff's default was therefore turned by Moore to his own advantage, and the Recumbent Figure was shown in the British Pavilion at the New York World's Fair in 1939. It was stranded in New York until 1945, shown meantime in the courtyard at MOMA where it suffered some damage from weather and vandalism.[9]

**Bentley Wood, terrace with Barbara Chermayeff in reclining chair.**

At Bentley Wood, the wooden frame against which the Figure was seen from certain angles helped to ease its transition between the realms of culture and nature, providing a geometric background similar to the frames which appear in the visionary paintings of Paul Nash. The lower panels of the frame were glazed to block the wind, the upper ones being unglazed, offering a variety of metaphorical interpretations. Moore's suggestion of a humanising presence is very apt. One of the most often reproduced views of the terrace shows Barbara Chermayeff reading in the foreground in a tubular-framed wicker chair, while Moore's Figure reclines at the other end of the terrace in a companionable manner.

The hint of classicism in the figure seems to correspond to the mood of Chermayeff's architecture, at Bentley as at Gilbey's, while its cutting away and opening up of solid mass has a closer analogy to the way that the structural frame at Bentley Wood is brought into play as a major architectural element. We are so used to seeing Henry Moore's reclining figures on plinths in open air settings, that the photographs of the sculpture at Bentley have lost the impact that this, the first such occurrence, would then have had. Familiarity framed structures in the architecture of the 1950s has in a similar way distracted our attention from the box-like character of most modern buildings before this time. There was little apparent interest in modernism's ancestry in the doctrine of structural rationalism, as transmitted through Viollet-le-Duc. Indeed, there is no evidence that Chermayeff knew it from a historical point of view, although his description of modern as 'Gothic' in 'A Hundred Years Ahead' seems to suggest something of the kind. Most modern buildings of the 1930s concealed their construction, often by hiding brick beneath a coat of render as in 64 Old Church Street, but at Bentley Wood the aesthetic use of the frame was indivisible from its structural requirements. The exposed elements of the Australian Jarrah wood are the major support members, painted white to distinguish them, while the timber cladding is of Western Red Cedar, weathering to grey and providing a tonal contrast and a rougher surface. The first-floor balcony enables the joists to be 'read' as a secondary grid, and the whole structure casts attractive shadows inside. The nearest analogue to this elevation is the south-facing solarium of the Heliotherapeutic Institute at Legnano, Italy, by BBPR, 1938 which has a similar two-storey grid with solid end walls.

After the Moore, the other major work of art, hanging over the piano at Bentley Wood, was John Piper's Forms on Dark Blue, 1936, a canvas slightly over 5ft x 6ft, exhibited in the same year in the important 'Abstract and Concrete' group show at the Lefevre Gallery.[10] Piper's abstract period lasted only two or three years but it was an important stage in his development, during which he came to know some of the community of modern architects. Another small abstract by Piper can be seen in photographs in one of the cupboard display areas in the living room, where there were also displayed Edward Wadsworth's Three Forms, 1932–33, Barbara Hepworth's Nesting Forms, 1937 (white marble), probably a loan from the artist, and a small 'stabile' by Alexander Calder.[11] The colour schemes of Piper's abstract paintings, with small touches of red against sombre backgrounds, relate to some of Chermayeff's experiments with interior colour. The purpose-made settee by the fire at Bentley Wood, a sort of high-backed Chesterfield, was upholstered in dark blue, the same colour as the linoleum top of the dining table, around which were grouped honey-coloured Thonet chairs. A small Picasso head of a sleeping woman hung upstairs, a detail closely related to the larger painting which Chermayeff bought for the Heywood-Lonsdales.[12]

It is interesting to compare Chermayeff's use of the term 'Gothic' for modern with Piper's inspiration from mediaeval stained glass which he copied in watercolour early in his career, an influence he traced in his abstract work as much as in any of his other modes. Both men shared an admiration for the work of Moholy-Nagy, which they discussed in a short television programme on 27 January 1937, called 'Art in Modern Architecture'. Piper introduced a reference to a construction by Moholy-Nagy with cut-away celluloid, to which Chermayeff responded by saying 'this picture appears to be letting light into a painting in the same way that a modern architect lets light into his building'.[13]

The television programme was broadcast a few weeks after a discussion at the RIBA, led by Chermayeff, with a loan of works by Piper and Nicholson, probably from his own collection. The other participants were Naum Gabo and Moholy-Nagy, with a written contribution sent by Piper's ex-wife, Eileen Holding. In his introduction, Chermayeff stressed the relationship between modern architecture and the deeper aims of abstraction, saying that 'Artist and architect were each in their own spheres framing the general contemporary aesthetic. Their relationship and spiritual alliance must be a working alliance if they were to enjoy to the full the creative alliance to which they were entitled.'[14] Moholy's contribution emphasised the spiritual attributes of space that were much discussed by this group of artists. One of the aspects that can be related to Bentley Wood was the idea of transparency and shifting parallax produced by movement. He stated that a fully-developed feeling of space was as important as the more normal functions of a house. When this is achieved, he believed, 'architecture will be understood, not as a complex of inner spaces, not merely as a shelter from the cold and from danger, nor as a fixed enclosure as an unalterable arrangement of room, but as a governable creation for mastery of life, as an organic component of living'.[15]

The third artist represented at Bentley Wood was Ben Nicholson, one of whose rectilinear abstract paintings hung initially over the fireplace. Chermayeff also owned one of his white reliefs of 1937 and other minor works.[16] Nicholson's paintings had a strong appeal for many modern architects, and the artist himself had been active since the beginning of the decade in stimulating the architects he knew to liberate themselves from conventional constraints. In 1937, Nicholson was co-editor of the book *Circle, an international survey of constructive art*, together with the sculptor Naum Gabo and the young architect Leslie Martin (1908-2000). The book aimed to show the unity of architecture, science and the arts through the means of abstraction and included examples of Chermayeff's work.

At the end of the 1930s, Nicholson took a special interest in a younger generation of architectural students, based at the AA school, among whose leaders were the founders and editors of Focus magazine, Anthony Cox (1915–93), Leo de Syllas (1917–64) and Tim Bennett (1918–42). The magazine only reached four issues before the war but was an articulate defence of the purity of modern architecture and abstract art at a time when it was winning acceptance but threatened by over-richness of expression. This concern was expressed most strongly in Cox's review of Lubetkin's Highpoint II, 1938, in *Focus* 2, and again in a severe criticism of 'formalism' in the MARS Group exhibition at the beginning of 1938 in the *AA Journal*. Bobby Carter and Leslie Martin also encouraged these left-wing ex-public school boys in various ways at the time and in the years ahead. They seemed, more than earlier generations, to have grasped the totality of what the modern movement meant, holding in delicate balance its social, technical and aesthetic demands with a fiery conviction. While fully international in their sympathies, they also perpetuated the morality of the English Arts and Crafts movement, evident in their mistrust of 'formalism' and their desire to make the production process evident in buildings.

Chermayeff found their concerns reflected his own, and this may have contributed to his desire to become a teacher. He lectured in November 1938 to the Edinburgh Architectural Students' Association and in March 1939, was invited to address the congress of the Northern Architectural Students Association, held at the Hull School of Architecture where Leslie Martin was professor, as part of a symposium on 'The architect's place and purpose in modern society', together with Bobby Carter, Maxwell Fry and Herbert Read. 'The new architect, I would consider, is not so much an artist as a craftsman who is operating in an ever-broadening complex of design generally', Chermayeff explained.[17] Martin later wrote that he regarded Chermayeff's lecture as 'a turning point in student thought; it was largely as a result of this stimulating address that a policy was introduced into the organisation which may have far-reaching beneficial effects on architectural education in this country'.[18] J. D.

Bernal was one of the other speakers, calling for systematic research into 'human social needs in a scientific way'.[19]

The students of the AA who had emerged victorious from an ideological battle against conservatism which, coinciding with the Munich Crisis in the summer and autumn of 1938, discovered a new political signifiance in architectural education. Chermayeff was the first speaker at an AA General Meeting on 23 May 1939, on 'The Architectural Student - Training for what?' Confessing that he had no architectural education himself, he proceeded to question the term 'architecture', proposing in its place 'some other general term such as "design" which would cover town-planning, construction . . . industrial design, the study of materials and so on'.[20] In a later passage, he may have been the first person to use the word 'ecology' in a school of architecture in England when he listed this as one of necessary additional studies for a design school forming part of a contiuum:

> Then there would be landscape gardening as an indissoluble part of the architectural elements with which one builds, and then the study of art forms and forms generally, texture, colour, the study of contemporary development in a strict historical sequence, sculpture, painting, typography and layout, photography and films.[21]

Acknowledging Gropius as a pioneer in this kind of general education, Chermayeff seemed to give back to the Bauhaus educational project a new kind of urgency, or at least an English dimension, with his suggestion that 'a Henry Moore or a Ben Nicholson could give infinitely more to the potential architect in terms of their specialised knowledge than perhaps an architect could give'.[22] In this speech are already contained the seeds of Chermayeff's teaching programmes in the USA.

It was these AA students, with Bobby Carter in attendance, who drove Frank Lloyd Wright down to see Bentley Wood during his first ever visit to England that spring. As well as his remark about the height of the upper rooms, he said, 'It'll take a little time for God to make it click', a typical example of the patronising comments he seemed able to draw from an inexhaustible supply. However, he appeared generally to approve and drank tea on the terrace, in a Lock's hat lent by Chermayeff which was too small for him.[23] Another student visitor was a German émigré student at the AA, Gerhard Kallmann, who remembers Chermayeff as 'very Russian, very hospitable, very much in the grand manner, the grand seigneur. He liked having students at Halland, so whenever we could, we would pile into the little MGs and off we went to the heavenly landscape'.[24] Chermayeff summoned Kallmann to teach under him at the Chicago Institute of Design in 1947.

Chermayeff mentioned landscape gardening as one of the elements he expected to teach. Landscape Gardening, or Landscape Architecture, as its practitioners preferred to call it, was a

Frank Lloyd Wright at Bentley Wood, May 1939, photo Serge Chermayeff.

relatively new profession and Bentley Wood fitted into its landscape, with the graciousness of a Georgian villa, enjoying a lively but relaxed relationship with nature. As John Summerson famously wrote in 1959, Bentley Wood 'whose beautifully sited hollow rectangles suppressed every vanity of "style" and merely touched the environment into conscience of form', was 'the most aristocratic English building of the decade'.[25]

**Bentley Wood, seen from the newly-cleared woodland, Spring 1939.**

Much of this achievement must be attributable to Chermayeff's configuration of the house and placing it on the site but the detail of the landscaping was partly achieved with the specialised professional help of Christopher Tunnard, who had worked on a landscape in relation to a new house by Raymond McGrath at St Ann's Hill, Chertsey, Surrey in 1935–6, where he lived with his rich benefactor, Gerald Schlesinger. He was a contributor of lively articles to the *Architectural Review* which gave the magazine its first substantial coverage of historical landscape issues. He therefore already belonged in Chermayeff's milieu and was a natural choice as a landscape designer. Tunnard wrote that 'Chermayeff had thought out some of the development himself before we discussed plans together. He fixed the position of the drive and started clearing the corner of the wood nearest the projected site of the house, leaving pleasant groups of trees in open glades.'[26] Tunnard discussed further work with him, probably in the spring of 1937 following the pubic inquiry decision, advising on more tree clearance and development of a dell garden where surface water and house overflows terminated in the wood. 'This gave us a frame. Inside it the house would rise beautiful and well anchored by its terrace, screen walls and careful siting in a green sea of grass and yellow daffodils. But it needed the extra stability that new planting alone could bring.'[27] New tree planting is recorded on a site plan published in the *Architectural Review*. Tunnard seems to have suggested two different ways of approaching the question of a garden as such, either a geometric structure or a knowing cultivation of 'irregular, atmospheric planting based on a scheme as carefully drawn as the other'. He continued:

Chermayeff who is a man of intellect, chose the method predominantly emotional in its appeal; but with the eye of his profession, he declared in favour of an atmospheric planting showing an architectural character; a free yet controlled scheme, related but in contrast to the formality of the building. It was a subjective and essentially picturesque scheme which we eventually made.[28]

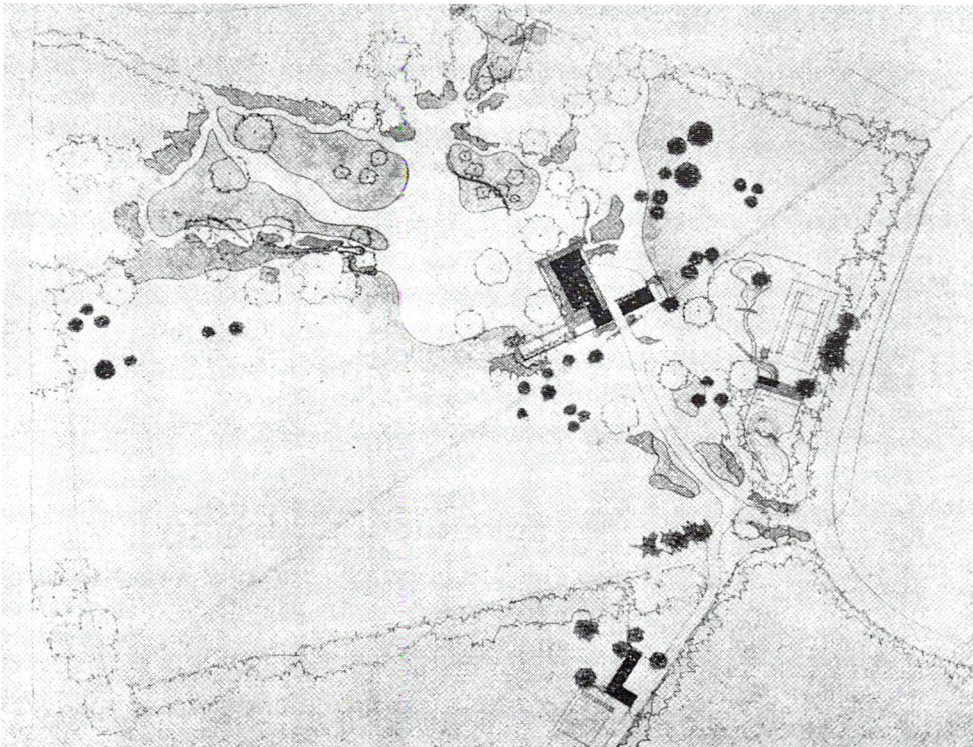

Bentley Wood, site plan showing newly-planted trees (dark) and replanted areas (grey), with views opened up through woodland. This plan also shows the intended gardener's cottage on the drive and tennis court in an old quarry.

Tunnard and Chermayeff added new trees to define the edge of the wood, and chose plants for a long border along the wall, backing the terrace extending out to the glazed screen and the Recumbent Figure, with a mixture of delicate plants for the sheltered position, and 'bedding plants - in the summer the scent of nicotiniana is carried into the house through the open windows'.[29] The result was a more relaxed conception of 'modern gardening' than earlier efforts that tended to go for excessive geometry or an absence of form, although the modest landscaping of Shrub's Wood already suggested a way in which house and planting could work together. Tunnard summed up this reciprocal relationship when he wrote:

> To me, the architect's point of view has been of the greatest value, particularly that of an architect who believes that planting is a part of architecture. In this problem, planting was architecture, and the oak tree on the terrace had as great an importance in the whole design as any timber support within.[30]

Serge Chermayeff
entertaining at Bentley
Wood, 1939.

Chermayeff later felt that Tunnard's contribution was in danger of being overstated. The collaboration came between spells in which Chermayeff was making his own decisions about planting. He wrote to the landscape architect, Sir Geoffrey Jellicoe (1900–96), after the latter had made a flattering reference to Bentley Wood in a lecture in 1957, to state that, 'The site plan, the architectural design, in its entirety had been completed by myself; and Christopher Tunnard, whose services at the time cannot be underestimated, contributed plant material and advice on plant arrangement exclusively to form my own specific landscape plans.'[31] Even if this is only one side of the story, it does not conflict with Tunnard's account.

The thinning out of existing trees, while far from being the whole extent of landscape work, offers an interesting analogy to the opening out of Moore's sculpture, the exposure of the structural frame, and the implication in Moholy's statement at the RIBA that the life of a work of art resides in the negative spaces and the eye that moves around them. While Bentley Wood is far from dematerialised, it seems to have grasped the paradox of a figure-ground reversal in which the negative void or ground can, in certain conditions, be perceived as the positive figure in the subtly balanced equation.

The critical literature on Bentley Wood is extensive. Charles Reilly, who lived not far away at Brighton, brought Clough Williams-Ellis over to visit, and described the house soon after occupation in his column, 'Professor Reilly speaking' in the *Architects' Journal* as 'Chermayeff's lovely crystal, white and golden thing', and 'a regular Rolls-Royce of a house'.[32]

Ivan Chermayeff shows Bentley Wood to the architectural assistants, John Eastland Fortey (left) and Birkin Haward (right), Spring 1938.

The house was finished too late to be included in the MARS Group exhibition in January 1938 but it fitted the new look of modernism that emerged from this presentation, being less concerned with the aesthetic effect of white architecture, and more closely involved with social issues.[33] Bentley Wood was, however, one of the favourite buildings elected by a group of distinguished non-architects who were polled by the *Architects' Journal* early in 1939. Including the votes cast for the De La Warr Pavilion, Chermayeff emerged in popularity third only to Berthold Lubetkin and Charles Holden.[34] The canonic role of the house was further reinforced in J.M. Richards's book, *An Introduction to Modern Architecture*, published by Penguin in 1940 and the first popular book on the subject. Richards forecast an increase in national characteristics of modern architecture, suggesting that the result should be called 'regionalism'. Of all the examples illustrated, Bentley Wood represented this trend most clearly.

Other articles gave a strictly factual presentation but the most discursive, by Christopher Hussey in *Country Life*, appeared on 26 October 1940 when Chermayeff had already sold Bentley Wood to Dorothy Elmhirst's son, Whitney Straight, and moved with his family to America. Hussey had greeted the Waring and Gillow exhibition in 1929 with lavish praise but remained ambivalent about the enduring value of modern architecture at the end of the decade. As a natural conservative, he emphasised in Bentley Wood a reconciliation with the past, and a relationship to place, unlike 'architecture designed purely to illustrate an intellectual thesis and without relation to its setting or national tradition'.[35] As the first historian of the picturesque, Hussey appreciated the success of the landscape design, noting the colour relations between the 'warm mauvish-grey' of the Western Red Cedar and the buff-coloured brick, merged with the purple-leaved berberis in the terrace, while the white verticals of the frame corresponded to the silver birches on the edge of the wood.

Englishness and its relationship to modernism was one of the recurrent topics of *Axis* magazine between 1935 and 1938, in which John and Myfanwy Piper, together with regular contributors such as Geoffrey Grigson, struggled to reconcile these apparent opposites, redefining much about Englishness in the process and returning, as they hoped, to a more vigorous native tradition that had been overlaid by sentimentality in the Victorian and Edwardian periods. Bentley Wood seems like the architectural equivalent of this argument, warming the covert classicism of the modern movement to a point of romantic tenderness without allowing it to become expressionistic or formless. Appearing as a 'token modernist' in a three-man symposium on 'Whither the English House?' in 1937, Chermayeff repudiated the clichéd notion of the modern house expressing 'patterns of speed, efficiency or science', while agreeing that it should incorporate whatever technology was appropriate and available.[36]

Another Penguin book, *The Scientific Attitude*, by the scientist C. H. Waddington welcomed the idea of 'a romantic view of life' as compatible with 'a scientific society', suggesting that 'The substitution of a romantic ideal for our recent pallid and inhibited one would, I think, in itself simply release enormous potentialities of action which have been suppressed. It would be incompatible with the myriad vested interests, large and small, which sit on our heads like tin-pot or cast-iron lids. They would go flying.'[37] It was probably not coincidental that Waddington's wife, the architect Justin Blanco-White, built another modern timber house, Shawms, Cambridge, in 1938, and was a friend of the Pipers. The way in which the works of art hung in the living room at Bentley Wood convinced Hussey that 'works of this type' were 'decoratively related to something I could grasp! They look right here'.[38] The sense of rapprochement illuminates his conclusion, 'Where so much is unfamiliar and new, it is something of an effort taking it all in, but a most educative experience. It is also packed with ideas and works out so many experiments that I venture to think that it will continue for some time to be a source of stimulus to those wishing to live abreast of the times.'[39]

We are now familiar with the idea of an architect's own house as a programmatic statement but there were relatively few examples in the 1930s, compared to the great richness of architects' own houses built after the war. Bentley Wood is most directly comparable to Ernö Goldfinger's 2 Willow Road in Hampstead, completed in 1939, where works of art and the architect's own furniture designs from previous years came together in a more personal statement of modernism than would have been possible for an ordinary client. Lubetkin's bungalow at Whipsnade, Hillfield, 1936, was an expression of its architect's lifestyle (with an outdoor fireplace for barbecues), and Patrick Gwynne's The Homewood, Esher, 1938, built for his parents, became the house where he lived in later years. Bentley Wood, as a statement of house, landscape and contents, was more complete than any of these, however, and its reasonableness and lack of quirky individualism may have commended it specially to contemporaries.

**Bentley Wood, living area at night.**

Chermayeff, like Grigson and the Pipers, was able to see the distant past as being closer to the present than the recent past, so that in going forwards there might also be an element of going backwards. This, at least, seems to be the meaning in his television talk, 'Rebuilding England' of 8 April 1937, in which he showed excerpts from the film, The Face of England by Paul Rotha. Having made the case for modern architecture's contribution to the environment as a whole, he states that 'The most commonplace and cheapest modern building may have infinitely greater beauty than the oldest and the rarest, and some ancient cottage perfectly conceived may be infinitely superior to the latest, largest and most expensive modern structure.'[40] The paradox of this view of progress, in terms of conventional linear time, was made more manifest in the closing words of the film, in which Chermayeff said that 'the modern architect is no vandal but the lover of all that is best in all periods, who is anxious in rebuilding to preserve beauty and to recapture for us today and for the future some of the preindustrial orderliness and quality which we are rapidly losing.'[41]

At the end of the 1930s, there was a concern shared by conservatives, such as Hussey and Kenneth Clark, as much as by left-wing thinkers, as to whether modernism could become popular and widespread without losing its integrity. After ten years of small-scale experiment, the credibility of the 'project' of modernism depended on this. Bentley Wood seemed, on many levels, to offer the desired resolution. It satisfied Tim Bennett's demand for 'a time when architecture will again be fine building, just as old manors and churches were "fine" cottages and barns'.[42] At the time when Hussey was writing, shortly after the evacuation from Dunkirk, the value of English culture was one of the motives which inspired the seemingly hopeless resistance to Hitler, and it may not be too far-fetched to suggest that what Bentley Wood stood for was precisely a modern form of Englishness, a fusion that reactionaries and revolutionaries alike had failed to predict.[43]

Notes
1 Reprinted as Building the Wooden House, Technique and Design, with new contributions by Christa and Michael Grüning and Christian Sumi, translation by Peter Reuss, Basel, Boston, Berlin, Birkhauser Verlag, 1995.
2 For a detailed discussion of the Inquiry, see Barbara Tilson, 'The Battle of Bentley Wood', Thirties Society Journal, No.5, 1985, pp.24-31.
3 'What kind of house?' Listener, 10 March 1937, pp.444-5.
4 Serge Chermayeff, 'Film shots in Germany', 1931, p.132. This illustrates houses by the Luckhardts with Alfons Anker in Schorlemerallee, Dahlem. A closer comparison are the houses by the same architects in 55 Heerstrasse and 24 Am Rupenhorn, Charlottenburg, 1928, both with a blank panel of wall at one end of the elevation and bands of windows extending to the other corner. Since these houses were close to Mendelsohn's own house, it is very likely that Chermayeff saw them.
5 Goldfinger's visit is recorded in snapshots in the collection at his home, 2 Willow Road, London NW3, now owned by the National Trust. His modular system is described in James Dunnett and Gavin Stamp, eds.(1984), Ernö Goldfinger, London, Architectural Association.

6 Arnold Whittick (1974), *European Architecture in the 20th Century*, Aylesbury, Leonard Hill Books, p.368.

7 Philip James, ed. (1966), *Henry Moore on Sculpture*, London, Macdonald. In The Nude, 1956 (London, John Murray), Kenneth Clark described the sculpture as having 'the feeling of the menhir and the memory of rocks worn through by the sea'. (p.356).

8 ibid., p.99.

9 Details of this story are taken from Roger Berthoud (1987), *The Life of Henry Moore*, London, Faber & Faber, pp.155-66. During the same period, Berthold Lubetkin 'half-commissioned' an elm wood sculpture for his Highpoint II penthouse, although he relinquished his claim to it on finding that its intended location, eight feet above floor level, was not appropriate for the work. A bronze cast of the maquette for Recumbent Figure is in a private collection, illustrated in James Peto and Donna Loveday, eds. (1999), Modern Britain 1929-1939, London, Design Museum, p.36.

10 Reproduced in colour at Plate 1 in Anthony West (1979), *John Piper*, London, Secker & Warburg, and as a catalogue cover for Piper's exhibition at Marlborough New London Gallery, 1964. See also Tate Gallery, *John Piper* (1984), catalogue entry 23, p.86. This records Chermayeff's ownership of the painting and states that it was destroyed by fire. The painting was damaged rather than destroyed when Chermayeff's possessions, which were stored at Powell's Depositories, Gate Wharf Road, Paddington, were bombed during the war. He made his own repairs to it, and it hung in his various houses in the USA, latterly in his home at Wellfleet, Cape Cod. The painting is seen in a photograph of a specially arranged room at Bowman's furniture shop, Camden Town, in *RIBA Journal*, 9 January 1937, p.215. If it was already owned by Chermayeff at this time, he may have been happy to lend it for exhibition prior to the completion of Bentley Wood. Edward Wadsworth's Three Forms, c.1932, was completely destroyed in the fire at Powell's Depositories. See P. & D. Colnaghi & Co. Ltd. (1974), *Edward Wadsworth 1889-1949, Paintings Drawings and Prints*, London, catalogue no.62 Study for Three Forms). Between the *Architectural Review* photo shoot in 1938 and the *Country Life* shoot in 1939, there were a number of changes in the works of art, probably as a result of sales made by Chermayeff. Some spaces may have been filled with loans, as with a large painting by Jean Hélion hung over the fireplace. The work is illustrated in *Axis* 1, January 1935, p.20 as 'Peinture 1934'. Hélion encouraged Myfanwy Piper to start *Axis* as an English equivalent to his own magazine, *Abstraction-Création*.

11 I am grateful to Dr Sophie Bowness for confirming the identification of the Hepworth piece.

12 This was probably a copy made by John Piper from an original in a private collection in Belgium, which was shown to Picasso who apparently signed it. Piper gave it to Chermayeff, but it was destroyed in the Blitz. See Victoria Milne, 'Nothing Trivial', 1994-6, based on interviews with Chermayeff, p.31.

13 Typescript in Avery Library.

14 Chermayeff at Informal General Meeting of RIBA, 'Modern Art and Architecture', 9 December 1936, *RIBA Journal*, 9 January 1937, p.209.

15 Moholy-Nagy, ibid., p.213.

16 The white relief was one of three versions of the same composition. It is described as 'Décor for 7th Symphony Ballet (4th movement)', 1939, in Herbert Read intr. (1948) *Ben Nicholson*, London, Lund Humphries, plate 62, and in Nobert Lynton (1999), *Ben Nicholson*, London, Phaidon, p.145. Nicholson made several designs for a proposed ballet of Beethoven's Seventh Symphony, commissioned by Leonide Massine for the Ballets Russes de Colonel De Basil, but never carried out on stage. The first version belonged to the architects Leslie and Sadie Martin (now in the Norton Simon Museum, Pasadena), and a 'project' version to Barbara Hepworth's sister, Elizabeth and her husband, the architectural writer, John Summerson (now in the Tate Gallery, London). The Chermayeff white relief hung in the study at Bentley Wood and is seen in photographs of Chermayeff's house in New Haven in the 1960s, together with a small abstract painting of the 1930s. Chermayeff sold it through the Marlborough Galleries in 1974. The larger painting appears to have been destroyed by bombing and is not recorded in any publications on Nicholson's work. A small silkscreen print by Nicholson remained in Chermayeff's collection in Cape Cod at the end of his life.

17 Unidentified newspaper cutting, Avery Library.

18 Testimonial for Chermayeff from Dr. J.L. Martin, 13 July 1939, included in Chermayeff's letters of commendation, Avery Library, SC Box 5 (40-4c).

19 ibid.

20 'The Architectural Student – Training for What?: A discussion opened by Serge Chermayeff FRIBA.', *Architectural Association Journal*, June 1939, p.6.

21 ibid.

22 ibid.

23 Photographs of Wright at Bentley Wood in Avery Library and Chermayeff family collection. Information about the visit and Wright's utterance from Susan Cox (née Babington-Smith), one of the group.

24 Author interview with Gerhard Kallmann, September 1997.

25 John Summerson, 'Introduction', in Trevor Dannatt (1959), *Modern Architecture in Britain*, London, B.T. Batsford, p.17.

26 Christopher Tunnard, 'Planning a Modern Garden, an experience in collaboration', *Landscape and Garden*, Summer 1939, p.24.

27 ibid. p.25.

28 ibid., pp.25-6.

29 ibid., p.26.

30 ibid., p.26.

31 Chermayeff to Jellicoe, 17 April 1957, Avery Library. Jellicoe wrote in 'Building in the Landscape', *RIBA Journal*, April 1957, p.210, 'The clarity of thought takes one back immediately to Greece, the source of all intellectual art of Western civilisation'.

32 'Professor Reilly Speaking', *Architects' Journal* , 28 September 1938, p.479.

33 Percy Horton remembered Chermayeff introducing him to Le Corbusier at the opening of the MARS Group exhibition in January 1938: 'Chermayeff's dynamism seemed to overwhelm the little man.' Percy Horton to Walter Strachan in *The Living Curve*, 1984, p.190.

34 Votes for Bentley Wood came from 'William Hickey' (*Daily Express* columnist), Henry Moore, Henry Morris (Education Officer, Cambridgeshire), Dr Vevers (Superintendent to Zoological Society, London) and Richard Wyndham (painter and socialite). These five votes placed Bentley Wood joint sixth in ranking order of all buildings polled. *Architects' Journal*, 25 May 1939, pp.851-62.

35 'A Modern Country House, Bentley, near Halland, Sussex, Part I', *Country Life*, 26 October 1940, p.370.

36 'Whither the English House? A discussion', *Design and Construction*, August 1937, p.372.

37 C.H. Waddington (1941), *The Scientific Attitude*, Harmondsworth, Penguin Books, p.123.

38 Christopher Hussey, 'A Modern Country House, Bentley, near Halland, Sussex, Part II', *Country Life*, 2 November 1940, p.393.

39 ibid.

40 Serge Chermayeff, 'Rebuilding England', MS, p.5, Avery Library.

41 ibid., pp.5-6.

42 Tim Bennett, 'The Contribution of the Thirties', (review of Alfred Roth, *The New Architecture*), *Architectural Review*, July 1940, p.30.

43 After the war, Bentley Wood was bought by the owner of the *News of the World*, Sir William Emsley Carr, who made additions to the house, including a billiard room in a single-storey structure linked to the west end of the house. Two central bays of the upper balcony were in-filled to extend the guest bedrooms, and an upper storey was added over the servants' flat at the east end of the house. Chermayeff revisited in 1959 and declared the changes 'a disaster' (see Milne, 1996, p.18). Of the garden, he wrote to Robert Harling, the editor of *House and Garden*, 'For my part I find that what remained of the Capability Brown concept was very difficult to extract from the Sutton Seed Catalog type of gardening which has been imposed over it.' (Chermayeff to Harling, 30 September, 1959. Avery Library.) A subsequent owner made further changes, which are illustrated in Lance Knobel, 'The Tragedy of Bentley Wood', *Architectural Review*, November 1979, pp.310-11. As a result of this article, the owner refused all subsequent requests to visit the house. Bentley Wood was sold in 1999, and the new owners have begun to remove some of the added features.

# California, New York and Chicago 1940–51

A letter from C.H. Reilly, dated April 1939, survives among Chermayeff's papers. It is an open letter to accompany job applications, for Chermayeff's theoretical enthusiasm for the employment of the best architects in salaried positions with national or local government was suddenly changed into a financial necessity. The collapse of the ICI project in Huddersfield, combined with the costs and delays of Bentley Wood, seem to have been contributory causes to Chermayeff virtually closing his practice and being declared bankrupt in June 1939.[1] For a man of his pride, it must have been a traumatic event, although most of his colleagues in modern architecture, notably Raymond McGrath, Wells Coates and even the apparently successful Oliver Hill, had been required to live close to the financial edge and were in similar straits, due to banks calling in loans. The likelihood of war from the autumn of 1938 onwards led to many cancelled projects, and Chermayeff's office had always been run with an ideal of perfection rather than a discipline of cost control, so that it is likely that overheads consumed much of the fee income from his projects. One of his recourses was to write formally to Lord De La Warr, then in the Ministry of Education, in December 1938, proposing to undertake a research programme on school building, in order to 'eliminate the possibility of hasty repetitive building on an obsolete pattern' when the 'present state of emergency' was over.[2]

Chermayeff asked  Maxwell Fry and Patrick Gwynne, a former assistant of Wells Coates, if they would go into partnership with him but the offers were declined.[3] In March 1939, he arranged to take space in Wells Coates's office, and they entered a competition together for School and Holiday Camps, organised by the Building Centre and announced on 16 March. Their entry was awarded a joint third premium of £25 but the bankruptcy led to his enforced departure, and a considerable strain on their old friendship.[4] Chermayeff failed to obtain any salaried employment before the outbreak of war, which is perhaps not surprising given that he would not have taken easily to a subordinate's role, despite Reilly's assurance that 'he would be a charming colleague with whom to work'.[5] However, he had some speaking engagements in Hull and at the AA, as described in the last chapter.

Early in 1939, Frederick Muller Ltd. published Chermayeff's small booklet, *Plan for Air Raid Precaution: A Practical Policy*, with an introduction by J.B.S. Haldane. As Felix Samuely summarised it, 'he lays great stress on the fact that all ARP services throughout the country should be coordinated, and that the most important issue at present is that there should be a joint programme embracing all protective measures, to which everybody would have to work (whether or not the individual agrees with that particular programme.)'[6] ARP was one of the long standing campaigns of the ATO, in which Lubetkin and the engineer Ove Arup were also involved. They believed that the government measures were inadequate for the aerial bombardment that was predicted.

If Chermayeff was trailing his coat in a search for employment, he was unsuccessful. The sale of Bentley Wood to Whitney Straight was arranged and some of the contents put into store, while an auction was held among friends for the remainder of the items.[7] The *Builder* magazine carried the following notice in its issue of 14 July 1939: 'Mr Serge Chermayeff FRIBA is shortly to leave for the United States where, it is stated, he will make his home.'[8] It is not certain what plans were made at this stage. A further letter from Reilly, dated July, announces Chermayeff's search for teaching jobs in America, recommending him as 'a first-class lecturer with a quick, clear mind [who] can put his thesis to his audience in a most convincing way'. This is the first definite evidence of Chermayeff's intention to teach, which at this stage seems a matter of expediency, although it had sufficient background in his method of practice and his public engagement in educational questions – not least the European Academy of the Mediterranean eight years earlier – rather than specific experience in a school.

The outbreak of war on 3 September found the Chermayeffs, accompanied by an alsatian, minus Peter and Ivan who were at school at Dartington, homeless and staying as the guests of the novelist Rebecca West and her husband Henry Andrews at Possingworth Manor, Sussex. She turned the visit to account in an article in the *Ladies' Home Journal*, describing how Neville Chamberlain's announcement on the radio 'meant that a lovely future was torn up under their eyes. They were not going to a new country to enjoy exciting professional opportunities and form exciting new friendships. They were stranded in England without a stick of furniture and without a roof to shelter them.'[9] Barbara Chermayeff found a job, leaving Serge behind, afflicted with the unpleasant skin complaint, impetigo, while the alsatian howled as it had sympathetically contracted mange. During the autumn Chermayeff found some temporary work on government evacuation hostels, and wanted to make a more significant contribution to the war effort, but felt that he was being discriminated against, writing later that 'I guess socialist-minded reformers with Russian names had no priority.'[10] By December the Chermayeffs were planning their departure to America, despite the absence of job offers from across the Atlantic, and living temporarily at Old Kennards, Leigh, near Tonbridge.[11]

Chermayeff's motive for going to the USA was evidently questioned. A letter of February 1942 by the Labour MP George Strauss, a friend and client of Wells Coates, was written to refute a rumour in New York that Chermayeff left the country 'in her hour of peril'. Strauss explains that 'I know personally that he applied to go on the American quota long before the outbreak of war, and that when the war broke out he wanted to abandon his plans and stay in England until it was all over, and meanwhile do some useful work here.'[12] Strauss said that in the absence of useful work, he advised Chermayeff to leave, even though he was reluctant to go.

Because the USA immigration quotas were full for those of Russian origin, the Chermayeffs booked a passage to Canada, sailing from Liverpool. Prior to departure, they stayed with the architect and planner, William Holford (1907–75), losing their smaller dog, Ham, a Westmorland terrier (one of a pair called Ham and Eggs), in the blackout. They called out his name up and down the street, causing several residents to open their windows thinking there might be a sudden supply of black-market ham.[13] They sailed on 13 January 1940 but the ship, the Duchess of Bedford, was attacked by a German submarine and the passengers were ordered to the lifeboats. The damaged ship managed to get back to harbour, and there followed a delay of nearly two weeks before they successfully made the crossing between 24 January and 1st February.[14] Staying in Montreal, Chermayeff made contacts with Canadian architects (which he remembered with affection years later), giving a lunchtime talk to architects in Toronto on 11 March, in which he described the architectural profession in England as 'preoccupied with the preservation and prolongation of the past while the present stormed around them'.[15] With a visa for the USA issued on 19 March, they made their way to Lincoln, Massachusetts, with some 35 pieces of luggage – mostly left at Lincoln station – to stay with Walter and Ise Gropius in the house Gropius had built in 1938 on arriving from England to teach at Harvard. Chermayeff was quick off the mark with his new career, broadcasting on CBS on 26 March on 'Why Modern Architecture?' and giving lectures at Harvard and Yale, both places at which he taught in later years. In Lincoln, the Chermayeffs made contacts and then spent five weeks in New York, where Howard Myers, the publisher of *Architectural Forum*, threw a party for them on the top of the Rockefeller Centre. Chermayeff lectured in Chicago and Detroit, visiting the Ford Motor Works with its architect, Albert Kahn, and also at the University of Ann Arbor, Michigan, where he evidently thought that he would get a teaching post, suffering an unexpected disappointment.

As Barbara explained in a letter to the Pipers, 'the race against time, of finding a job before the bank balance vanishes is rather nerve-wracking, it doesn't exist as compared to what people are going through in Europe now.'[16] It was cheaper to be on the road than to take a house, so in June they set out on a long cross-continental trip in a recently purchased car, leaving the boys behind in the care of the the Gropiuses. The Chermayeffs were keen to see Indian country, and areas which were being developed under the agencies, such as the Farm Security Agency, established by Roosevelt in the New Deal. They went south to New Orleans and through to New Mexico, meeting Frieda Lawrence, the widow of D.H. Lawrence in Taos. In Philadelphia they met Louis Kahn (1901–74), and his colleagues Oscar Stonorov (1905–70) and Edmund Bacon (b.1910), also George Howe (1886–1955), an older supporter of modernism. As

Barbara described the trip, 'We examined U.S. housing projects and visited all the universities en route, the Boulder and several of the T.V.A. [Tennessee Valley Authority] dams, the Grand Canyon and Canyon de Chelly, and went right off the main roads into the Navajo and Hopi Indian country, camping out on several occasions, though Serge doesn't take very kindly to it.'[17]

Reflecting a few months later on his visit to the stone ruins of Pueblo Bonito, where the Indians both danced and built, Chermayeff quoted the statement by the English scientific and social writer Havelock Ellis that 'Dancing and Building are the two primary and essential Arts. Dancing stands for the source of all the Arts that express themselves in the human person – building is the beginning of all the Arts that lie outside it.'[18] It is tempting to think that he saw this in relation to his own beginnings as a dancer. At the end of the trip, the boys, now eight and five, came across the continent to join them in San Francisco, where they found support from a community of architects and like-minded people, and where Chermayeff hoped to be able to get a teaching job.

In the Bay Area, there was a group of architects, including William Wurster (1895–1973), whose timber houses and industrial buildings of the later 1930s appealed to Chermayeff for their simplicity and sensitivity to nature. Gardner Dailey's Owens House, 1939, with its timber frame elevation, glazed double-height, is like a more open version of Bentley Wood.[19] In 1940, Wurster married the planning expert Catherine Bauer (1905–64), some six years after the breakup of her long-running affair with Lewis Mumford. She inspired him to take a fresh interest in the social issues of architecture, which she had explored in pre-Nazi Germany. Vernon DeMars (b.1908), a young architect in the 'Second Bay Region tradition', was involved in New Deal housing for the Farm Administration with a young landscape architect, Garrett Eckbo (b.1910). The landscape architect Thomas Church (1902–78) was a frequent collaborator of Wurster's, and author of the book *Gardens are for People* in 1955. These were among the fifty or so members of the group Telesis, founded in 1939, a West Coast equivalent of MARS in England but less riven by faction. The group held an exhibition, 'Space for Living' at the San Francisco Museum of Art soon after Chermayeff arrived, and in an article of 1942 he acknowledged that without their 'understanding, encouragement, loyalty and help in the last year or so, the transition period would have been immeasurably harder'.[20] John Entenza was editing the magazine *California Arts and Architecture* (after 1943 just *Arts and Architecture*), which in 1945 embarked on its programme of 'Case Study Houses', but Chermayeff advised John Piper in November 1940, 'So far all the ingenious and good jobs in Contemp. Planning, Houses, furniture, and what have you are so few and far between (don't be deceived by the tech. and art press) that they have no impact value.'[21]

In his first year in California, Chermayeff obtained commissions for two private houses, each in association with an established architect, described in Chapter 8. These indicate the friendly feeling towards him but also the likely difficulty of getting building work, even in the months before Pearl Harbour. In September 1940, not long after his arrival, Chermayeff met Eric and Louisa Mendelsohn in the street, and, as Barbara wrote, 'we were glad to see them, old troubles now having been forgotten'.[22] In a moment of optimism, Chermayeff sketched some plans and perspectives for a new family house somewhere in the San Francisco area, not unlike Bentley Wood but differing significantly in being a single-storey courtyard house of the kind that occupied his mind greatly during the next thirty years (see page 164). A great many of his stored possessions, including the whole pre-war archive of his practice, were destroyed by a bomb on the storage warehouse at Paddington on 1 September 1940, and the remnants were sent over later in the month.[23] By November, he was depressed by the slim chances of getting the teaching he wanted, and wrote to the Pipers, 'For my part, I have lost all desire to build, to practise here in making more houses for the well-to-do or to repeat anything approaching a successful career or Bentley for oneself. It is quite a relief to have got all that out of one's system.'[24]

Dr Grace L. McCann Morley, the director of the San Francisco Museum of Art and one of the sponsors of Telesis, invited Chermayeff to lecture on 'Crisis in Architecture' on 18 September, a talk later repeated at Portland, Oregon. She also gave him the opportunity to present a course in design, consisting of five seminars, which enrolled mostly qualified professionals on the basis of Chermayeff's reputation.[25] Chermayeff liked the independent quality of the Northwest, writing to John Piper, 'It is my belief that the West has to break away from being the second hand clothes market of the East. It has all the potentialities of a real contribution, a number of energetic people are here already and it still has all the defects and virtues of a frontier. It is anxious to do things on its own, particularly in matters of art without the patronising help of the Mus.Mod.Art N.Y.'[26] On the same trip he made contact with the Pacific Northwest Regional Planning Commission and its chairman, B. H. Kizer, who thought that Chermayeff had a concept of architecture and the arts so broad that 'he sees their relationship with the world of natural resources and the plans for their conservation and development with a fresh and clear vision'.[27] Catherine Bauer wrote to the Director of the Northwest Regional Council supporting Chermayeff as a suitable collaborator and employee. In April 1941, Kizer offered Chermayeff a part-time consultative position, in the hope that he might also be able to get a part-time teaching post at the University of Oregon at Eugene, where members of the faculty were 'deeply impressed' by him, but lacked funds.[28] The architects of Portland, Oregon, led by Pietro Belluschi (1899–1994), were also keen to get him to teach there, and Belluschi reported that the Dean of the School of Architecture, Ellis Lawrence, was surprised and impressed that 'a person who had made such a mark in pure design, would be so deeply interested in the social implications of present day architecture as you are'.[29]

Chermayeff was also hoping that the restructuring of the School of Architecture at the University of California, Berkeley, might give him the teaching opportunity he sought, writing that 'if this materialised it would provide a place from which one could operate in the good cause with the full backing of respectability, it seems the best place at the moment, if the fever of war does not make them close down on Art, foreigners and all as indeed they closed down on me in Ann Arbor after everything had been fixed.'[30] He was again disappointed, for as Catherine Bauer explained, 'it is a slow and complicated process, and a much bigger problem than merely getting one person into one job.'[31] Meanwhile, he was diverted by the first of several visits to Frank Lloyd Wright at Taliesin West, Arizona, at the end of March 1941, where he complained about the low ceilings and observed Wright's Napoleonic management of a desert picnic party.[32]

In the summer of 1941, Chermayeff met the German-born art historian Dr Leo Balet at the home of Jan de Graeff in Oregon. Balet was teaching at Brooklyn College, New York, having been supported in his immigration to the USA by the art historian Meyer Schapiro. Balet recognised in Chermayeff a potential ally in his almost lone stand as a liberal and modernist in the Bauhaus mould against a highly conventional establishment. The President of the College, Harry Gideonse, an economist, was an ally of Balet, and intended to appoint a new Chairman of the Department of Art, so Balet urged Chermayeff to apply.[33] As Chermayeff wrote to Lewis Mumford, 'The task, as I understand it, is to build the whole thing up on an entirely new model . . . what Balet has told me, suggests that here is an opportunity to translate into action the various ideas we have discussed.'[34] There was considerable local opposition to the appointment of a non-American but Chermayeff gathered letters of support from America and England.[35] Gideonse met Mumford at a dinner party, who reported to Chermayeff:

He is an old fashioned Manchester liberal . . . but he is also, queerly, a man of social principle and, in a way, of social vision: part of his reaction consists in his revolt against the a-moral materialism which usually went with collectivism in the twenties. So I think he is capable of respecting those who hold different opinions, provided they are also men of principle; which means that I think you will find it possible to get along with him – and vice-versa.[36]

Sibyl Moholy-Nagy reported to Ben Nicholson in December 1941, 'Serge Chermayeff came twice through Chicago when trying to get a Professorship at Brooklyn College which by now he has managed. I guess they'll be happy to settle down again after all these years of roaming around and I'm sure he'll do an excellent job in New York. He was full of good plans, and glad about the recognition this appointment means.'[37] The Chermayeffs moved their possessions to a small apartment at 301 East 21st Street, where visitors, like Peter Blake, were surprised to find puff adders, brought back from trips to Cape Cod by the Chermayeff boys, curled up asleep on the sofa cushions.

In a circular letter asking for the support of old friends and colleagues, Chermayeff explained his aims: 'It is apparent that the continued development in Design and the contribution this can make to the post-war reconstruction period depends largely on our ability to prepare for this work now by integrating the Social, Technical and Art problems, into one organic whole in the minds of those who will have the job of carrying it out.'[38]

Brooklyn College already had some art classes but Chermayeff had been selected in order to remodel the whole curriculum, so that it became the first American version of modern design teaching integrated within a liberal-arts college, rather than standing alone, like the 'New Bauhaus' in Chicago under Moholy-Nagy; or in the form of a summer school, like the famous one at Black Mountain College, organised by Josef Albers; or the less well-known Mills College, where Robert Jay Wolff, Chermayeff's colleague and then successor at Brooklyn, held a summer session in 1940. Chermayeff prepared himself for teaching by attending a summer session of the Chicago Institute of Design at their country 'campus', a farm at Somonauk, Illinois, in 1942.[39] Wolff later called Chermayeff's five years in Brooklyn a 'heroic and successful effort to transform a hopelessly backward and conservative department into the first Bauhaus oriented manifestation in American public education'.[40] The heroism was manifested in the face of some vocal opposition, as the reform of the Department involved getting rid of a number of the existing staff. Gideonse stood by Chermayeff and described it fifteen years later:

> We had quarrels . . . with the local newspaper, the *Brooklyn* [*Daily*] *Eagle*, which for some three weeks and every single day on the front page ran a story. They couldn't really make up their minds what they objected to, but it was clear they objected. One day he was a Fascist, the next day he was a Communist and one day he was a nudist! There was always something! . . . Then gradually by patience and letting ourselves be eroded by the wind and the storm and the sand it wore off and at last Chermayeff got a chance to rebuild the department.[41]

Chermayeff personally found it a thoroughly satisfactory place to work and recalled that 'what gave me the taste for teaching, really, was the fact that New York had a very large Jewish minority and as there were only four colleges, the four colleges had the top one and a half per cent of intellectual quality in the whole of the United States, so by pure chance I was suddenly given the opportunity to rub minds at this college level with the most excellent students.'[42]

Chermayeff described his aims for the new Department of Design in terms of what he felt to be the urgency of the situation in the outside world, 'study leading to action' as he described it in words taken from Paul Hanna, producing a certain kind of skilled generalist, 'required to possess intelligence that takes the over-all view rather than the partial approach'.[43] Chermayeff believed fervently in the connection between abstract art and political freedom. The example of Hitler's Germany could not have been a clearer demonstration of the opposite case. The usefulness of abstraction lay in part in its applicability to real problems of design, and as Chermayeff wrote in his report to Gideonse in 1942:

> . . . art, or more specifically design, because the word 'art' has become degraded and meaningless through misuse, must inevitably play an increasingly large part both in the educational process directed towards constructive objectives and in Life itself as one of the most vital instruments with which to shape a better environment.[44]

Rather unusually for a Bauhaus approach, the course began with History of Art, taught by Leo Balet, one of whose units examined 'The origins in the 12th century of the culture in which we are still living'.[45] It also included Basic Design and Mechanical Drawing. The course gradually extended into other skills, photography, crafts, colour, printing, architecture and applied design among them. The applications of design skill, which the Department tried to implement through projects for the college and on campus, included stage design and city planning. Intensive courses were offered for those awaiting military call-up, or released from service. Chermayeff particularly recalled three students who made careers outside the field of design, Oscar Brandt, Leo Bogart and Isidore Goldiamond, who followed him to Chicago as secretary before becoming a Professor of Sociology at the University of Chicago. Chermayeff was insistent upon the importance of spreading and opening up visual culture, as a kind of social therapy, in terms of which Eric Gill would have approved:

> Art must cease being considered as a commodity provided by mysteriously endowed specialists for the delectation of an equally exclusive body of patrons and must become an activity in which all participate. Then art can become an instrument of social therapy as potent as security and health.[46]

The craft basis of the Bauhaus was perpetuated through the study of Basic Design, in which the experience of handling materials was the primary foundation of the student. Chermayeff saw the activity in the college as a whole in terms of an ideological war effort. As he wrote in October 1942, 'we must continue a vigilant, unceasing fight against stupidity, complacency, intolerance, greed and in whatever forms they appear, which are breeding here at home, the replacements for those gaps in the fascist ranks which our soldiers might create.'[47] Chermayeff was able to come closer into contact with the Bauhaus through working with György Kepes, a fellow-Hungarian, born in 1906, who worked with Moholy-Nagy in London as his assistant, before accompanying him to Chicago, where he headed the Light and Colour department. Kepes taught at Brooklyn from 1943 to 1945, before moving to MIT. This was the period in which he published his first major didactic work, *Language of Vision*, 1944. In an introduction to the book, S. I. Hayakawa of the Illinois Institute of Technology explained the link between the political and the visual which was so strongly felt at this time:

To cease looking at things atomistically in visual experience and to see relatedness means, among other things, to lose our social experience . . . the deluded self-importance of absolute 'individualism' in favour of social relatedness and interdependence. When we structuralise the primary impacts of experience differently, we shall structuralise the world differently.[48]

Among Chermayeff's colleagues in the early years were the abstract painters Burgoyne Diller and Harry Holzman, both of whom had links with Mondrian and Neo-Plasticism. They brought in other members of American Abstract Artists, a group organised in 1936, including the painter Ad Reinhardt, who began teaching at Brooklyn in 1947, just after Chermayeff had left. Another of these artists, Arshile Gorky, became a friend of Chermayeff over many years. The Department was never the preserve of one artistic group, and there were representatives of realist photography and even of surrealism.[49]

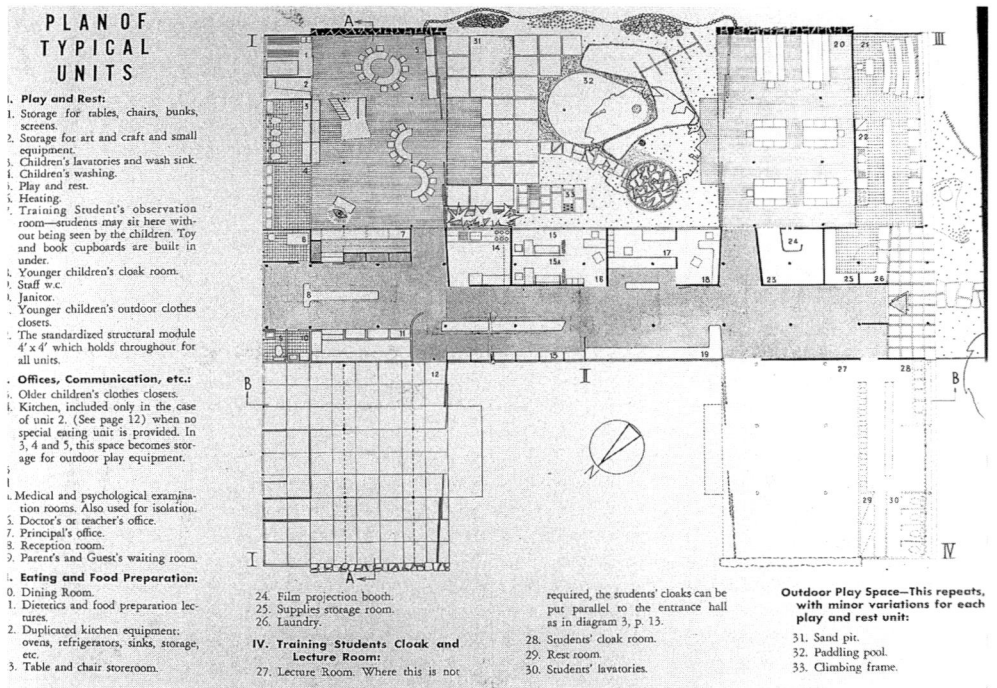

PLAN OF TYPICAL UNITS

I. Play and Rest:
1. Storage for tables, chairs, bunks, screens.
2. Storage for art and craft and small equipment.
3. Children's lavatories and wash sink.
4. Children's washing.
5. Play and rest.
6. Heating.
7. Training Student's observation room—students may sit here without being seen by the children. Toy and book cupboards are built in under.
8. Younger children's cloak room.
9. Staff w.c.
10. Janitor.
11. Younger children's outdoor clothes closets.
12. The standardized structural module 4' x 4' which holds throughout for all units.

II. Offices, Communication, etc.:
13. Older children's clothes closets.
14. Kitchen, included only in the case of unit 2. (See page 12) when no special eating unit is provided. In 3, 4 and 5, this space becomes storage for outdoor play equipment.
15.
16.
17. Medical and psychological examination rooms. Also used for isolation.
18. Doctor's or teacher's office.
19. Principal's office.
20. Reception room.
21. Parent's and Guest's waiting room.

III. Eating and Food Preparation:
22. Dining Room.
23. Dietetics and food preparation lectures.
24. Duplicated kitchen equipment: ovens, refrigerators, sinks, storage, etc.
25. Table and chair storeroom.

24. Film projection booth.
25. Supplies storage room.
26. Laundry.

IV. Training Students Cloak and Lecture Room:
27. Lecture Room. Where this is not required, the students' cloaks can be put parallel to the entrance hall as in diagram 3, p. 13.
28. Students' cloak room.
29. Rest room.
30. Students' lavatories.

Outdoor Play Space—This repeats, with minor variations for each play and rest unit:
31. Sand pit.
32. Paddling pool.
33. Climbing frame.

The levelling and integration of different areas of specialist knowledge was one of Chermayeff's main aims, the other being the engagement of students in real projects in their local community. In 1943, students worked on the need for preschool education in the neighbourhood, a study which resulted in the production of a booklet, *A Children's Center and Nursery School* in 1944, reflecting the interest in this building-type as an essential aspect of social improvement which had been current among British modernists in the 1930s. The text describing the nursery school emphasises the importance of socialising the children at an early age, as well as giving the parents a break. In the proposal, the schools were intended for community use outside hours, like the 'Village Colleges' in Cambridgeshire, one of which was designed by Walter Gropius and completed shortly before the war. 'The Children's Center is the minimum educational, recreational and health-promoting instrument; the important first link in the chain of such other social instruments as schools, hospitals, recreational centers, universities, concert halls, etc,, which serve to develop and maintain our physical, social and cultural well being.'[50]

The college campus itself was also studied, with the aim of turning the college into a local cultural centre. Public opinion was surveyed, in the manner of the English organisation, 'Mass Observation', which Chermayeff admired for its detailed study of ordinary people's views. A model was made so that the scheme could be easily understood by the local community. Plans were made for building a new theatre and concert hall on campus, to which Chermayeff contributed his specialist knowledge, overcoming obstructions from the Professor of Music in a typically forthright way.[51] Chermayeff designed seating for the theatre and for the lounges in the new library which was made in Momoronack, New York.[52] After Chermayeff left in 1947, this aspect of the work was briefly taken over by the exiled Catalan architect and CIAM President, José Luis Sert (1902–83).

One of the most distinguished students to come from Chermayeff's period of teaching at Brooklyn was the potter Karen Karnes, who later wrote 'I loved you very dearly, and learned so much from you. Always afterwards I have been very conscious of the great part you played in those important years - not only in Brooklyn, where your voice was the first that I heard from the adult art world, but afterwards . . .'[53] Another student was Albert Szabo, from a Hungarian immigrant family in Brooklyn, who entered the college to study sculpture in 1945. He recalls 'I met this tall Englishman and was very impressed, because he spoke with such a special accent . . . he said "Before you study painting and sculpture you must study architecture" . . . I became quickly convinced that I had no alternative but to become an architect.'[54]

In April 1943, Chermayeff presented his work in England to the University of the State of New York Board of Examiners in Architecture in support of his application to become a licensed practitioner in the USA. He was proud to emerge with a score of 92%.[55] When the war ended, he set up an office in New York, shared with Konrad Wachsmann, as much as anything as a showroom for a display of his work, which was illustrated with photographic blow-ups and a few models, such as that of the Gilbey building.

Between 1943 and 1945, Chermayeff maintained his involvement in the wider world of architectural politics through his active membership of the American Society of Planners and

Architects (ASPA), an informal American outpost of CIAM, with Joseph Hudnut, Dean of Architecture at Harvard as its President and George Howe as Vice-President. One of Chermayeff's specific contributions was to organise a day conference on 20 January 1945, at which Le Corbusier and Claudius Eugene Petit were the speakers. Hudnut wrote to congratulate him, saying 'it is hard to imagine any one doing a better job or any one seizing this splendid opportunity at just the right moment, as you have done.'[56]

Much like the MARS Group, ASPA wanted to combine political pressure for improved housing with research inside the profession on industrialisation. A new element was a desire to form local planning workshops.[57] One effect of Chermayeff's involvement was contact with José-Luis Sert, later his Dean at the Graduate School of Design at Harvard. Together they outlined an urban project which would offer the unwilling American public an alternative to the suburbs. Varying the pre-war assumption in CIAM circles that public housing of the future would mostly be in the form of large-scale flats, this 'New York Project Committee' recommended that a new district should be composed of high and low apartment buildings, and that 'possibly row houses would predominate in such a development'.[58] This is also a precursor of Chermayeff's growing interest in low-rise individual housing, at a time when the New Deal housing programmes were rapidly coming to a halt, and the AIA was taking a conservative stance on this issue.

Chermayeff was also active, through this uneasy period of change, in the Architects' Committee of the National Council of Soviet-American Friendship, an organisation which, as Richard Plunz notes, was listed in 1952 as subversive by the US Attorney General. In 1949, he addressed the Planning and Building Panel at the Cultural and Scientific Conference for World Peace in New York, known as the 'Waldorf Conference'. He later explained that his knowledge of Russian made him useful to this organisation as on an occasion when he acted as interpreter for Dmitri Shostakovitch at a dinner.

Richard Plunz suggests that involvement in such organisations may have told against the career prospects of anyone concerned. In fact, Chermayeff seems to have confined his ambitions largely to the academic sphere, where the atmosphere was in any case more liberal. The general conservatism of the 1950s was inimical to his own intentions in education but for reasons far beyond any specific action on his part. His political background was questioned when he wanted to visit the Soviet Union in 1959 to participate in the large exhibition, 'Graphics USA', on which his son Ivan worked as a designer. Chermayeff was initially denied a visa. By this time, McCarthyism was in decline and Chermayeff was able to get a high-level interview in Washington with the Director of the United States Information Agency, who confirmed that he had been officially 'investigated' three years earlier and that the Agency, 'found no reason to question his loyalty or qualifications for work with our exhibition in the USSR'.[59] Unfortunately, by this stage there was no longer an official position on the exhibition team for him, although Chermayeff visited England that summer in order to be closer to hand if a call came.

In March 1943, Chermayeff discussed with the Trustees of the Museum of Modern Art in New York the possibility of himself becoming director of a Department of Industrial Design, which the museum wished to establish. The intention was for the museum to act as a link between designers and manufacturers, giving its approval to certain products. A trial was to be made with radios, to be manufactured by the Montgomery Ward company.[60] This was probably intended to be additional to his work at Brooklyn College, rather than a replacement for it. The job never materialised as such, but as a preliminary exercise Chermayeff was commissioned to design and curate, in collaboration with René d'Harnoncourt, the exhibition 'Design for Use' which opened in May 1944, as part of the 15th anniversary celebrations of the museum. As Chermayeff stated, 'The purpose was to present industrial design in a comprehensive way as a historical development in industrial society and not as a catalogue of fashionable shapes or gadgets.'[61] In particular, he pursued his theme of the unity of the modern home, writing that 'The growing recognition that the house is a problem of interrelated function makes us now think of home equipment as components of a unit of living space rather than as separate aesthetic and technical problems. Modern industrial technology applied to this field will give Industrial Design its greatest opportunity.'[62] The issue of industrial design in the USA was different to that in Britain, because of the existence of an influential and commercially successful group of designers, such as Raymond Loewy, whose application of 'styling' to products had different priorities to the high-minded puritanism of the Modern Movement, as exemplified in the Museum. As one of the captions in the exhibition catalogue expresses it, 'The desire to make objects look "up-to-date" by borrowing forms from unrelated modern machinery often leads to absurdities such as this pencil sharpener streamlined to resemble an airplane.'[63] The exhibition made a particular feature of technology developed in wartime, like the double-curved plywood forms by Charles Eames (1907–78), using techniques originally discovered for making light-weight splints, and the development of plastics. The exhibition therefore carried forward the message of the 1941 Organic Design show, with a more penetrating interpretation of the word 'organic' to cover a holistic relationship between the separate items of a home, as well as the curved forms which were appearing through a mixture of technology and fashion.

'Design for Use' was part of a continuing struggle between the essentially European values of the Museum of Modern Art, and what might be described as the American values of the industrial design firms. As Chermayeff put it in a draft of the catalogue text, later excised, 'In order to prevent the wider spread of illiterate and vulgar design which might parallel the cultural disaster of the 19th century, we must ensure that in the postwar period at the least the safeguard of adequate education for designers is established.'[64] Links to Chermayeff's pre-war world were made by the inclusion of a photograph of the wall of cupboards in the living room

'Design for Use' exhibition, Museum of Modern Art, New York, 1944.

'Lady's bedroom', Modern Art in French and English Furniture and Decoration, Waring and Gillow, 1928. 'The effect of the room is obtained by a simple combination of a clean fresh green and the dignity of the dark furniture in Macassar ebony relieved by a thin band of walnut.' (Text from exhibition catalogue.) Flower painting by Maud Klein.

Studio flat for Anthony Gibbons Grinling, Chelsea Court, Swan Street, London, 1931.

Handknotted rug
(153x139.7cm), Royal
Wilton Carpet Factory,
1930.

Foyer bar, Cambridge
Theatre, 1930.

Broadcasting House,
eighth floor waiting room,
1932.

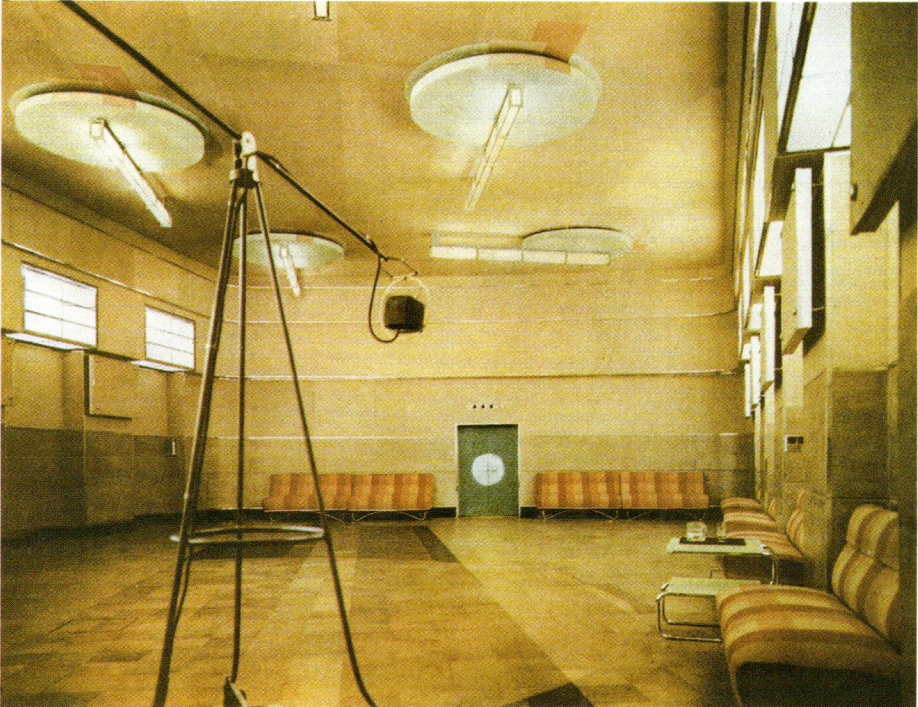

Broadcasting House,
Orchestral Studio 8A,
1932.

157

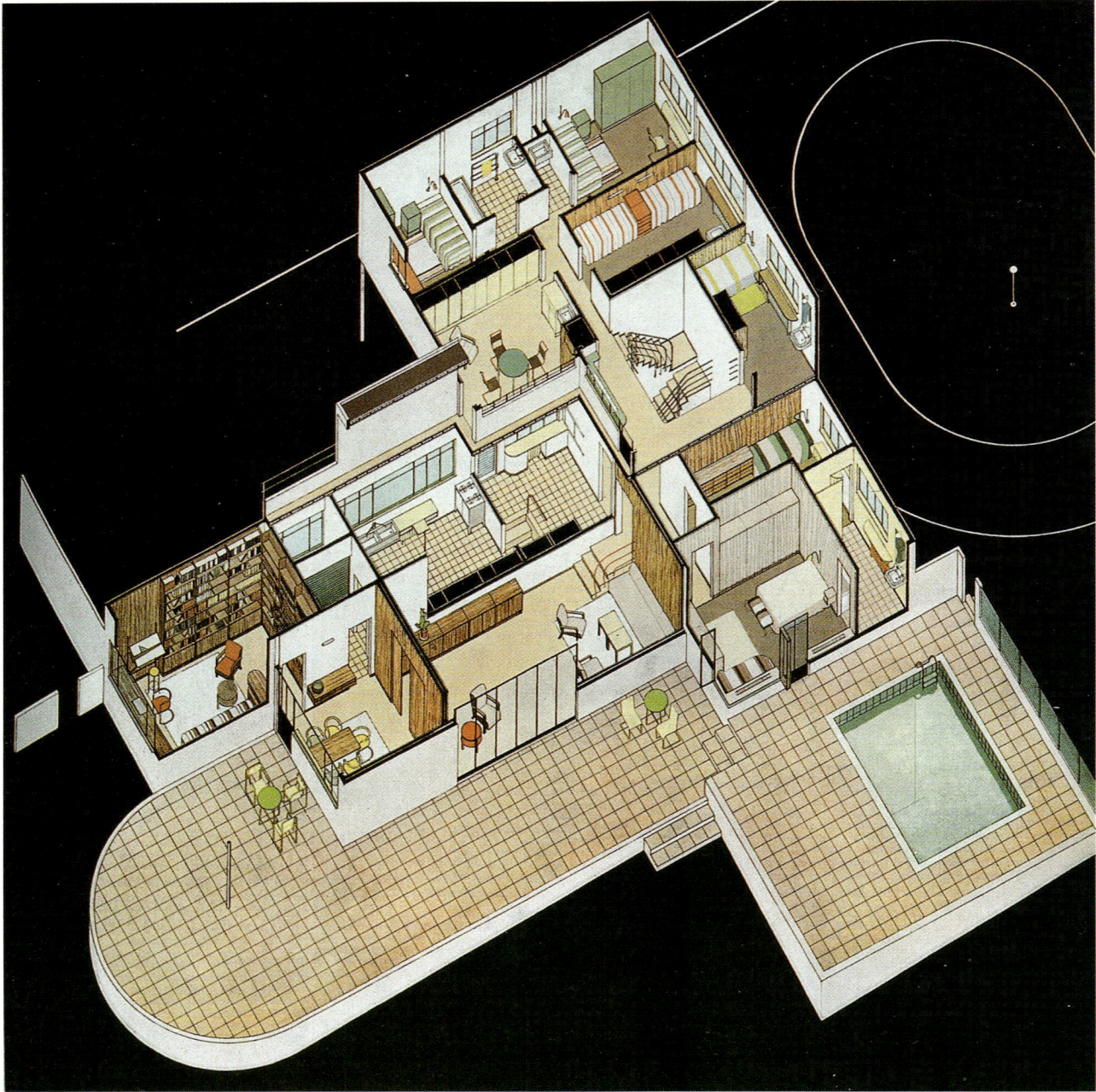

Bedroom designed by Miss P.E. Humphries for William Whiteley Ltd. with PLAN unit furniture.

Right: De La Warr Pavilion, colour scheme for theatre interior, from Serge Chermayeff (1935), *The Application of Colour in Modern Buildings*.

Opposite: Country House at Puttenham, 1932.

|  |  |
|---|---|
| WHITE | Reflective plaster ceiling and proscenium opening. |
| PALE BLUE | Proscenium curtain. |
| CREAM | Absorbent building board on North, South and East Walls. Proscenium flank. Gallery curtain. |
| SYCAMORE | Gallery woodwork. |
| RED | Gallery seating. |
| DARK BLUE | Stalls seating. |
| BROWN I | Steel window frames and tubular framework of seating. |
| BROWN II | Curtains at stalls level. |
| WALNUT | Woodwork at stalls level. |
| BROWN III | Close cover carpet throughout stalls and gallery. |

Elmhirst apartment, interior.

Bentley Wood, garden terrace with Henry Moore's *Recumbent Figure* in foreground, from 1939 colour slide.

Bentley Wood, living room with painting by Ben Nicholson, from 1938/9 colour slide.

Chicago Plans exhibition, 1949, installation.

Peter Chermayeff
(designer), Serge
Chermayeff and
Christopher Alexander,
Community and Privacy,
1963, book jacket.

Opposite: Harvard Patio
House, model.

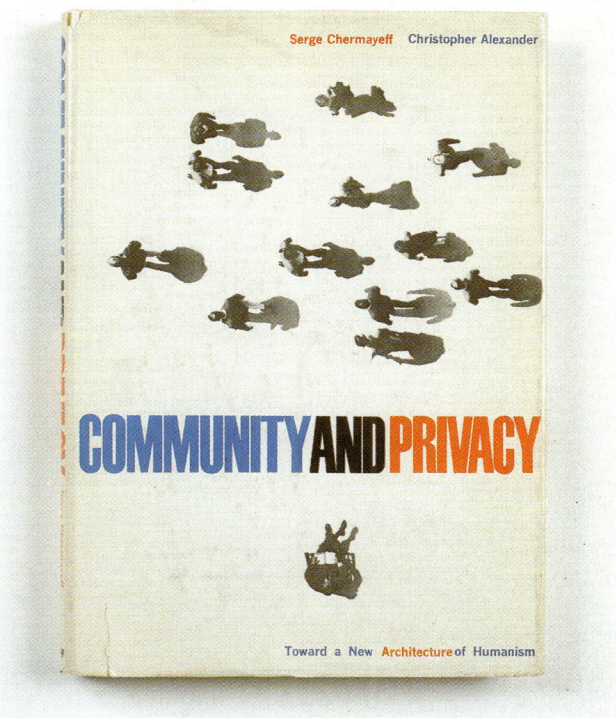

S. Chermayeff and E. Born,
Horn House, Richmond,
California, 1942.

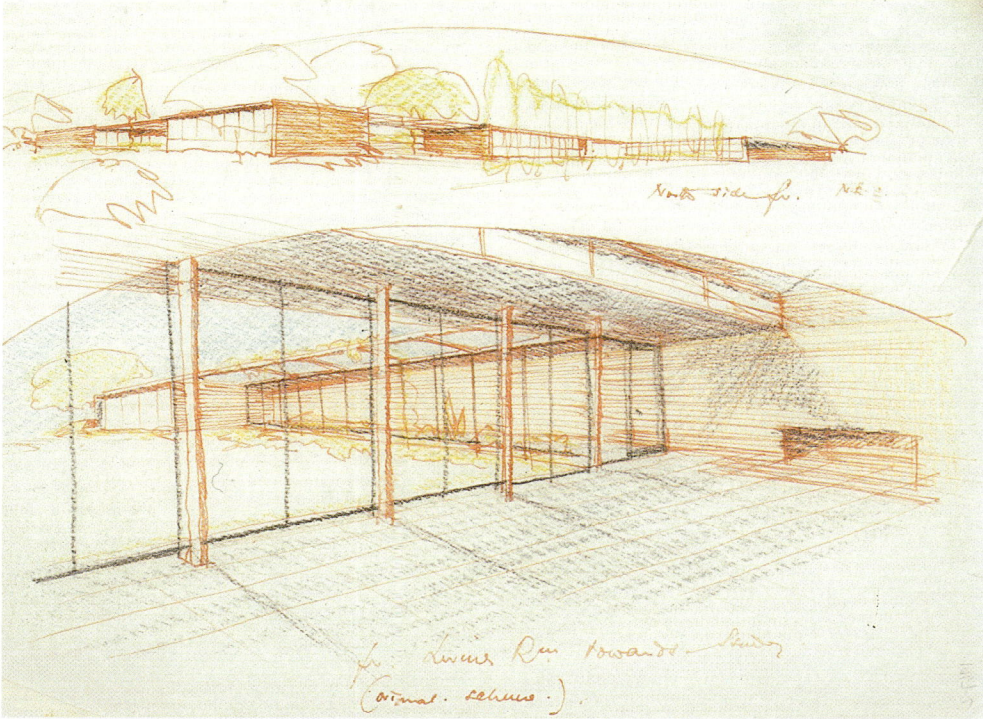

Proposal for Chermayeff
house in San Francisco
area, c.1942, street
side perspective and view
from living room.

*North side fr. N.E.?*

*fr. Living Rm towards Study
(original. scheme.)*

Proposal for Chermayeff
house in San Francisco
area, view in courtyard.

*Courtyard from Study wall. (S.W.)*

Serge Chermayeff and Raphael Soriano, Ciro Jewellery Shop, San Francisco, 1942, interior.

Navajo textile displayed with a Chermayeff painting in exhibition at Baldwin-Kingery Gallery, Chicago, 1951.

Payson House, Portland, Maine, 1952 garden front.

Payson House, interior.

166

Chermayeff Cottage, Cape Cod (Truro, Massachussetts).

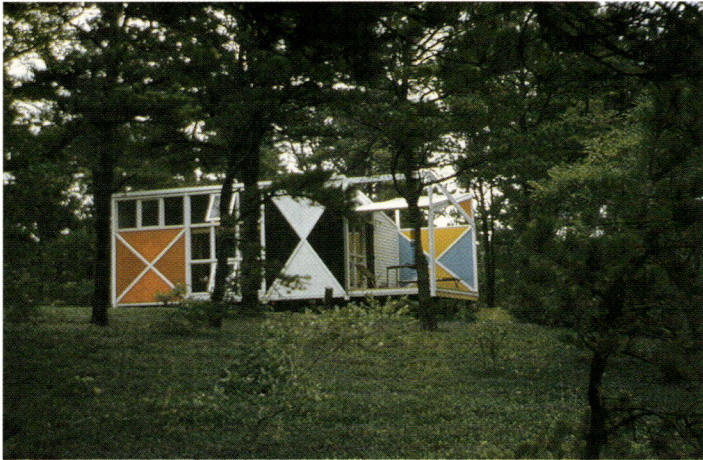

Chermayeff studio, Cape Cod (Truro, Massachussetts), original building, 1951.

Sigerson House, Cape Cod (Truro, Massachussetts), sketch designs.

Cape Codder printing offices, Orleans, Massachussetts.

Opposite: 28 Lincoln Street, exterior.

28 Lincoln Street, interior.

28 Lincoln Street, Serge Chermayeff sitting in main room.

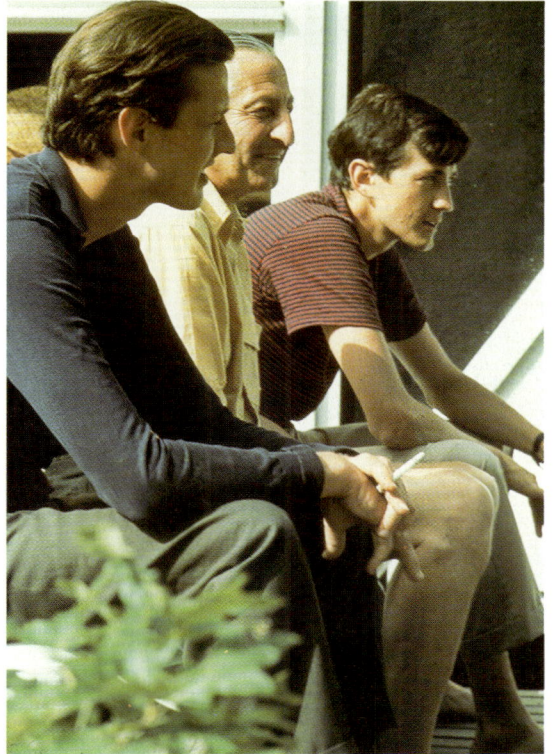

Serge with Ivan and Peter
Chermayeff at Cape Cod,
1966.

Serge Chermayeff, Barn
Dance, oil painting, 1948.

Serge Chermayeff, The Lonely Crowd II, oil painting, 1950.

Serge Chermayeff, In the forest of Night , oil painting, c.1950.

172

Serge Chermayeff, Morning
Window oil painting, 1950.

Serge Chermayeff,
montage with shingles.

Serge and Barbara Chermayeff at Cape Cod, 1991.

Serge Chermayeff drawing at Cape Cod, 1991.

at Bentley Wood. No long-term job for Chermayeff emerged from the Byzantine internal politics of MOMA, although he took part in the exhibition, 'Tomorrow's Small House' in 1945, with a joint scheme with Vernon de Mars and Susanne Wasson-Tucker.

His work at Brooklyn continued through the allied victory in Europe and the more ambiguous ending of the war in the Pacific a year later. Chermayeff was not likely to stay at Brooklyn forever, feeling that the courses there were too far removed from his own 'taste, talent and experience'.[65] In the autumn of 1946, László Moholy-Nagy, who had contracted leukemia, came from Chicago on an unacknowledged farewell visit to New York, where his friends rallied round him. He died, sooner than expected, back in Chicago on 24 November 1946, aged 51. The original New Bauhaus which he had founded in Chicago in 1937 had run into difficulties with its original backers in the course of its first year, and Moholy had refounded it as the School of Design, with most of the original staff, working heroically for nine years without a holiday. In 1944, the school became the Institute of Design (ID), with financial backing from Walter Paepcke, Chairman of the Container Corporation of America, who employed Herbert Bayer, the Bauhaus typographer, directly for his publicity, along with other avant-garde designers. In 1946 the Institute of Design had acquired its own building, an 1892 Armoury by Henry Ives Cobb in the style of H. H. Richardson at 632 North Dearborn Street.

In July 1946, Moholy put forward various names as possible successors in a letter to Paepcke, starting with Marcel Breuer. Paepcke devolved the selection process to Walter Gropius, who himself had spotted Moholy's potential as a teacher when appointing him to the Bauhaus in 1923. Breuer was ruled out, because he had recently had a bitter quarrel with Gropius. Other candidates, some from Moholy's list, some not, included José-Luis Sert (Moholy's second choice), Eero Saarinen, György Kepes, Charles Eames, Konrad Wachsmann and Robert Wolff.[66] Gropius was keen on giving Chermayeff the job, and he was appointed in December, to start on 15 January 1947.[67]

The Institute of Design had a remarkable group of staff running its foundation course and other departments, including the architects George Fred Keck and Ralph Rapson, although for various reasons the study of architecture was not as significant as it later became under Chermayeff. Other teachers were the photographer Nathan Lerner, Charles Niedringhaus, James Prestini, maker of exquisitely thin wood-turned bowls, and, as an occasional visitor, the composer John Cage. Chermayeff had contact with the school through his attendance at the summer foundation course in 1942 and enjoyed being in 'an extremely vigorous, not to say arrogant city'.[68] Some previous accounts of the 'Chicago Bauhaus' omitted to mention Chermayeff's role, and a recent writer says that after Moholy's death, 'the school lost its vision and resolve'.[69] In fact, it flourished considerably for a period of three years until the falling off of ex-servicemen brought financial and institutional problems. Unlike the Brooklyn department, Chermayeff inherited a 'going concern' at Chicago, and his early years were helped by the number of good students coming out of the forces with GI grants for higher education. He also took onto his staff some of Moholy's former students, such as Richard Filipowski, who had a specialism in three-dimensional design. Hans Schleger (1898–1996), a German who had worked in London after 1932, was a visiting lecturer in the year 1950–1. The photographer Harry Callahan also made a notable contribution. Hugo Weber and Otto Kolb were both Swiss, and recommended by Siegfried Giedion. Weber was a sculptor, and Kolb an architect and industrial designer. Weber taught drawing in an innovative, highly physical way and sculpted the head of Mies van der Rohe.

Perhaps the most famous teacher brought to Chicago by Chermayeff was Buckminster Fuller (1895–1983) who had previous experience of teaching at Black Mountain College under Josef Albers, but appreciated the breadth and freedom of the Institute of Design. Fuller 'occupied the whole of the basement, and made it a sort of Merlin's cave of wonderful devices, and expositions and models of his various mathematical and basic components'. A student working with Fuller, Kenneth Snelson, succeeded in giving actual form to Fuller's theoretical idea and invented the original 'tensegrity structure', a way of creating a lightweight solid form based on tension rather than compression. Chermayeff told the Bauhaus historian Hans Wingler that 'it was, I think, fair to say [the ID was] the real "launching pad" for Fuller, although he had started a similar workshop, with less success, at Black Mountain College a year before'.[70] Fuller was an intermittent visitor during 1949, living in a caravan in a parking lot as an experiment.

The atmosphere was pervaded by jazz, then rife in the Chicago 'underground'. Chermayeff, reliving a little of his dancing twenties, went to hear Ella Fitzgerald at the Blue Note, and to other jazz clubs, with the artist and teacher Emerson Woelffer, sometimes accompanied by Buckminster Fuller. As Chermayeff related, 'Bucky loved jazz, he could do his little beats and stuff, and I loved dancing . . . it was not relaxation from the other work, it was a continuation in another medium'. Fuller found an analogy between 'jazz beat and geometry made visible.'[71] When Peter Blake visited and met Fuller for the first time, he insisted that 'bebop has the same beat as the mathematical shorthand I have been working on', and demonstrated it by jumping on top of one of the drafting tables to dance while calling out a sequence of numbers.[72] Sometimes the school itself laid on jazz parties, at the regular auctions of work by staff and students that were held to raise funds. Following Moholy's lead, the Institute's work had a strong leaning towards kinetic art and design. Konrad Wachsmann came in 1950, his teaching crossing between architecture and product design. 'He could draw like an angel and he could do all sorts of things which other people couldn't do . . . I invited Wachsmann to come because he had an extremely disciplined way of steel structuring.'[73]

As at the Bauhaus itself, where Moholy had taken personal charge of it, in succession to Johannes Itten, the Foundation Course was a key element of the Institute of Design, involving a reorientation based on visual experiment and direct experience of materials. This led the way towards other more specialised areas but still ensured a principle of potential crossovers in many directions, including product design, probably the strongest area in Moholy's time. By getting students to work on 'hand sculptures', the forms no longer had the geometric rigidity associated with the 1920s Bauhaus but expressed Moholy's later enthusiasm for the 'organic' in its widest sense.

In a lecture in 1949, Chermayeff explained how he saw the Foundation Course at the Institute of Design as essentially remedial:

Serge Chermayeff, portrait photo c.1947.

> the students . . . arrive so completely inhibited by their previous training that they have absolutely no courage at the 'awareness', 'early adult level'. They are, from the viewpoint of any kind of organisational or creative activity at a far more primitive stage as a result of this thing which we ironically call 'education' than they were at a much earlier age. So we have to spend from about a year to a year and a half undoing the immense harm that our educational system has done to the people who we consider will become important functionaries in our society . . . in other words, we have to start all over again. This is not, I assure you, a piece of arrogance or egotism on my part. It is not a magnificent conceit of the Bauhaus mind. It is not any kind of special situation at all but rather a very commonplace, ordinary situation which is being faced by any school at an advanced level anywhere, which faces its responsibilities with integrity and intelligence.[74]

Institute of Design, Chicago, Foundation Course, 'Architectonic space construction for experiment with elements within a given space'.

Some of the most inspiring teachers taught on the Foundation Course, including Filipowsky, Weber and Woelffer, the school's jazz specialist, of whom Albert Szabo, summoned by Chermayeff from Brooklyn College to complete his training, wrote, '[his] paintings are as wonderful as he is'.[75]

The value of this Foundation Course was, in Chermayeff's mind, set against the increasingly mechanical processing of large numbers of architectural students in other schools. 'The conventional curriculum is inadequate in time and content for the task', he wrote, 'and it is becoming apparent that the economy cannot employ the vast number of "degree" and "license" holders supposedly adequately trained for their exacting work in a contemporary industrial society.'[76] Even the architecture course itself tried to avoid too much specialism, declaring that 'it is not the sole purpose of the architectural department's training to produce specialists in this field alone'.[77]

In running an architectural curriculum on a more comprehensive scale than at Brooklyn, Chermayeff came close to realising his ideal of the integration of science and art, starting from first principles without reference to existing methods of architectural teaching. This was the first occasion when Chermayeff used the term 'Environmental Design' as a description for architecture in this wider frame, 'a designation of a wider spectrum of design and planning and modern technologies. That is: in reality to bring the original intention of Gropius up to date, and to make it possible for fresh minds to develop the methodology toward new purposes.'[78] One of the projects involved designing a house in a jungle or a desert, justified because it meant dropping all the preconceptions that would have arisen in a localised project. The result went a long way towards Chermayeff's aim of avoiding a self-conscious style. Projects illustrated in an article in 1948 include a two-storey row house on a 16ft plot, developed in terms of economy of labour and materials, for 'rest, play, view and traffic'.[79] This can be related to Chermayeff's pre-war concerns with the planning of domestic space, complete with all furniture, and the potential of the unit house. It also looks forward to his work on the relationship between house form and urban form. Advanced students worked on an apartment house project (similar to work done under Moholy-Nagy's directorship), working down from the unit of the whole block to the furnishing and equipment of a model apartment. Coping with larger numbers of students, Chermayeff became more systematic in his approach to teaching than he had been at Brooklyn. Students were introduced to their first achitectural problem in the fourth semester, when they had already mastered some aspects of technique and design methodology. As Chermayeff described the process, 'the problems of design are first broken down into their elements and thus presented to the student in intelligible form'.[80] One of the most revealing of the published designs is not for a building as such but a diagram, by the student Hal Esten, described as 'typical analysis of dwelling function, traffic diagram between activity zones'.[81] In its use of language as much as in its visual form, this diagram appears as a direct precursor of the ideas that Chermayeff developed at Harvard nearly ten years later, which were incorporated in his book, *Community and Privacy*.

Chermayeff invited Gerhard Kallmann (b.1915) to come from England and teach architecture, establishing a system of standardised building elements which would enable the development of flexible space and planning. In technical studies, Chermayeff's aim was to place the architect in a position of knowledge so that without taking over the function of specialist consultants, he could design with an anticipation and awareness of their contribution to a building, rather than asking them to provide technical support for something already determined. This was a development of Chermayeff's practice as a designer in London, particularly on the Gilbey Offices and the Blackley Laboratories.

A purely technical approach to architecture would have fulfilled the caricature-like expectation of 'Bauhaus' but this was balanced at Chicago by an element of imaginative creativity, which Moholy supplied in his lifetime and which was reinforced by Chermayeff's invitation to the Austrian architect and theorist, Frederick Kiesler (1890–1965), to teach at Chicago in 1950. Kiesler defined his position in 1949 in the words, 'Form does not follow function. Function follows vision. Vision follows reality.'[82] Although Kiesler was not a close associate of

Institute of Design, Chicago, Foundation Course, 4, 'Drawing discipline, ruling pen exercise' by Isobel Masmotte. 6, Composition in natural wood grain.

institute of Design, Chicago, Foundation Course, 'Architectonic space model for study of movement within the space' by Dorothy Riley.

Institute of Design, Chicago, Foundation Course, 'Entrance side of typical row house development' by Tetsuo Takayanagi.

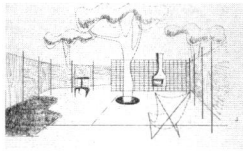

**Institute of Design, Chicago, Foundation Course, 'Perspective sketch of typical private outdoor area in row housing open to community park' by Tetsuo Takayanagi.**

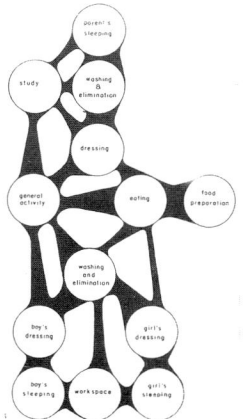

**Institute of Design, Chicago, Foundation Course, 'Typical analysis of dwelling traffic diagram between activity zones' by Hal Esten.**

Chermayeff, his position is interesting as one that Chermayeff himself may have sympathised with but have been unable to articulate through his own much more rationalist way of talking about architecture and design. As Yehuda Safran explains, 'Kiesler was seeking to embrace two contradictory impulses of our time: the notion that the deepest ground of our being is individual, and the equally strong desire for collectivity, to be achieved through the universality of experience. Kiesler's attempt to coordinate all dimensions and levels, what he called "continuity" and "correlation", was to overcome the dichotomy which characterised the entire Romantic movement and led to noble visions of fraternity as well as to terrible forms of collectivity.'[83]

Chermayeff's personal sympathy for the romantic does seem to have brought a genuine vigour and revival to the Bauhaus idea, even though it seems incompatible with his stricter pronouncements. No longer tied to Dessau by the personal histories of any of its staff, the ID introduced new elements and adapted to changing conditions. 'I think he was more liberal than the Bauhaus', Gerhard Kallmann says.[84] In 1951 the Institute was hoping to include film and television in its curriculum. Chermayeff explained:

> We are particularly anxious to extend our work in visual communications, which now covers all graphic, photographic and film media, into television. I do not feel, however, that this may be usefully done in a water-tight compartment; rather do I see this as part of a larger framework of mass communication study in which our visual emphasis would bring to other means and derive from these a useful pollinating effect.[85]

In 1952, following his resignation from Chicago, Chermayeff explained in a letter to Douglas Haskell how he felt he was carrying through the original ideas of Gropius from the 1920s in opposing an introverted and self-sufficient culture of architecture, but that Gropius himself had gone over to the enemy side:

> Gropius and Belluschi want to perpetuate the myth of the Architect's superiority. The Architect is to be the 'coordinator', the 'leader of the team' etc, etc. What endows the Architect, apparently automatically, with such advantages over his fellow-men? The fact of choosing the now-fashionable 'profession'? The traditional training, the validity of which is being questioned everywhere by honest educators? The ability to sketch charmingly? The claims to creative leadership can hardly be established ipso facto, on such a slippery basis. Architectonic genius is as likely to reside in an engineer or manager or scientist.[86]

As at Brooklyn, the Institute became involved in current local planning issues. In 1949, the invitation came from the large Chicago firm SOM (Skidmore, Owings and Merrill), with whom Chermayeff had friendly links, to mount an exhibition 'Chicago Plans', a typical scheme of its time inspired by CIAM thinking, showing the poor existing conditions of

**179**

crowded streets and noise in the city as a contrast to a utopian vision of linked slab blocks among trees with the Chicago River flowing through, making a traffic-free space with federal government, city and civic centres all brought together on reclaimed land where railway sidings and marshalling yards cut off the Chicago 'Loop' from the southern part of the city. The value of proximity to the existing railway stations was stressed, even at a time when cars were beginning to take over from train travel. It was not until 1973 that SOM produced a plan for this space that was adopted for action in the creation of Dearborn Park. The scheme itself is perhaps now less interesting than the lively exhibition design (see page 161).[87]

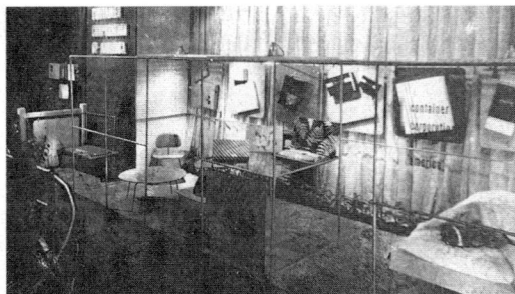

**Chicago Plans exhibition, 1949, panels.**

**Middle: Institute of Design, Chicago, Foundation Course, Group Project for Museum of Modern Art International Furniture Competition, Masonite and aluminium frame knockdown cabinet for easy shipment.**

**Left: institute of Design, Chicago, Foundation Course, 'Exhibition stand for the Container Corporation of America' by Robert Brownjohn.**

By 1950, Chermayeff had achieved a great deal at the Institute but there were also underlying causes of instability. The principal one was financial. During the first years of the returning GIs, there was a source of good, well-funded students. A new phase was inevitable and in 1950 Walter Paepcke felt that he had done enough to support the Institute of Design. He was interested in developing the summer school at Aspen, Colorado, as a new project. Chermayeff sympathised with him and they worked together to find other sponsors, but found that Foundations, while generally sympathetic, 'never understood either the contribution to liberal or professional educational implication [sic]'.[88]

Chermayeff's own personality also played a part. He said of himself, 'I could bring out the best in people by being ruthless. In other words, not tolerating anything under standard, top standard or nothing.'[89] The historian Alain Findeli writes that 'Chermayeff's relationship with the students was unsatisfactory, suffering from a lack of personal attention, availability and patience.'[90] People inevitably compared this to Moholy's less abrasive manner but as one of the students, Martin Myerson, wrote later, this had positive as well as negative aspects, 'Moholy was avuncular and supportive of his students. They were very devoted to him, but that benign approach did not always have helpful results. Serge, on the other hand, had tremendous bite. To some students it was devastating, but to others, as he marked up their near-finished drawings with a greasy pencil, the results could be electrifying. Brilliant students knew they had a brilliant master.'[91]

Hans Wingler, historian of the Bauhuas, writes that 'he achieved his authoritative position to a large extent by his astute criticism, in which he postulated the genuine and knew how to justify this criterion, rejecting whatever was half-conceived or imitative.'[92] Directly to Chermayeff, he wrote, 'I can only repeat again and again that in a most admirable way you differentiated and at the same time concentrated the curriculum of the ID. I know a lot of schools of design. The ID had in your time the best program which I know of.'[93] Even so, a journalist covering the fortunes of the school in 1955 later referred to Chermayeff solely in terms of his 'explosive and eloquent temper'.[94] Robert Wolff wrote to him personally in 1949, 'You are a strange guy and you know it. Any relationship with you is going to have its ups (very pleasant and rewarding) and its downs (more disagreeable than you yourself could possibly imagine).'[95] To quote Myerson again, 'Serge always reminded me of a Shakespearean character, larger than life. He also reminded me of a specific Shakespeare play, The Tempest. Serge himself was tempestuous.'[96] Chermayeff asserted himself intellectually among staff and visitors. Gerhard Kallmann recalls that 'whatever colloquium he would establish, whether with economists or scientists, Chermayeff always dominated them even in their field. Not just with verbal ability but intellectually – in his insights. He had very much of a focussed vision of what architecture should do.'[97] Kallmann also remembers the sparrowhawk that Peter and Babara Chermayeff kept at home, flying freely from room to room and swooping down on the heads of visitors from time to time. It seemed an apt familiar. As at Brooklyn there were staff he got rid of by one means or another. He deliberately had a violent argument with the well-known Russian-born sculptor, Alexander Archipenko, who was on the staff when he first arrived, and who consequently left.

One reason for the ambiguous historical record was Chermayeff's quarrel with Sibyl Moholy-Nagy, the widow of his predecessor, which resulted in her leaving her job as librarian and lecturer in 1948. The financial and personal aspects of the Institute's instability became linked and Robert Jay Wolff, while admitting that Chermayeff had made the Institute grow, wrote that it was 'crumbling under the pressure of internal strife and as a result of the disintegration that sets in when inexperienced but ambitious people lose the collective security that emanates from a powerful leader'.[98]

Against these adverse judgments, we can set many opinions of the high quality of the teaching and student work. Visiting around 1950, William Johnstone, the principal of the Central School of Arts and Crafts in London, who had developed his own highly successful course of 'Basic Design', recorded that 'The Chicago Institute still continues to be a school of ideas and along with the Frank Lloyd Wright Foundation is the most outstanding form of art education in America.'[99] Chermayeff noted with particular pride the special Silver Medal Award at the Sao Paolo Art Institute awarded in 1948 for an exhibition of the Institute of Design curriculum and examples of work and the 'almost clean sweep' of Institute students in a competition for industrially produced system furniture at the Museum of Modern Art, New York.[100]

The development of the Institute of Design took place against a background of growing conservatism in American art and society which made Chermayeff increasingly embittered as he swam against the tide in future years. A reviewer of the 58th Annual exhibition, 1947, of the Chicago Art Institute in *Progressive Architecture* (where Chermayeff was awarded a prize for his abstract painting, New York 2), wrote: 'If rumour had it that a wave of reaction was sweeping the country, and if designers have been considering retrenching in the face of a new conservatism, you can tell them to "come out now".'[101] This was only a temporary and localised respite, however. Despite its high standards, the Institute of Design looked too free and unacademic to more conventional eyes. As Paepcke and Chermayeff searched for an institution which would incorporate the Institute, their first discovery was that the President of the University of Chicago believed that art had no place in a university. Instead they settled on the Illinois Institute of Technology (IIT), which already had its own school of architecture under Mies van der Rohe (1886-1969), himself the third and final director of the Bauhaus in Germany. This was highly formalised, unlike the free-wheeling creativity of the Institute of Design. In spite of their differences of approach, Chermayeff claimed that he and Mies got on well together, partly, as he explained, 'because we both liked to drink'.[102] Indeed, during his visit to Chicago in 1941, Chermayeff claimed to have acted as a peace-maker between Mies and Moholy, who had used the name 'Bauhaus' illegally, in Mies's view. The merger was announced on 17 April 1950. On the other hand, Franz Schulze, Mies's biographer, claims that Mies was hostile to the Institute of Design during the presidencies of both Moholy and Chermayeff, and he was 'put off by the dubious efforts of . . . Chermayeff to insinuate architectural courses (called "shelter design") into an ID curriculum supposedly restricted to interior design'.[103] This is surely to misunderstand the intention at the ID to include architecture within the other design disciplines. The split between Mies and Chermayeff was, in effect, a replay of the unresolved issue at the original Bauhaus about the proper place of architecture in a general school of design. Mies always took its primacy and autonomy for granted, while Chermayeff and Moholy saw it as part of a continuous exchange of information and skills between different design fields. Mies and his teaching colleagues resisted the merger with ID but without success. At the outset, the two schools were administratively separate, but the authorities could see no justification for this and wanted an amalgamation. As Kevin Harrington writes, 'While this made sense to the administration at IIT, the fundamental difference in attitude between ID and Mies's curriculum was not understood by them, or if understood, thought to be inconsequential. Both Chermayeff at ID and the faculty in the architecture department reported their inability to make clear the philosophical differences of the two programmes to the central administration.'[104] In making recommendations for the Dean of the combined college, each side proposed candidates to their liking, with little hope of agreement.

Chermayeff's mood of antagonistic depression is evident in his lecture 'The Profession of Architecture', delivered at the Institute of Design on 2 November 1950, when the future was already looking clouded, over four months into the Korean war, with McCarthyism getting into its prime. Undeterred, Chermayeff attacked the President of the American Institute of Architects, Ralph Walker, for his forthcoming book, *Collectivism Versus Individualism*, which was a symptom of the right wing reaction in the USA, claiming that Walker 'sneers at every true issue and really has done nothing else but jump on the bandwagon of popular politics'.[105] In general, Chermayeff noted 'the passing of a brief age of clarity and the entering of a new age of babbling and confusion . . .'[106]

The difficulties of the new regime at IIT were increased by the attitude of Henry Heald, the President of IIT, and his successor J. T. Rettaliata who hoped that the Institute would offer cut-price design services to industry in return for sponsorship. This was totally incompatible with Chermayeff and his colleagues' educational aims. As Chermayeff believed, their intention all along had been 'to turn a subtle educational system for designers into a very crude catch all for "project grants" by local industry'.[107] There were additional problems over incompatible academic methods and standards, since the Institute of Design had continued Moholy's practice of not grading student work, and selecting students without high paper qualifications. Chermayeff's initial response was to appoint his wife Barbara as registrar 'because she knew what kind of students we wanted'.[108] The pressure from IIT was towards technical studies rather than the artistic and social aspects of the Institute's programmes that had previously prevailed.

Chermayeff related that he 'became quite unacceptable' with his 'constant complaints for their interference [sic], and was therefore forced to resign'.[109] He resigned as President of the ID at the end of the 1950–1 academic year while retaining his professorship until, on return from a visit to England, he finally cut all his ties with Chicago. No successor was appointed for three years, until Jay Doblin, a designer from the office of Raymond Loewy, was brought in to carry out IIT's expectations, amidst much complaint from the survivors of the earlier regime. Once Mies's School of Architecture building, Crown Hall, on the IIT campus was completed in 1956, the ID moved into its basement and its symbolic subjection was complete. Chermayeff commented later, 'I was very relieved I wasn't going to spend the rest of my life fighting two idiots', but it must have been an extreme situation to provoke this move.[110] In effect, Chermayeff was never again the head of his own institution after Chicago, probably because institutions feared his high principles, seemingly inseparable from his ferocious temper.

## Notes

1 Bankruptcy notices were published as follows: *London Gazette*, vol. 447, 13 June 1939, pp.4024-5 and 30 June 1939, p.4544; vol. 448 7 July 1939, p.4738; vol. 449, 10 October 1939, p.6840 and 28 November 1939, p.8009. Information from Tilson, 1984, p.31, fn.40. See also 'An Architect's Affairs', *The Times*, 24 June, 1939, p.3, which records liabilities of £4,929 against assets valued at £727.
2 Chermayeff to Lord De La Warr, 6 December 1938, Avery Library.
3 Information from conversation with Patrick Gwynne, October 1995 and letter from Maxwell Fry to Gavin Stamp, c. 1979.
4 See exchange of letters in Laura Cohn (1999). *The Door to a Secret Room: A Portrait of Wells Coates*, Aldershot, Scolar Press, pp.219-20. Announcement of competition, *Architects' Journal*, 16 March 1939, p.441, results 25 May supplement.
5 Reilly, open letter April 1939, Avery Library.
6 Felix J. Samuely, 'Aspects of A.R.P.', *Focus*, 3, Spring 1939, p.48.
7 The young architects Herbert Tayler and David Green bought four of the Thonet dining chairs. A fictionalised version of the empty Bentley Wood and the absent Chermayeffs occurs in the story 'Fin de Siècle' by Mollie Panter-Downes, one of Chermayeff's closest friends and wife of his Harrovian contemporary, Clare Robinson. First printed in the *New Yorker*, 12 July 1941, reprinted in *Good Evening, Mrs Craven: the Wartime Stories of Mollie Panter-Downes*, London, Persephone Books, 1999, pp.67-76. I am grateful to the author's daughter, Virginia Chapman, for drawing my attention to this reference.
8 *Builder*, 14 July 1939, p.50.
9 Rebecca West, 'The First Fortnight', *Ladies' Home Journal* (New York), January 1940, p.14.
10 Chermayeff to Anthony Jackson, 13 December 1963, Avery Library.

11 Temporary address on letter from Chermayeff to Ben Nicholson, 19 December 1939, Tate Gallery Archive 8717.1.2.690. The letter discusses how Nicholson could send examples of his work to the USA for exhibition and sale as part of the Chermayeffs' baggage: 'I truly hope that we shall meet again soon with lights blazing.'

12 G.R. Strauss to H. Gideonse (President, Brooklyn College), 17 February 1942, Avery Archive.

13 Chermayeff interviews with Richard Plunz, 1975-80.

14 Dates taken from Chermayeff's passport, family collection.

15 Notes of speech, Avery Library.

16 Barbara Chermayeff to John and Myfanwy Piper, from 1801 Highland Place, Berkeley, San Francisco, 9 August 1940. Copy kindly supplied by the late Myfanwy Piper.

17 ibid.

18 Lecture text, 'Crisis in Architecture', 18 September 1940, Avery Library.

19 See Marc Treib, ed.(1995), *An Everyday Modernism, the houses of William Wurster*, San Francisco Museum of Modern Art, p.165. In the interview between Chermayeff and Betty Blum (Chicago Architects Oral History Project, 1985), Chermayeff mentions 'fresh friends, people like Gardner Dailey, for instance', p.21.

20 Serge Chermayeff, 'Telesis, the birth of a group', *Pencil Points*, July 1942, p.45.

21 Chermayeff to John Piper, 14 November [no year given], kindly communicated by the late Myfanwy Piper. Datable to 1940 from internal evidence.

22 Barbara Chermayeff, letter to Ben Nicholson, 4 September 1940, Tate Gallery Archive, 8717.1.2.691

23 The date 1 September is taken from the Chermayeff interview with Betty Blum, p.118. In this, Chermayeff gives the year as 1941, but other evidence suggests that it was 1940.

24 Chermayeff to John Piper, 14 November 1940.

25 See testimonial by Morley for Chermayeff's application to Brooklyn College, reference below, note 35.

26 Chermayeff to John Piper, 14 November 1940.

27 Testimonial, see below, note 35.

28 Kizer to Chermayeff, 25 April 1941 Avery Library, filed under National Resources Planning Board.

29 Belluschi to Chermayeff, 14 November 1940. Copy of letter, Avery Library, filed under National Resources Planning Board. Chermayeff's proposal can be found in the MS, 'Outline for Planning and Design Department in a Western University', SC Box 5 (40-44). Later dated 1942/3 by Chermayeff, but almost certainly written in late 1940.

30 Chermayeff to Piper, 14 November 1940.

31 Catherine Bauer to Kenneth C. Warner, 3 March 1941.

32 'Frank really liked to torture people, so off they went with stainless steel cups and the latest picnic equipment and radios with loudspeakers which could pick up the symphony in New York and relay it and with tires blowing left and right. Everybody stripped in order to pull him out of a hole or whatever. He was standing by in a large straw hat admiring the sweating young men.' Chermayeff interview with Betty Blum, 1986, Chicago Architects Oral History Project, p.54.

33 See Morris Dorsky, (Chairman, Art Department, Brooklyn College of the City University of New York), 'Preface', *Brooklyn College Art Department, Past and Present 1942-1977*, organised by Mona Hadler and Jerome Viola, Brooklyn College, 1977, copy kindly provided by Professor Albert Szabo.

34 Chermayeff to Mumford, 18 August 1941, Avery Library.

35 Testimonials from Ian McAllister, William Holford, Dr J. L(eslie) Martin, Lewis Mumford, Grace L. McCann Morley, Lawrence Anderson, B.H. Kizer, Alfred H. Barr, Pietro Belluschi. The first three date from the summer of 1939. All became part of a cumulative CV, with additions from Harry Gideonse.

36 Mumford to Chermayeff, 10 November 1941, Avery Library.

37 Sibyl Moholy-Nagy to Ben Nicholson, 31 December 1941, Tate Gallery Archive, 87171.1.2.2983.

38 Chermayeff to Ben Nicholson, 1 October 1940, Tate Archive 8717.1.2.692.

39 Chermayeff recorded this attendance in various interviews. Date confirmed in Alain Findeli (1995), *Le Bauhaus de Chicago. L'oeuvre pédagogique de László Moholy-Nagy*, Sillery, Quebec, Editions du Septentrion, p.96.

40 Robert Jay Wolff to Hans Wingler, Director Bauhaus Archiv, 31 March 1976. Copy in Avery Library.

41 Gideonse, speech at Brooklyn College, May 1957, MS in Avery Library, SC Box 6 (55-59).

42 Tape 'Environmental Design is our task', Pidgeon Audio-Visual, 1980.

43 Serge Chermayeff, 'Excerpts from Report to the President of Brooklyn College 1942', Avery Library.

44 'Department of Design Brooklyn College. Excerpts from Report to the President of Brooklyn College 1942'. MS, Avery Library.

45 *Brooklyn College Bulletin*, 1946, 11.1 'Art centred on the 12th century', p.68.

46 Serge Chermayeff, 'The Social Aspects of Art', in Julian Harris, ed. (1946), *The Humanities: An Appraisal*,

University of Wisconsin Press, pp.141-2.

47 Serge Chermayeff, 'The Necessity of a Second Front', (October 21), 1942, *Observer-Kaleidoscope*, Brooklyn College, October 1942.

48 S.I. Hayakawa, 'The Revision of Vision', in György Kepes (1944), *The Language of Vision*, Chicago, Paul Theobald, p. 10.

49 See statement by Chermayeff dated 10 February 1947 in SC Box 6 (45-49) 1947, on the catalogue of the recent AAA exhibition, suggesting a new title acknowledging the new breadth of the organisation.

50 [Serge Chermayeff] *A Children's Center and Nursery School*, Revere Copper and Brass Inc., 1944 .

51 Blum interview, 1985, pp.26-7.

52 ibid., p.104

53 Karen Karnes to Chermayeff, 20 Sept [no year, c.1962], Avery Library.

54 Author interview with Professor Albert Szabo, Harvard, 24 September 1997.

55 See papers filed under N in Chermayeff correspondence, Avery Library.

56 Hudnut to Chermayeff, ASPA papers, Harvard University Archives.

57 Report to the executive, AGM, from sub-committee (Foreman, Haskell, Chermayeff and Stonorov), n.d. ibid.

58 Report to ASPA by New York Project Committee, February 1945. ibid.

59 George V. Allen to Mrs John Carter Vincent, 14 August 1959. Avery Library (under Joseph Rauh correspondence).

60 See 'Memorandum based on conversation between Mr Jalkut, Mr Abbott and Mr Chermayeff. Held at the Museum of Modern Art on March 11, 1943. Avery Library.

61 Chermayeff letter to Richard P. Lohse, Zurich, 26 December 1951.

62 ibid. Similar wording is found in the exhibition catalogue, Museum of Modern Art, *Art in Progress*, New York, 1944, p.194.

63 ibid., p.195.

64 Design for Use, 'Historical Data', MS, SC Box 5 (40-45), Avery Library.

65 Richard Plunz interview, Side 8, p.2.

66 Findeli, 1995, pp.141. Information from Moholy's letter to Paepcke, 31 July 1946, University of Illinois at Chicago Archives.

67 Chermayeff applied for leave of absence from Brooklyn in December 1946 and formally resigned in February 1947.

68 plunz interview, Side 8, p.2.

69 Paul Betts, 'New Bauhaus and School of Design, Chicago' in Jeannine Fiedler and Peter Feierabend (2000), *Bauhaus*, Cologne, Könemann, (English Edition), p.72.

70 Chermayeff to Hans Wingler, 6 October, 1957, Avery Library.

71 Blum interview, 1985, p.38

72 Peter Blake (1993), *No Place like Utopia*, New York, Knopf, p.94.

73 ibid., pp.45-6.

74 Serge Chermayeff, 'Fine Arts in General Education', contribution to conference at Midwestern College of Art, 10-12 November 1949, Avery Library.

75 Albert Szabo to Robert Wolff, n.d. Avery Library.

76 Serge Chermayeff, 'Chicago Institute of Design', text originally published in *L'Architecture d'Aujourd'hui*, February 1951, reprinted in Plunz 1983, pp.251-7.

77 Report to Board of Directors of the Institute of Design, 1947, Avery Library.

78 Chermayeff to Hans Wingler, 5 December 1977, Avery Library.

79 'Architecture at the Institute of Design', *Interiors*, November 1948, p.121. Design by Esten.

80 Serge Chermayeff, 'The Institute of Design integrates Art, Technology and Science', *Interiors* CVIII, September 1948, p.148.

81 'Architecture at the Chicago Institute of Design', *L'Architecture d'Aujourd'hui* X, February 1950, p.55.

82 Frederick Kiesler, 'Pseudo-functionalism in Modern Architecture', *Partisan Review*, July 1949, No.2, pp.733-42, reprinted in Yehuda Safran, ed. (1989), *Frederick Kiesler 1890-1965*, London, Architectural Association, pp.56-61.

83 Yehuda Safran, 'In the Shadow of Bucephalus', in Safran, 1989, p.10.

84 Gerhard Kallmann interview, September 1997.

85 Chermayeff to C.A. Siepmann, Department of Communications, New York University, 21 March 1951, Avery Library.

86 Chermayeff to Douglas Haskell (*The Magazine of Building*), 4 June 1952, Avery Library.

87 Made in collaboration with Homer Grooman, Don La Vine and Harry Smith. See Richard P. Lohse (1954), *New Design in Exhibitions*, New York, Praeger, pp.182-7.

88 Chermayeff to Hans Wingler, n.d. (c.1972), Avery Library.

89 Blum interview, 1985, p.107.

90 Findeli, 1995, p.142. [Author's translation.]

91 Martin Myerson, 'Reminiscences', letter to Peter Blake, 20 August 1979, Avery Library.

92 Hans M. Wingler(1978), *Bauhaus*, Cambridge MA and London, MIT Press, p.205.

93 Hans Wingler to Chermayeff, 18 October 1967, Avery Library.

94 John Chancellor, 'Institute of Design, the rocky road from the Bauhaus', *Chicago*, July 1955, p.34.

95 Wolff to Chermayeff, n.d. (c.1949). Avery Library.

96 Myerson, 20 August 1979.

97 Milne, 1996, p.35.

98 Robert Jay Wolff, letter to Charles E. Whitney, ed. *Industrial Design*, dated 4 November 1956, Avery Library.

99 William Johnstone, 'Survey of American Art Teaching Methods', n.d. MS in Johnstone papers, Lawrence Batley Centre for The National Arts Education Archive (Trust), Bretton Hall, W. Yorkshire.

100 Chermayeff to Hans Wingler, 5 December 1977, Avery Library.

101 Maude Kemer Riley, 'Art is Everywhere', *Progressive Architecture*, December 1947, p.8.

102 Blum interview, 1985, p.24.

103 Franz Schulze (1985), *Mies van der Rohe, a critical biography*, Chicago & London, University of Chicago Press, p.235.

104 Kevin Harrington (1986), 'Mies's curriculum at MIT' in *Mies van der Rohe: Architect as Educator*, Chicago, IIT, p.65.

105 Plunz, 1983, p.152.

106 ibid., p.157.

107 Chermayeff to Hans Wingler, n.d. c.1972, Avery Library.

108 ibid., p.44.

109 Richard Plunz interview, Tape 8, p.9.

110 Blum interview, 1985, p.81.

# 'Towards a New Architecture of Humanism': MIT, Harvard and Yale 1951–69

On leaving Chicago in the summer of 1951, Chermayeff made his first return trip to England, where the Festival of Britain coincided with the eighth CIAM conference in the Hertfordshire village of Hoddesdon. He lectured at the Institute of Contemporary Arts, recently established by Herbert Read and others in fulfilment of many of the cultural objectives of the 1930s. This lecture was described by Martin Myerson, one of Chermayeff's friends and supporters at MIT, as 'so brilliant and so meaningful that I remember all of his principal points after a decade'.[1] At the same time, Chermayeff renewed his contacts with London architects, some of them old friends like Wells Coates, others of a younger generation, such as H.T. Cadbury-Brown, one of the organisers of the CIAM conference, both of whom he invited to be visiting teachers at Harvard. He returned to take up a temporary teaching post at the Massachusetts Institute of Technology, in Cambridge, organised through the Chairman of Architecture, Lawrence Anderson. Chermayeff's Brooklyn colleague, György Kepes, was already teaching there. Chermayeff recalled, 'I had a wonderful year at MIT, with splendid students … which made me soon forget my sense of frustration of the later days of the Institute of Design.'[2] The students included Maurice Smith, later a Professor at the school, and the Indian architect Charles Correa. Chermayeff's teaching programme reflected the technical orientation of the school, with a study of solar heating systems and reflectors for use on tall buildings.[3]

This eastward move was welcome in that it placed the Chermayeff family closer to their summer cottage on Cape Cod than they had been in Chicago, or even when they first bought it in 1942, during their time in New York. The removal of onerous administrative duties enabled Chermayeff to set up a new architectural practice in Cambridge and build the Payson House at Falmouth Foreside, near Portland, Maine (described in Chapter 8), as well as a studio for himself near his cottage on the Cape.

Chermayeff's long-term ambition in coming to Cambridge was to teach at Harvard, where he had been informally offered a three-year contract by Hudnut in 1946, although he had turned down. Both Hudnut and Gropius, one of Chermayeff's staunchest allies, retired in 1952, the former being replaced as combined Dean and Chairman of the Graduate School of Design by José Luis Sert, from January 1953, on Gropius's recommendation.[4] He also recommended Chermayeff as one of the future members of faculty, and Sert worked to achieve his appointment, while Chermayeff offered suggestions for other teachers. The two architects even discussed finding a building plot which they could share.[5] The President of Harvard, Nathan

Pusey, had maintained a successful resistance to McCarthyism, and so Chermayeff was in a sympathetic liberal environment, at a time when Sert wished to relieve the severity of Gropius's curriculum with teachers more sympathetic to his own Corbusian background. The historian Siegfried Giedion (1893-1968) was a member of the faculty, and was soon joined by the Viennese architect and historian, Eduard Sekler, who worked successfully alongside Chermayeff, who valued his broad teaching of architectural history as a necessary background for students.[6]

The Graduate School of Design (GSD) took students with college degrees not necessarily in architecture. Chermayeff liked to insist on the special status and responsibilities that this implied. Visiting as a critic from Chicago early in 1951, he said in his summing up:

> I am a little bit suspicious of graduate schools, or any schools at all, which undertake to solve completely realistic problems. I would prefer to think of graduate schools generally as places in which great dreams are dreamed, where great concepts are formed and where great principles and performance standards are established, leaving it to the harsh realities of the thereafter to force compromise with one's conscience and with the financial possibility.[7]

Chermayeff himself chose to teach the first year and was given a free hand to invent a new course, and insisted that students from the three branches of the GSD – Architecture, Landscape and Planning – should all work together in his first year programme to achieve a shared base of knowledge and skill under the title 'Environmental Design'. This was not popular with the Professor of Planning, Reginald Isaacs but Chermayeff and his teaching team resisted incursions on their students' time. As at Chicago, he imposed tough standards and demanded a lot of work from students. The typical pattern of work which he developed over nearly ten years was to divide students into teams and set them research tasks. There was an emphasis on initial fact-finding, as Chermayeff described in an interview with Richard Plunz:

> A community plan ... would involve various aspects of a known and reachable environment – an exercise in reconnaissance to find out the major factors, physical and social, and to see whether they represent a special pattern to be encountered in a particular place chosen for the investigation, such as: patterns of movement, of pedestrians, of traffic, of places of encounter, of meeting places in communities, of various noise levels throughout the particular environment; to report and organise these various results obtained by students in small groups ... so that these might then be presented to the class at large who would share all the information so obtained.[8]

This was the first of ten exercises making a progression through simple individual structures, moving to a survey of existing 'housing clusters', and a study of windows for outlook and ventilation purposes, dealing with Chermayeff's theme of privacy. The fifth exercise examined stairs: 'outdoor stairs, indoor stairs, public stairs of ceremonial character to stairs of mundane daily use such as for school children on their way to school or just stairs or steps in a landscape which give you a particularly pleasant way of going from one level to another without fatigue.'[9] The emphasis on people as users of buildings continued through the study of 'Dwelling Cluster Design and Structure', as students looked for the determinants of different problems and their potential solutions. This was followed by a project on the design of private exterior space, an issue addressed in Chermayeff's pre-War houses and subsequently an increasing preoccupation, in which issues of landscaping and architecture were addressed together, with an emphasis on views into and out from the space. An interior design exercise was less domestic than technical, often taking the form of a demountable exhibition design. These exercises, all one week apart from the first which was longer, led to two extended studies, first 'The Planning and Sector Designs of a Community', an integration of the factors affecting movement, noise, and the contrast of places of quiet and 'places of intense use and community encounter.'[10] Secondly, 'typical groups of dwellings or the community as a whole' were presented in the form of models and drawings. Chermayeff recalled the intensity of work through the year, 'people didn't sleep much. We really kept pushing, and this had many rewards'.

The Environmental Design course combined specific local observation with a general approach to problem solving. Chermayeff hoped that this would give students a sense of realities outside the normally introverted world of an architecture school. The concentration on the home rather than on any other building type was typical of his thinking but he always placed this in a communal urban context. His main teaching colleagues on this course were the English planning expert, Jaqueline Tyrwhitt (1905–83), the editor, with Constantine Doxiadis, of the magazine *Ekistics* which sought a new breadth of vision in planning in line with the vision of Patrick Geddes and Lewis Mumford. Chermayeff described Tyrwhitt as 'A kind of walking human encyclopaedia of immense breadth of knowledge of both technical and planning and social and urban issues, which are rarely stored in one single mind.'

Tyrwhitt had spent the previous year collaborating with Sert and Ernesto Rogers (1909–69) on a publication of the proceedings of CIAM 8 (1951), on the theme 'The Core of the City', which formed a background to the GSD's attention to urban issues during the 1950s. The third member of the team, Albert Szabo, described her as, in many ways, Chermayeff's female equivalent, having a remarkable memory, highly refined critical faculties and an utterly blunt manner that almost matched his. Szabo, already noted as a student of Chermayeff at Brooklyn, had followed him to Chicago to continue his studies, later completing them at Harvard. He had gone back to Chicago to teach and remained there for three further years until invited back by Chermayeff to teach at Harvard. Within a few days of his arrival, Chermayeff said such devastating things to him in front of the students, that he sent his resignation in to Sert. The Dean convinced Szabo to withdraw his resignation, explaining that

Chermayeff had already caused two previous teaching assistants to resign, and that Chermayeff himself would have to be dismissed if it happened again. Chermayeff never apologised to Szabo but relations improved markedly thereafter.[11] Such behaviour was typical of Chermayeff. At least once he entered into a sort of collusion with a student, Bill Drake, explaining that he wanted to use him as the target of his abuse in order to make his educational meaning clear to the other students.[12] His own son, Peter, was one of the students, and performed well, without receiving any special treatment. As Martin Myerson describes it 'Studying with Serge might at times be painful; but studying with Serge has always been stimulating and memorable and often exalting.'[13]

One effect of Chermayeff's apparently rather humble position in the teaching hierarchy was that all students underwent his influence, with the result that his work had a more widespread influence than it might have had in other conditions. One of his students, Catherine Herzog Powell, wrote to him in 1971, regretting the later changes at Harvard, contrasted with 'the famous first year as taught by you, Al Szabo, and Jaqueline Tyrwhitt' with its 'clear message that this was the presentation to all students of "the tools of the design trade" so to speak'.[14] Richard Plunz writes that Chermayeff's courses 'became the glue which held the Graduate School of Design together'.[15] Martin Myerson wrote, 'every word, every look, every stroke of his pen, inside the studio or out, was a tool for teaching. His students were his pupils of course; but his friends, his professional peers (and few equal him), his family, his university colleagues were also privileged to be his students.'[16] Louis Bakanowsky, a student and later a teacher at Harvard, saw Chermayeff as an outstanding figure in the faculty:

> It was difficult not to admire him in those days, because he stood alone, often. Even as a student it was clear that he was solitary among the faculty. A lot of backbiting and competition that occurs in faculties anywhere was aimed at Serge here. And not for the highest reasons. But it was obvious to everyone that he was isolated. He did have a really interesting, innovative, programme that was working and he was solely in charge of. A lot of it was based on jealousy, I think.[17]

Chermayeff found himself increasingly in collision with Sert who would not accede to Chermayeff's requests for an enlarged teaching role, based on research.

Chermayeff was often at his best in a 'crit', a review of student work at the completion of a project. On these occasions, his comments could be most unforgiving but he was also apparently able to summarise a discussion memorably, cut through confused thinking and find exactly the right words to express a thought. He held regular seminars for first year students, in which he answered students' questions. Chermayeff was keen to have these taped and transcribed, perhaps feeling that some of his best ideas came spontaneously. By today's standards they are very one-sided affairs but a lively feeling still comes across.

Chermayeff was a troublesome member of Sert's team in other ways. On one occasion, while Wells Coates was teaching in 1956, Chermayeff left his briefcase behind after a meeting. Looking inside to identify the owner, Sert discovered a scheme for reorganisation of the GSD, with Chermayeff himself as chairman. He returned it with amusement but his conciliatory and pragmatic approach began increasingly to irritate Chermayeff who felt that the school was failing to set high enough standards, and was admitting students without sufficient ability. By the mid 1950s, Chermayeff was no longer content with his first year teaching and wanted to establish a research department at Harvard. He warned against 'the pitfalls of pseudoresearch when conclusions and premises are hastily arrived at and monuments built on a false base', but believed strongly in the real thing.[18] Design research was an almost mystical goal among English architects and design reformers who looked up to the left-wing scientists in London in the 1930s. Now in Harvard, he was surrounded by a community of researchers in many fields into which, he believed, architecture and planning should extend themselves. In a parallel venture, his old friend Leslie Martin, perhaps the only English architect with a doctorate in his subject, left the London County Council in 1956 to become Professor of Architecture at Cambridge, England. Here, one of his projects was to set up a post-graduate research programme, with a strongly mathematical and scientific basis.

The concept of research to PhD level was still unfamiliar in architecture, even though the GSD had been empowered to offer doctorates since 1950. In a paper in November 1953, Chermayeff proposed three main areas for possible research, the first being for architects to increase their skill in technical aspects of building services. The second theme, entitled 'The Core', as in CIAM 8, was 'as a theme for enquiry into the civic design of all times and at all levels of scale and purpose'.[19] After this came the study of housing and planning in under-developed areas of the world, a timely suggestion given the expansion of western firms and the increasing number of international students. He concluded his proposals with the belief:

> It is highly desirable that Design Research, clarification of elements and semantic aesthetics, as well as the refinement of visual sensibilities, should be carried on under the direction of world figures, artists and philosophers, such as Gabo, as a way to feed back through the Graduate School of Design a more serious understanding of the issues involved and a more disciplined approach to design than is generally now the case.[20]

Chermayeff had welcomed Naum Gabo and his wife when they landed in New York in November 1946, and offered the former a job at the Institute of Design, which was declined. Gabo did, in fact, teach at Harvard in the autumn of 1953 and spring of 1954, although he preferred to return to his own work thereafter.[21]

In 1955, Chermayeff submitted another paper on Design Research, more emotively phrased, stressing the importance of this work, its complexity and richness. He proposed a seminar of three hours per week, involving distinguished visiting scholars or practitioners, with studio activity. He also expressed caution about the development of teaching in the visual arts which materialised in the form of the Carpenter Center for Visual Arts, designed by Le Corbusier and opened in 1963. He could only imagine it having educational value if it was conducted in the form of a Bauhaus-inspired foundation course, involving craft workshops and design problems.[22] Two years later, as Chermayeff wrote to a friend in New Zealand in the summer of 1957, 'my own advanced work plans at Harvard thwarted for the coming year – and I remain in charge of the kindergarten.'[23]

Chermayeff found scope for his research in the Joint Center for Urban Studies, a project shared between Harvard and MIT, and directed by Martin Myerson. It was through the Joint Center that Chermayeff developed the work which culminated in the publication of his book with Christopher Alexander, *Community and Privacy* in 1963. One preliminary step towards it, following on from Chermayeff's earlier work for the MOMA exhibition, 'Tomorrow's Small House', 1945, was the Harvard Patio House, developed by Chermayeff and a group of his students and launched in 1957 with a press release and some coverage in magazines for the general reader. This was a single-storey courtyard house concept, intended to provide some of the benefits of suburban low-density without their adverse effects in terms of land use. It may have developed in part from a genuine project for developing a site in Bowdoin Street, Cambridge, on a corner with Hudson Street, surrounded by conventional free-standing houses of various dates. Here twelve small houses were intended to be grouped on a site that normally would have held three at most. Drawings show variants on the architectural form, such as concrete barrel vaults, which do not figure in the more diagrammatic models publicised in 1957, but the concept of the houses is part of the same exploration.[24]

As Chermayeff wrote, 'The front yard on most conventional houses is an expensive and useless facade. The equally useless setbacks around the house tend to become dirty alleys, noise traps and difficult parking lots. The city dweller needs and prizes green space, trees and the peace that is associated with natural growth. He doesn't obtain them from the yards of most conventional houses. To reap the full advantage of such areas, they need to be incorporated into the home, not lie outside it.' To these advantages, he added his favourite themes of privacy in the home and zones of silence. On another occasion he described the alternative more graphically as 'the American open plan, in which television, radio, the screaming child, homework, reading, mother, father, grandfather, all find their uneasy kind of being – this sort of human garbage pail sort of plan'.[25]

The proposal to remove the 'front yard' and 'porch' from the American house was a radical break with the practice of the previous hundred years, and for this reason had little appeal to the normal home buyer, but Chermayeff justified it on the grounds that the noise and smell of the passing cars had made the front porch no longer a pleasant place to sit, and the front yard no longer the proper site for ceremonial arrivals and departures, as it once had been. 'When the little town with its porches facing the little quiet street with promenading people under lovely shade trees planted in memory were there, when all these contacts were made at this kind of first-hand level, this was all very fine. But now we have a tremendous disruption of this kind of thing'.[26] After several decades of intense car traffic, the standard form of the American suburban house has indeed reflected the inhospitable character of the street by presenting a garage door and little else towards the street.

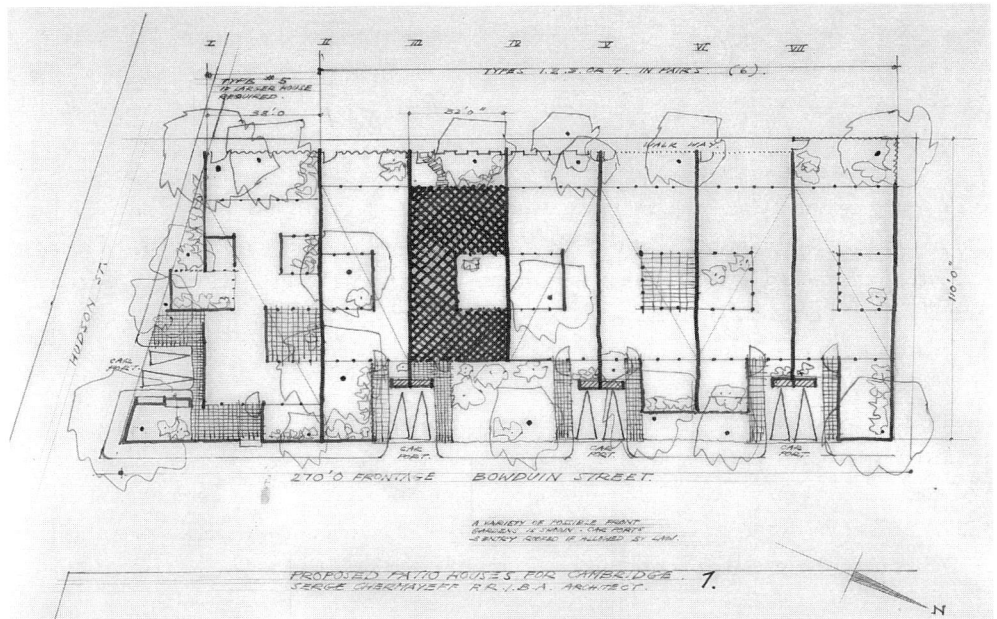

**Bowdoin Street housing project, 1956, site plan.**

Why should the patio house have absorbed so much of Chermayeff's attention during this period, to the exclusion of other types of housing, let alone other types of building? We can see his interest developing from the time of the Kernal unit houses of 1933 but perhaps it can be traced even further back to the many single-storey houses in Grozny at the beginning of the century. More recently, a number of architects had demonstrated the value of turning the free-standing villa form of modernism 'outside in', beginning, perhaps, with Le Corbusier's house for his parents on Lac Leman of 1923, even though this was designed to control access to the beautiful view, rather than to prevent overlooking by neighbours. The incipient courtyard form of the Mendelsohn and Chermayeff project for Frinton of 1936, and the more pronounced enclosure of outdoor space at Bentley Wood have been noted as forerunners, while Chermayeff's two houses in California – discussed in the following chapter – both established a definite relationship between the house and the space around it, although this was normal for small modern houses by architects, such as the California Case Study houses. The 'binuclear' character of the plan of the Mayhew House of 1942 established Chermayeff as an early exponent of the idea of breaking up the mass of the house, although in that instance the levels on the site were conducive to splitting the house in two. This was one of the principal determinants of a new type of patio house in the 1950s. In writing a history of the courtyard house in 1973, Duncan Mackintosh listed a succession of plans by architects in New England which would have have been known to Chermayeff and which would possibly have been influenced by his concerns, such as the linear patio house plans of Morse Payne, a member of TAC (Gropius's firm, The Architects' Collaborative), in 1956, and José-Luis Sert's house in Cambridge of 1958 which was binuclear in plan, with a central atrium. Richard Plunz describes the Harvard Urban Houses as 'perhaps the only really "new" low-rise house-type to be produced since the nineteenth century row house', an opinion which helps to justify Chermayeff's obsession with this form.[27]

The schemes for patio houses by Chermayeff and his students were never in the form of a complete, four-sided courtyard, but were instead divided into three or four nuclei with pockets of garden in between, so that the outdoors was in a dynamic relation to the rooms, achieving acoustic insulation and outdoor space that could be adopted by individuals or groups in the household. These forms emphasise the importance which Chermayeff attached to privacy and the elimination of noise from the home.

While such concerns were evident in his diagrammatic explanation of Bentley Wood in 1939, recent social changes had made this an issue of increasing importance. The 'invention' of the teenager in the post-war years was accompanied by portable record players and transistor radios, as well as television. The modernist ideal of the open plan house was ill-adapted for all the occupants of a growing family. Parents, adapting more slowly to social changes, probably still wished to retain seclusion and some formality in the home, requiring a differentiation of territory. The psychological mood of the 1950s, with the semi-permanent state of cold war, may also have encouraged a turning inwards from the optimistic transparency. More obvious factors were the increasingly extended commuting journeys and the decline in public transport which meant that more cars were using the roads at rush hours. To prevent this in a period of rising population, more houses would be needed at higher densities in the inner suburbs. The Bowdoin Street scheme opened up the possibility of using the internal space of a building lot much more economically by grouping the car spaces at one end of the site, with a pathway between the houses, not revolutionary in terms of modernism but still a provocative gesture in 1950s America. The idea of freeing the immediate surroundings of the house from traffic was developed in schemes such as Radburn, New Jersey, by Henry Wright (1878–1936) and Clarence Stein (1882–1975) in the 1930s, and commended by their colleague Lewis Mumford. Some of the student projects from the Chicago Institute of Design show patio houses with access to communal public spaces, not unlike those provided in the houses by Stein and Wright at Sunnyside Gardens, Queens, in the late 1920s, but this aspect of the planning idea seems to have been dropped from Chermayeff's later theoretical proposals. The

Bowdoin Street housing project was accompanied by a diagram with two parallel lines of verbal description, showing the flow of people through the different 'realms' of the house from the street at one side and pedestrian footpath on the other, with the house designated as a container in the centre with its own internal variations between zones of privacy for parents and children, and their shared 'hearth' in the centre.

The patio house evidently commended itself to Chermayeff as a pedagogic device, as it provided a focus on the social planning of space in a form which did not require any great knowledge of building construction. He felt that it was a microcosm of all other forms of planning, saying:

> I suspect that the more architects think in this more or less abstract way of the general good of humanity at all stages of its development, the more they will recognise the extraordinary similarities and continuities in our life at all scales ... It [was] with this notion of variety in expression but similarity in principle that I would leave the final jury of the year in environmental design: a particular solution but at the same time a generalised purpose to be kept in balance during the processes of design.[28]

The newspaper launch of the Harvard Patio House created only a mild effect. In the summer of 1957, Chermayeff talked of having a publisher and planned to write through the vacation 'in the hope of producing something acceptable (and lucrative)'.[29] This was a proposal for the publishers, Harcourt Brace, with a wide-ranging content, drawing on lectures given and articles published since his arrival in the States.[30] There is no evidence that Chermayeff carried this project through but several parts of the Harcourt Brace proposal went towards the book *Community and Privacy, Towards a New Architecture of Humanism*, by Chermayeff and Christopher Alexander (b.1936), published by Doubleday in 1963. A further ingredient came from 'The Urban Family House Project' issued as a mimeographed text in 1959, which became the section in dealing with the courtyard house, on which Alexander worked. He was a young English architectural student, of Viennese birth, who had come from Cambridge to Harvard on a scholarship to be one of the first PhD students in the GSD. He was already recognised as a brilliant mathematician, but was at odds with his architectural training at Cambridge. His presence was a stimulus to Chermayeff, and something of their 'rubbing minds' (to use one of Chermayeff's phrases) can be seen in an annotated copy of 'The Urban Family House Project' in the archives of Yale University.[31] Chermayeff reflects on the theme of the eventual book that man cannot necessarily change in accord with developing technology, 'There are limits beyond which man may not safely be changed – and it is our belief that certain presently existing forms threaten to jump these limits, to induce changes in man that are not permissible.'[32] Alexander seems to have been particularly strong on methodology, writing that 'our purpose is to work our way to pressures so specific that they are obvious and unequivocal; and need no support from argument.'[33]

The introduction to *Community and Privacy* was written by the poet Kenneth Rexroth, defining the book's wider purpose as 'the creative reconstruction of our ecology'. 'Ecology' (first coined by the German biologist Ernst Haeckel in the previous century) was the word Chermayeff used when speaking at the AA in London in 1939, long before it became fashionable, but by the beginning of the 1960s it was beginning to take on its present significance. It may be appropriate to remember that the Greek root of the word means 'house' or 'home', and Chermayeff used his book to demonstrate that the right relationships of space in the home can form a pattern for a larger scale in society. The eight sections of the first part, 'Mass Culture', surveyed contemporary America and described the shortcomings of its way of life, which had their effects in urban and domestic design. The opening quote in the section 'Background', from Kenneth E. Boulding speaking at Harvard in 1960, used the term 'post-civilisation' to describe the immediate future condition. Further quotes, spread over three pages, moved from Patrick Geddes and Le Corbusier to James Thurber, and thence to President John F. Kennedy. These excerpts, used effectively through the book, indicate the breadth of Chermayeff's reading in literature, popular science and current affairs.

The broad statement of the problems of over-population is followed in the second chapter by a discussion of 'Vanishing Nature', opening with the observation that 'Elderly persons who regret the passing of the urbane way of life have observed with equal pain the increasing penetration of the countryside by the car, the helicopter's invasion of the wilderness, and the disappearance of plants and beasts they loved well. They have witnessed the passing of many intimate contacts with nature which, like the arts, once gave them unequalled pleasure.'[34] Chermayeff invoked an unspoiled natural or man-made environment that we have since ceased to hope for, writing of 'the tragedy of tourist buses in the piazzas of Tuscany or Coca-Cola barges on the Grand Canal of Venice'. Under the subheading 'A New Ecology', the then novel idea of a total control of the environment on earth was related to the sense of responsibility not to create further destruction, so that the more pessimistic disaster plans for 'survival capsules' did not have to be implemented. The third chapter moved into the issue of the city, once more invoking through Chermayeff's own lifetime memories, the more civilised urban world he had known. 'Some people are old enough to have enjoyed the life of urbanity that existed in the well-defined, individual cities of the past. They remember these cities as possessing forms and characteristics which were peculiar to each, as being capable of rousing memorable delights or even positive – not apathetic – delight.'[35] It was a call for a better-defined urban environment with a sense of visible order.

The fourth chapter is entitled 'The Suburban Flop', and considered the shortcomings of the meeting place of town and country. This was part of the growing criticism of the American way of life through books such as William H. Whyte's *The Organisation Man*, 1956, echoing similar, often snobbish, criticism of the English suburbs by architects of all persuasions in the 1930s. The prefatory quotations to this chapter range from the eighteenth century English architect, Isaac Ware, claiming that 'The art of building cannot be more grand than it is useful; nor its dignity a greater praise than its convenience', to an article 'Good-Bye suburbs' of 1958 by Mary McLaughlin, announcing the author's return to New York city, 'Those fierce canyons hold no terrors for me: I've known the battlefield of Suburbia and I'm not going to re-enlist.'[36] In a statement parallel with research being conducted at Cambridge, England, under Leslie Martin, the chapter ends with the claim that 'If the total land area were to be carefully planned for maximum use at every scale, the inner city could accommodate both vertical buildings for all-purpose use and short-term occupancy, and dwellings on the ground for families with children. Such dwellings on the ground could, as functioning parts of the urban technological context, succeed where suburbia has failed.'[37] Improved privacy was a historical reason for preferring the lower densities of suburban development to urban forms. The proposals at the end of *Community and Privacy* aimed to show that through intentionally designing for this end, the advantages of privacy could be maintained at much higher density. As summarised in Chermayeff's later book, *Shape of Community*, 'the idea that this desirable state could only be obtained in areas of low density was demonstrated to be illusory; the book argued that design could produce the desired results anywhere.'[38]

**Urban patio house plan.**

**Right: Peter Chermayeff, 'Noise', chapter-opening graphics for *Community and Privacy*, 1963.**

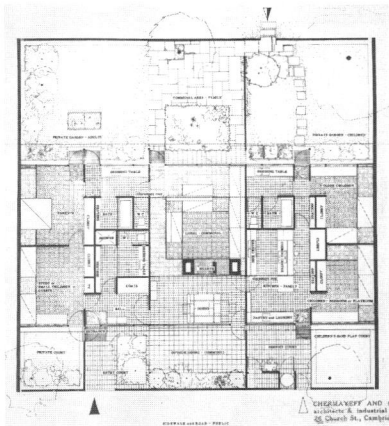

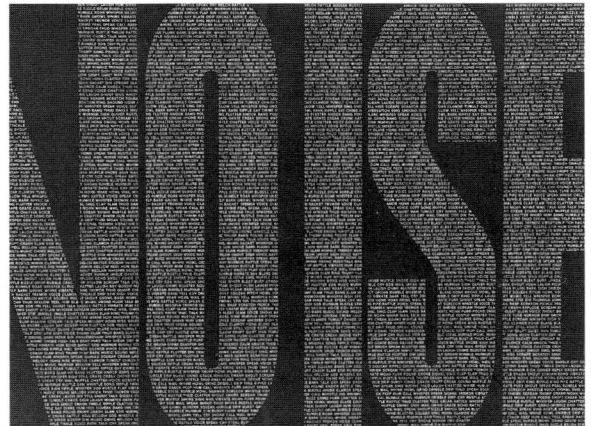

Chapter Five, 'In Search of the Small' deals with the boredom and depression induced by the uniformity of 'the air-conditioned nightmare', leading on to 'Enemy Number One: Car'. This was a relatively early incidence of what has since become a commonplace, although it is ironic that in 1961 Chermayeff was commissioned to write an article on 'the automobile as an object' in which he fondly recalled 'my young road-racing days in the twenties' as the 'peak of excellence in car design'.[39] Enemy number two is noise, much of it produced by cars but then overlaid by radio and television. This was Chermayeff's particular preoccupation, not necessarily widely shared by a younger generation. It recalls his intolerance of Mendelsohn's Bach recordings in their London office, and his concern to give the Gilbey building acoustic isolation. Control of noise was one of the main justifications for his preferred form of patio house.

Chapter Eight, 'Faith and Reason', is a hinge point in the book, where the solutions begin to appear. It concentrates on the value of design method rather than 'taste', in a reprise of familiar modern movement doctrine which was nonetheless a necessary reminder at a time when these ideas had become corrupted or lost their appeal. In the new conditions of the 1960s, Chermayeff and Alexander proposed that problem solving had now become much more complex than before, and yet, as the chapter title suggests, there was a non-scientific dimension to getting the right approach, not without a touch of professional arrogance: 'A commitment of faith is not less valuable for being a personal commitment or, as it is sometimes termed, a prejudice. Presumably, it is the prejudice of a highly skilled and gifted individual able to sort out the particular aspects of his culture that need, to be reflected in form.'[40]

This leads into the second half of the book, which begins on the scale of the city with a proposition about the specific uses of particular spaces, and their corresponding position on a scale between public and private. This is explored through a number of worldwide traditional and vernacular building forms, leading to an explanation of the inadequacy of the standard suburban house, particularly when provided with a modern 'open plan', so visually beguiling but unconcerned with the sense of hearing and the question of personal space. The link is made back to the city through the need to connect the private to the public in a more effective way. From Chapter 11, 'The Problem Defined' onwards, the design methodology begins to become clearer, showing how, in words Chermayeff used in describing his pre-war practice, 'no problem is too small to receive attention'. The radical nature of this process is to challenge some of the received meanings of words such as '"Apartments", "row houses", "single-family houses", "yard", "garden", "garbage", "parking lot", "living room", "kitchen", "dining room", "bedroom", "bathroom",' which, as the authors comment, 'are all heavily loaded words that make any number of irrelevant images spring to mind. Designer and user alike may imagine that these words stand for something immutable, though in fact they are just names for the familiar'. This goes on to describe how the meaning of the word 'house' had been broken down into components by Chermayeff in the course of his seminars since 1952, to which Alexander had contributed since 1960. The proposition 'Every problem has a structural pattern of its own' is an important demonstration of the revision of categories and their spatial manifestation. The chapter lists 33 'basic requirements' for the entry area to a family house, from 'efficient parking for owners and visitors; adequate manoeuvre space' to 'partial weather control between automobile and dwelling' and then proceeds to plot their intersections on a chart, where two 'requirements' coincide, showing the overlapping aspects of function.

From this, a broader pattern can be deduced but, the authors suggest, this cannot be done only by eye, experience or intuition. The requirements are so numerous that only a computer can process it, 'The IBM 704 computer at The Massachusetts Institute of Technology, given appropriate instructions, found the major cleavages for our attachment problem in a few

Peter Chermayeff, section opening spread design, Ch.9, 'Anatomy of Urbanism', *Community and Privacy.*

minutes. A galaxy on closer scrutiny is seen to be composed of stellar systems. The collection of thirty-three items given on our list is similarly arranged: apparent chaos is resolved into coherent groupings.'[41]

**Apparent Chaos, the problem structured',** *Community and Privacy.*

**Right: 'Diagram of interaction between the thirty-three requirements of the problem',** *Community and Privacy,* **p.163.**

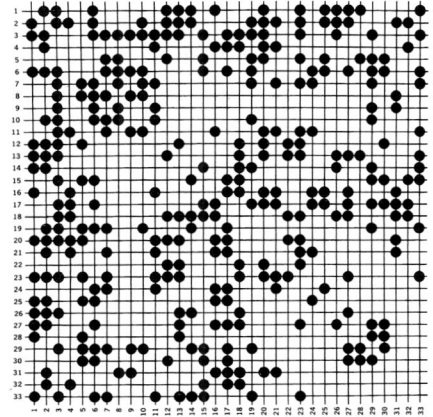

Such an early use of a computer in design work now appears primitive, but it was in character that Chermayeff should have welcomed the new possibilities, encouraged by Alexander's own mathematical mind. He felt that the discipline the computer required of asking the right questions was 'long overdue in a profession which has adopted attitudes and made pronouncements on very slender evidence indeed'.[42] Alexander shared his view about the arbitrariness of current architectural aesthetics, in his own case arising from the architecture course at Cambridge under Leslie Martin, which he felt represented a formalistic ossification of the principles of modernism.[43] Alexander recalled that in their work together, he and Chermayeff listed more and more 'requirements', sticking them on a noticeboard on the wall, until he felt that Chermayeff was overwhelmed by the complexity of the problem.[44]

The rather abstract use of the computer begins to become more real as the analytical technique is applied more graphically to the chosen problem of the small house, leading to a series of critiques of real and imaginary planning schemes, examined under a small list of criteria and adjudicated. In the following chapter, the nature of the transitions from one type of space to another is examined again, with the introduction of the concept of the 'lock' (by analogy with rivers and canals rather than with keys and doors) which can be introduced to improve the privacy aspects of a house plan without necessarily sacrificing useful space, provided its multiple possibilities are kept in mind. A series of plans is examined, some of them by Chermayeff and his students offering alternative design solutions.

The final chapter 'New Planning Blocks' is the most original, with its opening graphics demonstrating a 'sequence of development from the barrier to the lock.'[45] A later one, 'the lock emerges as a realm and an activity zone'[46] shows how dynamic and original the whole process of analytical thinking can become, by re-allocating functions from one part of the house to another. This perhaps contains a distant recollection of Chermayeff's planning of the Heywood-Lonsdale apartment in 1937, where convention was not allowed to stand in the way of the best uses of the space.

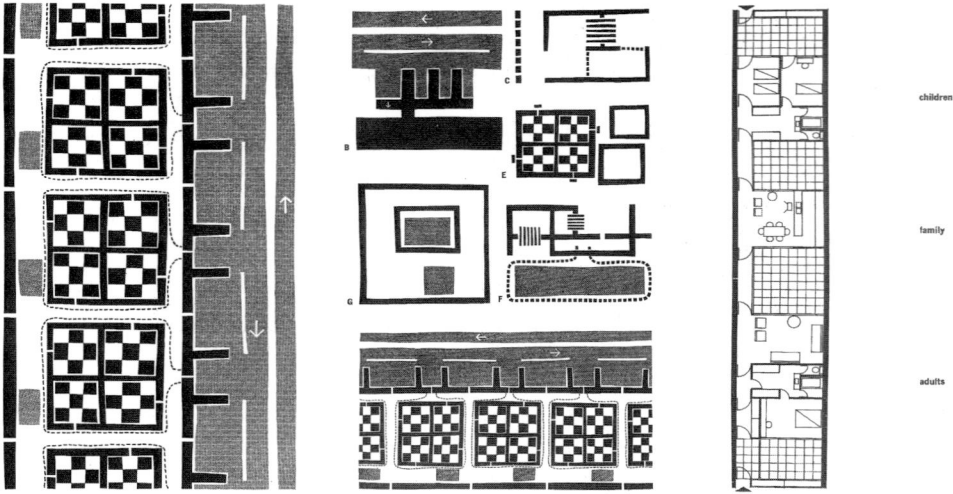

Far left: 'Composite Diagram', *Community and Privacy*, p.175.

Middle: House clusters: B 'Solid wall of alternating transfer points', C 'Entrance lock', E 'Inner nature of the cluster - open and closed space', G 'Cluster surrounded by pedestrian circulation', F 'Service zones', *Community and Privacy*, p.183.

Left: Court House, Harvard, design by Robert Reynolds and Serge Chermayeff, *Community and Privacy*, p.226.

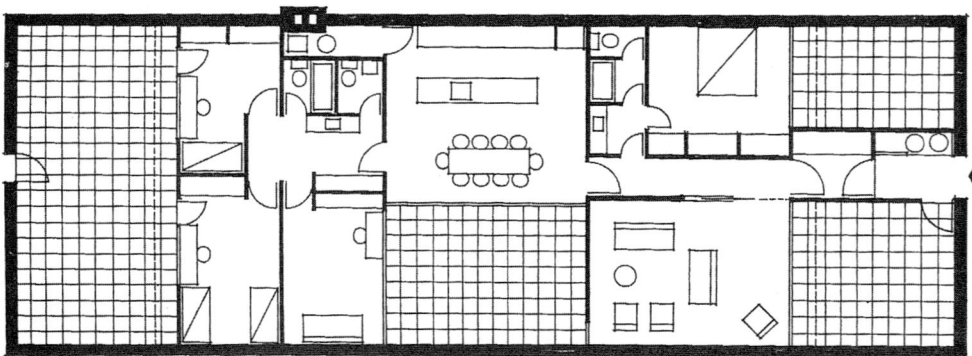

Court House for a Cluster, design by Serge Chermayeff, *Community and Privacy*, p.224.

The operations described in the book appear so simple that their significance may easily be overlooked. Richard Plunz sees them as the 'logical result of fifteen years of experimentation with programmatic structure', recognisably linked to the diagram of zoned uses at Bentley Wood, with its 'intermediate language' bridging the gap between verbal functional requirements and the final built form, a language whose task is to be sufficiently abstract and generalised as to be suggestive of new possibilities.[47]

Opposite: Urban Cluster, design by Christopher Alexander, John Meunier, Peter Chermayeff, Robert Reynolds and Alden Christie, *Community and Privacy*, p.196.

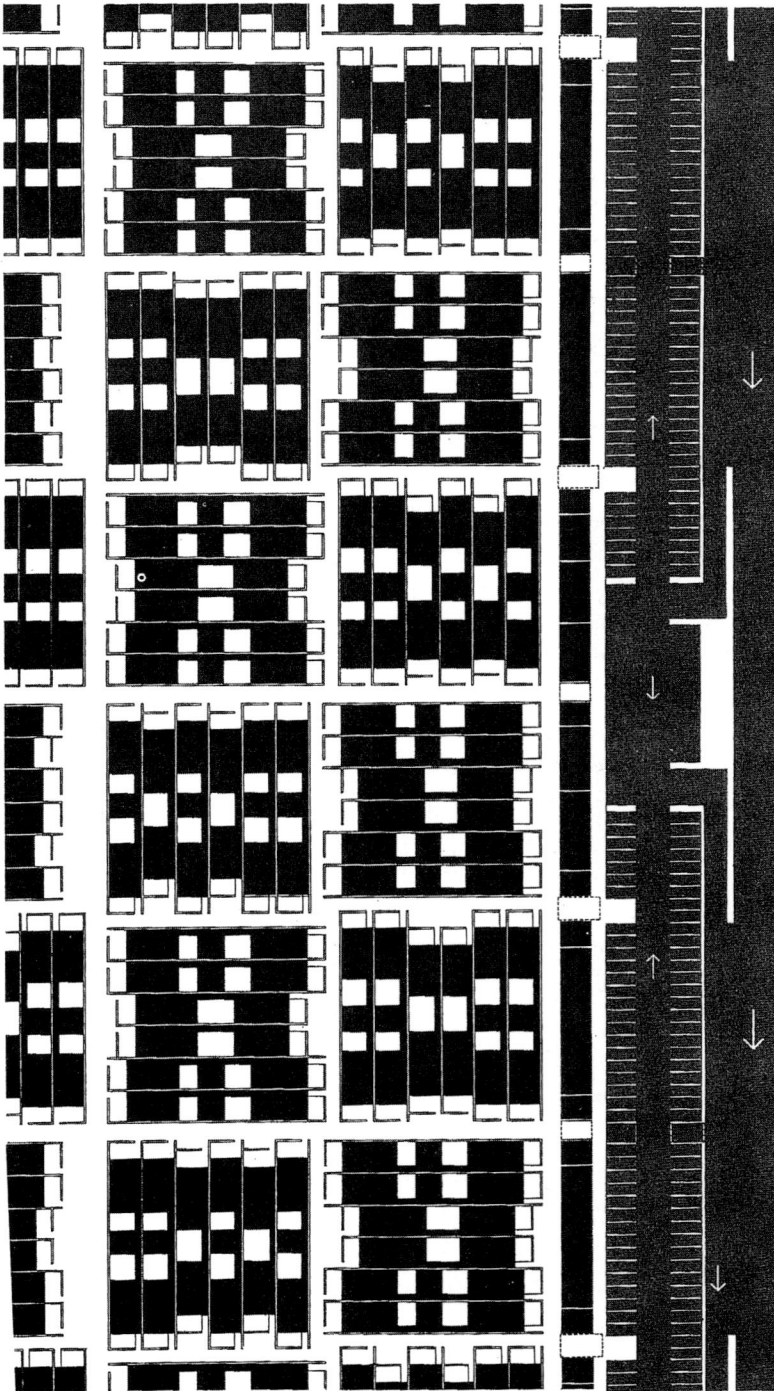

entry

doorbells, mail, waiting

community space


emergency access

tenant bulk storage

cart storage

entry
doorbells, mail, waiting

vending machines,

laundromat

service entry
garbage

shop and maintenance
equipment storage

cart storage
entry
doorbells, mail, waiting

community gathering


emergency access

tenant bulk storage

cart storage

entry
community gathering

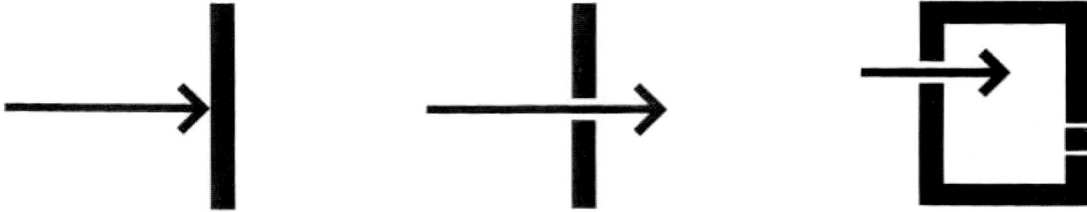

'Diagram of sequence of development from the barrier to the lock', *Community and Privacy*, pp.230-1.

Chermayeff made a summary of the contents in a letter to Saul Steinberg (1914–99) in October 1960, seeking permission to use his drawings, 'It is a polemic against the Look-Listen and auto-crazy culture with some professional remedies coming at the end in a desperate attempt to kill artiness as well with the same prophylactic (stone)! I won't paraphrase myself except to tell you that I am deeply concerned as a planner with Vanishing Nature, the atrophy of first-hand experience for man, and the suburbanisation of the human habitat.'[48]

*Community and Privacy* is thus almost two books in one, a statement of a general problem, and a much more specific form of solution. As a number of reviewers remarked, the emphasis is much more on privacy, particularly in the second half, than on community. Its 'New Architecture of Humanism' sounds all too readily like misanthropy, reflecting Chermayeff's own ideas about the need for a defensive family unit, in which well-being depends on the ability of individuals to get away from each other. This emphasis on a personal as well as an architectural interiority is one of the consistent themes of his design career. As he explained in a preface for the Italian and Japanese editions in 1967, 'a model yardstick was deliberately limited to the neglected Private end of the spectrum', since he was already projecting another book to cover 'the Community end to the Metropolitan area scale'.[49] The word 'community' had been emphasised by Paul and Percival Goodman in their book *Communitas*, published in 1947, and Chermayeff sent Percival Goodman a draft of his text, which Goodman applauded as 'an old urban dweller, an exponent of the architecture of streets and a believer in land conservation'.[50] On the other hand, the new exponent of traditional street forms, Jane Jacobs, whose book, *The Death and Life of Great American Cities* was published in 1961, wrote to Chermayeff that, 'this second theme you deal with is, to put it baldly, how to make denser suburbs for people professing the values, needs and standards of middle-class professionals. I do not really think it has much greater application than that.'[51] If its prescriptions were followed, she felt that the problems she was addressing of the alienating quality of public housing projects might indeed be intensified. There is indeed a sense of academic detachment in *Community and Privacy*, along with a determination not to see all sides of the question. In a correspondence with Marshall McLuhan, the Canadian pioneer of media studies, Chermayeff wrote, 'You suggest that architectural form might become especially expressive of the new forces at work. I suspect that the opposite would be advantageous. I retreat from continuing pressures of communication into undated solitude and simplicity.'[52]

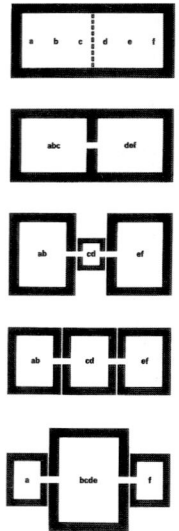

'The lock emerges as a realm and activity zone', *Community and Privacy*, p.234.

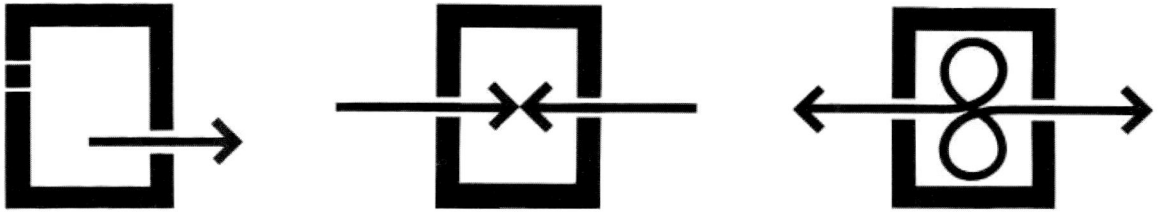

The book was designed by Peter Chermayeff to a generous page size. Bold double-page graphics opened each chapter, drawn lettered and photographed, representing concepts such as noise, nature and hierarchy. There are a number of cartoons by Saul Steinberg, whose work Chermayeff greatly admired. Specially drawn plans of cities illustrate their variety of abstract form, and towards the end of the book specimen plans of houses are joined to graphic demonstrations of thought processes and transformations in planning, some graphically presented as systemic loops. Many of these features were unfortunately lost in the Penguin paperback edition, issued in 1966, through which *Community and Privacy* became most widely known.[53]

As Bernard Rudofsky noted in reviewing *Community and Privacy* for *Domus* magazine, it was one of a number of books of its time attacking aspects of the American way of life. The devastating effects of man on nature were beginning to worry many people. In 1962, Rachel Carson published *Silent Spring*, one of the landmarks of the environmental movement, and one of the many texts quoted in *Community and Privacy*. There was a growing concern about the deterioration of city life, expressed in the book *The Exploding Metropolis: A study of the Assault on Urbanism and How Our Cities Can Resist It*, 1957, with contributions by William H. Whyte, Jane Jacobs and others. The movement for the conservation of monumental urban buildings was just beginning, and although Chermayeff was never very active in this field, he was persuaded by Douglas Haskell, the editor of *Architectural Forum*, to write a letter in support of the retention of Grand Central Station concourse, New York, in 1955, referring sentimentally to the position 'under the clock' as the site of lovers' trysts, and knowing that 'it would be difficult to recreate again, except after the passage of many, many years, an equivalent symbol and familiar place.'[54] On a more personal level, he was active in seeking the designation of Cape Cod as a National Seashore Park in 1960 in the early period of the Kennedy presidency, following a threat to build a nuclear power station on the Cape. In his development of *Community and Privacy*, he not only displayed his own lifelong love of the direct experience of nature, but also the warnings of Marshall McLuhan about the growing substitution of vicarious experience of the world through new media.

Alexander Tzonis places *Community and Privacy* in a context with Thomas Kuhn's *The Structure of Scientific Revolutions*, 1962, J.K. Galbraith's *The Affluent Society*, Michael

Harrington's *The Other America*, and Kevin Lynch's *The Image of the City*, all of which in differing ways were critiques not only of American society, but of the inherited belief systems on which it had developed in the previous century, without actually casting aside a basis of scientific rationalism, as did many of the counter-cultural movements of the later 1960s.[55]

Four years after the notorious lament over the split between the arts and the sciences in C.P. Snow's lecture, *The Two Cultures*, *Community and Privacy* was a convincing demonstration that in architecture at least, each could contribute towards a common social purpose. It reflected new ideas about the role of science as a study of the nature of connections between things, such as the principles of Cybernetics, promoted by Norbert Wiener in his book of that name in 1948 and featured prominently in *Shape of Community*. Richard Plunz, writing in 1980, believed that the importance of the book was less in its specific methodology than:

> as a kind of manifesto that creativity and rationality in design might both reach new heights. Of even greater significance was the attempt at an understanding which the words of the title seemed to express; the problem of 'function' and 'form'. Function was described in terms of the private activity and communal activity, rather than private and communal space. Thus activity and form were correlated in a manner which broadened considerably for architects the possibilities of a behaviour-oriented understanding of design.[56]

The historian Nan Ellin sees *Community and Privacy* as part of a long-term phenomenon of 'Postmodern Urbanism', beginning after the war and including groups such as Team X, the young members of CIAM who broke away from what they saw as the detached and over-theoretical views of the Gropius and Le Corbusier generation.[57] None of them would probably accept the label 'Postmodern' with any pleasure but it serves to distinguish what may in retrospect be seen more as a current within modernism that emerged in response to the changing conditions in the second half of the century. This involved a recognition of the full complexity of the urban problems that had previously been oversimplified, together with a renewed affection for the existing urban fabric. One of the Team's members, Jerzy Soltan, who had worked with Le Corbusier after the war, was a colleague and friend of Chermayeff at Harvard in the 1950s. *Community and Privacy* resembles Team X texts in its shift of emphasis from relatively rigid views of the city plan to a definition of a city in terms of systems and flows of information. Chermayeff's ideas were acknowledged as influential by the Team X members in partnership as Josic Candilis Woods, especially in their designs for the Free University of Berlin, won in competition in 1963. Shadrach Woods (1923–73) wrote to Chermayeff from Berlin in February 1965, 'We wish you were here, to whom we owe so much.'[58] Alexander Tzonis comments that Chermayeff 'had great admiration for the ideas of Shadrach Woods and Gian Carlo de Carlo [another member of Team X], which he viewed with great sympathy for their urbanistic targets but with some reservations for their admirable but intuitively-reached typological solutions'.[59]

Urban design was a new issue in America, and Richard Plunz sees Chermayeff's contribution as one of several which questioned the design-oriented approach deriving from the middle years of CIAM, citing Chermayeff's address to the first Urban Design conference at Harvard in 1958, in which he stressed the need to understand the structuring principles of cities which would underly their physical form, particularly in respect of communication, information handling and mobility. 'He saw hierarchies of communication in general, and movement in particular, as the primary functional basis for urban infrastrucure.'[60] In this, Plunz observes that Chermayeff was one of three major theorists of the period, the other two being Louis Kahn, with his Philadelphia circulation network, and Shradrach Woods with his 'stem principle', each a different way of seeing the invisible forces at work in a city.

*Community and Privacy* is significant for the involvement of Christopher Alexander, who remains, nearly forty years later, one of the most significant architectural theorists of the twentieth century. His trilogy of books in the 1970s, *The Timeless Way of Building*, *A Pattern Language*, and *The Oregon Experiment*, is based on an investigation into the importance of feeling in architecture which is missing from *Community and Privacy*, but the trilogy shares with it a belief in breaking down problems into small components and providing a means of building them back up into new forms of solution. Patterns such as 'Intimacy Gradient' from *A Pattern Language* are similar to the concerns for organising the space of the home in *Community and Privacy*, together with an interest in providing new names for aspects of architectural organisation. Alexander's frequent pessimism about the state of the world is similar to Chermayeff's and, like his, must be interpreted as a call for action. The two men formed a close bond at the time and Alexander wrote to Chermayeff, 'If I ever get somewhere in the problems of modern urbanism, it will always be because of you – it was you, not Cambridge, who opened my eyes to the real problems.'[61] In a testimonial for Alexander, Chermayeff wrote, 'He has a brilliant mind, and is fortunately unorthodox and inventive in the manner of applying his remarkable intelligence.'[62] Chermayeff evidently found it difficult to crystallise his thoughts into words, and seems to have enjoyed working collaboratively. Alexander wrote to him in 1966, 'When we worked together in Cambridge, part of the little help I was to you came from the fact that I tried to re-state, more clearly, your own thoughts as you saw them.'[63] Their shared European background may have contributed to the success of their relationship. As Chermayeff wrote to his editor at Doubleday, responding to a phrase in a review by the English planner Peter Hall, 'I love to think of myself as an "American Puritan". Both Christopher and I have been more often accused of being unrequited Europeans – ah well the shrinking world.'[64]

*Community and Privacy* also contains a critique of the architectural profession in America, more by implication than by explicit reference. Chermayeff resigned from the American Institute of Architects in 1954, partly in protest against its lack of commitment and initiative in the field of architectural research, its neglect of housing, and as a stand against the

**207**

increasing formalism in American modern architecture, represented by the changing direction in the work of architects he knew personally, such as Philip Johnson (b.1906) and Edward Durrell Stone (1902–78). He even privately criticised Gropius for remaining associated with TAC as it grew into a large-scale commercial practice. For Chermayeff, the intention and programme of a building gave it a claim to cultural validity, not the external manifestation. 'The reason for our own failure lies in the programme behind the act, the consideration of true purpose, the "why" of building, which has been overlaid by obsolete cliches in a backward-looking culture. We are faithless cowards of the worst kind.'[65] In a later writing, Chermayeff quoted his friend, the economist and diplomat J.K. Galbraith who looked back to see how planning had become a dirty word during the Cold War period, encouraging architects to narrow their focus:

> The Communist countries not only socialised property, which seemed not a strong likelihood in the United States; but they planned, which somehow seemed more of a danger. Since liberty there was circumscribed, it followed that planning was something that the libertarian society should avoid.[66]

Reviewing *Community and Privacy* and Alexander's first solo book, *Notes on the Synthesis of Form* in his own book, *Towards a Non-Oppressive Environment*, 1972, Alexander Tzonis wrote:

> both ... created a great controversy when they were first published. Certainly for those whose commitment was to manipulating visual form as a purpose in itself, both books represented meaningless words, incapable of providing any help to the designer. For those who lived to see the scientisation of architecture, both books were the turning point they had been dreaming about. Lethaby's pronouncement that design was no longer a mystery and that it consisted of a conscious process whose goal was to fit form to a programme seemed to have become a reality.[67]

By the time that *Community and Privacy* was published, Chermayeff was a Professor at Yale. His frustration with Dean Sert, and the obstacles to developing post-graduate research in architecture at Harvard had reached a peak. Peter Chermayeff, who founded the design firm Cambridge Seven Associates in 1962, says that he suggested that his father should consider going to Yale, where his friend Paul Rudolph (1918–97) was Chairman of the School of Architecture from 1958 to 1965. Chermayeff was a visiting critic in 1960 and as Rudolph later explained, 'It was my notion to get people who didn't agree with me ... and he was certainly a good candidate. It was never dull when you were near Serge.'[68] Rudolph made the distinction between a critic, an observer and a teacher, saying that Chermayeff made his most acute insights as an observer, 'someone who perhaps makes more connections with society in general and a given subject ... He also had the ability to think beyond the problem of the moment. And he was there as a complement to the faculty, as a thoughtful provocateur.'[69]

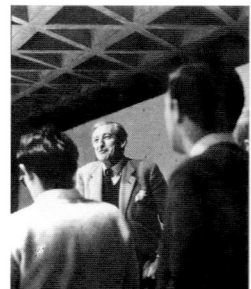

Serge Chermayeff teaching at Yale, 1960s.

Chermayeff himself wrote to Rudolph two years into the job and recorded his own reasons for moving, 'When I asked you if I could come to Yale, I told you that I had started a line of enquiry which I hoped to finish before the rules of the game closed the academic career I had deliberately chosen long ago, and while I could still be useful.'[70] He expressed his 'unequivocal admiration for your gifts but also for your integrity and forthright acceptance of other view points as a deliberate policy for the school', seeing himself in the English parliamentary mode as 'the loyal opposition'.[71]

Chermayeff's departure from Harvard at the beginning of 1962 was a sensitive matter, as he had been awarded a sabbatical year at the time, and was expected to continue in post. The news reached Harvard first in the form of a press release from Yale, and Chermayeff wrote what must have been the most apologetic letters of his career to smooth over the affront.[72] At Yale, he enjoyed the smaller size of the university and the greater capacity to mix with faculty members from other schools. The move was surprising, though, as Paul Rudolph's architecture, then highly fashionable, tended to be formal and expressive, entirely unlike Chermayeff's. By coincidence, Christopher Tunnard, the landscape architect who worked at Bentley Wood, was a long-standing member of the university faculty, now specialising in planning and urban history, although no friendship was rekindled. Chermayeff enjoyed meeting Louis Kahn as one of the frequent visiting critics in the school, even though their architectural ideas seemed so different. He also enjoyed the company of James Stirling (1926–92), who had been a visiting teacher first in 1958, and returned in 1961 and several times thereafter. He found that Stirling was someone he could drink, laugh and talk with in a relaxed way. A further benefit of the move (discussed in Chapter 8) was the possibility, which arose soon after Chermayeff's move, of building a house on an urban plot in New Haven, which could demonstrate the principles of *Community and Privacy*.

Rudolph's building for Art and Architecture on the New Haven campus was completed in 1964, with its heavy bush-hammered concrete and wide open spaces, which Chermayeff would go round, when he was semi-retired, turning off students' radios.[73] After its severe damage in an unexplained fire in 1969, Chermayeff commented 'It may be unusable as a working space; it certainly would be usable, as I recommended to the president only recently, as an extension of the Art Gallery'.[74] There was a large open space for 'crits' in the middle of the building, where people passed by, and Rudolph enjoyed making these occasions into theatrical events, with deliberately contrasting personalities. The atmosphere in the school was always intense, with students frequently working all night.

1961 was known as 'The English Year', with Richard Rogers (b.1933) (a relation of the Italian architect Ernesto Rogers), his wife Su, Norman Foster (b.1935) and Eldred Evans (b.1937) making a conspicuous group of students. Rogers has recalled that Chermayeff, 'could have persuaded us to do anything. He was a dominating figure, hugely intellectual in the best

**209**

European mould and just as much of an influence on me as Rudolph.'[75] Foster designed a scheme for a whole city, with rows of terrace housing, punctuated by towers, which demonstrated the thinking of *Community and Privacy*.[76] As Foster describes his experience at Yale, 'My timing … was more fortunate than I could ever have foreseen because it marked the change in leadership to Serge Chermayeff. He was as European as Rudolph was American. It was not just in dress or manners, but deeply rooted in differences in philosophy. For Chermayeff, debate and theory took precedence over imagery. Questioning was to the fore, analysis dominated action.'[77] On another occasion, Foster has described Chermayeff as 'philosophical to the point of "a building – why design a building?"'[78] Chermayeff invited him to stay on as a research student and teaching assistant but he returned to England, where he and the Rogers, with Foster's wife Wendy, worked together as Team 4 Architects. One of their important early projects was a development of housing for the developer-builders, Wates, on a site at Croydon, Surrey. This was designed on the model of *Community and Privacy*, and they wrote to Chermayeff, 'we had some gruelling interviews where we not only quoted your book *ad infinitum* but also gave them a copy. They were so impressed with our social mindedness as against our competitor's architectural art approach that with a little luck we shall get the job.'[79]

This did not happen, although in their early small house designs, such as Creek Vean, Cornwall, 1964-6, there are definite echoes of Chermayeff's ideas about domestic space planning. The resemblances remain in the standard house type developed by Richard and Su Rogers in the early years of their practice together after Team 4, of which the built examples were the Humphrey Spender Studio house in Essex, 1968, and the better-known Rogers House in Wimbledon, completed in 1970. Both of these consist of twin pavilions, enclosing a courtyard space. They added in a postscript, 'We are now in the middle of trying to explain locks and realms to our students at the Regent Street Polytechnic where we both teach.'[80] Foster wrote to Chermayeff in 1966, 'We're realising more and more the value of the Yale studies and now that the practice and our teaching here is a little more organised we'd like to follow some of the ideas further.'[81]

At Yale, Chermayeff had reached the final stage of his work towards a curriculum in 'Environmental Design', with the kind of freedom he had hoped for when first outlining curricular schemes in the early 1940s. He wrote to Kingman Brewster, the President of Yale, 'I sense a growing appetite among the younger people for the broadening of current offerings to enable the visual arts to expand more freely through new media such as film and TV into the general field of Communications.'[82] With post-graduates in the fields of architecture and planning, he was able to move into research-based teaching on a higher level than at Harvard. He commented on the amount of money you would need to pay such talented and enthusiastic staff, had they not been paying themselves as students.[83] From his 'Master' classes, Chermayeff developed what he termed the Yale 'model', a form of collaborative work between resident faculty, visiting experts and the students themselves, examining existing urban schemes or proposals – such as the early versions of Milton Keynes or the unbuilt Hook New Town in England –  and assembling a 'mosaic' of comments on them, using tape recordings to capture the spontaneous flow of discussion, and afterwards circulating extracts from the transcripts, sorted under different categories. It was a stimulating method, giving students an important role and narrowing the gap between them and the staff, by giving them the feeling of doing work of real importance. As Alexander Tzonis, who was first his student and later faculty assistant at Yale, writes, 'it was easy for Chermayeff to turn to large-scale issues of urban planning and to receive grants from the US National Bureau of Standards and the Twentieth Century Fund with whose help he could set up a true multidisciplinary laboratory for research based on computational and systems design thinking.'[84]

Yale, School of Arts and Architecture, c.1965, 'Student housing proposal, levels 3 and 4'.

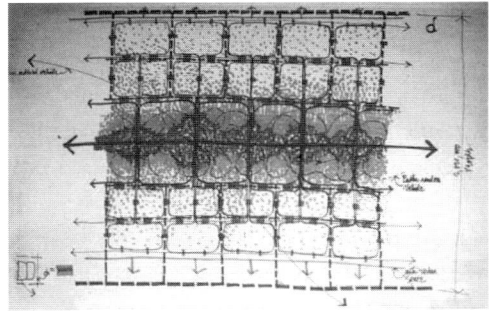

Right: Yale, School of Arts and Architecture, c.1965, 'Urban linear growth Study'.

Yale, School of Arts and Architecture, c.1965, 'Urban settlement study'

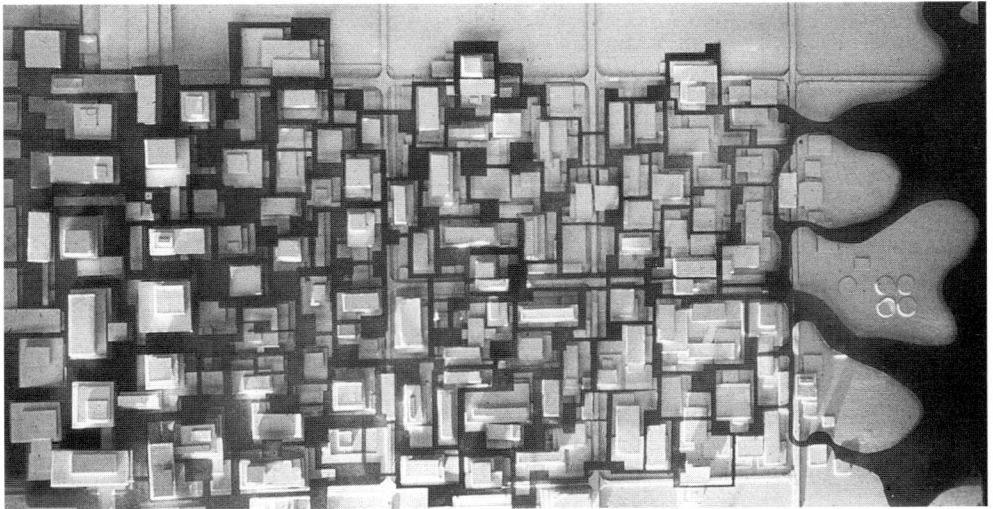

The theme of Chermayeff's teaching carried on from *Community and Privacy*, but now addressed the community end of the spectrum, using similar techniques of surveying a wide range of issues before beginning to reach conclusions. Alexander Tzonis contrasts the differing assumptions of urban theory on the East and West coasts, the latter being represented by Melvin Webber who 'took for granted the inevitable liquidation of what they called, oddly, "cityness" and promoted a chaotic free-wheeling, private automobile dominated paradigm'.[85] This was the thinking that produced in the mid 1960s in England the concept of the new town of Milton Keynes as a loosely-spread network of transport routes, unrelated to the familiar concentric concept of a city. Tzonis continues, 'The East Coast theoreticians, of whom Chermayeff was one of the most active representatives, remained committed to the idea of "urbanity", and to developing techniques for nurturing it. An interesting debate developed between these two schools of thought at the time …'[86]

At the same time, Chermayeff sensed a new danger close at hand in the form of incipient post-modernism, which paraded itself in the 1965 issue of the annual Yale architectural journal, *Perspecta*, edited by one of Chermayeff's students, Robert Stern. In retrospect, it is a brilliant piece of editing, including the first appearance of long extracts of Robert Venturi's *Complexity and Contradiction in Architecture*, before its publication in book form, and articles by Vincent Scully, Louis Kahn, Philip Johnson and Charles Moore, who became Paul Rudolph's successor in 1965. Chermayeff took violent exception to the tone of the magazine, with its emphasis on monumentality and the value of history, accusing the editors of complicity in a 'private cabal or conspiracy aiming to promote private power or personal advantage'.[87] Stern, currently the Chairman of Architecture at Yale, has recently described Rudolph's appointment of Chermayeff as 'a deliberate, if misguided, attempt to lodge an anti-heroic anti-aesthetic point of view in the curriculum'.[88]

The modern movement was undergoing a profound and necessary revaluation, but Chermayeff was playing his own part in it, not as a seeker after outside alternatives like Philip Johnson, but by going more deeply into the underlying problems and their methods of solution. Chermayeff's Yale teaching, carrying on many of his themes from Harvard, was embodied in the book *Shape of Community, Realisation of Human Potential* which he wrote jointly with Tzonis, and which was published in 1971. The project had a number of alternative titles, including 'Planning Places', and 'Mobility and Tranquillity', but Chermayeff took the title from an epigraph from Martin Buber, 'Shape the Shapeless Community', adapting it originally for a series of lectures given at Harvard. The book has a number of similarities to *Community and Privacy*, with its text broken up into separately titled paragraphs and sections, its 'hypertext' of quotations, this time set at right angles to the main text and running in the margins, and in the ironical light relief offered by the graphics, in this case drawings by Ivan Chermayeff. These make it easier to dip into than to read consecutively, and the authors began by proposing that their text was more like a crystal with facets than a sequential linear argument. Although comparatively simple in its language and frame of reference compared to later architectural theory, it failed to win much acclaim on first publication and has never achieved the same reputation as *Community and Privacy*.

The prologue to *Shape of Community* announces that the book is not about architecture as normally understood, revealing in fact the failure of modernism, as much as the still-nascent post-modernism in architecture, to address the important issues, 'Most of the changes in the last half-century, somewhat speciously described as the period of the "modern movement" in applied arts, were in the realm of aesthetic form rather than in the substance of a great transition in human affairs. With very few honourable exceptions, most of the protagonists in the movement were ignorant of, or indifferent to, the changes in need and potential that were generated during the same period.'[89] Chermayeff believed that he and his collaborators had developed a genuinely new method for dealing with urban problems, by attending to new thinking in the methodology of science, particularly in the field of cybernetics with its attention to alternations between contrasting conditions, rather than the earlier scientific model of selecting one of a series of possible choices as 'correct'. This was the point made in one of the marginal notes in *Shape of Community*, a text by Arthur Glikson (taken from *Ekistics* magazine of 1967): 'The integration of opposite elements in the urban units should not be conceived as the establishment of static syntheses but as the initiation of meaningful dialogues carried on in the 'language' of environment. Where such opposites are induced to co-exist, the urban 'breath' is set in motion and an urban quality may be achieved.'[90] From this concept, Chermayeff had developed what seems to have acted almost as a universal diagram, in the form of a figure of eight, which flowed ever outwards towards its limits and then back towards a centre, where the contrary conditions crossed over. He described this as 'dynamic order-interaction; continuous pumping between related phenomena', and found the same pattern in the 'twofold ecological problem of structuring one side and conserving the other side, not separately but simultaneously, and always in direct interaction'. As he said in 1974, 'All the apparent contradictions are really complementarities'.[91]

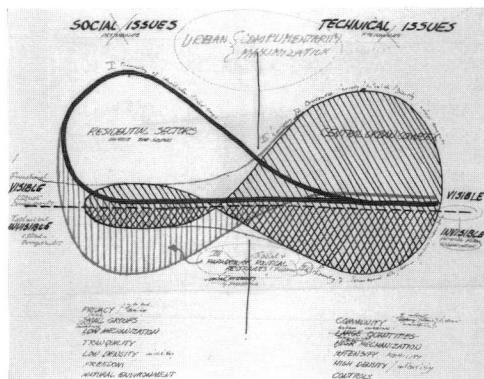

In a letter shortly after the publication of his book, Chermayeff made a reference to the book *A God Within* (1972), by the scientist René Dubos, which, he said 'gives scientific evidence to support ideas which in my case were amateurishly arrived at'.[92] This was one of several books which moved significantly away from mechanistic and behaviourist models of man. Dubos, a microbiologist, argued for 'the creation of new positive values through the development of environmental and human potentialities'.[93]

Writers on urbanism such as Edmund Bacon and Kevin Lynch had been addressing similar problems for some years before *Shape of Community*, and the book does briefly discuss issues such as urban squares which had emerged as symbolic of the difference between the settled ways of the old world, and the placelessness of the new. Chermayeff and Tzonis suggest that the 'Modern Agora' may be recreated in a controlled indoor climate, although one from which the forces of commerce are absent. There is a rejection of ready-made solutions, however: 'pseudo-professionals of all kinds (their number is growing as more and more people jump onto the "urbanology" band wagon) produce pseudo-realities to deceive innocent men further. Pseudo-plans produce pseudo-reconstruction, urban renewal and, worse, pseudo-cities.'[94]

Chermayeff and Tzonis believed that the situation was grave, and required a new form of professional training such as they were developing at Yale. Their book has little to say directly about issues of pollution and finite resources, although these factors are always in the background. It is perhaps too academic in its approach, despite its moment of caustic and aphoristic Chermayeff wit. Most reviewers failed to get the point at all. Perhaps *Shape of Community* was ahead of its time, or perhaps, as in his earlier book, Chermayeff found community a difficult subject to write about. The idea at the heart of the proposal that the method would increase the number of possible human interactions seems to get lost in the thickets of argument. It was ahead of its time, and five years after publication, Chermayeff wrote to an editor at Harvard University Press: 'The media have finally caught up with the concerns and conclusions of my book. Everyday almost identical phrases on Urbanism, Public Transportation and People-Mix appear in liberal magazines and even the *New York Times*.'[95]

Chermayeff's emphasis on the crucial role of public transport has been confirmed in all kinds of subsequent urbanistic practice, as expressed by him in a letter to the *New York Times*, 15 April 1971. 'Any "station" in any mass-transit system is a potential "exchange" between movement sub-systems, old and new, including the neglected walking. These exchanges can become forceful structuring devices in determining the location of housing, health, education and other community facilities. Mass transit is thus directly complementary to all essential community components.'[96]

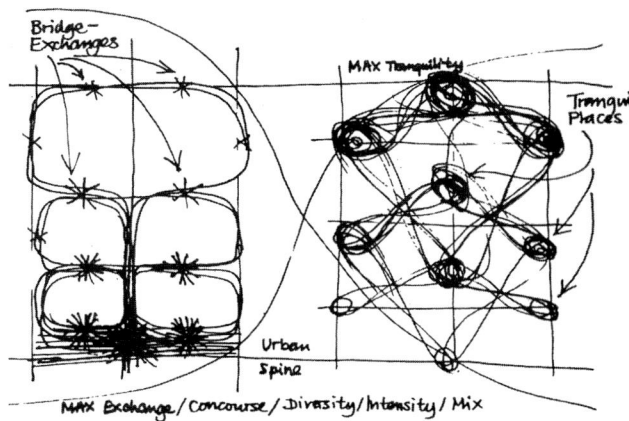

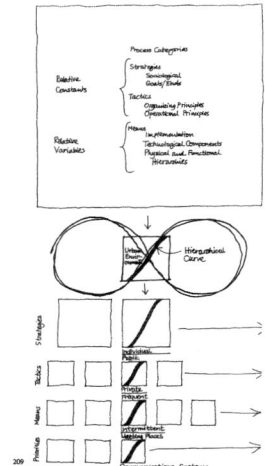

On the other hand, although the importance has only belatedly been recognised by a wide public, architectural and urban theory have gone in very different directions since the 1970s, tending either to the neo-traditional or the self-indulgently avant-garde. In Britain, the proposals of the Urban Task Force, chaired by Richard Rogers between 1997 and 1999, did make an attempt to introduce certain ideas which may be traced back to Chermayeff's influence on Rogers, who has stepped out of his role as a maker of seductive buildings to deal with these more intractable and less glamourous issues.

One can see the pulling together of many themes from Chermayeff's life and work in *Shape of Community*. There is the fruition of his early engagement with the work of Patrick Geddes, through his friendship with Andrew Messer. Geddes was a biologist before becoming an advocate of town planning, and an important exemplar of a non-architectural mind applied to environmental questions. Since he did not produce formalist solutions, Geddes's message has evaded those who wish their cities to be encapsulated in an image, but Chermayeff acknowledged his importance in 'putting man and his works in direct relationship with nature' in a way that was later overtaken by technological change as well as being over-simplified by the Garden City Movement.[97] Chermayeff would have learnt more about Geddes from his follower, Lewis Mumford, whom he spent a significant time with soon after his arrival in the States, in the summer of 1940, before beginning his new vocation of teaching. They rarely met in later years but their ideas followed similar paths, growing in disenchantment with what was happening in post-war society. Mumford felt that the possibilities of technology were being used for inhuman purposes, although he did not turn against it entirely. Chermayeff's hopes for a better world which he expressed in the 1930s had in some cases fulfilled some of his parodic projections in 'A Hundred Years Ahead' within his own lifetime.

One of Chermayeff's supporters in Yale teaching, the British artist and Independent Group member John McHale (1922–78) of the State University of New York at Binghampton, gave one of the best explanations of the importance of the late phase of Chermayeff's theoretical work. This, ironically, echoes the terms 'either/or' and 'both/and' used by Venturi in *Complexity and Contradiction* to introduce a post-modernist position in terms of architectural style but, as McHale explains, Chermayeff's thinking:

> goes far beyond architecture and planning per se. It provides practical examples of the ways in which we may move from the earlier polarities of either/or to the more inclusive both/and. Those earlier dichotomous choices belonged to historical periods of marginal survival when our alternatives were more impoverished and our life strategies correspondingly meagre. The human condition was essentially a zero-sum game. If I won, you lost ... Chermayeff's multi-dimensional planning grid uniquely illustrates this conceptual change. The choices are not between community or privacy, uniformity or variety, the closed or the open, but lie within a spectrum of varying degrees of value commitment.[98]

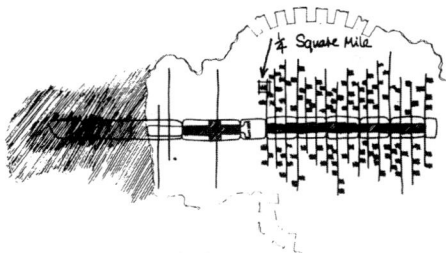

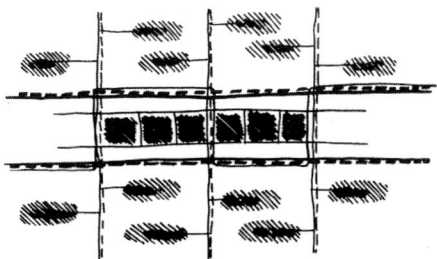

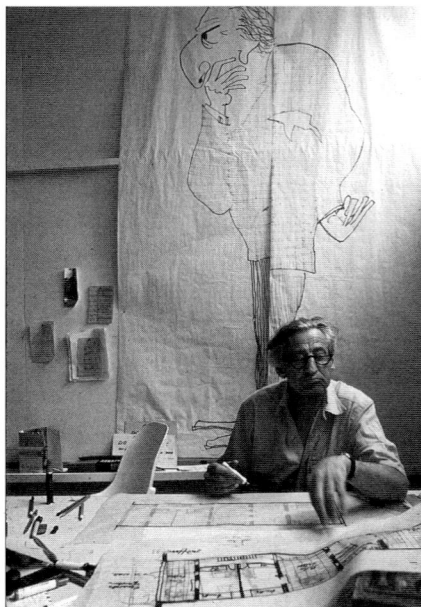

Left: Tokyo Metropolitan Bridge Extension, Kenzo Tange Team, diagrammatic plan and diagram of organisation, *Shape of Community*, 1971, p.237.

Serge Chermayeff working on theoretical house plans, Yale University, 1966, backed by a cartoon by students.

Perhaps the last word should be left to a much earlier witness, the painter Walter Bayes, whose son Alexander was one of Chermayeff's early collaborators at Waring and Gillow. Speaking in the discussion at the AA that followed Chermayeff's paper on education of 23 May 1939, Bayes said, 'Mr Chermayeff had started as a painter, but had found that painting was not big enough for him and had gone spirally outwards into other fields, which again were not big enough, until he became an architect; and now he seemed to complain that architecture was not big enough, and if the President [of the AA] had not put a stopper on the spiral Mr Chermayeff's ambition would have embraced the recasting of the whole political and economic system.'[99] It is no exaggeration to say that Bayes correctly prophesied the future of Chermayeff's intellectual trajectory in embracing ever-wider fields.

## Notes

1 Martin Myerson to Edward Echeverria, The Ford Foundation, 2 June, 1961, copy in Chermayeff file, Harvard University Archives. No text for this talk survives, but in his Foreword to Plunz, 1983, Myerson says that 'he sketched the character of postwar Britain as a framework for its art, architecture, and urban design.' (p.xi) The exhibition presented during the summer of 1951 at the ICI was 'Growth and Form', organised by Chermayeff's friend, the scientist Lancelot Law White.
2 Richard Plunz interviews, 1975-80, side 8, p.10.
3 See illustration in Plunz, 1983, p.186.
4 See Reginald Isaacs (1991), *Walter Gropius*, Boston, Toronto, London, Bullfinch Press, p.271.
5 Chermayeff to Sert, 10 February 1953, Harvard University Archives.
6 See Chermayeff memo to Sert, 5 November, 1953, SC Box 6 (50-54), Avery Library. 'It is particularly important at this moment in world history to get a course of a more universal character than is accustomed. Certainly we should know of the western heritage, but not to the total exclusion of the rest of the world.'
7 'An Approach to Redevelopment', panel discussion. Community Appraisal Study, A Collaborative Project Sponsored by the Departments of Regional Planning, Landscape Architecture and Architecture, Graduate School of Design, Harvard University, Spring 1951, pp.1-2. SC Box 6 (50-54) Avery Library.
8 Interview, 11 October 1975. Typed transcript courtesy of Professor Richard Plunz, p.1.
9 ibid., p.3.
10 ibid., p.4.
11 Conversation with Professor Albert Szabo, 2 July 2000.
12 Conversation with Ivan Chermayeff, 23 May 2000.
13 Foreword to Plunz, 1983, p.xii.
14 Catherine Herzog Powell to Chermayeff, 20 October 1971, Avery Library.
15 Richard Plunz, 'Chermayeff as Educator, TSS, E.1980, p.5.
16 Foreword to Plunz, p.xi.
17 Quoted in Victoria Milne, 'Nothing Trivial', 1994-6, p.42.
18 Chermayeff memo to Sert, 11 December, 1957, Harvard University Archives.
19 Chermayeff memo to Sert, 3 November 1953, p.4, Avery Library.
20 ibid.
21 See Martin Hammer & Christina Lodder (2000), *Constructing Modernity, The Art and Career of Naum Gabo*, New Haven & London, Yale University Press.
22 See Chermayeff memo to Sert, 14 April 1955 and letter to Archibald MacLeish, 31 March 1955, Avery Library.
23 Chermayeff to Maurice Smith, 5 July, 1957, Avery Library.
24 Drawings in collection of Peter Chermayeff.
25 Seminar with Chermayeff and Wells Coates, Harvard University Environmental Design Seminars, Fall/Spring 1954-5. Transcript, Avery Library.

26 First Year Seminars, Harvard GSD, 1955-6. Transcript, Avery Library.

27 Richard Plunz, 'Chermayeff as Educator', 1980, p.7.

28 Richard Plunz interview, 11 October 1975.

29 Chermayeff to Maurice Smith, 5 July, 1957 Avery Library.

30 See book proposal dated 1957 in Chermayeff correspondence files under Harcourt Brace.

31 Yale University Archives, Sterling Memorial Library, Serge Chermayeff 1240, Box 1, Folder 3.

32 ibid., p.3.

33 ibid , p. V21.

34 Serge Chermayeff and Christopher Alexander (1963), *Community and Privacy, Towards a New Architecture of Humanism*, New York, Doubleday, p.45.

35 ibid., p.55.

36 ibid., p.66.

37 ibid., p.72.

38 Serge Chermayeff and Alexander Tzonis (1971), *Shape of Community*, Harmondsworth, Penguin Books, pp.25-6.

39 Serge Chermayeff, 'Design of the Automob le', *Canadian Art*, XIX, January 1962, p.20.

40 *Community and Privacy*, 1963, pp.116-7.

41 ibid., p.166.

42 Chermayeff, speaking at Architecture and the Computer conference, Boston, 5 December 1964. Printed proceedings in Avery Library.

43 See Stephen Grabow (1983), *Christopher Alexander, The Search for a New Paradigm in Architecture*, Stocksfield, Oriel Press, pp.30-31.

44 Conversation with author, February 1992.

45 *Community and Privacy*, 1963, pp.230-1.

46 ibid., p.234.

47 Plunz 1983, p. xxvi

48 Chermayeff to Saul Steinberg, 13 October 1960, Avery Library.

49 Serge Chermayeff, *Community and Privacy*, preface to new editions, 1967. Avery Library SC Box 6 (55-59) 1959-61.

50 Paul Goodman to Chermayeff, 5 May 1960, Avery Library.

51 Jane Jacobs to Chermayeff, 10 June 1960, Avery Library.

52 Chermayeff to Marshall McLuhan, 30 November 1960, Avery Library.

53 By the beginning of 1969, the American hardback had sold 20,000 copies and the 'miserable' paperback 30,000. Chermayeff letter to Timothy Seldes, 23 January 1969, Avery Library.

54 Chermayeff to Douglas Haskell, 27 September 1954, Avery Library.

55 Alexander Tzonis, 'Serge Chermayeff, humanist', *Spazio Società*, July/Sept. 1997, pp.19-20.

56 Richard Plunz, 'Chermayeff as Educator', 1980, p.9.

57 See Nan Ellin (1996), *Postmodern Urbanism*, Cambridge, Mass and Oxford, Blackwell.

58 Shadrach Woods to SC, 11 February 1965, Avery Library.

59 Tzonis, 1997, p.23.

60 Richard Plunz, 'Chermayeff as Educator', 1980, p.7.

61 Christopher Alexander to Chermayeff, n.d., Avery Library.

62 Chermayeff to Charles Moore, 11 March 1963, Avery Library.

63 Christopher Alexander to Chermayeff, 3 June 1966, Avery Library.

64 Chermayeff to Anne Freemantle, 1 June 1966, Avery Library.

65 SC 'Random Thoughts on the Architectural Condition', Cranbrook, 9 June 1964, in Plunz, 1983, p.189.

66 J.K. Galbraith (1967), *The New Industrial State*, Boston, Houghton Mifflin Co., quoted in Chermayeff and Tzonis, *Shape of Community*, 1971, p.65.

67 Alexander Tzonis (1972), *Towards a Non-Oppressive Environment*, Boston, ipress, p.99.

68 Milne, 1966, p.49.

69 ibid.

70 Chermayeff to Paul Rudolph, August 1964, Avery Library.

71 ibid.

72 See Chermayeff to Sert, 24 January 1962, Avery Library.

73 Information from John McAslan.

74 Serge Chermayeff, 'Shape of Community Revisited' in Plunz, 1983, p.198.

75 Kenneth Powell (1999), *Richard Rogers, Complete Works*, London, Phaidon, p.11.

76 Illustrated p.358 in Deyan Sudjic, ed. (2000), *On Foster … Foster On*, Munich, Prestel.

77 Norman Foster, Pritzker Prize Address, in Sudjic, 2000, p.729.

78 Norman Foster, Royal Gold Medal Address, ibid., p.485.

79 Richard Rogers and Norman Foster to SC, 2 September 1964, Avery Library.

80 ibid.

81 Norman Foster to Chermayeff, 22 March 1966, Avery Library.

82 Chermayeff to Kingman Brewster, 17 November 1964, Avery Library.

83 Chermayeff tape recording 'Environmental Design is our task', Pidgeon Audio Visual, 1980.

84 Tzonis, 1997, p.21.

85 ibid., p.23.

86 ibid., p.23.

87 See Chermayeff, 'Open Letter to the Editors', *Perspecta*, 5 May 1965, Avery Library.

88 Robert A.M. Stern, 'The Impact of Yale', in Sudjic, 2000, p.359.

89 *Shape of Community*, p.xxx

90 Arthur Glikson, quoted in *Ekistics*, August 1967, *Shape of Community*, p.30.

91 Chermayeff (1974) *In Search of Questions* (the John William Laurence Memorial Lectures, the Tulane University School of Architecture), pp.3–5

92 Chermayeff to Richard Power, Sumachita Center for Cultural Innovations, 14 September 19 72, Avery Library.

93 René Dubos (1972), *A God Within*, New York, Charles Scribner's Sons, p.192.

94 *Shape of the Community*, p.177.

95 Chermayeff to Arthur Rosenthal, Harvard University Press, 30 November 1976, Avery Library.

96 Chermayeff to the *New York Times*, 15 April 1971, Avery Library.

97 *Shape of Community*, p.63.

98 John McHale, SUNY, Binghamton, 11 March 1975, Avery Library.

99 *Architectural Association Journal*, June 1939, pp.10-11.

# Building in America

Chermayeff's attitude to the practice of architecture during his time in the USA is ambiguous. Sometimes he would say that he did not wish to build very much, whilst at other times one has the impression that if he had been able to, he might have returned to a level more like his pre-war practice, and more equal to some of his architect colleagues in the university departments where he taught, such as J.L. Sert and Paul Rudolph, both of whom continued to build prolifically.

His productivity from the 1940s to the 60s was certainly nothing like the pre-war level but he produced a reasonable body of work. He was able to build more, for example, than his old friends Raymond McGrath and Wells Coates, for the former went into government service in Ireland and missed the opportunities for major buildings, while the latter, before his death in 1958, had many disappointments. Although most of Chermayeff's projects were small houses – many of them holiday homes – they formed a counterpoint to the development of his theoretical ideas, culminating in the last of the series of houses designed for himself, 28 Lincoln Street, New Haven, in 1962, which made the same points that Community and Privacy made in its way the following year. In addition, there were larger unbuilt projects to demonstrate Chermayeff's evolving ideas at an urban scale.

'He wasn't a bad architect, he was simply afraid of his wife,' was how Chermayeff explained his unusual involvement in the house for Clarence Mayhew in Oakland, California, one of a pair in the Bay that he designed in 1941 before moving east to New York.[1] Mayhew was presumably one of the circle of local architects he encountered when he settled in California in 1940, and he was lucky to gain his collaboration in this enterprise because although he would have needed a locally licensed associate for any building work, he could hardly expect that the associate would also be the client. The stress was laid on Mrs Mayhew's role as client and she was evidently a formidable lady. 'I reasoned that two heads would do a better job in designing a house for my wife than just one', Mayhew said. 'I tried out the idea on several of my architect friends, who thought I was crazy. Their reaction convinced me that the idea was sound.'[2] Chermayeff responded by saying that 'if you design a house for yourself, it is likely to become an experiment', even though he had avoided the negative connotations of this at Bentley Wood.[3]

The site, at 330 Hampton Road, Piedmont, formed part of a large estate, and was steeply sloping, with fine live oak trees which the house was designed to thread around. A series of alternative schemes are illustrated in an article in *Architectural Forum*, showing Chermayeff's concern to advertise a heuristic method for reaching a solution. The first version, an L-shape with a two-storey wing on the uphill part of the site oversailing a lower cross wing, is captioned 'Little adaptation to slope … lack of intimacy between house and garden … outdoor living shadowed in afternoon … some good trees lost.'[4] By stages, the design worked itself out into a series of three single-storey linked blocks stepping down the hill, with some kinks on plan to add interest and to avoid the trees. This breaking down also reflected Chermayeff's increasing interest in zoning domestic space, specially in order to regulate the interaction of adults and children, since the Mayhews had two daughters. Although all the bedrooms were in the upper block, the children and adults are separated by a passage. The playroom was in the L shaped main block, at an angle to the living room and well separated acoustically by the whole of the kitchen quarters. Its own access to outdoors was tucked away around a corner, with a terrace over the garage which creates the third and lowest level on the site.

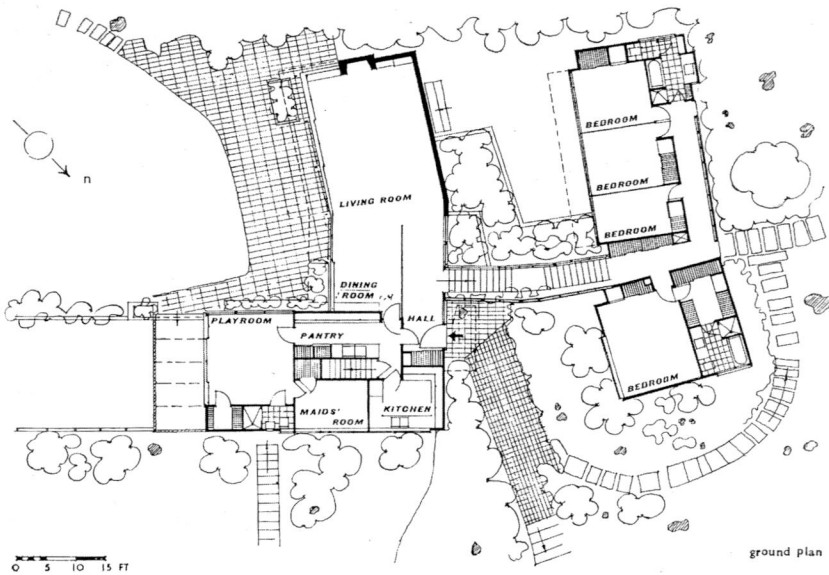

S. Chermayeff and C. Mayhew, Mayhew House, Piedmont, California, 1942, plan.

Resemblances to Bentley Wood are evident in the timber construction (more remarkable in Sussex than in the Bay Area) and the devices used to give the greatest sense of linkage between indoors and out. Ceilings were continued from interior to exterior in the form of overhangs and windows to the living room could slide back and virtually disappear from view. External materials were continued into the interior, so that the redwood planking of the children's playroom exterior was continued on the same plane as an internal treatment of the dining end of the living room.

Mayhew House, entrance.

Right: Mayhew House, bedroom terrace, interior of staircase and glass wall of living room.

Chermayeff seems to have taken a lot of trouble with the entrance, which is separate from the garage. There is a pathway through natural-seeming greenery approaching the front door obliquely. A live oak stands beside the door, and one of its stems pass though the projecting canopy over the door. Chermayeff offered an 'organic' solution for the canopy but a rectilinear alternative was preferred as being less competitive with the freedom of the natural tree shapes. This pedestrian approach was deliberately made more attractive than the garage approach, and although the glazed door is flanked by a large glass panel, the view through the house at this point is partially blocked by a screen of Japanese woven grass, blanking off most of the view between floor and ceiling.

Mayhew House, living room.

Right: Mayhew House, terrace outside living room.

The article in *Architectural Forum* saw the Mayhew house as 'a subtle blending' of the contrasting points of view of the two architects, one Californian, the other 'one of the leaders in the English school practising in the crisp, so-called International Style'.[5] This dichotomy

223

was the basis of a controversy launched by Lewis Mumford with an article in the *New Yorker* 'Skyline' column in 1947 in which he contrasted the émigré modernists on the East Coast unfavourably with the newly emerging regionalist tradition in the West.[6] The Mayhew House does indeed sit with some poise on a boundary line between these two possibilities, although Mumford wanted to stress the pluralism of the West, rather than its production of one singular mode of building. As noted in Chapter 7, Chermayeff felt a strong sympathy for the independence of the West, as well as a personal devotion to Mumford. The treatment of the plan and the site express a form of organicism but the detailing remains strictly rational and almost everyday. A throwback to Chermayeff's earlier practice is the generous provision of built-in furniture. As at Bentley Wood, there was an inside line to the contractor, who in this case was Mayhew's father, a retired contractor, who ensured higher than average standards of work. Mrs Mayhew remained in residence until the early 1990s and the house is in excellent condition.

The Mayhew House was the loosest house plan Chermayeff ever made, although this can be explained by the need to deal with a highly specific site. When Bentley Wood was published in England, those who made a critical commentary were disinclined to stress its departures from a strict line of 'international modern'. Nearly ten years later, and in another continent, the polemical situation was much more polarised, and Chermayeff continued to act as a witness, sometimes tacitly through his buildings and more often explicitly through his writings and speeches, against any kind of hegemony issuing from the Museum of Modern Art or other arbiters of taste. He was one of the participants when this issue was debated at MOMA in February 1948 under the title 'What is happening in modern architecture?' In common with many other architects of his generation and older, he objected to the formulation of the 'International Style' as a style, instead of the presentation of modern architecture as a multifarious programme for practical and ideological change. He did not like expressive architecture for its own sake but expressed considerable enthusiasm in later life for Ralph Erskine, whose work in Sweden in the post-war years was part of a continuing Scandinavian challenge to excessive style-consciousness. Had Chermayeff remained in California, his work would probably not have continued in such a woody and romantic vein, since he also expressed enthusiasm for the Case Study houses, which manifested their appreciation of nature and the softness of the California climate in a more technological language.

The second Chermayeff house in the Bay area, the Horn House, at 339 Western Drive, Richmond, was carried out at much the same time as the Mayhew House. The contract was signed a week after Pearl Harbour in December 1942. The client, Walter Horn, was Professor of Art History at Berkeley, whose chief life work was the editing and interpretation of the ninth century San Gall plan, the earliest surviving architectural plan in the western world. His wife was an architect, but he employed Chermayeff in conjunction with Ernest Born, as well-known member of the Second Bay School who collaborated with Horn on the publication of the San Gall plan in 1979, with Garrett Eckbo as landscape designer.[7] The site, a cliff side overlooking the Bay and the Golden Gate Bridge, was unplanted and exposed to the weather. As the text in *Interiors*, doubtless contributed by Chermayeff himself, explained, 'The raw winds and rain which sweep in from the Bay made it unwise to place outdoor living area adjacent to the water unless a windbreak – certain to block the view – were also erected.'[8] As a result, the outdoor living area was placed on the landward side of the house, formed as a terrace deck overlooking an enclosed sloping garden. The climatic conditions allowed Chermayeff to introduce a cranked pedestrian entry around the garage, shut in by a high boundary fence, emphasising the privacy that he posited in opposition to the openness of the American suburb. The outer enclosure allowed a greater openness in the house itself and from the terrace on the land side, there is a view right through the living room, which shares the seaward prospect with the study and bedroom, the only one in the house, pending the building of a guest wing in the space between the kitchen and the garage.[9]

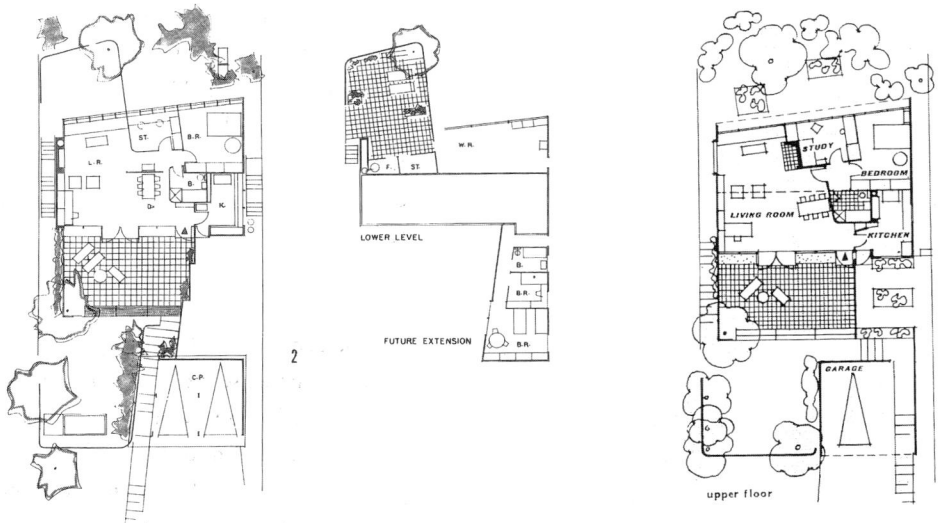

The US entry into the war meant that the scheme experienced some economies owing to the restriction of materials, while the extreme weather meant that after a trial double-timber boarding was changed to stucco over metal lathing for the outward-facing walls. Early versions of the plan show Chermayeff enjoying more of a freedom in abstract graphic treatment than before, in some ways more closely resembling Brazilian architecture of this time, or some of the designs of Berthold Lubetkin in England. Not all the devices were realised in the building. The south elevation of the Horn House leans forward from the vertical, rather like a ship's bridge, while it is also oblique to the side walls, and on an early version of the plan a line is shown which carries a sheltering wall to the terrace below the main living floor into the internal space as a partition between study and living room.[10] The interior is probably Chermayeff's most open plan, with one large, multi-purpose living space closing in towards a fireplace in the core of the house, close to the main view.

The site was also much smaller than that for the Mayhew House but the text in *Interiors* comments, 'Landscaping is very successful, though still incomplete, and in the lovely, secluded space, no view betrays the smallness of the whole lot (50' x 90', house and grounds).'[11] Although tailored to precise circumstances of site, the Horn house still has the essentials of a house type which could, if wanted, have been adapted to a standard urban or suburban site.

About this time, Chermayeff sketched out a proposal for a house for his family on the back of some duplicated sheets describing his proposed programme for a school of architecture. Chermayeff seems to have liked to organise the details of the future in his mind, and since existing trees are shown on the plan, this may have been a project for a real site. Like his executed projects in California, it shows how Bentley Wood was already going in directions that seemed to anticipate Californian conditions. It is a single-storey design, centred around three sides of a courtyard, with long extended routes to the master bedroom in one corner and a study, even more effectively isolated at the opposite end of the plan from the boys' rooms and play area. There are few solid walls, and privacy is created through making space between different functions. The design shows the reactions of a newcomer to the Californian climate with its promise of year-round warmth, allowing house and garden to interpenetrate in reality as well as in concept. The organisation of the street frontage, with a strong separation between the car port and the adjacent service and play area appears to anticipate the enquiry in *Community and Privacy* into these aspects of the home.

Chermayeff executed one other commission in the Bay area, a showroom for Ciro Jewellery, well-known as specialists in pearls, at 2763 Mission Street, San Francisco, executed in 1946 with Raphael Soriano, one of the participants in John Entenza's Case Study house programme (see page 165).[12] This commission, which was meant also to include a shop in Beverly Hills, came shortly before Chermayeff had his own New York office set up, but he also needed local help in the West. Mr Khoroche of Ciro was a client of Chermayeff's in London, when he designed a small shop for the company at 48 Old Bond Street in 1938. The San Francisco shop was also small, although double-height inside. The whole of the left-hand wall was mirrored, and a mezzanine gallery installed. Chermayeff worked on producing a combined spotlight and general diffused general light in one fixture.

On his arrival in New York in 1943, Chermayeff worked with his former assistant, Peter Blake, then on the staff of *Architectural Forum*, and Abel Sorensen, with collaborators Norman Fletcher and Henry Hebbeln, on a theoretical housing project for 'Park Apartments', part of a series of wartime proposals for different building types published in *Architectural Forum* in May. The design itself is a 2/3 section type, ultimately derived from experiments in Moscow in the 1920s but introduced to pre-war England by Wells Coates at the 9 Palace Gate flats of 1938. In the 1943 scheme, Chermayeff and his colleagues introduced a number of possible variants in apartment plans and sections to give the variety enjoyed in private houses in addition to the other benefits they thought that apartments could provide in terms of better light and air, and more open space. Mechanical services include air-conditioning for the bathrooms and other internal areas. The assumptions are purely Corbusian, and the overall form is a slab raised on piloti, although its architectural form shows no indication of the movement of Le Corbusier towards the béton brut and heavyweight look of the Unité at Marseilles. It is interesting to read in the text how Chermayeff's critique of the standard terrace house begins to suggest the solutions that he himself would bring forward in later years for reforming this type of house rather than rejecting it. 'Most typical developments involve waste of land and effort: The unproductive setback strips between houses; the front yard which becomes a maintenance liability in the struggle to "keep up with the Joneses" and offers little more than facade value; and the too-close-for-parents'-peace yard play area, or its dreary and dangerous street-play alternative. The provision of play areas in found space is an admirable palliative for the inherited chronic disorders of the past. It is not a prescription for the future.'[13]

Chermayeff, with Peter Blake, Abel Sorensen, Norman Fletcher and Henry Hebbeln, 'Park Apartments'.

Right: 'Park Apartments', interior of duplex apartment.

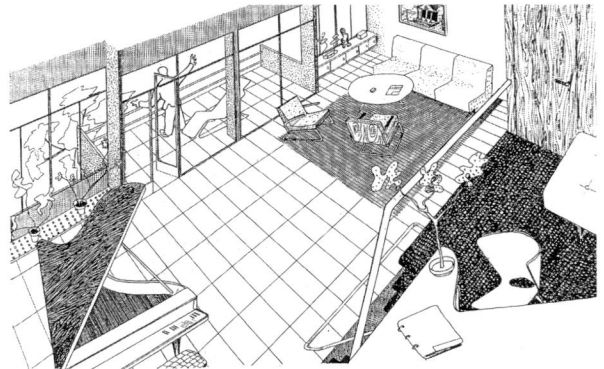

A Corbusian sketch diagram contrasts the 'Cramped, Rugged Individualism' of the house against the 'Free Cooperative Individualism' of the ideal apartment to emphasise the point. A comment on this scheme by Joseph Abel suggested that it would 'provide extremely attractive living quarters … superior to those which have thus far been built.'[14]

Two years later, Chermayeff, in association with the San Francisco architect Vernon DeMars and Susanne Wasson-Tucker, worked on a joint scheme for 'The House in its Neighbourhood' for the Museum of Modern Art exhibition, 'Tomorrow's Small House'. Chermayeff's main contribution was the design of two large slab apartment blocks on an imaginary hillside, a decent distance away from curving roads, where small row houses (designed by DeMars and Wasson-Tucker) were indicated in small groups, some of them examples of show houses in the exhibition itself. This was 'mixed development' of a kind advocated in England before the war and put into practice after it at sites like Alton East and West in Roehampton. The text proposes 'there is no sudden intrusion of giantism, and even the upper floors seem to retain some contact with the ground. Each apartment has its own balcony and opens widely to sun and view, and every tenant has access to the roof terrace.'[15] Communal buildings by Chermayeff and De Mars were grouped casually between the other main elements.

Chermayeff's joint office with Konrad Wachsmann in East 37th Street, New York involved a conversion of one floor of an existing building, with main rooms to front and back half linked by a narrower section around a light well. The brick party wall was left as exposed brick in a Corbusian gesture. Chermayeff described it as 'an office which showed things we could do photographically' rather than a working office. He recalled a visit from a Saudi Arabian who wanted to commission a hospital design, explaining that it was 'for the elite of Saudis'. Chermayeff replied on behalf of himself and Wachsmann, 'You know a hospital which is designed for the elite is not a hospital, it's a pleasure pavilion. I'm sure you can find an architect who would do this. We won't'.[16]

Wachsmann was in some ways an unlikely partner for Chermayeff, whether or not they intended to design joint projects, since the aspects of engineering structure developed in Wachsmann's work were never central to Chermayeff's social view of architecture. Apart from sharing a need to get started in a new country (Wachsmann came to the States in 1941), their common interest was probably in the mass production of housing. In 1946, Wachsmann launched his General Panel Corporation, with which Gropius's name was associated, which proved to be a commerical failure. Chermayeff believed it to have been impractical and unsuitable for the building culture of America because it involved building upwards from a slab, rather than in filling below a roof erected at an early stage in the process and giving protection from rain.[17]

In 1945, Chermayeff entered a competition organised by the Museum of Modern Art for Dormitories at Smith College, the women's college at Cambridge, along with other notable architects such as Marcel Breuer.

The only work Chermayeff executed in New York was a Travel Agency Office in the Rockefeller Center, with entrances off the lobby of the Time Life building as well as from the street, in 1946, for the newly created British Railways in association with Irish Railways. This was executed in association with the architects Ketchum, Gina and Sharp, with its egg crate ceiling masking air conditioning and strip lighting, it looks like a post-war space, despite the pre-war look of the railway posters framed on the wall as a form of panelling. There were specially-designed desks on angled tubular legs and a long kinked counter, which reflects some of the free-form ideas in the Horn House.

It is hardly surprising that Chermayeff had little time for running a practice during his period at the Institute of Design, dealing as he was with an unstable institution and also painting for the first time since he had taken up architecture. While in Chicago, Chermayeff did evidently design a model hospital which he described in an interview in 1985, 'A group of doctors, rather advanced surgeons, were very dissatisfied with the facilities in the existing hospitals. They asked me to design a hospital for them which was fundamental for heavy operations with the absolute minimum distance between nurse supervision, the operating room, and the patients waiting and convalescing rooms. That worked out of course roughly into spokes in a wheel with very short spokes so that the night nurse could see form her desk every door in her little domain.'[18] Chermayeff did not have a license to practice in Illinois, and so handed the scheme over to SOM, but without any further results.

The exhibition 'Design for Use' at MOMA in 1944 has already been mentioned. This achieved some reputation as an exhibition design among the many produced at this time in Britain and the USA. The exhibition plan was slightly skewed to the sides of the L-shaped room, and worked around a central rotunda space, with a ring of photographs of chairs suspended above head height, matched by samples of chairs on a curved base. Implements and objects were placed on shelves with explanatory and photographic panels, divided into grids, inclined back from the shelf tops. This plan was designed to give the visitors a sense of flowing around the space, and was descibed as 'a beautiful example of planning that gives visitors the feeling of complete freedom while in fact directing their movement.'[19] In the same statement, given in 1951 to the author of a book on exhibitions, Chermayeff stressed that the then-fashionable term 'organic' was to him more conceptual than stylistic, implying the integration of the elements of a house into a mechanical core.

Chermayeff claimed to have spent over half-a-year researching the exhibition, of which he wrote, 'The purpose was to present industrial design in a comprehensive way as a historical development in industrial society and not as a catalogue of fashionable shapes or gadgets.'[20]

The exhibition 'Chicago Plans' in City Hall, Chicago in 1949, also mentioned earlier, was presented for the Chicago Plans Commission by Chermayeff with Homer Grooman, Don La Vine and Harry Smith. This was also in an L-shaped space, giving onto a glazed lobby, with a system of floor-to-ceiling poles in aluminum, fixed in rings top and bottom and held in tension by springs. This was devised partly in order to assist in touring the exhibition. Richard Lohse commented: 'The exhibition was noteworthy for the logical organisation of its theme as well as for the careful and convincing selection of the pictorial and textual material and comprehensivle explanation of the statisticial tables.'[21] There were panels of photographs and texts, some tilting forwards from the wall in a V shape. The exhibition was centred around the proposal for a new government centre, but in order to make its case, it reviewed the urban history of the city, its previous plans, notably the one by Daniel Burnham of 1909: 'The informative character of the pictorial panels was underlined by the appeal to the visitor of the exhibition to lend support to the planning work of the Committee for the reorganization of the heart of the city and building of the Civic Centre.'[22] A dramatic set of photos showed the present difficulties of transport and living conditions in the city, with an enlarged photo of an injured girl lying on a pavement, with the caption 'Lives are lost on overcrowded city streets.' The presentation culminated in the model of the proposed Civic Centre, appearing to float in mid air, but it was clearly a much more comprehensive review of the state of the city.

'Japanese paper' textile for Anton L. Maix, 1950.

With his interest in industrial design demonstrated in the 'Design for Use' exhibition in 1944, and the orientation of the Institute of Design at Chicago, Chermayeff made some attempts to re-enter this field. The most productive was a series of designs for screen-printed furnishing textiles made for the New York firm of L. Anton Maix in 1950, in a collection that included work by the well-known graphic designers Alvin Lustig (1915–55) and Paul Rand (b.1914). Chermayeff contributed three abstract patterns, one, 'Japanese Paper' composition of chevrons, triangles and squares, with a rhythmic feeling, similar to Navajo and Peruvian traditional design, and 'Cross Hatch' which was more sober, with squares made of intersecting diagonal lines of grey, making a wide, rough-edged vertical and horizontal check pattern in between. The third pattern is called 'Inside Outside', a large-scale repeat, suggesting the view through the bars of a window, but effectively abstract, using the cross-hatch style for tonal areas. This was issued in Chermayeff's favourite colours of blue, yellow and white.[23] A fourth pattern, 'Navajo', was based on a vertical waving line which demarcated separate colour areas. The

'Navajo' textile for Anton L. Maix, 1950.

commercial success of these fabrics was variable. A letter from Maix to Chermayeff in 1955 indicates how little of 'Cross-Hatch' had been sold, while 'Japanese Paper' had to compete against many similar designs. However, Chermayeff was invited to make further designs and colourways for 'Inside Outside'.

In 1956, Chermayeff was invited to make some proposals for furniture designs for Eugene Schmidt of the Darmstadt firm of Polstermöbel Fabrik, following a meeting with him. Chermayeff wrote: 'We should like to develop a line which would include stools, dining chairs, easy chairs, reclining chairs, and couches, all capable of combinations and variations.'[24] All the evidence that remains is a series of sketches in the Chermayeff archive, showing reclining chairs with frames of elegant calligraphic form, and other chunkier ones with sides cut from plywood sheet. As with the PLAN furniture in the 1930s, Chermayeff seems to have been interested in the springing systems for these chairs. In a more modern vein, he drew arrangements for foam rubber cushions in covers that would allow different uses, with the pads stretched out as a mattress folded onto each other.

From 1950 onwards, Chermayeff's built work consisted almost entirely of small houses. Many of these were on Cape Cod, but one, the Herbert and Eileen Payson House at Portland, Maine, finished in 1952, should be considered first since it does not belong with the group of designs on the Cape. Michael Payson was a roommate and friend of Ivan Chermayeff at the boarding school, Andover, outside Boston. He invited Ivan to stay and this led to a friendship between both generations of both families. As Mrs Payson wrote in a memoir of the project:

> The Chermayeffs had heard that we were a very 'family' sort of group who made a fuss over birthdays and graduation ceremonies. We had learned (by understatement and implication) that they had no traffic with such nonsense, that they were held together by strong bonds of intellectual understanding and mutual respect, and they they had on one occasion found it practical to celebrate Christmas two days late. It looked as though we might have some fun together and we did.[25]

The family owned a nineteenth century summer house which had been demolished, leaving large brick cellars in a well-planted park, a setting of a kind familiar to domestic architects in post-war Britain. There was no need for a grand house, but it needed to live up to the scale of the site. The cellars were mostly filled in, leaving one small brick shed surviving above ground from the old structure.

To commission a modern architect such as Chermayeff was a bold move for a family not previously aware of contemporary arts, but he justified their faith by producing a design which Eileen Payson described as 'dramatic and breathtaking in its simplicity'.[26] In Chermayeff's words, 'The Herbert Paysons could not at this time afford, nor indeed wanted, a large establishment. They did agree, though, that however modest, the immediate accommodation had to be, the scale of the house should be worthy of the drama and scale of the unique site.'[27] Chermayeff designed a single storey house, which he described as 'a "large" small house on the "large" large site', with alternating full-length windows and wall panels of vertical boarding, painted in a range of colours, grey, white and deep red (see page 166). The plan is a T-shape with a main rectangular body, off which a smaller section forms a kitchen, dining-room and entrance wings. The main orientation is north-east, towards the view of the ocean, but the south-west corner is developed with a paved terrace outside the dining room to catch the sun. A living room, 20' square on plan with two columns in the centre, is the main space, with a wide opening into the hallway and wood strip flooring running all through. Two bedrooms, each with their own bathroom, are accessed from a corridor, and at the end of the main block of the plan, a generous study doubles as another bedroom. Each of these rooms has its own door onto the lawn in front of the house, an external louvred and screened door for summer, and a solid internal door for protection against storm and snow. The main block of the house gets additional south-western light from a long clerestorey to compensate for the otherwise frequently sunless aspect.

The rooms were partly furnished with antique pieces already owned by the family - many of them reupholstered to fit their new context - and partly with new pieces bought with Chermayeff's advice. The Paysons were model clients from his point of view, despite some private misgivings. In a letter to Douglas Haskell at *Architectural Forum*, Chermayeff wrote:

> They were exceptional clients for any architect and were in particular wonderful for me designing the first house in ten years and longing to be untrammelled - and untrammelled I was. The Paysons, having outlined their practical requirements and defined a budget, and being innocent and unspoiled architecturally speaking, accepted my design on the basis of my reputation and never questioned my judgments at any time either on matters of principle or detail. All this sounds Utopian, it is in fact true.[28]

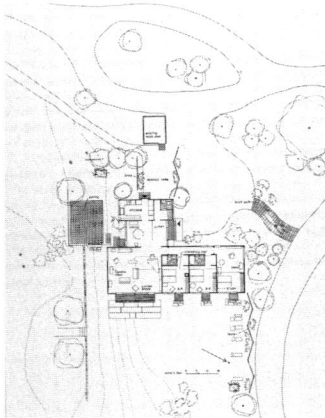

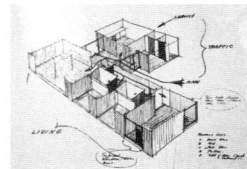

Payson House, diagram of use of colour.

Left: Payson House, outside dining room.

Far left: Payson House, plan.

Eileen Payson wrote:

> Our money was sparse and we had to think hard and ten times over, about everything. We discussed some inexpensive but charming modern settees, recovered our favourite pieces with bright sail cloth, and planned unbleached muslin curtains for the water side. Lovely clear colours – red yellow and blue – blossomed on doors throughout the house, while the main walls were calm grey or white. Suddenly, mysteriously, rhythm and meaning began to flow through the place –  imperceptible, unproveable, but there![29]

A considerable amount of earth moving took place to remodel the site, and Chermayeff made plans for moving some of the existing evergreens, with further shrubs and wild flowers in long grass.

The Chermayeff family became deeply attached to their own summer holiday home on Cape Cod. In 1942, Chermayeff leased a site from Jack Phillips, the owner of a beautiful piece of wild landscape near the Atlantic shore, where ponds occur amongst woodland. Phillips encouraged other modern artists and designers to build vacation houses on his land, and the sign boards, hand-painted and nailed to trees on the dirt track approaches, used to read as a lexicon of distinguished names, including Breuer, Saarinen and Kepes.

**Chermayeff Cottage, after second extension, 1951.**

**Right: Chermayeff Cottage, elevation and elevation of completed building.**

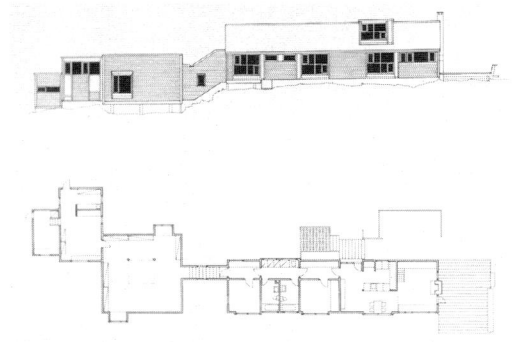

**Chermayeff Cottage, studio extension, interior, three views.**

The Chermayeff cottage looks westwards over the Slough Pond, on the crest of a bank. Timber framed, with grey-painted weather boarding and a pitched roof, it is close to the local vernacular 'saltbox' type. The cottage grew gradually as Chermayeff could afford to develop it. The main section has a brick chimney in a gable end, Inside, this makes the centre of the main double height sitting area, with a snug sense of enclosure. A door beside the fireplace opens onto a decking area where much summer eating, drinking and sitting took place, with views down a steep slope to the pond. There is a loft bedroom above for the boys and later for visitors. Chermayeff and Breuer built the steep ladder stair with their own hands in the summer of 1950. The kitchen has a 'bar counter towards the dining area, which has a typical Chermayeff table arrangement end-on to the large window, with the same Thonet bent wood and cane chairs that were used at Bentley Wood.

The plan was also extended in 1950 to include a bedroom wing, with two bedrooms overlooking the pond, acoustically buffered from each other by two bathrooms.[30] The partitions between the rooms and the passage only come a little above door height, with a void above to create an extra sense of space, but each suite becomes private when the doors across the passage to the bathrooms are shut. On the exterior of this wing, and on the blank dormer in the roof which provides headroom in the loft, Chermayeff introduced a device of diagonal timber framing with brightly coloured triangular panels in mulberry red, a cool yellow and grey.

Still later again, in 1971, a large studio was added, square on plan and lofty inside, with a big skylight and only two windows at lower level, arranged pinwheel fashion in opposite corners of the room. One of these is a bay window facing across the pond, which provided a place for Chermayeff to sit and watch the disc of the setting sun sinking among the trees, something which often appears in abstracted form in his paintings. The studio lies along the line of the existing linear plan but is reached by link stairs which operate rather like the stairs in the Mayhew house. This was built in order that Chermayeff could sell the house he had built in New Haven and retire with what he called his 'loot' – his books, pictures and objects collected when travelling – to live full time on the Cape. Beyond the studio, there was another small suite of rooms for Barbara's mother, Sybil Perry.

Sigerson House.

Middle: Chermayeff studio extended as guest house.

Far left: Chermayeff studio, original building, 1952.

Opposite: Wilkinson House, Cap Cod (Truro, Massachussetts), sketch designs.

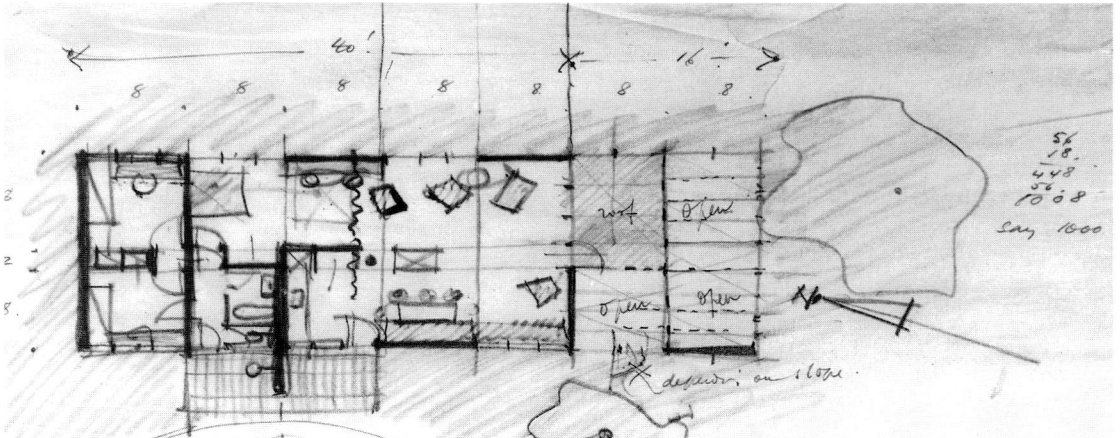

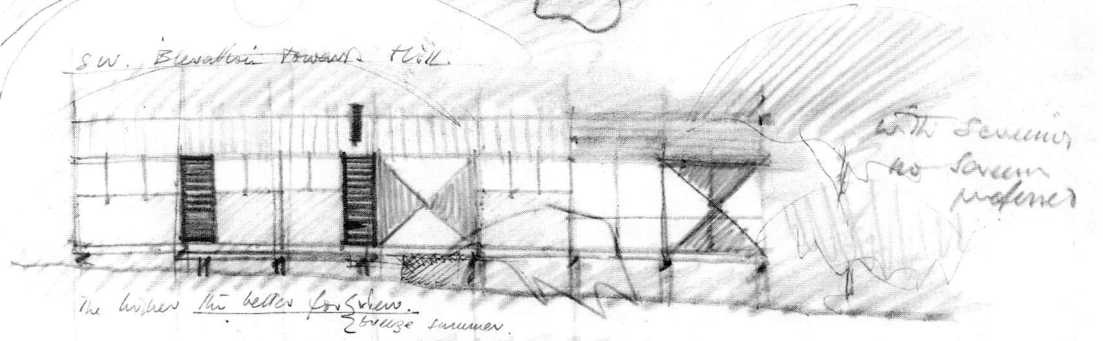

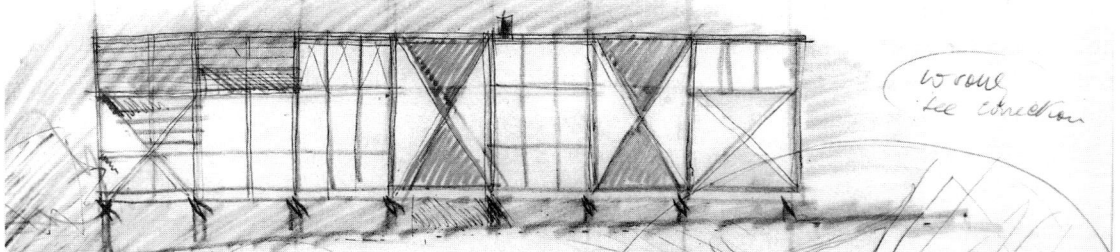

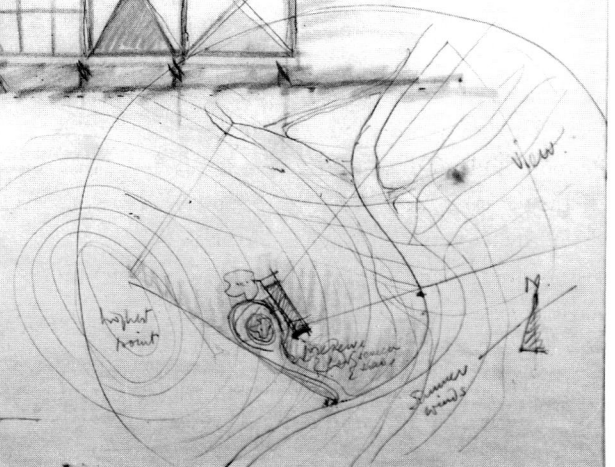

Bold external colour was used for Chermayeff's freestanding studio, near the cottage, built in 1952, and extended in 1957 to provide another area for guests. The frame is made highly legible, especially in section where a 'scissor' truss was used to create different possibilities of internal sky lighting. The panels are in bolder triangles of red, yellow, blue, black and white. A published text explained, 'no attempt has been made to place the house unobtrusively in the landscape. In fact, the building has been deliberately contrasted with its environment by the geometrical treatment of the facade and the bright contrasting colours of the rectangles with their gay informal atmosphere.'[31] As another writer (probably using Chermayeff's own words) put it:

Result: never a dead looking surface. Chermayeff's cottages look like lovely clusters of parasols, sails and flags, entirely fitting in a seaside vacation setting. In a curious way, these sophisticated and colourful abstractions show more respect for nature than many a 'woodsy' cottage.[32]

The scissor truss principle was used for two other houses on the Cape, the Sigerson Cottage and Wilkinson Cottage of 1954. The constructional diagram for the latter illustrates the principle with monopitch bays changing at the end of the house into scissor trusses which create a dramatic, semi-enclosed space for a veranda. The system was good for adding parallel bays to timber frame structures, because it naturally provided a means for sky lighting. This was appropriate for the offices of the local newspaper, *The Cape Codder*, in Orleans, Massachusetts, which Chermayeff also designed in 1954 (see page 168). He was often featured in the paper as a local celebrity. The scissor truss also appears in a project for a Harvard University Yacht club on the Charles River of 1954, made jointly with Peter Chermayeff, essentially a timber frame monopitch with a skylight.

One other house in the same cluster on the Cape was different, because of the nature of its site. The O'Connor House, built in 1956, is on the top of a hill, where the sea could be seen over the treetops. Chermayeff therefore designed a two-storey house with a roof deck on top

O'Connor House, 1956, upper floor interior.

Middle: O'Connor House, 1956

Far left: Wilkinson House, porch.

Opposite: O'Connor House, Cape Cod (Truro, Massachussetts), 1956, plans and elevations.

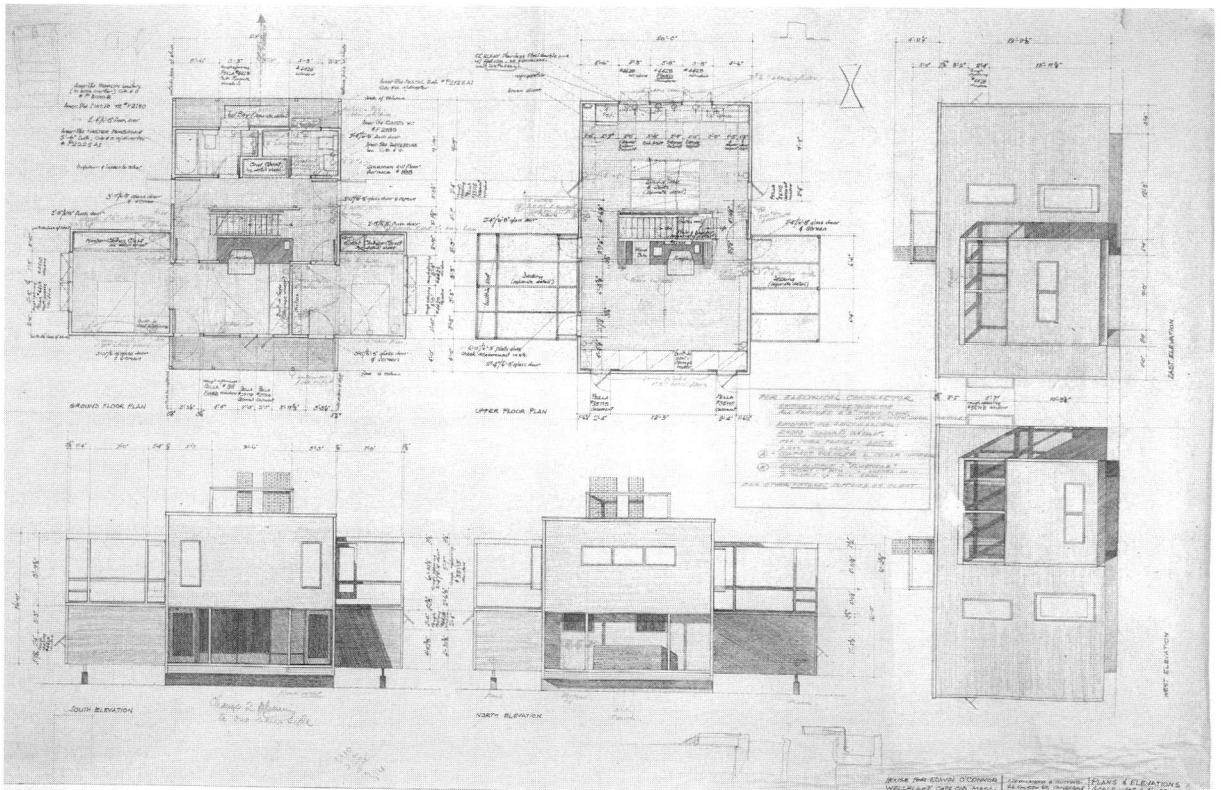

to get up to the view. Edwin O'Connor, the author of *The Last Hurrah*, chose the site with Chermayeff's collaboration and apparently said to a friend who asked what the house was to be like, 'I don't know but Chermayeff does.'[33] The same account continues, 'Essentially the design is outwardly in the classic clapboard tradition of New England and an unpretentious, square-cut form, relieved and partly camouflaged by the use of different colours, the classic grey, barn red and white trim, with the south porch interior a warm yellow.'[34] The basic two-storey rectangular solid of the house is lightened by extensions to the ground floor, each of which has an open porch above with a pergola over the top, creating a sense of interpenetrating geometry. A brick chimney rises up through the centre of the house and appears as two stacks on the rooftop. Main living room and kitchen are on the upper floor to get the benefit of the view, with bedrooms and study below. Most of the seating is on the form of benches with cushions around the wall, mostly in black and white, with 'brightly coloured loose cushions for porch and occasional use'.[35]

With an informality still unusual in 1956, the round dining table is in the kitchen area itself, with easy access to the raised side porches, one to the east for breakfast with a view of the ocean, the other over 'tree tops of the immediate slope towards the ponds, Thoreau's house and the magnificent sunsets'.[36] The stairs come up in the centre of the house, with an internal ladder ascending to the rooftop. The whole house is cantilevered about 4' north and south off raised foundations, which give it an extra sense of lift. A slatted screen conceals the bedrooms from the driveway and the front door is reached up a flight of four steps and along a short piece of decking.

The Payson House was carried out with some office assistance from TAC in Boston, but in the following year, 1953, Chermayeff set up a new office and partnership in Cambridge with Heyward Cutting. Peter Chermayeff writes that Cutting was an appealing partner, who had 'taste, a general aristocratic urbaneness and Britishness', as well as some capital to put into the partnership.[37] Chermayeff made the conceptual design for remodelling Cutting's house on Higgins Pond, Cape Cod by removing part of the first floor to create a double-height living space with a ladder stair, and a sunken sitting area with big cushions around a heating vent in the floor.[38]

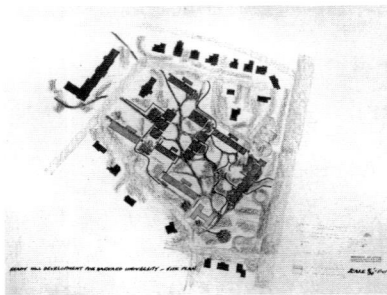

In Cambridge, the practice worked in 1954 on a scheme for the Shady Hill area between Francis Avenue, Bryant Street and Beacon Street, to the north of the Harvard University, who owned the site. The scheme involved private developers, with a mixture of dormitories and apartments. One of the existing roads was to be removed from the site, and perspectives show a pleasant series of paths winding among trees between the buildings, some of them guided by curving walls to create semi-private ground level spaces. Apartment buildings were projected up to eight stories, others forming four-storey walk-up clusters of small apartments with different accommodation on an overall square footprint. These were planned to be laid out in a series of open courtyards, not unlike Harvard Yard, and Chermayeff drew the diagonal routes which he wanted to develop through the site. As far as surviving drawings indicate, the elevations were partly in brick, with heavy access balconies and, in some cases, curved concrete roofs for the penthouse flats, presumably derived from Le Corbusier's Rob & Roq project of 1949. Had this scheme been built, one would have a different impression of Chermayeff's architectural character. The buildings themselves would seem typical of their time, but the use of divisions of exterior space to create a slightly mysterious sense of place would have been memorable.

**Shady Hill Estate, perspective.**

**Middle: Shady Hill Estate, Cambridge, Massachussetts, 1954, sketch plan.**

**Far left: Heywood Cutting House (conversion), Truro, Massachussetts, c. 1953.**

Plans for development of the 'Diamond K' Ranch, Sacramento, California, were made in 1955, a site on the edge of a freeway for which a mixed residential development was proposed, not unlike Chermayeff's scheme for 'Tomorrow's Small House'. There were to be two sets of slab blocks on the upper part of the site and lines of patio row houses quite closely clustered together, stepping down the slopes. This scheme went to a model stage but no further.

Over several years, Chermayeff was involved in a project for a new theatre at Harvard, claiming with some justification that he had experience and knowledge in this field. This formed part of a considerable programme of rebuilding under President Nathan Pusey, after 1953. A competition was proposed in 1954, and in 1959 Chermayeff was working with an English-born theatre designer, Horace Armistead, and the director, Stephen Aaron, but the project was not taken further.

**F.D. Roosevelt Memorial, competition design with Peter Chermayeff, Aram Mardirosiam and Robert Reynolds, 1960.**

At the beginning of 1957, Chermayeff wrote to Cutting to express dissatisfaction with the partnership, whose overheads he felt were eating up the proceeds of those projects which were executed. He seems to have expected Cutting to make introductions to clients. Cutting had only brought in one, while Chermayeff's own contacts produced most of the work. The partnership ceased in the course of the year. Chermayeff did not open another architectural office after this but when, after winning the competition for the Boston Aquarium in 1962, Peter Chermayeff set up Cambridge Seven Associates, including his brother Ivan as a graphic designer and Chermayeff's Harvard pupil, Louis Bakanowsky, the firm provided Serge with an infrastructure for design work, including his own house at 28 Lincoln Street, New Haven, begun in the same year.

One project undertaken jointly, with Peter and three of his fellow students at GSD, Aram Mardirosian, Jack Beyer and Robert Reynolds, was a competition design for a Franklin Delano Roosevelt Memorial in West Potomac Park, Washington DC, in 1961. A total of 574 designs were submitted and the jury, chaired by Pietro Belluschi, chose a rather expressionist romantic design by Pedersen and Tilney & Associates, which was later rejected by the Federal Commission. The Chermayeff design was conceived as abstract forms in landscape, with a giant triangular roof canopy in the form of a space-frame floating among over the tree-tops, sheltering a triangular pinwheel arrangement of stone walls, inscribed with texts from Roosevelt. The triangular theme was carried further out into the landscape, with low walls and lines of water beneath the trees. Peter Chermayeff recalls that 'Serge's scheme for the memorial had wonderful timeless qualities that we students worked out for him, creating a tranquil "place" under an elegant roof structure, floating and free standing ... the whole very rich, strong, understated.'[39] The text accompanying the competition submission speaks of a new era of humanism, served by high technology. It seems a sensitive and un-kitsch response to a difficult symbolic programme, with something of the modern monumentality of Louis Kahn about it.

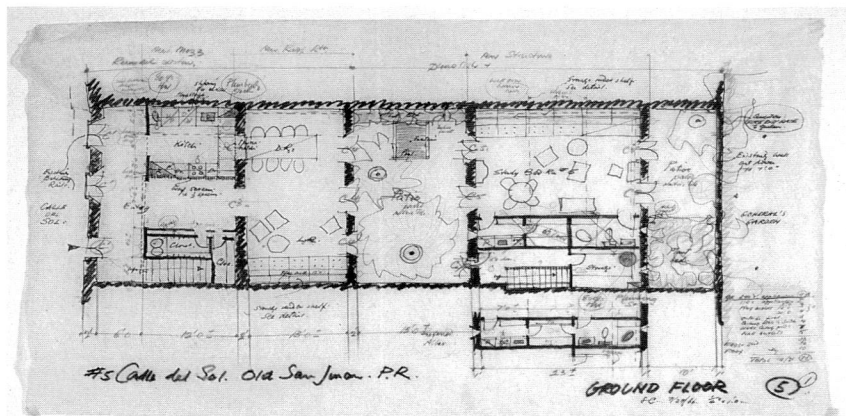

Project for alterations and additions for own residence at 5 Calle del Sol, Old San Juan, Puerto Rico, 1966.

Chermayeff's last and perhaps most interesting major unbuilt project was for infill housing in Wooster Square, New Haven, in 1967, prepared jointly with Cambridge Seven Associates. This area between the Yale University Campus and the rail station had become severely deteriorated by the early 1950s, and in 1954, the City Redevelopment Office and Wooster Square Renewal Committee began work of rehabilitation, with a mixture of new social buildings and action by individual property owners.[40] The Mayor of New Haven at the time, Richard Lindsay, and his Director of Development, Edward Logue, were involved in Chermayeff's teaching at Yale, and understood his ideas.

**Wooster Square, redevelopment study, with Cambridge Seven Associates, Inc., 1967.**

Peter Chermayeff recalls, 'We developed a very good scheme, modest in many ways, severely constrained by a tight site and the minimal funds and tight regulations of the federal housing programme. It was good because Serge was dedicated to amenity, to not only building good quality units but to provideing good social space, indoors and outdoors. He wanted the residents to have places for interaction, for bonding into some kind of community.'[41] The project had been fully designed and was out to tender when the Federal funding was withdrawn. Mayor Lindsay was no longer in office and Chermayeff had to go to the Federal District Court to get his fees for the job, succeeding in getting legal costs and damages as well but he was disappointed not to be able to build a scheme representative of his theories of inner urban development. In 1969, Chermayeff was involved in organising a protest movement against the State Street Highway project, involving an east-west street whose enlargement would have cut off Wooster Square and the struggling southern sector from the city centre.

As part of the Yale group research into housing of imaginary inner-city residential areas, a seductive set of perspective drawings were made, showing children sitting in the 'inner sanctum' of a patio garden, or safely playing in tree-lined pedestrian streets, onto which patio houses open, with their service functions facing onto the vehicular roads. Tall slabs of housing look down on this miniature paradise, which resembles some examples of European housing design of the 1960s in the 'New Casbah' style, such as the Siedlung Halèn near Berne by the Swiss practice, Atelier 5, 1959–61, and Bishopsfield at Harlow New Town by Michael Neylan, 1966.

Chermayeff's last major architectural work was his own house at 28 Lincoln Street, New Haven, 1962-3. He had been frustrated in his ambition to build in Cambridge, where he and Barbara lived in a rented apartment in a modern block at 45 Linnean Street. In New Haven, there appeared initially to be no sites available, but Barbara looked over a garden wall and saw the perfect site, a garden alongside an older house. Although it was not officially for sale, the Chermayeffs approached the owners of the house who were glad to sell it. The narrow strip of land was perfect for a demonstration of the principles of *Community and Privacy* and the fact that Barbara's mother was to live with them made it natural to add more rooms in a semi-independent grouping and the front of the site, rooms which could in theory be adapted for other family members at different times in their life.

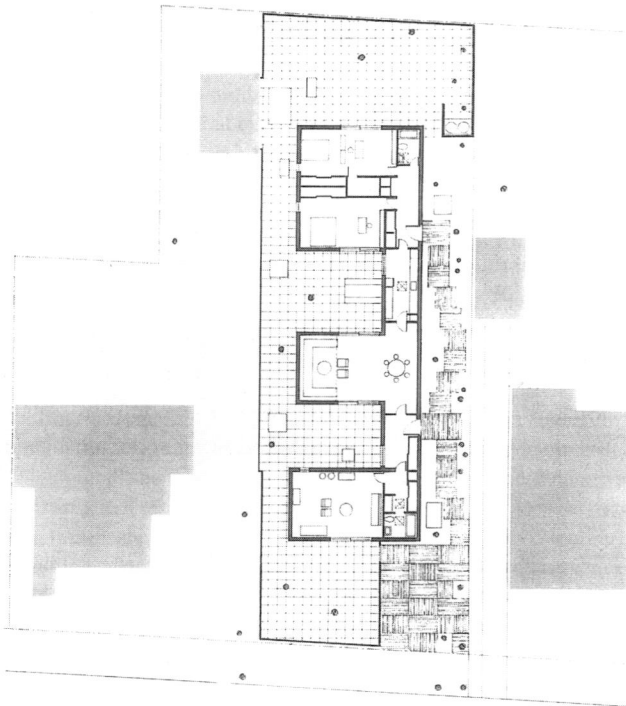

Chermayeff House, 28 Lincoln Street, New Haven, Connecticut, plan.

The house plan, with its three 'cells' linked by a continuous corridor, was able to permit the preservation of the existing trees on the site, giving it a pleasing landscape quality from the beginning. Construction was of concrete block, fairfaced inside and out, with simple door and window details, all of these spanning between the white vinyl tiled floor and the pine boarded ceiling. None of these were materials that Chermayeff would have used in the 1930s but the house is in many ways the fulfilment of his ideas about the planning of Unit Houses, simple and basic in its construction and detailing, while offering a variable set of planning principles. Although the construction gives it unity, the actual dimensions of the three main areas of the house show subtle differences, demonstrating the principle of flexibility within the system. The emphasis is on space and activity but there is also enough enclosure, indoors and out, to create a sense of interiority and focus.

The central section has a raised ceiling to allow for clerestorey lighting and the emphasis on height in the main living space that was a recurrent feature of Chermayeff's house designs. Beneath this upper space, the walls were lined on three sides by built-in bench seating, making an area of suitable scale for a conversational group around a low table, with pictures hanging on the walls above, pride of place going to the large John Piper from Bentley Wood, in its

243

restored condition. A further memory of Bentley Wood came in the form of five of the same pre-war PLAN chairs, which had survived the fire in the wartime store and been recovered after suffering from mildew in its aftermath. Beside the Piper hung a copy by Chermayeff of a late cubist Picasso still life of 1924 which belonged to a colleague in Chicago. He enjoyed these exercises both as a way of learning about the construction of a painting and in order to enjoy a reproduction at large scale as part of his furnishings. He also hung copies of paintings by Ben Nicholson (enlarged in scale from a postcard reproduction), Le Corbusier and Leger. In addition there were Chermayeff's own paintings, and a flatweave rug by Ivan on the floor in blocks of colour. A round dining table with Eames LCM plywood and metal chairs of 1946 was at the opposite end of the room from the sitting area, next to the kitchen and, along the wall there was a display area for hanging paintings and an enormous flat wicker basket, with a broad display ledge and box-like compartments below for pictures and objects (see page 170).

There is a parking space off the road, where the fence with the neighbouring house to the north was removed by mutual agreement, giving freedom to a double line of trees. The part of the garden nearest the road was enclosed by a 7ft high fence of rounded cedar, which Chermayeff said he would have liked to make as a 9ft high wall of the same 'Waylite' concrete blocks as the house. The approach to the front door is paved with in-situ concrete slabs, the 'front' and 'back' doors are the only openings in the wall, the latter giving separate entry to the private study and bedroom section of the house at the far end of the site, which has its own semi-private outdoor space, where Chermayeff painted an abstract mural on the intrusive back of a neighbour's garage, and a concrete low-relief on the ground in front. Making the kitchen into one of the narrow links between the main sections of the house resulted in a very narrow space which is also liable to be used as a passageway, but this configuration could probably have been altered. Ground floor windows faced each other to provide a view through the centre block across from one of the inner courtyards to the other, one peopled by a large upright sculpture, the other with a low outdoor picnic table under the shade of a tree.

The relationship between the house and Chermayeff's theories was emphasised in a text in the English magazine, *Architectural Design*, 'This single unit would therefore appear at mid scale in a hierarchical organisation of systems, ranging from the separation of conflicting elements of service in the dwelling, to the articulation of conflicting activities in the neighbourhood.'[42] This dealt with the large scale but also, 'At the smallest scale within each unit, this principle is reflected in the disposition of the separate components of the house into appropriate realms and integrities. For example, the services such as plumbing and heating are grouped in an accessible under floor trench which runs the full length of the house and over which are grouped all units such as bathrooms, etc. which require this service. Also all electrical circuits are kept separate from the structure, and are exposed (and accessible) but visually integrated into the detailing of the junction of the masonry walls and the wooden ceiling framing.'

The publication showed the house in the context of other studies for patio houses, and their possible assembly into residential neighborhoods.

> A parallel discipline dictates the planning into hierarchical groupings, grading community to privacy, loud areas to quiet, etc. By the grouping of areas into pavilions, these physical and social separations can be made, but visual continuity can be maintained, if desired, by the uninterrupted views across and through the open courts, which are themselves proportioned and as similar to the totally enclosed rooms. In a large project of this type of housing, units would be tightly clustered to demark similar principles of organisation, of private communal and public spaces, social and service access etc.

Chermayeff expressed his pleasure in the house in a letter of 1972 to his English friend, Mary Adams, the commissioner of his early television broadcasts, 'This place is the most livable house we ever had.'[43] English architects came to visit, including Leslie Martin who described it as 'the oasis you have built so skilfully for yourselves'.[44]

Two years later, Richard Sheppard picked up the way the house was an adverse comment on America of the mid-1960s, 'Everything you see is sumptuous, taste is display and architecture a prestige commodity. Concrete blocks, pictures, books, the lovely dogs and you and Mrs Chermayeff came to stand for something we didn't find elsewhere.'[45] This comment may explain why the house in Lincoln Street failed to have the impact that Chermayeff might have hoped for. While it was admired by a select few, it was not an expression of any set of American values, and house design soon began to move in the direction of various forms of post-modernism.

Before leaving New Haven in 1972, the Chermayeffs toyed with the idea of moving to San Juan, Puerto Rico, and bought a property in the centre of the old town, for which Serge made architectural proposals for conversion. Here he might have been able to participate in the kind of dense traditional city life that his books called for and hoped to recreate in the States, against such rooted cultural opposition.

Reviewing his built work after 1940 can only leave a sense of disappointment compared to the intense activity of the 1930s, and Chermayeff's mid-life career change has led to English commentators more or less disregarding the American buildings. Although small in scale and widely spaced over the years, the houses he built are varied, but all have his individual signature, most of all, perhaps, those on Cape Cod where he felt able to relax and develop his ideas about the relationship between architecture and painting, using structural forms and materials simple enough to be adopted by a self-builder.

**Notes**
1 Serge Chermayeff, 'Shape of Community Revisited' (1972), in Plunz 1983, p.194.
2 'A House Divided', *House and Garden*, May 1947, p.96.
3 ibid.
4 'House in Piedmont, California.', *Architectural Forum*, June 1946, p.118.
5 ibid., p.121.
6 Lewis Mumford, 'Skyline' column, *New Yorker*, 11 October 1947, pp.106, 109. Reprinted in Joan Ockman, ed. (1993), *Architectural Culture, 1943-1968*, New York, Rizzoli, pp.108-9.
7 On Eckbo, see Marc Treib and Dorothée Imbert (1997), *Garrett Eckbo, Modern Landscaping for Living*, Berkeley, Los Angeles and London, University of California Press.
8 'Cliff shelter', *Interiors*, September 1947, p.82.
9 Extensions were added by Ernest Born in 1966.
10 Plunz , 1983, p.148.
11 'Cliff shelter', *Interiors*, September 1947, p.82.
12 The list of works in Plunz, 1983 gives the date as 1942, but an exchange of letters between Chermayeff and Soriano in Avery Library of February and April 1946, suggests that this is the correct date.
13 *Architectural Forum*, May 1943, p.139.
14 Joseph Henry Abel, 'The Apartment House' in Talbot Hamlin, ed. (1952), *Forms and Functions of Twentieth Century Architecture*, New York, Columbia University Press, III, p.76.

15 The Museum of Modern Art (1945), *Tomorrow's Small House*, New York, p.19.

16 ibid., p.92.

17 Ibid., pp.3-4.

18 Interview with Betty Blum, 1985, p.90.

19 James Gardner and Caroline Miller (1960), *Exhibition and Display*, London, B.T. Batsford Ltd., p.44.

20 Chermayeff to Richard Lohse, 26 December 1951, Avery Library. In the books by Gardner & Miller and Lohse, the exhibition is misdated to 1949.

21 Richard P. Lohse (1954), *New Design in Exhibitions*, New York, Praeger, p.185.

22 ibid.

23 Ann Pringle, 'Maix shows work of 8 designers in regional fabrics', unidentified news cutting, Avery Library.

24 Chermayeff to Eugene Schmidt, 20 July 1955, Avery Library.

25 Eileen Payson 'Ascent into Architecture', text kindly contributed by Michael Payson.

26 ibid.

27 Serge Chermayeff, 'Home for Herbert Payson Jr., Falmouth Foreside, Maine', Avery Library.

28 Chermayeff to Douglas Haskell, 21 July 1952, Avery Library.

29 EileenPayson, loc. cit.

30 Dating from inscription on the reverse of a photograph in Chermayeff's collection.

31 Kurt Hoffman (1955), *Neue Einfamilienhaüser*, Stuttgart, Julius Hoffman Verlag, p.30.

32 *House and Home*, July 1954.

33 Unattributed text in Chermayeff papers, Oversize box 1, Avery Library.

34 ibid.

35 ibid.

36 ibid.

37 Email to author, 29 October 2000.

38 See article 'How to Remodel a Salt Box' from *Women's Day*, n.d., Chermayeff collection. Chermayeff was involved in further alterations to the house in 1982 for a subsequent owner, Raymond Nasher.

39 Email to author, 29 October 2000. Competition submission with photos and text in Chermayeff family collection. Designs published in Thomas Creighton (1962), *The Architecture of Monuments*, New York, Reinhold.

40 Don Metz and Yuji Noga (1966), *New Architecture in New Haven*, Cambridge MA, MIT Press, no.52. Drawings in Avery Library.

41 Email to author, 29 October 2000.

42 P.F., 'Architect's own house at New Haven', *Architectural Design*, October 1963, p.494.

43 Chermayeff to Mary Adams, 25 April 1972, Avery Library.

44 Leslie Martin to Chermayeff, 25 July 1963, Avery Library.

45 Richard Sheppard to Chermayeff, 29 November 1965, Avery Library.

# Conclusion

Chermayeff carried on working full-time at Yale until June 1969, when he became a Professor Emeritus. Despite the increasing tendency in the school towards post-modernism, his graduate classes remained popular. The 1969 issue of *Perspecta* was dedicated to him, and was prefaced by a tribute from Alexander Tzonis, which commended his consistent hold on the idea of a revolutionary architecture, even through the post-war time, which Tzonis characterises as a kind of proto-postmodernism when, 'the rest of the profession went back to the good old pre-revolutionary times, the times of the private jokes concerning questions of style and puzzles of ornament'.[1] Chermayeff had, however, stuck it out long enough to participate in the student revolution of the 1960s. Tzonis also commented on the institutional resistance in American universities to the kinds of programme that Chermayeff wished to start for architecture, that might have led them away from formalism, 'The academic and professional institutions were once again obscuring reality by tailoring it to their abilities and to the assurances that those abilities gave them. Chermayeff's main contribution was that he pointed the way, proposing new professional attitudes and priorities of commitment; committing his whole life to them without hesitating to sacrifice the comfort of a very professional un-professionalism.'[2]

In retiring officially and becoming a Professor Emeritus, Chermayeff certainly did not feel that his teaching life was over. J.L. Sert had just retired as Dean at the GSD, and in November 1969, the Acting Dean, Maurice D. Kilbridge, informed the President of the College that Chermayeff was 'still striding high, zealous to transform architecture to its new role'. Chermayeff's supporters at Harvard wanted to bring him back as a guest teacher, believing that 'he is one of the few academic architects in the country who has theories of what it's all about and can challenge students intellectually.'[3] Kilbridge added that, 'Some others say I am inviting a tiger into the compound, subdued by age and fate, but far from toothless.' In the event, Chermayeff returned to Harvard to give some seminars in 1974 and continued to work for several years as a guest teacher and lecturer in American universities, an activity which went back to the 1940s.

He was ideal as a visiting teacher or critic, articulate, unafraid of anything or anybody, and able to use a student's scheme to illuminate a general proposition about architecture and planning. An account by the architect and teacher Joseph Passonneau helps to explain the nature of his contribution:

When I was Dean at Washington University we started to have Serge on juries. He and George Anselvicius were great friends, which is how, I think, it all started. Serge was an accurate and devastating critic – with a remarkable memory for student work. He was frequently a thesis juror, which meant that he would come in at the middle of the semester and then descend on the students at the end. He would throw a fit if an issue that he had criticised at mid term was not addressed at the end. Juries … serve many functions. They serve some purpose in adjusting students' architectural skills and attitudes. More importantly, they are exhibitions – and we had some great exhibitions with Serge fencing with other polemicists, such as Aldo van Eyck. But they serve primarily as ceremonies, crowning the end of a long semester, demonstrating that serious architects care about all of the work and misery students go through to get all those drawings up on the walls.

One year, at the final jury, Serge was particularly savage. As always, almost the entire school crowded into our jury room to listen to Serge, and flay a group of (not completely defenceless) students. After a long day Serge had to leave to catch a plane. He had been so unkind that day I was relieved to take him to the airport before the jury was completed. When I got back I was met in front of the architectural building by two students whom Serge had not gotten to. One was in tears. Both were incensed that their work was not reviewed by Serge. I wrote Serge about this and he sent a brief but thoughtful note, commenting on each project – which he could not have spent more than a minute or two examining.[4]

University of Minnesota, Minneapolis, critique sketch, 1958.

Left: Chermayeff at the University of Miami, 1975.

Passonneau also recalled the circumstances in which Chermayeff, who threw his head back when talking, got his nickname at Washington University, 'One of our girl students, rebelling against his discussion of her project, muttered under her breath something like "Listen to old Sniff-sniff!" Serge overheard her, fixed her for a moment with a beady eye, and then cackled briefly and went on to the next project.'

Harris Sobin, of the University of Arizona, wrote:

> Either at desk crits or juries in his own First Year Environmental Design Studio [at Harvard] or at final reviews in later years on which he was frequently a guest juror, Chermayeff demonstrated what for me remains to this day an unparalleled ability to identify, articulate and explore relevant architectural issues with clarity, culture, elegance and wit. He always seemed to immediately and unerringly be able to go to the very heart of what was right or wrong with a student's scheme, conveying to the student, and in the process to the entire class, a firm understanding of exactly why what he identified as right was right, and why what he identified as wrong was wrong, always indicating in the latter case those alternatives open to the student which could improve either process or product.[5]

In some cases, Chermayeff's visits to schools of architecture served to generate controversy about local planning issues in the press. This could be stimulated by a press release about his lecture, or a subsequent reporting. In 1958, as a visiting teacher at the University of Minnesota, where his former Chicago colleague Ralph Rapson (b.1914) was the head of the School of Architecture, Chermayeff took the opportunity to criticise the new car-based plans for a university campus and propose in their place a compact pedestrian scheme which would also open up the river banks. Otherwise, as he wrote to Rapson, 'we shall postpone for more years than I dare to think of … the essential start to build a different and healthier environment for later Americans.'[6] At Tulane University, New Orleans in 1974, a press release gave Chermayeff's statement that 'Technology, industry and the family car have degraded cities, transforming them from havens for wealthy residents into ghettos for the new poor' and his proposal that the car should be treated as an emergency vehicle where population is thin and congestion is no an issue. 'It could be treated like a yacht. It could be something wealthy people put in harbour until ready to go on a cruise and when the pleasure cruise is over, shove it back in the harbour.'[7] He continued the anti-car theme in Columbus, Ohio in April 1978, being reported as saying, 'In no American city is anything spilling out onto the sidewalk or public square. The closest thing you get to that is a person surrounded by a moat of traffic eating his lunch from a brown paper bag in some little green place. It's ridiculous for the richest country in the world.'[8]

Chermayeff had a long-standing interest in developing countries and immediately after his retirement from Yale spent two months in India, at the invitation of the Indian Institute of Architects, visiting schools of architecture and making recommendations for the future of architectural education. He travelled with Barbara, stopping to lecture in Ankara on the way, where students waited a whole day for his arrival. Chermayeff had been invited to visit India in 1962, by Gautam Sarabhai, the founder of the National Institute of Design in Ahmedabad, where Le Corbusier had built a famous house for the Sarabhai family in the 1950s. Chermayeff had a low opinion of the National Institute of Design, of which he wrote privately, 'it appears to have no Indian (vital) priorities; in its "western" copycat programme'.[9] While in India, Chermayeff spent much of his time between engagements with the Sarabhai family, particularly with Gautam's brother, Vikram, scientist and head of the Indian Atomic Energy Commission, discussing the findings of his own research in India. Vikram died tragically young in 1971 at the age of 52 and Chermayeff wrote that 'the loss to science everywhere and to India in her immediate critical fortune is immeasurable.'[10] He also re-met his former student, Charles Correa, and the founder of the school of architecture in Ahmedabad, Balkrishna Doshi, a member of Le Corbusier's Paris atelier in the 1950s.

Chermayeff was funded by the John D. Rockefeller 3rd Fund, and produced a report which is a valuable summary of his general philosophy of environmental design as an interdisciplinary study, focussed on intentions and breadth of thinking rather than technological fixes.

> Growth and change in the human habitat and in human ecology require a theory of environmental design and means for its implementation, a dynamic system of order involving institutional adjustment to changing technological realities: environments to be conserved, modified, or in particular, to be designed having no historic, scientific or technological precedents.'[11]

In India, he found many institutional and economic inhibitions to the advancement of talented practitioners, as well as an inadequate appreciation of India's heritage of built environment, contrasted with the prominence given to new consumer goods.

Chermayeff's recommendations included the establishment of a National Centre for Environmental Studies, on lines similar to his Yale teaching and *Shape of Community*, combining long-term research of worldwide application with an attention to more immediate local problems. As he wrote:

> Learning though doing is probably the most effective way to discover existing realities, to modify these in the light of experience and to make meaningful innovations, however modest. Programs which involved the public in the problems of the currently neglected environment, might make more comprehensible even complex events and the relationship between them.[12]

The fact that Chermayeff deprecated the copying of aspects of modern building forms from magazines did not mean that he undervalued design ability for his 'environmental designers' of the future, and he states in the report that 'admission policies should be liberalised to the greatest possible extent and demonstrable intelligence or talent be given greatest opportunities for development. Design ability is not easily measured by quantitative tests.'[13] He evidently saw a parallel between the separation of the design professions and the absence of an ecological approach, writing that 'an ecological framework will build bridges between arbitrarily separated activities and join preservation, conservation and construction of immediate critical necessities with planning for the future.'[14] Although Chermayeff had an immediate impact on at least one school of architecture in India, where he caused the resignation of the newly-appointed English head, his report failed to have much impact although 'loot' from his Indian trip enriched the decoration of his new studio on Cape Cod on his return.[15]

For someone with Chermayeff's length of experience and acute understanding of the links between politics and the environment, there was plenty in the early 1970s to be depressed about. The 1960s may have rekindled the feeling of revolution but rationality was often lost in the process. One of Chermayeff's lecture engagements was for the 14th Milan Triennale of 1968, where protesting students occupied the exhibition building at the opening and the whole programme, including Chermayeff's lecture, had to be cancelled. His text included the statement that 'Many, including myself, welcome this new revolution of our transition period while at the same time praying that its expression will as quickly as possible become constructive and nonviolent.'[16] He wrote that he sympathised with the students in Milan and Venice, where 'both exhibitions are stale and commercialised' and where he deplored the 'brutal suppression by police'.[17]

In a lecture, delivered in several versions in different places between 1967 and 1971, Chermayeff reflected on how his own experience had led him to deepen his understanding of design. He stressed the development of overlapping concerns that made painters, for example, want to read about politics.

> In architecture, where I uneasily spent some years of my life after having started as a painter, the transition was more precisely measured. It was away from formalism which was really a residual stage of historicism. Eclecticism distinguished the work all around me when my life began. Then, very soon, as I began to think about these things and became interested in them, this was replaced by a kind of structuralism; the influence of the miraculous engineering which was making its appearance at the turn of the century, so that people could see how things were structured and tried to bring this structuring to every creative act from painting and sculpture all the way to architecture, sometimes not too successfully to my mind.[18]

He described how the doctrine of functionalism had mutated from being a concern with over-simplified, mechanistic programmes towards the understanding of dynamic systems, from 'the ideal of a utopian completed master form, lasting forever, perfect and immovable and of course dead, towards systems, towards life which is process.'[19]

His travels in early retirement were for Chermayeff a form of escape. As he said in 1972, he sought 'old friends in old countries or glimpses of "innocent" hope further afield (underdeveloped)! where perhaps humanity will skip the "Modern Age" coming to its dismal conclusion.'[20]

On 1 May 1974, Chermayeff returned to Harvard to deliver the annual Gropius Lecture at the GSD, an occasion he felt was symbolic, in relation to the memory of Gropius himself, who died in 1969, and his own relationship to Harvard. The lecture was entitled 'Institutions, Priorities, Revolutions' and was a compelling statement of his position, emphasising how architecture always lags behind social changes, having failed to foresee the emerging problems of the car. Contemporary critics tried to engage with social issues, he said, thus condemning (without naming directly) Reyner Banham's praise of Los Angeles which, as Chermayeff writes, 'on closer inspection turns out to be the highest density suburban super-cluster with maximised travel time, in the sun, for the affluent. The poor public remains unrecognised. You will recall the closing line in Brecht's "Threepenny Opera": "Die im dunkeln sieht man nicht" (Those in the darkness can't be seen).'[21]

In the short space of a lecture, Chermayeff's priorities and commitments, to borrow his own frequently used phrase, emerged more clearly than in the longer text of *Space of Community*, with a sense of urgency and pathos, reinforced by a Swiftian wit, whose 'savage indignation' had been a consistent feature of his utterances over many years but, with the accumulation of human folly (the Watergate Scandal was beginning to break, leading to the resignation of President Nixon in August 1974). 'We have lost contact with nature, while building our man-made environment too fast', Chermayeff said, 'In the process we lost our sense of wonder and compassion for other living things.'[22] He still foresaw a research-based profession of environmental designers, holding this as a hope for the future, and in a passage which he subsequently quoted as his credo, said:

> I hope that our 'shape makers' will, like old soldiers or the Cheshire Cat, fade away along with their 'creations'. I hope to see these replaced by 'problem-solvers'. I hope to see an international space agency established for here below. I continue to believe that artistic independence is not a myth. I am therefore confident that the beauty of nature and art will join the elegance of science in a new amalgam. And I feel that once this is achieved, this new excellence will be recognised.[23]

Privately, however, Chermayeff did not express such optimism, writing to his son Ivan after the lecture:

> I have come to the conclusion I am no longer good for the young - my world to which I was sent and where I later became an immigrant; the Western World old and new Europe

and N. America with all their imitators everywhere is falling apart quicker than the eye or thought can follow. I look out on the dissolution with distaste. Whatever may replace it on a global scale will take much agony and time. I shall not be there and cannot now imagine its lineaments.[24]

To an interviewer on the *Cape Codder* newspaper, he said in 1973 that he hoped his speech at Montreal, accepting the gold medal of the Royal Canadian Institute of Architects, would be his last public appearance, 'actually I've sworn this to myself because I'm really fed up with going out and I hate architects en masse. They're a dreary bunch, just like doctors.'[25]

In 1980, as a result of much lobbying by his supporters, which generated some of the comments quoted earlier in this chapter, Chermayeff was awarded the AIA and ASCA (American Institute of Architects and Association of Collegiate Schools of Architecture) Award for Excellence in Architectural Education. His speech on receiving the award is a good summary of his interests at the end of his active career, with a broad schematic overview of the twentieth century and his own place in it:

> Over the years, my own preoccupation changed from things one imagined could be personally mastered, such as a painting or a sculpture, to structures of use, such as industrial design or architecture in which you could perhaps master the client first. But then one found, of course, that in addition one had to master the economy and compromise with the existing culture, in which you were supposed to be making an independent, creative judgment. Designing cities is even more difficult.[26]

Compared to this, he described Philip Johnson's recent AT&T Tower in New York as 'a black comedy of contempt'.

Among the last public lectures given by Chermayeff followed the award of the Misha Black Memorial Medal for education in design, at the Royal Society of Arts in London on 20 October 1980, the occasion for his last visit to Europe. In the winter of 1979–80, a large exhibition on the 1930s in Britain was held at the Hayward Gallery, creating a renewed but distinctly nostalgic interest in early modernism, among a public which had decisively rejected its later manifestations. Chermayeff contributed a reminiscence to a special issue of the *Architectural Review* in November 1979, a modest and tender piece of writing, expressing the reality of the hopes of the period as well as their fragility.[27] He could have played along successfully in the role of a 'period piece' and he entertained the journalist Jonathan Glancey, then working at the *Architectural Review*, with reminiscences of his tango dancing days, but when among fellow-professionals – including survivors from the pre-war period – Chermayeff said, 'I will address myself to immediate and rather grimmer problems.'[28]

Ronald Reagan was shortly to enter the White House, and Chermayeff was not wrong in his prediction that 'We are approaching a crisis; violence and abuse of nature and humanity have increased all over.'[29] The talk was called 'The Third Ecology', the term Chermayeff had adopted in *Shape of Community*, where he defined the first ecology as 'the ecology of the sea', the second that of the land, and the third ecology as the man-made one of the cities which was becoming universal for the future, but still very little understood. The fourth ecology would be that of space. Chermayeff emphasised the huge gap between the trivial obsessions then current in the architectural profession and the unavoidable, urgent and largely neglected issue of the environment, in ways that sounds at times like the extremist 'deep ecology' writers of the same period:

> An 'affluent' society now faces the need for austerity instead of galloping consumerism. Non-renewable fuel no longer flows like water and water itself is no longer in endless supply. Even clean air is at a premium. The developed nations like dinosaurs have overcropped their pastures and polluted their environment.[30]

The advantage in foresight which Chermayeff gained from his close following of trends in scientific thinking is particularly demonstrated in this lecture, reasserting his faith in science in the 1930s. He quoted from Jacob Bronowski, one of his long-time friends who had recently become a familiar figure to English television viewers through his series, *The Ascent of Man*, as well as from the biologist Heinz von Foerster, working at the Department of Electrical Engineering at the University of Illinois, Urbana, the author of the foreword to *Shape of Community*, who seems to have done most to introduce Chermayeff to the systems way of thinking and its basis in nature. These were perhaps Chermayeff's lifeline to the rationalist optimism of the 1930s, presented in a much-altered form, overcoming the difficulty of over-determined design and shifting the focus, as he said, 'in a progressive movement away from making "things" to the understanding of "systems". This new knowledge made it possible to discard simple analogies between living organisms and man-made things which were simply matters of organisation at a much simpler level.'[31] Nonetheless, the concluding tone of Chermayeff's speech was dark, quoting Auden's line, 'Seekers after happiness, it is later than you think.' His own holistic view of architecture in the context of environmental design still seems too radical for most professionals. His own comment was that 'my swan song in the US and England are sombre warnings, alas, to people who are rather complacent in spite of the evidence.'[32]

By the time of the Gropius lecture, Chermayeff had moved permanently to Cape Cod, selling the house in New Haven in 1972, and adding his large studio to the end of the summer cottage. Here, cutting down on Martinis for economy's sake, he and Barbara sat and listened to jazz records, Vivaldi and Stravinsky, amidst indoor tropical plants, after working outdoors chopping down dead trees, cutting firewood and fertilising shrubs and flowers, for although the surroundings of the house seemed entirely natural, they had, in fact, been the result of many years' careful attention.[33] As he wrote to a graduate student at Columbia in December 1974, declining a request to give a seminar on the nature of the architectural profession, 'I have rather deliberately (+ characteristically) returned to my first loves: painting, which I do myself, + poetry. I read others, mostly romantic Russians – Pushkin, Lermontov, Mandelstam.'[34] Chermayeff did, in fact, publish some of his own poetry, but did not expect it to be taken seriously. The title given to two of his collections, *Verses of Anger and Affection*, indicates well enough the nature of the loosely structured contents, interspersed with Chermayeff's abstract felt-pen drawings. 'Acknowledgment with tears' characterises these efforts as 'The doggerel of doomy thoughts.'[35]

A more important activity in Chermayeff's retirement was painting, something which was interwoven in his life with architecture. He enjoyed the company of painters from the 1920s onwards but gave up active painting during the 1930s. In the 1940s, his painter and sculptor colleagues at Brooklyn, as well as his New York neighbours like Fernand Leger and Ashille Gorky, provided a stimulus to start again, which coincided with a lull in his architectural work. Another of his artist friends was Constantino ('Tino') Nivola, a Chilean painter and sculptor who was host to Le Corbusier on several occasions in Long Island. Still more significant was the Mexican Sculptor, Enrique Alfarez.[36] Chermayeff produced some of his best paintings while at the Institute of Design in Chicago, exhibiting work in Paris in the *Salon des Réalités Nouvelles* in 1948 and in New York, as well as in Chicago itself. His work of this period, of which a good visual record survives in slide form, is almost entirely abstract, with the exception of a series of designs for a projected ballet, Barn Dance, dated 1947, which show farmyard barns in simple perspective colour planes. The works are often evocatively titled, with names like In the Forest of Night, Lonely Crowd and Morning Window, often suggesting a sense of architectural space (see pages 172–3).

Perhaps, as with Le Corbusier's paintings, it was not so much the paintings themselves that mattered but the ideas that this form of activity helped to release in Chermayeff. As evidence for this view, we have a note to Chermayeff describing how a young woman painter at one of his lectures in Chicago in 1949 was 'delighted with the thoroughly painterly way in which you expressed your ideas, and said she'd been given a tremendous amount to think about'.[37] Chermayeff liked having his paintings appreciated but was also defensive about them. Speaking at Brooklyn College on his return visit in 1957, he said:

> I painted for some seven or eight years, just like hundreds of other people painted who were not painters. To be a painter means to be a painter all the time. I was not a painter all the time, but I found considerable pleasure of a therapeutic kind in painting, in a manner which is sometimes described as Abstract Expressionism, and then I started to look again, at painters like Lorenzetti and Piero della Francesca, and I came to the conclusion that I

could turn them upside down and they were better and more simplified abstract forms than I had myself painted and they had many, many things which I had never even attempted to reach. So I suddenly saw myself in rather poor condition, and I stopped painting.[38]

Overlapping coloured forms are often seen hovering in space, in a way that can be related to John Piper's abstract paintings of the 1930s that Chermayeff admired and collected. This was a consistent influence, and in 1977 he wrote, 'I have only been a part-time painter in my adult life – influenced by my good friends and pioneer modernists in England: Ben Nicholson, Barbara Hepworth, John Piper & Paul Nash in particular.'[39] To Ben Nicholson, Chermayeff wrote in 1974, 'I am now re-encouraged to try my own clumsy hand at abstracting the colour/line-scapes of our woods. I have been drinking them in for decades.'[40] The paintings fall into recognisable groups, often favouring a yellow-blue colour contrast. The forms tend to be vertical, with occasional Nicholson-like circles. Chermayeff experimented with collage (a series uses the stock prices from the *Wall Street Journal*, evidently with a satirical intention), and a series of montages with wooden shingles, wittily playing with the 'eyes' made with the nail-holes. He also had a phase of using forms connected like dovetail joints, similar to the logo of the Center for Urban Studies in Cambridge. These and other images prompt the idea that the paintings were indeed some kind of metaphysical investigation, in which the forms could be seen to have meaning, although always a meaning beyond words. The almost obsessive production of drawings, to which Chermayeff transferred his energy in his last years, suggests that they served as some kind of communication through abstract form, close to the automatic drawing of the doodle, repeated like a dance.

The house on the Cape continued to be a place for summer holidays for members of the family, of whom Chermayeff was intensely proud. He enjoyed swimming in the pond, which in earlier summer holidays had been a place for raucous jousting between home-made rafts. In those days, many creative activities took place spontaneously in the open air, making impromptu mobiles and sculptures, some evidence of which remained. The cottage itself became decorated not only with its typical Chermayeff colours of deep red, yellow, grey and blue, but with paintings nailed onto the weather-boarding, dappled with light or bisected by diagonal shadows. Living year-round in a holiday home in a remote place may not be the ideal for a retirement of twenty-five years. Apart from his painting and drawing, Chermayeff found less and less to enjoy as his old age stretched our almost indefinitely, and his mobility declined. Norman McGrath captured him on video, wearing his red dressing gown and going out onto the sitting deck in early spring, grumpily refusing to answer bland conversational questions. Apparently perennial, he died of no particular ailment, but seemingly more by an act of will.

How can Chermayeff's long career be summarised? When he died, the obituaries in the English newspapers were more extensive than the American ones, indicating that the revival of interest in his work of the 1930s had given it an established place in the canon of the period.

The second half of his career has necessarily always been more difficult to explain, since teaching cannot be easily summarised, and its influence is felt over long periods of time. The buildings of this period are not so dramatic, interesting and enjoyable though they undoubtedly are. Jerzy Soltan, his colleague and admirer at Harvard, believed that Chermayeff had martyred himself to teaching, suppressing his own creativity. 'I suspect that his enormous talents and success as pedagogue became almost a tragedy in his life. The activities of an educator are inscribed mostly in the heads (brains), emotions (hearts) and general culture of his students and disciples. Let us face it, these are not the most permanent witnesses of a man's greatness.'[41]

The ambiguous nature of his achievement was emphasised by Soltan in another letter in which he wrote:

> I was on several juries reviewing the work of Serge's students in his advanced programme at Yale. I was disheartened by the quality of his work (it was the first time I was there some vast city redesign project) and by Serge's intellectual position … I felt that Serge could teach a superb elementary course because he was so broadly and deeply knowledgeable about the fundamental issues in architecture. But in addressing complex issues late in his career he was not effective. The world had passed him by.[42]

Chermayeff might perhaps have been able to design important late buildings, but he never overestimated his ability as an architect, perhaps because he had never undergone the professional formation that for many architects makes their own mystery a task compelling above all others. Instead he was able, for a term of thirty years or so, to show architects that they had tasks other than the production of pure architecture.

The failure of *Shape of Community* to make an impact looks like evidence that, even if Chermayeff had been asking the right questions, he was not in the end able to formulate answers that had sufficient appeal or applicability. Perhaps it came at the wrong time, yet former Yale students writing in *Perspecta* in 1997 identified the shortcomings of the architecture course at the university in the 1980s in just the terms that Chermayeff would have chosen to describe his own intentions as a teacher:

> As we know to have been true throughout architectural discourse over the last quarter-century, our graduate training was almost entirely disengaged from the social and professional dimensions of design. While form and formal theories were analysed exhaustively, questions of social planning, technological innovation, user participation, and professionalism – concerns that naturally arose in our thoughts and conversations – were largely ignored in the studio and classroom. Missing too was any sense of architecture as a vehicle of opposition to the social and economic directions of the nation as a whole.[43]

Since this was an issue reviewing the 1960s, it might have been expected that in the year after his death, Chermayeff's name would have occurred several times in the texts but it is absent. Architectural theory has recently become central to the study of the subject but Chermayeff is equally absent from the anthologies of theoretical texts covering the period.[44]

It is not yet easy to judge whether the views of Chermayeff's former pupils, colleagues and supporters is special pleading. Alexander Tzonis wrote a long obituary on Chermayeff which concluded:

> many of the ideas of Chermayeff no longer shock. They have become absorbed quietly into the mainstream of design practice and education, justifying his decision to devote a considerable period of his life to research and teaching, to theory and methodology of design ... But there are also other aspects of Chermayeff's thinking that remain as fresh, unfulfilled, topical and demanding as at the time of their inception in the 1960s, 1950s or even the 1930s. A book about them is urgently needed and perhaps even more urgently needed is further work along lines of this thinking.[45]

It is impossible not to trace the activity of Richard Rogers as a promoter of urban renewal on a high political level back to Chermayeff's early influence on him, whatever other strands may have contributed to his thinking.

At the present time, when the idea of modernism in architecture is readily commodified and reduced to a set of images, Chermayeff's own images are themselves established as a part of this process. The persistence of these images, particularly of Bentley Wood, which has caused it to be the subject of recent articles in both French and Japanese magazines, indicates that something deeper was afoot. To find this, one might return to the influence of Eric Gill on Chermayeff's thinking at the beginning of the 1930s, exemplified in the phrase he liked to quote, 'Beauty looks after herself'. Gill did not invent this idea, for it is articulated in the writings of Aristotle, and Gill absorbed it through the writings of the French philosopher, Jacques Maritain. Chermayeff testified to the importance of his conversations with Gill, which were in effect his substitute for a formal training in art theory and there is no evidence that he had any single stronger influence to form his view of the purpose of art, and although he made no other connection to this neo-Thomist tradition, it offers one form of explanation for his beliefs.

As Thomas Dilworth describes it, 'the artist must not try to produce emotion, even delight. He must focus only on the thing he is making. This is the essence of artistic integrity.' As Maritain claimed, the artist 'sees deeper than others and ... discovers concrete spiritual radiances, which others are unable to discern.'[46] Although Chermayeff was in no conventional sense a religious man, he, like many others in the twentieth century, channelled this rigorous search for truth into artistic activity, in his case architecture and design, and later teaching. This was the impulse, which led first to architecture, and then beyond it. To quote Maritain again:

> the artist must ... of his own free will abandon fertile tracts for the arid and the perilous ...
> in the order of making and from the point of view of the beauty of the work of art,
> he must be humble and magnanimous, prudent, upright, strong, temperate, simple,
> pure, ingenuous.[47]

These qualities are set apart from contingencies of time and place, and can be seen in relation to Chermayeff's remarkable unity of life and work, the wild diversity of his early biography notwithstanding.

The resulting consistency was something he was himself able to recognise, writing about the collection of his essays and writings assembled by Richard Plunz:

> I was pleasantly surprised by the first RIBA lecture (Giles Gilbert Scott in the chair, et al).
> I can now honestly say with Mies: 'I don't change my mind every day' – or even in four
> decades.[48]

**Notes**

1 Alexander Tzonis, in *Perspecta*, vol.12, 1969, p.15.

2 ibid.

3 Maurice D. Kilbridge to Nathan Pusey, 12 November 1969, Harvard University Archives.

4 Joseph Passonneau to Peter Blake, 12 March, 1979. Chermayeff family collection.

5 Harris Sobin, Professor of Architecture, University of Arizona, Tucson, to John Clancy, President, Boston Society of Architects, 21 January 1980. Chermayeff family collection.

6 Chermayeff to Ralph Rapson, 30 January 1958, Avery Library.

7 Tulane University Press Release, 6 May 1974, Avery Library.

8 Chermayeff to Rolf Goetze, 28 December 1971, Avery Library.

9 Chermayeff to Mrs Sarabhai, n.d., Avery Library.

10 *Columbus Dispatch*, 13 April 1978, p.C2, cutting in Avery Library.

11 Serge Chermayeff, 'Design of the Physical Environment in India, Professional Standards and Education', 31 March 1970, Avery Library.

12 ibid., p.19.

13 ibid., 23.

14 ibid., p.24.

15 As described by Chermayeff in 'Environmental Design is our goal', Pidgeon Audio-Visual.

16 'Formal and Structural Changes in Human Settlement', p.4, Avery Library,
Box 8 (65-69).

17 Chermayeff to M.J. Rossant, 5 July 1969.

18 Serge Chermayeff, 'Shape of the Urban Community: Humanistic Considerations', talk at New York Academy of Sciences, October 19 1967, repeated as 'Urban Commitments and a Theory of Design', talk to Yale University, Department of City Planning, October 1968, and as 'Design as Catalyst', A.S. Hook Memorial Lecture, Centenary Convention, Royal Australian Institute of Architects, 1971, pp.1-2. Texts in Avery Library.

19 ibid., p.2.

20 Serge Chermayeff to Albert Eide Parr, Director Emeritus, The American Museum of Natural History, 23 January 1972, Avery Library.

21 Serge Chermayeff, 'Institutions, Priorities, Revolutions', Gropius Lecture, Harvard, 1974, in Plunz, 1983, p.207.

22 ibid., p.209.

23 ibid., p.211. This passage is quoted in Muriel Emanuel, *Contemporary Architects*, St James's Press, New York, London etc. editions 1980, 1994.

24 Chermayeff to Ivan Chermayeff, dated 14 April 1974, but context shows clearly that it came after the lecture, Avery Library.

25 Betsy Cochran and Gwen Hobbs, 'A Reflective Serge Chermayeff shows his paintings, writes his grandchildren', *Cape Codder*, 26 July 1973, Section 2, p.3.

26 Serge Chermayeff, 'Thinking before Acting', *AIA* Journal, April 1980, p.60.

27 See edited version 'An Explosive Revolution' in *Architectural Review*, November 1979, p.309. The full text appears as 'Thinking about the Thirties' in Plunz, 1983, pp.213-7.

28 Serge Chermayeff, 'The Third Ecology', *DIA Yearbook*, (Design and Industries Association) 1981, pp.5-10 and, with excisions, in Plunz, 1983, pp.93-100.

29 Plunz, 1983, p.92.

30 *DIA Yearbook* 1981, p.5.

31 ibid. p.8; Plunz, 1983, p.97.

32 Chermayeff to Mehmet Doruk Pamir, Ankara, 5 November 1980, Avery Library.

33 See Chermayeff's letter to Clare and Molly Robinson, 28 March 1973, Avery Library.

34 Chermayeff to Linda Yowell, 26 December 1974, Avery Library.

35 'Acknowledgment with Tears' in *Anger and Affection II*, 1990, p.33.

36. Peter Chermayeff writes that Chermayeff probably met Alfarez in 1940 in California. 'Serge and he bonded, and remained close to the end, though they saw each other infrequently. Ricky as an artist/craftsman was one reason for the bond, but their close tie had more to do with enjoying each other as personalities, both sharing a maverick background. Ricky, with peasant background, was a wild spirit. He rode as a young man with Pancho Villa and afterwards emigrated to the US and settled in New Orleans, where he became a popular figure, given many commissions by museums and the city, responsible for an amazing production of substantial pieces of public art. Serge and Barbara, when they first met, left Ivan and me with Ricky for several weeks, ages about 8 and 4 or so, and told us many times how astonished they were to return and find us working in Ricky's studio making myriad things in wire and wood and plaster and paper.' Email to author, 1 January, 2001.

37 Ben Park (President, The Documentary Company) to Chermayeff, 30 November 1949, Avery Library.

38 Chermayeff's talk at Brooklyn College, May 1957, SC Box 6 (55-59) 1957, Avery Library

39 SC to Viola Hadler, Art Department, Brooklyn College, 4.8.77. Avery Library.

40 Chermayeff to Ben Nicholson, 22 June 1974, Tate Gallery Archive, Ben Nicholson papers 8717 1.2.699.

41 Jerzy Soltan to John M. Clancy, 4 January 1980, Chermayeff family collection.

42 Jerzy Soltan, letter to Peter Chermayeff, n.d. (c.1980), Chermayeff family collection.

43 Editorial, *Perspecta* 29, 1997, p.xiii.

44 For example, Joan Ockman, ed. (1992), *Architecture Culture 1943 to 1968*, New York, Rizzoli, and Kate Nesbitt, ed. (1996) *Theorising a New Agenda for Architecture*, New York, Princeton Architectural Press.

45 Alexander Tzonis, 'Serge Chermayeff, Humanist,' *Spazio e Società*, July-Sept 1997, p.25.

46 Thomas Dilworth, 'David Jones and the Maritain Conversation' in Belinda Humfrey and Anne Price-Owen, eds. (2000), *David Jones, Diversity in Unity*, University of Wales Press, Cardiff, p.45, quoting Jacques Maritain (1923), *The Philosophy of Art*, Ditchling, St Dominic's Press, p.90.

47 Maritain op. cit., p.119-20.

48 Chermayeff to Jaqueline Tyrwhitt, 20 October 1974, Avery Library.

# Chronology

Information for this chronology, including list of works, publication references and unpublished texts, is largely drawn from Richard Plunz, ed. (1983) *Design and the Public Good, Selected Writings 1930-1980 by Serge Chermayeff*, MIT Press. I have made some additions and corrections. Some additional biographical information is drawn from the Chermayeff papers, interviews, etc. but much of the earlier information remains dependent on Chermayeff's own account as given to Richard Plunz.

## 1900
Born 8 October, near Grozny.

## 1907
Made clay head of Tolstoy for his grandfather.

## 1910
Entered Peterborough Lodge School, Hampstead.

## 1915
Entered Harrow School (house: The Knoll).

## 1916
Won the Henry Yates-Thompson prize for Design and Colour.

## 1918-20
Won the Henry Yates-Thompson prize for Design and Colour.
Left Harrow School.
Gazetted briefly into British Army as interpreter for General Maynard, at Murmansk. Worked for Amalgamated Press, London as an illustrator.
Left to teach and compete in ballroom dancing; wrote and edited *The Dancing World*.

## 1921
Visited Berlin briefly to meet mother and father, who came from Moscow.

## 1922-23
Sailed to Argentina to a friend's estancia; later becomes a partner in a dance hall in Buenos Aires.

## 1924
Changed name to Chermayeff by deed poll.

Worked for Ernest Williams Ltd. as an interior designer.

## 1925
Introduced to playwright Frederick Lonsdale, and to actor and producer Gerald du Maurier; made acquaintance of George Bernard Shaw.
September: *The Last of Mrs Cheyney*, play by Frederick Lonsdale, starring du Maurier and Gladys Cooper, opened at St. James's Theatre with sets by Chermayeff.

## 1927
International Tango Competition, London Palladium, 1927.
Met Barbara Maitland May.

## 1928
Took British nationality.
Married Barbara Maitland May.
Employed by Waring and Gillow as Director of Modern Art Studio, London.
11 November: opening of exhibition Modern Art in French and English Furniture and Decoration, Waring and Gillow.
### Works
• Interiors and furnishings for the exhibition Modern Furnishings, Waring and Gillow, London (in association with Paul Follot).
• Modern Art in French and English Decoration and Furniture exhibition, Waring & Gillow Galleries. Catalogue, 1928.
• Robertson, Howard, 'Modern Art in Decoration and Furnishing', *Architect and Building News*, CXX, 30 November 1928, pp.693-97.
• *Architects' Journal*, LXVIII, 26 December 1928, p.918; LXXIV, 4 November 1931, p.606.
• Christopher Hussey, 'The Modern Home', *Country Life*, LXIV, 8 December 1928, pp.840-43; 15 December, p.846, 22 December, p.915.
• Rogers, J.C. 'Modern Decoration at Warings', *Design in Industry Quarterly Journal*, December 1928, pp.3; 4-6.
• *Architectural Review*, LXV, January 1929, p.51; LXVIII, December 1930, p.266; LXXII, October 1932, pp.148, 151.
• *Decorative Art Yearbook 1929*, London: The Studio 1929, pp.101-15

• Wainwright, Shirley B., 'The Waring Exhibition', *Creative Art*, February 1929, pp.131-35.
• Cabinet Maker, 28 June 1930, p.735.
• Rogers, John C. *Modern English Furniture*, Country Life, 1930, pp.24, 26, 30, 52, 76-77.
**Unpublished texts**
(With Paul Follot) 'The Evolution of Decorative Art: its motives, its history and its present tendencies'. Talk at Exhibition of Modern Furnishings at Waring and Gillow, London

## 1929
June: took lease on house at 52 Abbey Road, London NW8 and designed new interiors.
Met Mansfield Forbes and Raymond McGrath.
**Works**
• With Paul Follot, 'Interiors for L'Atlantique' (destroyed).
• Guardian, G.B. 'La Decoration de l'Atlantique', *Beaux Arts* XI, October 1931, p.11.
• Chavance, R., 'Le Paquebot l'Atlantique et les beaux métiers', *Art et Decoration*, LX, November 1931, pp.153-64.
• Office for C. Derry at Ambrose Wilson Ltd., Vauxhall Bridge Road, London, SW1 (destroyed)
• *Design in Industry Quarterly Journal*, No.10, (December 1929), second photo following p.14.
• *Decorative Art Yearbook 1930*, London: The Studio, 1930, p.88.
• *Architectural Review*, LXVIII, July 1930, p.40.
• *Design in Industry*, No.1 (New Series), Spring 1932, p.9.
Miscellaneous projects and items of furniture, Waring and Gillow, London, 1928-30.
• *Decorative Art Yearbook 1929*, London: The Studio, 1929, p.118.
• Yerbury, F.R. (1929) *Small English Houses*, London, Victor Gollancz Ltd., Pl.CXXXVI.
• *Decorative Art Yearbook 1930*, London: The Studio, 1930, pp.59-62, 88, 91, 98.
• *The American Federation of Arts, Decorative Metalwork and Cotton Textiles*, New York, 1930-1931; illustration no.41. Catalogue of the Third International Exhibition of Contemporary Industrial Art.
• Rogers, J.C., *Modern English Furniture*, Country Life, 1930, pp.30, 32, 59-60, 92, 95, 129.
• Wichmann, Hans, *Design contra Art Déco, 1927-1932*, Jahrfünft der Wende, Munich, Prestel, 1993, p.194.
• Brohan, Torsten, and Berg, Thomas (1994) *Avant-Garde Design 1880-1930*, Cologne, Benedikt Taschen, pp.132-33.

## 1930
Foundation of Twentieth Century Group.
Meeting with Charlotte Perriand, arranged by Jack Pritchard.

Lecture to Cambridge University Architectural Society.
3 December: Meeting of Exhibition Sub-Committee of Twentieth Century Group.
**Works**
• Chermayeff Office, 173 Oxford Street, London W1 (destroyed).
• *Architectural Review*, LXVIII, July 1930, p.36.
• Chermayeff house interiors, 52 Abbey Road, London NW8 (destroyed).
• *Decorative Art Yearbook 1929*, The Studio, 1929, p.115.
• *Architectural Review*, LXVII, May 1930, pp.270-72, 288-89, 292; LXXI, February 1932, p.74; LXXII, October 1932, p.154.
• *Country Life*, LXVII, 21 June 1930, pp.919-20.
• *Creative Art*, VII, August 1930, pp.144-45.
• *The Studio*, C, August 1930, pp.144-45.
• *Innen Dekoration* (Darmstadt) XLI, August 1930, pp.318-23.
• *Decorative Art Yearbook 1931*, The Studio, 1931, pp.74-108.
• Aloi, Roberto (1934) *L'Arredamento Moderno*, 6 vols., Milan, U. Hoepli, I, Plate 547.
• Hoffmann, Herbert (1930) *Die Neue Raumkunst in Europa und Amerika*, Stuttgart, J. Hoffmann Verlag, pp.92-93.
• Morning Room at Bath House, Piccadilly, London W1 for Lady Ludlow (destroyed).
• *Architect and Building News*, CXXIX, 1 January 1932, pp.2-3
• *Architectural Review*, LXXI, February 1932, p.76.
• *Decorative Art Yearbook 1932*, The Studio, 1932, p.32.
Cambridge Theatre, Seven Dials, London WC2 (altered but largely surviving).
• *Architect and Building News*, CXXIV, 10 October 1930, pp.484, 491-96, 508; CXXV, 9 January 1931, pp.76-77.
• *Architectural Review*, LXVIII, October 1930, pp.159-64; LXIX, May 1931, pp.181-82
• *Architects' Journal*, LXXII, 8 October 1930, pp.539-42.
• *Creative Art*, VII, November 1930, p.383.
• *Architecture Illustrated*, II, April 1931, pp.119-29.
• *Moderne Bauformen*, XXX, May 1931, pp.208, 217-24.
• *Architectural Design and Construction*, II, June 1932, p.325.
• 'London's Longest Run', *Theatrephile*, II, No.6, 1985, pp.59-63.
• Perspective of foyer in Victoria and Albert Museum.
**Publications**
'Modernism. 1880-1930. Phases of Furnishing Fashion.' *The Cabinet Maker*, 28 June 1930, pp.734-35 (extract in Richard Plunz, ed. (1983) *Design and the Public Good*, Cambridge MA and London, MIT Press, pp.9-11).
**Other texts**
• 'Brief Statement of the 20th Century Group Beliefs.',

1930, (extract in Richard Plunz, ed. (1983) *Design and the Public Good*, Cambridge MA and London, MIT Press, pp.109-110).
• 'Artificial Light. A Few Remarks on Power, Position and Use', c.1930.
• 'Furniture and Decoration', c.1930.
• 'Harmony in the House', c.1930.
• 'Originality vs. Plagiarism, or Alternatively, Creating vs. Copying', c.1930.
• 'Private Lives - Private Lights', c.1930.

## 1931
January Elected to executive committee of Twentieth Century Group.
26 February: meeting of Twentieth Century Group at the Savoy Hotel.
Left Waring and Gillow to set up independent practice.
Summer: visited Germany with Jack Pritchard and Wells Coates.
Beginning of Broadcasting House project.
**Works**
• Competition entry for exhibition stand for Venesta Plywood Company, Building Trades Exhibition, Olympia, London.
• *Architect and Building News*, CXXV, 13 March 1931, p.376.
• Office for a Dermatologist (unidentified client), London (destroyed).
• *Architectural Review*, LXXII, July 1932, p.33.
• *Design for Today*, III, June 1935, p.228.
• Flat for Dudley Tooth, 41 Gloucester Square, London W2 (destroyed).
• *Studio*, IV, July 1932, pp.48-9.
**Publications**
• 'German Furniture. Notes on the Exhibition at Leipzig . . .' *The Cabinet Maker*, 28 March 1931.
• 'Contemporary Decoration', letter to the editor, *Architects' Journal*, LXXIII 1 April 1931, p.486.
• 'Film Shots in Germany with some Notes on the Film', *Architectural Review*, LXX, November 1931, pp.131-33.
• 'A New Spirit and Idealism', *Architects' Journal*, LXXIV, 4 November 1931 (talk given at Heal and Sons, 26 October – extract in Richard Plunz, ed. (1983) *Design and the Public Good*, Cambridge MA and London, MIT Press, pp.227-31).

## 1932
6 June: birth of Ivan Chermayeff.
June: opening of Broadcasting House.
14 September: BBC radio broadcast.
October: Fellowship application, RIBA.
December: formation of PLAN Ltd.
**Works**
• Interiors for Broadcasting House, London (entire eighth floor and third floor talk studios - destroyed).

• *Architect and Building News*, CXXX, 20 May 1932, pp.258-66; CXXXII, 14 October 1932, 'The Architect's Portfolio, no.188', following p.44; 21 October 1932, 'The Architect's Portfolio, no.189', following p.76.
• *Architects' Journal*, LXXV, 25 May 1932, pp.689-93.
• *Architectural Review*, LXXII, August 1932, pp.53-6; 64-5; 68-70; 72, plates V, VI; LXXIII, March 1933, pp.133-5; LXXXIII, May 1938, p.256.
• *Country Life*, LXX, 28 May 1932, pp.596-603.
• *Design for Today*, I, May 1932, pp.26, 28; II, November 1934, p.421.
• *British Broadcasting Corporation, Broadcasting House, London*, 1932, booklet.
• Proposal for Chermayeff House, Puttenham, Surrey. *Architectural Review*, LXXII, November 1932, pp.214-15.
• Chermayeff, Serge, *The Architectural Application of Colour*, London, Nobel Chemical Finishes, January 1936.
• Nesting Armchair with steel frame, Model R.P.7, for Pel, Ltd.
• *Architectural Review*, LXXIII, July 1932, p.65 and Pl.64 (with attribution to Leopold Quittner of Vienna); LXXVIII, December 1935, p.261.
• Read, Herbert (1934) *Art and Industry: The Principles of Industrial Design*, London, Faber and Faber Ltd., p.79.
• MacCarthy, Fiona (1972) *All Things Bright and Beautiful*, London, Allen and Unwin Ltd., Plate 108.
• Sharp, Dennis, Benton, Tim and Cole, Barbie Campbell (1977) *Pel and Tubular Steel Furniture of the Thirties*, London, The Architectural Association.
• Studio for Anthony Gibbons Grinling, Swan Court, Chelsea, London SW3 (destroyed).
• Patmore, Derek, *Colour Schemes and Modern Furnishing*, The Studio, 1945, p.23, Plate 21.
**Publications**
• 'Review of the Daily Express Building, Ellis and Clarke, architects', Architectural Review, LXXII, July 1932.
• 'Away with Snobbery, Sentiment and Stupidity', *Listener*, VIII, 21 September 1932, pp.393-5 (extract in Richard Plunz, ed. (1983) *Design and the Public Good*, Cambridge MA and London, MIT Press, pp.13-16).
**Unpublished texts**
• 'A Tonic for Architecture', remarks made in a discussion following a talk by Joseph Emberton, given at the Design and Industries Association, 26 January, 1932 (extract in Richard Plunz, ed. (1983) *Design and the Public Good*, Cambridge MA and London, MIT Press, pp.113-114).
• 'Modern Furniture', Talk at Victoria and Albert Museum, London, 17 November 1932.

## 1933
Mendelsohn and Wijdeveld in London to discuss Académie Européenne Mediterranée.

Autumn: establishment of Mendelsohn and Chermayeff partnership at 173 Oxford Street.

October: Ekco Radio 74 launched.29 December: closing date for Bexhill competition.

**Works**

• 'Kernal' House prototype and furnishings (Week End House).

• *Architects' Journal*, LXXVII, 29 July 1933, pp.868-70; LXXVIII, 6 July 1933, p.14; 30 November 1933, pp.691-5.

• *Architectural Review*, LXXIV, July 1933, pp.20-1; LXXVI, September 1934, p.105.

• *Design for Today*, I, July 1933, pp.94-5; II, February 1934, p.59.

• *Decorative Art Yearbook 1934*, The Studio, 1934, p.53. Exhibition of British Industrial Art in Relation to the Home (catalogue), London, Dorland Hall, 1933, pp.22-24.

• Summerson, John and Williams-Ellis, Clough (1933) *Architecture Here and Now*, London, Thomas Nelson & Son, Ltd., p.44.

• Exhibition Modern Living for Whiteley's, London (including model 'Week End House').

• *Architects' Journal*, LXXVIII, 30 November 1933, pp.691-95.

• Astragal (pseud.), 'Review of the Year', Architects' Journal, LXXIX, 11 January 1934, p.93.

• *Design for Today*, I, November 1933, p.285; December 1933, p.322; II, January 1934, pp.32-3; February 1934, p.105.

• *Architectural Review*, LXXVI, September 1934, p.105. Joel, David (1933) *The Adventure of British Furniture 1851-1951*, London, Ernest Benn, Ltd., p.117. Interiors for the BBC Broadcasting House, Birmingham (destroyed).

• *Architects' Journal*, LXXIX, 22 February 1934, pp.268.280-6.

• *Architectural Review*, LXXV, February 1934, p.72; March 1934, pp.106, 108.

• *Architectural Forum*, LXIV, June 1936, p.486. Furniture for PLAN Ltd.

• *Architectural Review*, LXXIV, July 1933, pp.28, 30; August 1933, p.72; LXXVIII, December 1935, p.265, 272; December 1935 pp. 261, 262, 272; LXXX, November 1936, p.229.

• *Architects' Journal*, LXXVIII, 6 July 1933, pp.26-27.

• Chermayeff, Serge, 'Letters from Readers: Plan Furniture', *Architects' Journal*, LXXVIII, 6 July 1933, p.12.

• *Design for Today*, II, July 1933, pp.94-5; April 1934, p.144; October 1934, pp.378-9; December 1934, pp.454-5, 459.

• *Decorative Art Yearbook 1936*, London, The Studio, 1936, p.89.

• Read, Herbert (1934) *Art in Industry: The Principles of*

*Industrial Design*, London, Faber & Faber Ltd., pp.86-7, 106.

• Pevsner, Nikolaus (1937) *An Enquiry into Industrial Art in England*, Cambridge, Cambridge University Press, pp.37, 41.

• Bakelite Radio Cabinets for Ekco, E.K. Cole, Ltd., London (until 1935).

• *Design for Today*, I, October 1933, p.239 (Model 74). Chermayeff, Serge, Letter to the editor, *Design for Today*, I, November 1933, p.282 (Model 74).

• Littman, Frederic H., 'The Evolution of the Wireless Receiver and its use in the home', *Design for Today*, IV, March 1936, p.97 (Model AC 86).

• *Decorative Art Yearbook 1934*, London, The Studio, 1934, p.126 (Model 64).

• *Architectural Review*, LXXVIII, December 1935, p.282 (Model AC 86).

• Pevsner, Nikolaus, 'Broadcasting Comes of Age', *Architectural Review*, LXXXVII, May 1940, p.190 (Model 74).

• *Trend in Design of Everyday Things*, II, Summer 1936, p.83. Quarterly of the Design and Industries Association (Model 74 and Model AC 86).

• Games, Stephen, 'Wireless Workshop', *Listener*, XCVIII, March 30 1978, p.414 (Model 74).

• Pevsner, Nikolaus (1937) *An Enquiry into Industrial Art in England*, Cambridge, Cambridge University Press, pp.104-6, 199 (Model 74).

• Wichmann, Hans, *Design contra Art Déco, 1927-1932, Jahrfünft der Wende*, Munich, Prestel, 1993, p.112.

**Publications**

• 'The Modern Approach to Architecture and its Equipment', *Architects' Journal*, LXXVII, 8 March 1933, pp.337-80.

• Talk to West Yorkshire Society of Architects, 2 March 1933. Synopsis and excerpt of talk in *Builder*, CLVI, 7 April 1933, p.589.

• 'Design Demonstrated in the Exhibition of British Industrial Art', *Design for Today*, I, July 933, p.92.

• 'Thoughts on Modern Architecture. A Review by Serge Chermayeff' (Review of R.A. Duncan, The Architecture of a New Era), London, D. Archer, 1933, *RIBA Journal*, XL, 8 July 1933, p.689.

• 'The Grammar of Groundwork', *Architectural Review*, LXXIV, October 1933, pp.147-8, 153-4.

• 'New Materials and New Methods', *RIBA Journal*, XLI, 23 December 1933, pp.165-79.

• Talk and Discussion at RIBA General Meeting, 18 December 1933. Excerpts from talk in *Architects' Journal*, LXXVIII, 21 December 1933, pp.784, 786.

• Excerpts from talk with summary of discussion in *Builder*, CVL, 22 December 1933, pp.984-5 (extract in Richard Plunz, ed. (1983) *Design and the Public Good*, Cambridge MA and London, MIT Press, pp.19-24.

## Other texts

• 'Unit Building', talk at the Architecture Club, London, 26 October 1933.
• 'Planning the House for Modern Living', talk at Exhibition of Contemporary Domestic Architecture in the West, 1933.

## 1934

February: announcement of Bexhill competition result. Mendelsohn left for extended visit to Palestine.
March: Mendelsohn returned to England.
April: Public Inquiry at Bexhill.

### Works

• Shann House, 116 Dunchurch Road, Rugby, Warwickshire.
• *Architects' Journal*, LXXIX, 19 April 1934, pp.564-5; 26 April 1934, pp.605-6; 10 May 1934, pp.685-8.
• *Architectural Review*, LXXV, June 1934, p.221; LXXVII, March 1935, p.106.
• *Architectural Design and Construction*, IV, October 1934, pp.19-20.
• *Decorative Art Yearbook 1936*, London, The Studio, 1036, p.26.
• McGrath, Raymond (1934) *Twentieth Century Houses*, London, Faber & Faber Ltd., pp.102-3.
• Yorke, F.R.S. (1934) *The Modern House*, London, Architectural Press, pp.164-5.
• 'Model Living Room', Exhibition of Contemporary Industrial Design in the Home, Dorland Hall, London. Bertram, Anthony, et. al., 'Letters from Readers: The Dorland Hall Exhibition', *Architects' Journal*, LXXX, 1 November 1934, p.641.
• Frost, A.E., 'The Exhibition of Contemporary Industrial Design in the Home', Architects' Journal, LXXX, 1 November 1934, pp.642-4.
• Bertram, Anthony, 'Contemporary Industrial Design. The Dorland Hall Exhibition.', *Design for Today*, II, December 1934, p.451.
• Elmhirst Flat, 42 Upper Brook Street, Mayfair, London W1 (destroyed).
• *Architecture Illustrated*, IX, December 1934, pp.196-8.
• *Architectural Review*, LXXVII, May 1935, pp.269-71.
• *The Studio*, 1935, pp.269-71; CXXI, January 1941, p.19.
• *Decorative Art Yearbook 1936*, London, The Studio, 1936, p.51.
• W.B. Corset Showroom, Maddox House, Regent Street, London W1 (destroyed).
• *Architectural Review*, LXXV, March 1934, pp.79-81.
• *Design for Today*, II, April 1934, pp.136-7.
• *W.B. Corset Showrooms*, London, Maddox House, January 1936, advertising Brochure.
• Clocks manufactured by Garrard Clocks Ltd., London 1934.
• *Exhibition of British Art in Industry*, London, Royal

Academy of Arts, 1935, pp.72-3.

### Publications

Letter to the Editor, *RIBA Journal*, XLI, 10 February 1934, p.371.

### Other texts

'Noise Prevention in Buildings', c.1934.

## 1935

Birth of Peter Chermayeff.
3 February: lecture at Karl Marx House, Clerkenwell.
March: Mendelsohn returned from Palestine. Quarrel with Mendelsohn.
18 March: 'The Architect and the World Today', lecture to students section, ATO.
Commission for 64 Old Church Street.
Purchase of site for own house at Bentley Farm, Halland, East Sussex.
25 November: opening of De La Warr Pavilion by HRH The Duke of York (later King George VI).

### Works

• Competition entry for Working Men's Flats, Cement Marketing Company.
• Denby, Elizabeth, 'Competition for Workingmen's Flats: the Designs Reviewed', *Architects' Journal*, LXXXI, 21 March 1935, pp.438-40.
• *Architects' Journal*, LXXXI, 28 March 1935, pp.482-5. Cement Marketing Company, Ltd., *Working-Class Residential Flats in Reinforced Concrete*, London, 1937, pp.32-5.
• Drawings in RIBA Drawings Collection.
• Proposal for a hotel complex at Craneswater Park, Southsea, Hampshire (in partnership with Erich Mendelsohn).
• Martin, J.L., Nicholson, Ben and Gabo, N. (1937) *Circle: International Survey of Constructive Art*, London, Faber and Faber Ltd., Section 3, plates 11, 12.
• Whittick, Arnold (1956) *Erich Mendelsohn*, London, Leonard Hill Books Ltd., pp.102, 107; Plates 33A, 33B.
• Zevi, Bruno (1970) *Erich Mendelsohn. Opera Completa*, Milan, Etas Compass, pp.231-3.
• Photos of drawings in Avery Library.
• Proposal for flats in Chiswick Mall, London, W4 (in partnership with Erich Mendelsohn).
• Zevi, Bruno (1970), *Erich Mendelsohn. Opera Completa*, Milan, Etas Compass, p.227.
• Photos of drawings in Avery Library.
• R.J. Nimmo House, Shrub's Wood, Chalfont St Giles, Buckinghamshire (in partnership with Erich Mendelsohn).
• *Architectural Review*, LXXVIII, November 1935, pp.174-8; LXXX, December 1936, pp.299-301; LXXXII, December 1937, p.250.
• *Architects' Journal*, LXXXIII, 2 January 1936, pp.9-14.
• *Decorative Art Yearbook 1936*, London, The Studio, 1936, pp.16-17, 36, 38, 46, 76, 79.

• *Revista de Arquitectura*, January 1937, pp.14-22.
• Yorke, F.R.S. (1937) *The Modern House in England*, London, Architectural Press, pp.109-11.
• Abercrombie, Patrick, ed. (1939) *The Book of the Modern House*, London, Hodder and Stoughton, pp.209, 218, 232-3, 246-7.
• Whittick, Arnold (1956) *Eric Mendelsohn*, London, Leonard Hill Books Ltd., p.99.
• Zevi, Bruno (1982) *Erich Mendelsohn*, Bologna, Zanichelli, pp.130-31.
• Drawings in RIBA Drawings Collection.
• De La Warr Pavilion, Bexhill-on-Sea, East Sussex (in partnership with Erich Mendelsohn).
• *Architect and Building News*, CXXXVII, February 2 1934, pp.161-4; February 9 1934, p.196; CLXIV December 20 1935 f.p.322,352; December 27, 1935,f.p.372.
• *Architects' Journal*, LXXIX February 8, 1934, pp.197,205-6,213-7; LXXXII December 12 1935, f.p.352; December 27 1935, f.p.372.
• Charles H. Reilly 'The Bexhill Pavilion', *Manchester Guardian*, 13 December 1935.
• Helsby, C., Hamann, C.W., Samuely, F.J. 'Welded Structural Steelwork for Entertainment Hall, Bexhill, Sussex', *The Welder*, X (April 1935), pp.529-33; May 1935, pp.559-65; XI October 1935, pp.716-22; November 1935, pp.751-9; December 1935, pp.783-9.
• *Architectural Design and Construction*, VI, January 1936, pp.90-3.
• *Cinema and Theatre Construction*, XIV January 1936, pp.35-8.
• Quigley, Hugh 'Bexhill and its pavilion', *Design for Today*, IV, February 1936, pp.49-54.
• Chermayeff, Serge (pseud. Peter Maitland), 'Leisure at the Seaside IV: The Architect', *Architectural Review*, LXXX, July 1936, pp.19, 21-8, 50; pl.iii.
• *Architectural Review*, LXXXIV, December 1938, p.309.
• *L'Architecture d'Aujourd'hui*, VII, October 1936, pp.45-53.
• *Building Research Station Notes, no.D781. Long Term Durability of Buildings XIV: The De La Warr Pavilion, Bexhill-on-Sea, Sussex*. Garston, Watford, Hertfordshire: Department of Scientific and Industrial Research, July 1962
• Benton, Charlotte, and Benton, Tim, *De La Warr Pavilion, Bexhill-on-Sea Summer School Booklet A305 History of Architecture and Design, 1890-1939*, London, The Open University, 1976, pp.5-21.
• Benton, Tim, 'The De La Warr Pavilion. A Type for the 1930s', in *Leisure in the Twentieth Century. Fourteen papers given at the 2nd conference of 20th century design history*. London, Design Council Publications 1977, pp.72-80.
• Zevi, Bruno (1982) *Erich Mendelsohn*, Bologna,

Zanichelli, pp.132-7.
• Brook, Jeremy et. al. eds. (1987) *Erich Mendelsohn 1887-1953*, London, Modern British Architecture.
Stevens, Russell and Willis, Peter 'Earl de la Warr and the competition for the Bexhill Pavilion 1933-34', *Architectural History*, XXXIII, 1990, pp.135-66.
• Drawings in RIBA Drawings Collection.
• Proposal for redevelopment of the White City Exhibition Grounds, London (in partnership with Erich Mendelsohn).
• Towndrow, F.E., 'A Scheme of National Importance', *Architectural Design and Construction*, V, April 1935, pp.192-9.
• *Architectural Review*, LXXIX, April 1936, plate ii, following p.164.
• Astragal (pseud.) 'Notes and Comments', *Architects' Journal*, XC, 27 July 1939, p.128.
• Whittick, Arnold (1956) Eric Mendelsohn, London, Leonard Hill Books Ltd., pp.102-6; plates 33c, 34a, 34b.
• Zevi, Bruno (1970) Erich Mendelsohn. Opera Completa, Milan, Etas Compass,p.226.
• Pianos with harp by Steinway and cabinetry by Whiteley's (1935-37).
• *Builder*, CLI, 18 September 1936, p.518; September 25 1936, p.571.
• *Architectural Review*, LXXXII, December 1937, p.261.

**Publications**
• With J.M. Richards, 'A Hundred Years Ahead: Forecasting the Coming Century', *Architects' Journal*, LXXXI, 10 January 1935, pp.79-86.
• With J.M. Richards, Letter to the Editor, Architects' Journal, LXXXI, 31 January 1935, pp.189-90.
• 'The Architect and the World Today', *Architects' Journal*, LXXXI, 21 March 1935, pp.435-6.
• Talk to students' section of the Architects and Technicians Organisation, London, 18 March 1935 (extract in Richard Plunz, ed. (1983) *Design and the Public Good*, Cambridge MA and London, MIT Press, pp.117-21).

**Other texts**
• 'Design for Selling'. Talk at the Publicity Club, London, 21 January 1935.
• 'The Architect in Society', Talk for A.T.O., repeated for Harrow School, 9 July 1935.

## 1936

September: submission of designs for planning permission.

19 November: refusal of planning permission for Bentley Wood.

December: formal announcement of dissolution of Mendelsohn and Chermayeff partnership. Chermayeff moved his office to 19 Grosvenor Place, SW1.

**Works**

• Proposal for a house, Frinton Park Estate, Essex (in partnership with Erich Mendelsohn).
• *Architects' Journal*, LXXXIV, 1 October 1936, p.461.
• *Architectural Design and Construction*, VII, August 1937, p.387.
• Carter, Ella (1937) *Seaside Houses and Bungalows*, London, Country Life Ltd., p.40.
• Gould, Jeremy (1977) *Modern Houses in Britain, 1919-1939*, Architectural History
• Monographs No.1. London, Society of Architectural Historians of Great Britain, p.31.
• Proposal of a house for an unidentified client, Dorney, Buckinghamshire.
• *Architectural Design and Construction*, VII, August 1937, p.388.
• Dennis Cohen House, 64 Old Church Street, Chelsea, London SW3 (in partnership with Erich Mendelsohn).
• *Architects' Journal*, LXXXIV, December 24 1936, pp.872-4; LXXXVII June 2 1938, pp.945-6; (June 9, 1938, pp.985-6, June 16, 1938, pp.2025-6, June 23 1938, pp.1065-6.
• *Architectural Review*, LXXX, December 1936, pp.254-5. R. Myerscough-Walker, 'Two Houses in Chelsea'.
• *Building*, January 1938, pp.15-19.
• F.R.S. Yorke (1937) *The Modern House in England*, London, Architectural Press, pp.36-37.
• Patrick Abercrombie, ed. (1939) *The Book of the Modern House*, London, Hodder and Stoughton, pp.94-5.
• Arnold Whittick (1956) *Eric Mendelsohn*, London, Leonard Hill Ltd.
• Bruno Zevi (1970) *Eric Mendelsohn. Opera Completa*, Milan, Etas Kompass, pp.
• Bruno Zevi (1982) *Eric Mendelsohn*, Bologna, Zanichelli, pp.138-41.
• Brook, Jeremy et. al. eds. (1987) *Eric Mendelsohn 1887-1953*, London, Modern British Architecture, ('Recollections' by Birkin Haward pp.71-2).
• 'Chelsea row rumbles: Don't put architecture in aspic.'
• *Building Design*, no.1115, 12 March, 1993, p.24.
• Music Room with piano for the Piano Exhibition, Dorland Hall, London.
• *Builder*, CLI, 18 September 1936, p.518; 25 September, 1936, p.571.
• *Architectural Review*, LXXX, October 1936, p.185.
• Project for Science Block for Gordonstoun School, Morayshire.
• Single drawing in RIBA Drawings Collection.

**Publications**

• *Colour and its Application to Modern Building*, London, Nobel Chemical Finishes, Ltd., January 1936. Booklet written and designed by Serge Chermayeff, reviewed and quoted by Philip Scholberg in *Architects' Journal*, LXXXIII, 23 January 1936 pp.175-6.
• 'The Architect's Duty to the Modern World', *Builder*,

CL, 24 January 1936, p.205.
• Excerpts from talk to the Manchester Society of Architects, 8 January.
• Review of *Specification* 1936 (London, The Architectural Press, 1936),
• *Architectural Review*, LXXIX, March 1936, p.138.
• 'The Queen Mary', Letter to the Editor, *Architects' Journal*, LXXXIII, 23 April 1936, pp.616-17.
• Peter Maitland (Chermayeff pseud.) 'Leisure at the Seaside: IV. The Architect', *Architectural Review*, LXXX, July 1936, pp.18-28.
• 'Modern Art and Architecture', *RIBA Journal*, XLIV, 9 January 1937, p.209.
• Summary of remarks made by Chermayeff at a RIBA general meeting, 9 December 1936, following talks by L. Moholy-Nagy, N. Gabo, Eileen Holding and Herbert Read.

**Unpublished texts**

'Television talk between Mr John Gloag and Mr Serge Chermayeff.' Broadcast live by BBC, 11 December 1936.

## 1937

26 January: public inquiry on Bentley Wood.
8 May: surrendered lease on 52 Abbey Road.
June: travelled to Paris to visit International Exhibition.
September: final working drawings for Bentley Wood. Construction began.

**Works**

• Office building for W. & A. Gilbey, Ltd., Oval Road, London, NW1.
• *Architects' Journal*, LXXXV, 15 July 1937, pp.98-108; 19 May, pp.849-51; CLXXII, 15 October, 1980, p.738.
• *Architect and Building News*, CLI, 30 July 1937, pp.149-54.
• *Architectural Review*, LXXXII, July 1937, pp.11-22; LXXXIV, September 1938, p.134.
• 'The Building that stands on Cork', *Ferroconcrete*, July 1937.
• Martin, J.L., Nicholson, Ben and Gabo, N. (1937) *Circle: International Survey of Constructive Art*, London, Faber and Faber Ltd., Section 3, plates 9, 10.
• Casson, Hugh, 'Façade, A View of Architecture: Good Building and Bad Theatre', *Night and Day*, 9 September 1937, p.118.
• *Architecture Illustrated*, XVI, February 1938, p.51.
• McCallum, Ian, *Pocket Guide to Modern Buildings in London*. London, Architectural Press, 1951, pp.23-5, 27.
• *Building Research Station Notes no.D814. London Term Durability of Buildings XV: The Offices of Messrs. W. and A. Gilbey, Ltd., Gilbey House, Oval Road, London W. 1.*, Garston, Watford, Hertfordshire: Department of Scientific and Industrial Research, July 1962.
• *Thirties. British Art and Design before the War*,

London, Arts Council, 1979, p.196.
• Gallery Lingard, London, *Architectural Books, Prints & Drawings*, n.d. (1999), pp.22-23.
• Drawings in RIBA Drawings Collection.

**Publications**
• 'Whither the English House? A Discussion', *Architectural Design and Construction*, VII, August 1937, pp.370-2. In conjunction with articles by M.H. Baillie-Scott and Naseby Adams.
• 'Circulation: Design: Design: Display: The Architect at the Exhibition', *Architectural Review*, LXXXII, September 1937, pp.91-104.

**Other texts**
• 'Art in Modern Architecture', Television disussion between Chermayeff and John Piper, broadcast live, 27 January.
• 'Rebuilding England', Television talk, broadcast live, 8 April.

## 1938
January: opening of MARS Group Exhibition, New Burlington Galleries.
January: opening of ICI Dyestuffs Research Laboratories, Blackley, Manchester.
Several key staff left Chermayeff office owing to cancellation of major projects.
Bentley Wood completed and occupied for summer.

**Works**
• Laboratory building for Imperial Chemical Industries Ltd., Blackley, Manchester.
• *Architect and Building News*, CLIII, 21 January 1938, pp.92-4.
• *Builder*, CLIV, 4 March 1938, p.451.
• *RIBA Journal*, XLV, 7 March 1938, pp.440-6.
• *Architectural Review*, LXXXIII, March 1938, pp.117-26; LXXXVIII, August 1938, p.83.
• *Architects' Journal*, LXXXVII, 24 March 1938, pp.507-11; LXXXVIII, 6 October, 1938, pp.571-2; 20 October, 1939, pp.647-8.
• *Architectural Design and Construction*, June 1938, pp.240-1.
• *Progressive Architecture*, XXX, January 1949, pp.59-65.
• *Imperial Chemical Industries Ltd., The New Research Laboratories, Manchester, 1938.*
• Drawings in RIBA Drawings Collection.
• Chermayeff House, Bentley Wood, Halland, East Sussex.
• *Architects' Journal*, LXXXV, 18 February 1937, p.293; LXXXIX, 16 February, 1939, pp.293-300; 2 March 1939, pp.371-2; 9 March, 1939 pp.411-2; 23 March 1939, pp.491-2; 30 March 1939, pp.531-2.
• Astragal (pseud). 'Notes and Comments', *Architects' Journal*, LXXXVIII, 22 September 1938, p.255; March 11 1937, p.414.
• Reilly, C.H. 'Professor Reilly speaking', *Architects'*

*Journal*, LXXXVIII, 22 September 1938, p.479; 20 October 1938, pp.637-8.
• Aylwin, G. Maxwell 'Letters from readers: Professor Reilly and the Architect's house', *Architects' Journal*, LXXXVIII, 29 September 1938, p.529.
• *The Times* (London) March 2 1937, p.13c. *Architectural Review*, LXXXIII, April 1938, p.198; LXXXV, February 1939, pp.61-78.
• Myerscough Walker, R. 'The Reasons for this House', Ideal Home, May 1939, pp.384-8.
• Hussey, Christopher 'A Modern Country House', *Country Life*, LXXXVIII, 26 October 1940, pp.368-71; 2 November 1940, pp.390-3.
• *Construzioni Casabella*, XIII, December 1940, pp.39-41.
• Interiors, CIX, July 1950, pp.80-3.
• Tunnard, Christopher, 'Planning a Modern Garden, an experience in collaboration', *Landscape and Garden*, Summer 1939, pp.23–27.
• 'What kind of house?' *Listener*, XVII March 1937, pp.444-5.
• Tilson, Barbara 'The Battle for Bentley Wood', *Thirties Society Journal*, V 1985, pp.24-31.
• Kitson, Ian 'Christopher Tunnard at Bentley Wood', *Landscape Design*, December 1990/January 1991, pp.10-15.
• Tunnard, Christopher (1938) *Gardens in the Modern Landscape*, London, Architectural Press, pp.68, 76.
• Richards, J.M. (1940) *An Introduction to Modern Architecture*, Harmondsworth, Penguin Books, pp.114-5, pl.29.
• Yorke F.R.S. (1944) *The Modern House in England*, 2nd edition, London, Architectural Press, pp.82-5.
• Kassler, Elizabeth B. (1964) *Modern Gardens and the Landscape*, New York, Museum of Modern Art, p.84.
• James, Philip (1966) *Henry Moore on Sculpture*, London, Macdonald & Co.,p.98, pl.25; pp.99, 101.
• Cantacuzino, Sherban (1964) *Modern Houses of the World*, London, Studio Vista, pp.72-4.
• Knobel, Lance 'The Tragedy of Bentley Wood', *Architectural Review*, CLXVI, November 1979, pp.310-11.
• Neckar, Lance M., 'Christopher Tunnard: The Garden in the Modern Landscape',in Marc Treib, ed. (1993) Modern Landscape Architecture: A Critical Review,Cambridge MA and London, MIT Press.
• Powers, Alan, 'Une Maison Moderne de Serge Chermayeff', *le moniteur architecture amc*, (Paris), No.69, March 1996, pp.44-51.
• 'English Modern Houses of the 1930s 2: Bentley Wood, near Halland, Sussex, 1938', *A+U*, No.9 (324), September 1997, pp.3-9.
• Gallery Lingard, London, *Architectural Books, Prints & Drawings*, n.d. (1999), pp.22-23.
• Perspective and site plan in RIBA Drawings

Collection.
• Ciro Jewellery Shop, 48 Old Bond Street, London 1938.
• *Architect and Building News*, CLVI, 4 November 1938, pp.128-9.
• Office Buildings and Canteen for I.C.I., Huddersfield. No surviving visual record.
• Project for extension, 3 Sterling Street, London SW7.
• Drawings in RIBA Drawings Collection.

**Publications**
• 'Reinforced Concrete', *News Chronicle*, 24 March 1938, p.19.
'Contemporary Architecture', Synopsis of a lecture given on 4 November 1938, at the Edinburgh Architectural Association', unidentified publication, pp.21-4.

**Other texts**
'Government Employment of Architects in Connection with Rearmament and Defense', 1938.

## 1939
March: competition design with Wells Coates.
May: Frank Lloyd Wright visited Bentley Wood.
13 June: first bankruptcy notice.
14 July: announcement that Chermayeff to leave for USA.
August: sale of Bentley Wood. Possessions put in store.
September: stayed with Rebecca West at Possingworth Manor.
October-November: worked on government hostels programme.
December: stayed at Old Kennards, Leigh, nr. Tunbridge Wells.

**Publications**
• *Plan for Air Raid Precautions: A Practical Policy*, London, Frederick Muller Ltd., 1939.
• 'The Architect's Place and Purpose in Modern Society', *Northern Architectural Students' Association Journal*, III, February 1939, pp.21-2 (extract in Richard Plunz, ed. (1983) Design and the Public Good, Cambridge MA and London, MIT Press, pp.123-4).
• 'Windows in Germany', Review of Otto Volker, *Glas und Fenster*, Berlin, Bauwelt Verlag, 1939, *RIBA Journal*, XLVI, 8 May 1939.
• 'The Architectural Student, Training for What?' *Architectural Association Journal*, June 1939, pp.4-15; *Builder*, XV, 2 June 1939, pp.1045-6.
• Excerpts of talk and discussion, The Architectural Association, London, 23 May 1939. Complete text including discussion with Henry Morris and J.D. Bernal, in Focus 4, Summer 1939, pp.96-101 (extract in Richard Plunz, ed. (1983) *Design and the Public Good*, Cambridge MA and London, MIT Press, pp.233-8).
• Review of J.L. Martin and Sadie Speight, *The Flat Book*, London, Percy Lund Humphries & Co. Ltd.;

Focus 4, Summer 1939, pp.80-1.
**Other texts**
• 'Finsbury Borough Council A.R.P. Shelters, Report on suggested signposting of Shelters', 1939.
• 'The Furniture of Tomorrow', Talk at Art Workers Guild, London, 3 February 1939.

## 1940
13 January: abortive voyage. Went to stay with Barbara's mother.
24 January: actual sailing from Liverpool.
1 February: arrived in Halifax, Nova Scotia.
19 March: visa for USA; visited Walter Groipus at Lincoln, Massachusetts.
May: lecture at Ann Arbor, Illinois.
June: beginning of cross-continental trip in Ford convertible.
August: arrived in San Francisco.
September: London Blitz, Powell & Sons store bombed; remaining possessions from store arrived in San Francisco; meeting with Eric Mendelsohn; design seminars at San Francisco Museum; association with TELESIS group.
October: sought letters of recommendation for teaching positions.

**Publications**
• 'Architects and the Air Raid Precaution', *Pencil Points*, XXI, November 1940, special supplement.

**Other texts**
• Untitled Luncheon Speech.
• Talk to the Ontario Architectural Societies, Toronto, 11 March 1940.
• 'Why Modern Architecture?' CBC Broadcast, 26 March 1940.
• 'Present position in Architecture or the Crisis in Architecture', talk at Harvard University, Graduate School of Design, 18 April 1940; also given at Yale University (extract in Richard Plunz, ed. (1983) *Design and the Public Good*, Cambridge MA and London, MIT Press, pp.127-134).
• 'Crisis of Architecture', talk at the Museum of Fine Arts, San Francisco, 18 September 1940.
• 'Biographical Note', 1940.

## 1941
March: visited Frank Lloyd Wright at Taliesin West.
April: discussion with North West Regional Planning Commission.
August: meeting with Leo Balet at home of Jan de Graeff, Oregon.
November/December: visited New York to discuss appointment at Brooklyn College.

**Works**
• Project for Chermayeff House in Bay area, San Francisco (dated conjecturally to 1941).

- Drawings in RIBA Drawings Collection.

**Publications**

- 'Architecture and a New World', *Arts and Architecture*, LVIII, May 1941, pp.18-19, 38, 40 (extract in Richard Plunz, ed. (1983) *Design and the Public Good*, Cambridge MA and London, MIT Press, pp.27-30).
- 'Implications of Air Raid Precaution', *Pencil Points*, XXII, July 1941, pp.489-90.
- 'Air Raid Precaution (ARP) and our Office of Civilian Defense', *Pencil Points*, XXII, September 1941, pp.591-3.
- 'A Reply', *Pencil Points*, XXII, October 1941, p.656.
- 'Is High Explosive the Greatest Danger?' *Pencil Points*, XXII, November 1941, pp.725-6.
- 'Review of Civil Defense, Lt-Col. Augustin M. Prentiss', *Pencil Points*, XXII, December 1941, p.10.
- 'Textbooks and Actuality', *Pencil Points*, XXII, December 1941, pp.777-8.

**Other texts**

- 'False Gods?' Unpublished article prepared for *Task* No.2, November 1941. (extract in Richard Plunz, ed. (1983) *Design and the Public Good*, Cambridge MA and London, MIT Press, pp.137-40).

## 1942

1 February: appointed Director of Department of Design at Brooklyn College and initiated curriculum reforms; moved to New York.
July: attended Chicago Institute of Design Summer School at Somonauk, Illinois.

**Works**

- Mayhew House, 330 Hampton Road, Piedmont, Oakland, California.
- *Architectural Forum*, LXXXIV, June 1946, pp.117-23.
- *House and Garden*, XCI, May 1947, pp.96-9, 181.
- *Architectural Review*, CII, July 1947, pp.43-5.
- Creighton, Thomas H. (1947) *Homes*, New York, Reinhold, pp.160-1.
- Fisker, Kay, 'Den Funkionelle Tradition. Spredte Indtryk af Amerikansk Arkitectur', *Arkitekten*, LII, May-June 1950, pp.90-1.
- *Amerikanische Architektur seit 1947*, Stuttgart, G. Hatje, 1951, p.32.
- Lohse, Richard, Shader, Jacques, and Zeitschmann, Ernst (1954) *L'architecture International de Demain*, Rochecorbon, France, Les Editions Charles Gay, pp.124-7.
- Macintosh, Duncan, *The Modern Courtyard House*, London, The Architectural Association, Paper no.9, 1973, p.16.
- Horn House, 339 Western Drive, Richmond California.
- *Architectural Forum*, LXXXVI, January 1947, pp.72-5.
- *Architectural Review*, CII, July 1947, pp.45-6
- *Interiors*, CVII, September 1947, pp.82-3.
- *Architect and Building News*, CXCVI, 1 July 1949,

supplement pages follow p.16; 8 July, 1949, pages follow p.36.
- *Amerikanische Architektur seit 1947*, Stuttgart, G. Hatje, 1951, pp.26-7.
- Drawings in RIBA Drawings Collection, Avery Library.

**Publications**

- 'San Francisco Blackout', *Pencil Points*, XXIII, January 1942, pp.27-8.
- 'Telesis: the birth of a group', *Pencil Points*, XXIII, July 1942, pp.45-4.
- 'The Necessity of a Second Front', *Observer-Kaleidoscope*, Brooklyn College, 21 October 1942.
- 'Prof. Chermayeff clarifies position on Second Front', Letter to the Editor, *Brooklyn College Vanguard*, 20 November 1942, p.4.

**Unpublished texts**

- 'Modern Architecture in Palestine', lecture to Hillel Foundation, New York, 22 March 1942.
- 'Address to the Alumni Association', talk at Columbia University Architecture Alumni Association, 28 May 1942.
- 'A Summary of Report on Contemporary Planning, Architecture, Design and Design Education', 1942 (extract in Richard Plunz, ed. (1983) *Design and the Public Good*, Cambridge MA and London, MIT Press, pp.241-3).
- 'Outline for a Planning and Design Department in a Western University', prepared for Stanford University, 1942.
- Excerpts from Report to the President of Brooklyn College, December 1942.

## 1943

Passed NCARB examination in New York to practise architecture in United States and joined American Institute of Architects.

**Works**

- Proposal for 'Park Type' apartments (in association with Peter Blake, Abel Sorensen, Norman Fletcher, Henry Hebbeln).
- *Architectural Forum*, LXXVIII, May 1943, pp.138-45; LXXIX, July 1943, p.39.
- Abel, Joseph H. and Severud, Fred (1947) *Apartment Houses*, New York, Reinhold, pp.63-6.
- Hamlin, Talbot (1952) *Forms and Functions of Twentieth Century Architecture*, 3 Vols, New York, Columbia University Press, III, p.75.
- Children's Center project, Brooklyn College, Department of Design.
- *A Children's Center or Nursery School*, Revere's part in Better Living, No.20, New York, Revere Copper and Brass Company, 1944.

**Publications**

'Planning: Urns or Urbanism', *Progressive Architecture*,

XXIV, February 1943, pp.72-6.
**Other texts**
Memorandum based on a Conversation between Mr
Jalkut, Mr Abott and Mr Chermayeff. Held at the
Museum of Modern Art on 11 March, 1943.'

## 1944
Defended Brooklyn College curriculum against charges
of pro-communist and anarchist sympathies.
Co-founder of American Society of Planners and
Architects, with Walter Gropius, George Howe, Joseph
Hudnut, Louis Kahn, Oscar Stonorov and others.
**Works**
• 'Design for Use' exhibition at the Museum of Modern
Art, New York.
• Museum of Modern Art, Art in Progress, New York,
1944, pp.190-201.
• Notes on the Industrial Design Exhibition, May 1944,
Museum of Modern Art, 17 January 1944.
• Little, Helen, 'Modern Museum Opens Art in
Progress Show', *Retailing Home Furnishings,* XVI, 29
May 1944, pp.1, 25.
• *Plastics,* July 1944, pp.18-19
• Lohse, Richard P. (1954) *New Design in Exhibitions,*
New York, Praeger Publishers, pp.180-1.
• Gardner, James and Miller, Caroline (1960) *Exhibition
and Display,* London, B.T. Batsford, Ltd., p.44.
• Drawing in RIBA Drawings Collection.
• Chermayeff Cottage (and later additions), Truro,
Massachusetts (until 1972).
• *Architectural Record,* CXXVIII, November 1960,
pp.168-70.
• Kaspar, Karl (1967) *Vacation Houses. An International
Survey,* New York, Frederick A. Praeger, pp.30-1.
• Powers, Alan, 'Modernist Ambition fulfilled in a Cape
Cod cottage', *Architects' Journal,* CCIV, 31 October
1996, pp.40-1.
**Publications**
'Future Possibilities of Multiple Dwellings', in Paul
Zucker, ed. (1944) New Architecture and City
Planning, New York, Philosophical Library, pp.278-89.
**Other texts**
'Design for use', text developed in relation to the
exhibition at the Museum of Modern Art, New York,
1944.

## 1945
Commencement address at Brooklyn College by Joseph
Hudnut.
Continued activities on behalf of American branch of
CIAM, the architects' section of the National Council
on American-Soviet Friendship and the Federation of
Architects, Engineers, Chemists and Technicians.
20 January: organised conference for American Society
of Planners and Architects, with Le Corbusier as speaker.

**Works**
• Proposal for prototype apartments in a hypothetical
neighborhood, Museum of Modern Art (in association
with Vernon DeMars and Susanne Wasson-Tucker).
• The Museum of Modern Art, *Tomorrow's Small House*
(catalogue), New York, 1945, pp.3, 19-20.
• 'Art and the Industrial Designer', *Magazine of Art,*
XXXVIII, February 1945, pp.50-3.
• 'Mondrian of the Perfectionists', *Art News,* XLIV, 15
March 1945, pp.14-16.
• Review of exhibition at the Museum of Modern Art,
New York. Also published as 'Mondrian y si
Perfecionismo', *Revista de Arquitectura,* XXXII, January
1947, p.35-9.
• 'Chemical Research Laboratory'. *Proceedings. American
Soviet Building Conference,* New York, Architects'
Committee of the National Council of American Soviet
Friendship, 1945, pp.134-6.
• Talk given to Industrial Buildings Panel, American-
Soviet Building Conference. New York, Architects'
Committee of the National Council of American-Soviet
Friendship, 5 May 1945.
**Unpublished texts**
'Broadcast from Union College', radio talk,
Schenectady, New York, 25 February 1945.

## 1946
January: ASPA meeting, NYC, with Le Corbusier as
speaker; naturalised as US Citizen.
26 November: death of László Moholy-Nagy,
Chermayeff interviewed for post of President of
Institute of Design, Chicago.
**Works**
• Renovation of Chermayeff Office, East 37th Street,
New York City (in partnership with Konrad
Wachsmann).
• *Interiors,* CVI, February 1947, pp.83-6.
• Drawings and photos in Avery Library.
**Publications**
'Structure and the Esthetic Experience', *Magazine of Art,*
XXXIX, May 1946, pp.190-4.
**Other texts**
• 'Architecture, Painting and Sculpture', talk at
symposium at Hampton Institute, January 1946.
• 'Industry, Architecture and Design', talk at University
of Toronto, 26 January 1946.

## 1947
January: appointed President of Institute of Design,
Chicago.
Awarded prize for painting 'New York No.2' at
American Artists Annual, held at the Art Institute,
Chicago.
**Works**
• Renovation of interior, Ciro of Bond Street, Jewellers,

2763 Mission Street, San Francisco (in partnership with Raphael Soriano).
• *Architectural Forum*, LXXXVIII, May 1948, p.128.
• *Architect and Building News*, CXCVI, 5 August 1949, supplement pages following p.138.
• Drawing in RIBA Drawings Collection.
• Project for store, Ciro of Bond Street, Beverley Hills (in partnership with Raphael Soriano).
• Drawings in Avery Library.
• Plan for the Brooklyn College Community, Brooklyn College Department of Design. 'A Brooklyn college Plan', typed text for project report, January 1947 (Serge Chermayeff Archive, Avery Library).
**Publications**
• 'Education of Modern Design', *College Art Journal*, VI, Spring 1947, pp.,219-21 (extract in Richard P unz, ed. (1983) *Design and the Public Good*, Cambridge MA and London, MIT Press, pp.245-8).
• Inaugural Address to the Chicago Institute of Design, 4 February 1947
• 'Cultural Delinquency and how to prevent its Spread', *California Arts and Architecture*, LXIV, August 1947, pp.28, 51-2.
• Talk to Western Art Association, 30 April, 1947.

**1948**
**Works**
• 'Naum Gabo', *Magazine of Art*, XLI, February 1948, pp.56-9. Review of the exhibition at the Museum of Modern Art, New York, 1948.
• 'Painting towards Architecture', *California Arts and Architecture*, LXV, June 1948, pp.24-31. Review of the Miller Company Collection of painting and sculpture, Meriden, Connecticut.
• Introduction to the 'Case-Study House' issue, *Interiors*, CVII, September 1948, pp.96-119.
• 'The Institute of Design integrates Art, Technology and Science', *Interiors*, CVIII, September 1948, pp.142-51.
• 'The Institute of Design - A Laboratory for a New Education', *Interiors*, CVIII, October 1948, pp.134-40.
• 'Architecture at the Institute of Design', *Interiors*, CVIII, November 1948, pp.118-25.
• *Comments after judging 735 entries to the annual Exhibition of Design in Chicago Printing* (pamphlet), Chicago, The Society of Typographic Arts, 1948, also published in Hans Wingler (1969) *The Bauhaus*, Cambridge, MIT Press, p.205.
**Other texts**
• 'Report to the Board of Directors, Institute of Design', Chicago, 1947.
• 'Review of a publication of the American Abstract Artists', 10 February 1947.
• 'President's Report', Chicago Institute of Design, 11 March 1947.
• Invited to show in the Réalités Nouvelles' exhibition in Paris.

• Advertising work for the Miller Company.
**Unpublished texts**
• 'Safe at Home-or are we?' talk at American Designers' Institute, Chicago, 7 January 1948.
• 'Form in Design', talk given in the series, 'Society and Design', Chicago Institute of Design, 22 April 1948.
• 'Social Responsibility and the Artist', talk at the Minneapolis School of Art, 3 June 1948.

**1949**
**Works**
• 'Chicago Plans' exhibition for the Chicago City Planning Commission, City Hall, Chicago.
• Lohse, Richard P. (1954) *New Design in Exhibitions*, New York, Praeger Publishers, pp.182-7.
• Franck, Klaus (1961) *Exhibitions*, London, The Architectural Press, p.47.
• Chicago Plans (exhibition brochure), Chicago, Chicago Planning Commission, 1949.
• Drawing in RIBA Drawings Collection.
• Proposed addition to Institute of Design premises, North Dearborn Street. No surviving visual record.
**Publications**
Introduction to exhibition catalogue, *Exhibition of Designs* by Will Burton. Chicago, The Art Director's Club of Chicago, 1949.
**Other texts**
• 'Are our houses fit to live in?' talk at the Home Institute Meeting. The Minneapolis Institute of Fine Arts, 8 March 1949.
• 'Address to Planning and Building Panel', talk to the Planning and Building Panel, Cultural and Scientific Conference for World Peace, New York City, 26 March 1949 (extract in Richard Plunz (1983) ed. *Design and the Public Good*, Cambridge MA and London, MIT Press, pp.33-34).
• 'Architecture: Anonymity and Autonomy', Harvard University, Graduate School of Design. Fogg Art Museum, 11 April 1949 (extract in Richard Plunz, ed. (1983) *Design and the Public Good*, Cambridge MA and London, MIT Press,pp.143-7).
• 'Design in the Elementary and Secondary School Art Program', talk at Iowa State University, May 1949.
• 'Fine Arts in General Education', panel discussion (P.R. McIntosh, chairman, with H. Harvard Arnason, Arnold Blanch, C. Howard Church, Charles Parkhurst) Midwestern College Art Conference, Minneapolis and St Paul, 10-12 November 1949.

**1950**
Incorporation of Institute of Design in Illinois Institute of Technology
**Works**
• Office for British Railways Inc., Rockefeller Center, New York City (in association with Ketchum, Gina and Sharp).

• *Progressive Architecture*, XXXI, June 1950, pp.84-6. Fabrics manufactured by L. Anton Maix, New York, 1950-55.
• 'New Patterns shown by fabric designers', *New York Times*, 22 April 1950, Sect. 12, p.3.
• Pepis, Betty, 'Patterns for prints', *New York Times Magazine*, 28 May 1950, pp.38-9.
• *Current Design. A Quarterly Survey*, Spring 1951, Plate: 'Fabrics 14', published by the Department of Design in Industry, Institute of Contemporary Art, Boston.
• *Industrial Design*, II, December 1955, p.66.

**Publications**
• 'Architecture at the Chicago Institute of Design', *L'Architecture d'Aujourd'hui*, X, February 1950, pp.50-6 (extract in Richard Plunz, ed. (1983) *Design and the Public Good*, Cambridge MA and London, MIT Press, pp.251-7).
• 'Theatre Planning: A Symposium', *Educational Theatre Journal*, II, March 1950, pp.1-8. Written exchange with Norman Bel Geddes, Edward C. Cole, Arch Lauterer, and Stanley McCandless.
• Ludwig Mies van der Rohe, Serge Chermayeff, Walter Gropius. *Three Addresses at the Blackstone Hotel, April 17 1950, on the Occasion of the Addition of the Institute of Design to Illinois Institute of Technology, Chicago*, Illinois Institute of Technology, 1950.
• 'The Social Aspects of Art', in Julien Harris, ed. (1950) *The Humanities: an Appraisal*, Madison, University of Wisconsin Press, pp.140-2.
• 'Design Demonstrated', *Furniture Forum*, II, April 1951, Introduction.
• 'Symposium on How to Combine Architecture, Painting and Sculpture', *Interiors*, CX, May 1951, pp.100-5. Discussion includes remarks by Serge Chermayeff.
• 'The Technique of Architecture from an Educator's Point of View', *The Boston Society of Architects Record*, XXXVII, November 1951. Excerpts from a talk to the Boston Society of Architects, 9 October 1951.
• 'Education of Architects', *Perspective*, 1951, The Manitoba Association of Architects, Students' Architectural Society, 1951

**Other texts**
• Talk given at 'Fifty Books of the Year' dinner, American Institute of Graphic Arts, New York, 4 April, 1950.
• 'IIT-ID Formal Announcement of Merger', 17 April 1950.
• Untitled text attributed to Mies van der Rohe and Serge Chermayeff for fund raising for new Illinois Institute of Technology architecture building, 1950.
• 'The Profession of Architecture,' talk given at the Chicago Institute of Design, 2 November 1950 (extract in Richard *Plunz*, ed. (1983) *Design and the Public Good*, Cambridge MA and London, MIT Press, pp.149-58).

## 1951
Exhibited in a one-man show of paintings, drawings and textiles at the Baldwin Kingman Gallery, Chicago. Awarded prize in the Chicago Artists Show of the Art Institute, Chicago, later exhibited at the Whitney Annual and the Metropolitan Museum of Art.
May: resigned as President of Institute of Design while retaining professorship.
July: visited London to attend CIAM 8 conference, Hoddesdon.
August: resigned professorship on return to Chicago.
September: moved to Cambridge, Masachusetts, as visiting lecturer at MIT.

**Unpublished texts**
• 'An approach to Redevelopment', panel discussion, Harvard University Community Appraisal Study, Graduate School of Design, Spring 1951.
• 'Education for Designers', talk at Institute of Contemporary Arts, London, July 1951.

## 1952
Taught at MIT.
Exhibited in one-man show at Design Forum in Providence, Rhode Island.

**Works**
• Chermayeff Studio, Truro, Massachusetts, 1952, Guest House addition, 1957.
• *House and Home*, VI, July 1954, pp.121, 124.
• *Bauen & Wohnen*, XI, March 1956, p.98.
• *Revista informes de la Construction*, No.90, April 1957.
• *Architectural Record*, CXXVIII, November 1960, pp.168-70.
• 'The Architect's Eye', *Cooper Union Museum Chronicle*, III, September 1962, p.44.
• *House and Garden*, London, XXI, May 1967, pp.84-5. Kaspar, Karl (1967) *Vacation Houses. An International Survey*, New York, Frederick A. Praeger, pp.30-1.
• Drawings in RIBA Drawings Collection.
• Payson House, Portland, Maine.
• *House and Home*, III, January 1953, pp.108-115.
• *Architects' Journal*, CXVII. 9 April 1953, p.458.
• *Architectural Review*, CXV, June 1954, pp.370-4.
• *Architect and Building News*, CCVII, 14 April, 1955, supplement pages following p.30; 21 April 1955, pages follow p.30.
• Hoffman, Kurt (1955) *Neue Einfamilienhaüser*, Stuttgart, Julius Hoffmann Verlag, pp.84-5.
• Drawings in RIBA Drawings Collection, Avery Library.

**Publications**
• 'The Gropius Symposium', *Arts and Architecture*, LXIX, May 1952, pp.27-31, 36-38.

• Discussion with György Kepes, Pietro Belluschi, Walter Gropius and Charles Burchard at the American Academy of Sciences, Boston, 31 January 1952: 'Chermayeff seems to prefer 57th Street on 57th Street', *Cape Codder*, 12 June 1953, p.6.
• Review of opening of Mayo Galleries, Orleans, Massachusetts, 'The Art of Presentation', *American Society of Planning Officials Yearbook*, 1952, pp.22-25.
• Talk to the National Planning Conference, American Society of Planning Officials, Boston, 13 October 1952.

## 1953
Appointed professor of architecture at Harvard University and assumed responsibility for first year teaching of interdisciplinary 'Environmental Design'. Established architectural office in Cambridge with Heywood Cutting.
### Unpublished text
'Memorandum to Dean Sert', Harvard University Graduate School of Design, 3 November 1953 (includes a memorandum to the Committee on Design Research).

## 1954
Exhibited in one-man show at the Behn-Moore Gallery in Cambridge.
Resigned from American Institute of Architects.
### Works
• Offices and plant for The Cape Codder, Orleans, Massachusetts.
• *Architectural Forum*, CII, May 1955, pp.156-7.
• 'The Architect's Eye', *Cooper Union Museum Chronicle*, III, September 1962, p.45.
• Sigerson House, Truro, Massachusetts.
• *House and Home*, VI, July 1954, p.123.
• *Revista Informes de la Construction*, No.90, April 1957.
• 'The Architect's Eye', *Cooper Union Museum Chronicle*, III, September 1962, p.44.
• Drawings in RIBA Drawings Collection.
• Wilkinson House, Truro, Massachusetts.
• *House and Home*, VI, July 1954, pp.120-5.
• *Bauen und Wohnen*, XI, March 1956, pp.96-7.
• *Revista Informes de la Construction*, No.90, April 1957.
• 'The Second House', *Time*, LXXX, August 17 1962, pp.31-7.
• 'The Architect's Eye', *Cooper Union Museum Chronicle*, III, September 1962, p.44-6.
• Barran, Fritz R. (1961) *Ferienhäuser*, Stuttgart, Julius Hoffmann Verlag, pp.52-3.
• Project for Harvard University Yacht Club (with Peter Chermayeff).
• Drawings in RIBA Drawings Collection.
• Shady Hill Estate, scheme for housing for Harvard University.
• Drawings in Avery Library.

• Scheme for development of Diamond K Ranch, Sacramento, California.
• Drawings in Avery Library.
### Unpublished text
• 'Commencement Address', Rhode Island School of Design, 12 June 1954.
• 'Environmental Design Seminar', Graduate School of Design, Harvard University, 17 December 1954 (extract in Richard Plunz, ed. (1983) *Design and the Public Good*, Cambridge MA and London, MIT Press, pp.259-69).

## 1955
### Works
• Proposals for furniture for Polster-mobelfabrik Eugen Smith, Darmstadt.
• Drawing in Avery Library.
### Publications
• *Rude and Random Rhymes*, Orleans, Massachusetts, Cape Codder Printery, c.1955, Designed by Ivan Chermayeff.
• *Report on the future development of Diamond K Ranch, Cambridge, Massachusetts*, Chermayeff and Cutting, Architects, c.1955.
• 'Der Verantwortung des Gestalters', *Der Aufbau*, X, February/March 1955, pp.68-70.
### Unpublished texts
• 'The Visual Arts: Their relationships', transcript from a symposium (with Serge Chermayeff, Naum Gabo, Ben Shahn, James J. Sweeney, Siegfried Giedion, and José Luis Sert, moderator), Harvard University, Graduate School of Design, 8 February 1955.
• Environmental Design Seminar transcripts, Harvard University, Graduate School of Design, dated 1 October, 15 October, 22 October, 27 October, 5 November, 12 November, 3 December, 17 December 1954, and 7 January, 14 January, 11 February, and 7 April 1955.
• 'Memo to Dean José Sert. Comments on the Present Curricula', Harvard University, Graduate School of Design, Spring 1955.
• 'Environmental Design. First and Second Semester', Harvard University, Graduate School of Design, c.1955.

## 1956
### Works
• O'Connor House, Truro, Massachusetts.
• 'Late American on Cape Cod', *New York Times Magazine*, 29 September 1957, pp.50-1.
• Ivan Chermayeff (1972) *Observations on American Architecture*, New York, Viking Press, p.136.
• Harvard Urban Family Houses (project, 1956-60). Press release, Harvard University Graduate School of Design, to Sunday papers of February 24 1957; Serge Chermayeff Archive, Avery Library.

• *Boston Sunday Herald*, 24 February 1957, p.54.
• Foell, Earl, 'Harvard Professor Twins Privacy and Quiet in House for Urban Living', *Christian Science Monitor*, 25 February 1957, p.6.
• *Architectural Record*, CXXI, March 1957, p.404.
• *New York Herald Tribune*, 10 March 1957.
• *New York Times*, 10 March 1957, Sect.2, pp.1, 4.
• 'The Patio House', *Harvard Alumni Bulletin*, 16 March 1957, pp.464-5.
• *Post* (Houston, Texas), 1 April 1957.
• *Interiors*, CXVI, July 1957, p.200.
• *American City*, LXXII, July 1957, p.200.
• *Topeka Kansas State Journal*, 5 September 1957.
• Springer, John L., 'Revolution in City Living: The "Walled House"', *This Week Magazine*, 1 September 1957, cover, pp.8-9.
• *House and Home*, XII, October 1957, pp. 140-140A.
• Rowntree, Diana, *Guardian*, 29 April 1964, p.9.
• Schoenauer, Norbert, and Seeman, Stanley (1962) *The Court Garden House*, Montréal, McGill University Press, pp.88-9.
• Macintosh, Duncan, *The Modern Courtyard House*, London, The Architectural Association, Paper No.9, 1973, pp.17-19.

**Unpublished texts**
• 'Memo to Dan Sert', Harvard University Graduate School of Design, January 1956.
• Untitled transcript from NBC 'Home' telecast, 10 April, 1956 (extract in Richard Plunz, ed. (1983) *Design and the Public Good*, Cambridge MA and London, MIT Press, pp.37-9).
• 'To Dean Sert, Re: General Policy of the Graduate School of Design', Harvard University, Graduate School of Design, 8 June 1956.

**1957**
Dissolution of architectural partnership with Heywood Cutting.

**Publications**
'The Shell Game', Letter to the Editor, *Architectural Forum*, CIX, July 1958, pp.54, 56.

**Other texts**
• 'Design and Transition: Architecture and Planning Purpose Examined in the Light of Accelerating Events,' talk at Dartmouth College Great Issues Course, 22 April 1957 (extract in Richard Plunz, ed. (1983) *Design and the Public Good*, Cambridge MA and London, MIT Press, 198pp.41-5).
• 'Modes and Manners in Art', talk at Brooklyn College, 20 May 1957 (extract in Richard Plunz, ed. (1983) *Design and the Public Good*, Cambridge MA and London, MIT Press, pp.271-6).
• Unidentified notes for television broadcast on Harvard Urban Family House Project, May 1957.
• 'Memorandum to Dean Sert', Harvard University,

Graduate School of Design, 17 December 1957.
• 'First Year Design Curricula', Harvard University, Graduate School of Design, 1957.

**1958**
Attempted to implement a PhD. and advanced research programme in design at Harvard.

**1959**
Received grant from Harvard-MIT Joint Center for Urban Studies for further development of the Harvard Urban Family House.
Summer: visited England.

**Publications**
• 'Transportation as a Builder of Cities', *Planning for Urban Transportation*, Ithaca, New York, Cornell University Department of City and Regional Planning, 1959.
• Talk given to Second Annual Spring conference of the Organisation of Cornell Planners, Ithaca, 20 March 1950.
• 'A Star is Sought - Some Disturbing Remarks on the Propensity to Create Architectural Heroes', Architectural Forum, CXI, August 1959, p.174.
• 'The Shape of Quality', *Architecture Plus*, no.2, 1959-60, pp.16-23.
• Talk at Texas A&M University, Department of Architecture, 17 March 1959.

**1960**
**Works**
• Competition entry for Franklin Delano Roosevelt Memorial (in association with Peter Chermayeff, Aram Mardosiam, Robert Reynolds).
• Creighton, Thomas H. (1961) *The Architecture of Monuments*, New York, Reinhold Publishing Corporation, p.133.
• Photoprints in Avery Library.

**Publications**
• *Shape of Privacy*, Cambridge, Massachusetts, Harvard University Graduate School of Design, 1961.
• 'The New Nomads', *Traffic Quarterly*, XIV, April 1960, pp.189-98.
• 'Statement of Serge Chermayeff, Professor of City Planning, Harvard University', *Cape Cod National Seashore Park Hearing of the Committee on Interior and Insular Affairs*, U.S. Senate, Eighty-Sixth Congress, Government Printing Office, 21 June 1960, pp.357-59.
• 'Statement of Serge Chermayeff, Professor of Architecture, Harvard University', *Cape Cod National Seashore Park Hearings, Eighty-Sixth Congress, Washington D.C.*, Government Printing Office, December 16 1960, pp.101-110.

**Unpublished texts**
• 'Scale, Shape, Mobility', talk to Division of

Architecture, Texas A&M University, 17 March. 1959
• 'The Shape of Quality', talk given at the Graduate
School of Design, Harvard, 16 April 1959 (extract in
Richard Plunz, ed. (1983) *Design and the Public Good*,
Cambridge MA and London, MIT Press, pp.171-6).
• 'Center for Urban Studies. Proposal for a Research
Project at the G. S. D., Harvard', May 1959.
• 'The Urban Family House. First Report on Progress',
Harvard University, 15 October 1959.
• 'Center for Urban Studies. Proposal for a Research
Project at the G. S. D., Harvard.' 'Revision', November
1959.

## 1961
### Unpublished text
• 'The Shape of Privacy', talk at Harvard University,
Graduate School of Design, 9 May 1961 (extract in
Richard Plunz, ed. (1983) *Design and the Public Good*,
Cambridge MA and London, MIT Press, pp.47-55).

## 1962
Resigned professorship at Harvard and took up
professorship at Yale.
### Works
• Chermayeff House, 28 Lincoln Street, New Haven,
Connecticut.
• *Architectural Design*, XXXIII, October 1963, pp.494-5.
• O'Brien, George, 'Designed for Privacy', *New York
Times Magazine*, 13 September 1964, pp.117-19.
• *Proa*, CLXIX, February 1965, p.12.
• *Arkkitehi-Arkitekten*, no.7-8, 1966, pp.100-1.
• *Baumeister*, LXIV, May 1967, pp.604-8.
*Gas + Architektur*, no.20, 1968, pp.12-17.
• Metz, Don, and Noga, Yuji (1966) *New Architecture in
New Haven*, Cambridge, MIT Press, pp.46-7.
• Hoffmann, Hubert (1967) *One Family Housing:
Solutions to an Urban Dilemma*, London, Thames and
Hudson, pp.147-9.
• Macintosh, Duncan, *The Modern Courtyard House*,
London, The Architectural Association, Paper No.9,
1973, pp.17-19.
### Publications
• 'Design of the Automobile', *Canadian Art*, XIX,
January 1962, pp.20-3.
• Frederick Shearman, 'Our Architects Get the Point',
*Miami Herald*, 28 January 1962, pp.5-6. Summary of
talk given at Florida South Chapter, American Institute
of Architects, 27 January 1962.
• 'Mobility and Urban Design', Program, Columbia
University School of Architecture, Spring 1962, pp.3-
12.
• 'The Hub of the Mater', Review of *The Turning Point
of Building: Structure and Design* (New York, Reinhold
Publishing Corp., 1961) by Konrad Wachsmann,
Progressive Architecture, XLVIII, May 1962, pp.196,

202, 208, 212.
• 'The Designer's Dilemma', *Yale Reports*, No.255, 20
May 1962.
• Review of James Marston Fitch (1961) *Architecture
and the Esthetics of Plenty*, New York, Columbia
University Press, Scientific American, June 1962,
pp.183-7.
• Edward J. Zagorski, ed. *Serge Chermayeff, Heinz von
Foerster, Ralph Caplan, Sibyl Moholy-Nagy: A Panel
Discussion*, Chicago, Industrial Design Education
Association, 1962.
• Talk to second annual meeting of the Industrial
Design Education Association, University of Illinois, 17
March 1962.
### Other texts
'The Designer's Dilemma.' Talk to the Annual Spring
Convocation, Yale Arts Association, 14 April 1962
(extract in Richard Plunz, ed. (1983) *Design and the
Public Good*, Cambridge MA and London, MIT Press,
pp.179-184).

## 1963
### Works
• *'New Urbanity' Project*, Yale University School of Arts
and Architecture.
• 'Search for a New Urbanity', *Ekistics*, XVI, November
1963, pp.301-5.
• Tzonis, Alexander, 'Search for a New Urbanity:
Commentary', *Ekistics*, XVI, November 1963, p.306.
### Publications
• With Christopher Alexander (1963) *Community and
Privacy: Towards a New Architecture of Humanism*, New
York, Doubleday & Co. Ltd., (excerpts published in
'The Future of the American City', *Current*, No.42,
October 1963, pp.58-63).
• Review of *Guide to Modern Architecture*, (London: The
Architectural Press, 1962) by Reyner Banham. The
Architectural Forum, CXVIII, March 1963, p.145.
• 'Let Us No Make Shapes: Let Us Solve Problems',
*Four Great Makers of Modern Architecture*, New York,
Columbia University School of Architecture, 13 April,
1961.
### Other texts
• Unidentified radio interview. Minneapolis, April
1963.
• 'In Search of a New Urbanity', talk at the Walker Art
Institute, Minneapolis, April 1963; also given at
Baltimore Museum of Fine Arts, October 1963, and
University of Illinois, Chicago, November 1963.
• 'Some Thoughts on the Architectural Condition', talk
at University of California at Berkeley, 18 September
1963.
## 1964
March: lecture tour in England, sponsored by Williams
& Williams Ltd., including seminars at University

of Liverpool.

**Works**

• New Haven Redevelopment Study, Yale University School of Arts and Architecture.

• Drogan, Marc, 'Space for Improvement', *New Haven Register Sunday Pictorial*, 17 May 1964, p.4.

**Publications**

• 'From the other End of the Spectrum: Some Thoughts on the Architectural Condition', *Yale Reports*, No.309, 19 January 1964.

• 'Education and Architecture', Letter to the Editor, *Architectural Forum*, CX, February 1964, p.40.

• 'From the Other End of the Spectrum', *Image 2*, University of Texas School of Architecture, May 1964. Talk given at University of Texas School of Architecture, March 1963.

• 'Private Affluence and Public Squalor', *Punch*, CCXLV, 17 June 1964, pp.880-3 (extract in Richard Plunz, ed. (1983) *Design and the Public Good*, Cambridge MA and London, MIT Press, pp.57-61).

• 'The Architectural Condition', *The Architectural Association Journal*, LXXX, July/August 1964, pp.45-50. Talk and discussion, *The Architectural Association, London*, 29 April 1964. Also published as 'La Prosperidad

• Privada y la Desidia Publica', *Proa: Urbanisme Arquitectura Industriel*, CLXIX, February 1965, pp.30, 32, 34, 1965.

• 'Jury Discussion', *Progressive Architecture*, XLVI, January 1965, pp.126, 168-70. Comments on entries to 1964 Progressive Architecture Annual Awards Competition.

• 'Random Thoughts on the Architectural condition', Marcus Whiffen, ed. (1965) *The History, Theory and Criticism of Architecture: papers from the 1964 AIA-ASCA Teacher Seminar*, Cambridge, The MIT Press, pp.23-36.

• Talk given at Cranbrook Academy, 9 June 1964 (extract in Richard Plunz, ed. (1983) *Design and the Public Good*, Cambridge MA and London, MIT Press, pp.187-90; 279-87).

• 'A Dilemma of Our Times', *Basis*, I, Auburn University School of Architecture and the Arts, Spring 1965, pp.7-10. Talk given at 'Eyes West 1963' Conference, Monterey, California, 14 September 1963.

• 'Architecture and the Computer', *Architecture and the Computer*, The Boston Architectural Center, 1965, pp.21-22, 44, 48-49, 50-51. Talk and discussion, The Boston Architectural Center, 5 December 1964. Excerpts also appear in 'Foot-dragging?' *Architectural and Engineering News*, VII, March 1965, p.96.

**Other texts**

• 'No Style-Either Regional or International', talk at University of California at Berkeley, 20 February 1964.

• 'What should our Environmental Goals Be?' talk to State of Connecticut Sixteenth Annual Development Conference, 1964.

• 'The Architect and the Future', identified as talk given to secondary school pupils as part of a Careers Advising Seminar, 1964.

## 1965

Grant from Twentieth Century Fund for study of formation of urban place, leading to material published in 1971 in *Shape of Community*.

**Unpublished texts**

• 'The Computer and the Humanities', talk at Yale University conference, 23 January 1965.

• 'Urban Environment Studies. A Proposal for Yale University', 11 February 1965.

• Untitled, talk at Louisiana State University, 1965.

## 1966

Grant from United States National Bureau of Standards for development of 'Yale Model', collaboration with Alexander Tzonis.

**Publications**

• 'Yale Model', Yale University School of Arts and Architecture, 1966-67.

• With Alexander Tzonis (1967) *Advanced Studies in Urban Environments*, New Haven, Yale University, Report for the Institute of Applied Technology, U.S. Bureau of Standards.

• Review of Architecture and the Computer, Bernard P. Spring, 'Review: Concerning Computers', *AIA Journal*, XLV, May 1966, pp.87-8.

• 'Environmental Design and Adaptation to Change', Urban Exploration, Florida State University, 1966 (talk given at the Urban Exploration Conference, Florida State University, 28 October, 1966, extract in Richard Plunz, ed. (1983) *Design and the Public Good*, Cambridge MA and London, MIT Press, pp.63-70).

**Other texts**

• 'Advanced Studies in Urban Environments', Yale University, School of Art and Architecture, 15 March 1966.

• 'Technology and the City Matrix', talk at Conference of National Bureau of Standards, University of California at Santa Barbara, 24 August 1966.

• 'Advanced Studies in Urban Design. Proposals for New Courses in the Department of Architecture, Yale', Fall 1966.

## 1967

**Works**

• Proposals of infill housing on Wooster Square, New Haven, for New Haven Redevelopment Authority (in association with Cambridge Seven Associates).

• Drawings in Avery Library.

**Publications**

• With Alexander Tzonis (1967) *Advanced Studies in Urban Environments*, New Haven, Yale University. Report for the institute of Applied Technology. U.S. Bureau of Standards.

• 'Collage of Concern', *Eye: Magazine of the Yale Arts Association*, No.1, 1967, pp.20-4.

• 'Design as Catalyst', *Socio-Economic Planning Sciences*, I, 1967, pp.63-9.

• Talk at University of Illinois, Urbana, 13 March 1967 (extract in Richard Plunz, ed. (1983) *Design and the Public Good*, Cambridge MA and London, MIT Press, pp.289-95).

**Other texts**

'Shape of the Urban Community: Humanistic Considerations', talk at New York Academy of Sciences, 19 October 1967.

**1968**

Participated in organising protest against the State Street Highway Scheme in New Haven.

**Publications**

*'Urban Yardstick' Project*, Yale University School of Arts and Architecture.

**Other texts**

• 'Urban Commitments and a Theory of Design', talk to Yale University Department of City Planning. October 1968.

• 'Formal and Structural Changes in Human Settlements', undelivered talk for 14th Triennale, Milan, 1968.

**1969**

June: fire in top two floors of Art and Architecture Building, Yale University, coincided with Chermayeff's retirement as Professor Emeritus.

Invited to visit India, travelled via Ankara to deliver lecture.

**Publications**

• With W. Mitchell, ed. *Synopsis of Conclusions and Record of Process, The Chermayeff Studio, Autumn 1968-69* (photostated booklet), New Haven, Yale University School of Arts and Architecture, January 1969.

• 'Urban Commitments', *Novum Organum*, 3, Yale University School of Architecture, 6 January 1969.

• 'Physical Mobility and Social Change', *Yale Reports*, No.501, 2 February 1969.

• 'No Simple Answers', *Modulus*, 5, University of Virginia School of Architecture.

**Other text**

'Architecture of the Human Environment', talk at the Middle East Technical University, Ankara, 19 December 1969.

**1970**

Two-month research period in India.

**Publication**

'Mathematics at Yale: Readers Respond', Letter to the Editor, *The Architectural Forum*, CXXXIII, October 1970, p.65.

**Other text**

'Design of the Physical Environment in India-Professional Standards and Education', report to the JDR 3rd Fund, 31 March 1970.

**1971**

Travelled to lecture in Australia and New Zealand.

**Publications**

• With Alexander Tzonis, *Shape of Community. Realisation of Human Potential*, London and Baltimore, Penguin Books.

• 'After S.S.T.: A Look Ahead', letter to the Editor, *New York Times*, 15 April 1971.

• 'Design as a Catalyst', *Architecture in Australia*, August 1971, pp.631-7.

• The A.S. Hook Memorial Lecture given at the Australian Institute of Architects Centenary Convention, 22 May 1971.

• 'The Shape of Humanism', *Arts and Society*, VII, The Pennsylvania State University, 1971, pp.517-31, talk and discussion at the Pennsylvania State University, 17 November 1970.

• 'On Urbanisation, Broad Frameworks, and Commitment', Printout, The Australian Architectural Students Association, 1971; talk and discussion, the Australian Architectural Students Convention, 16-23 May, 1971.

• 'Shape of Community', Transportation, Proceedings of the Fifth Boston Architectural Center Lecture Series, 1971, pp.7-14; talk and discussion at Boston Architectural Center, 27 January 1971 (extract in Richard Plunz, ed. (1983) *Design and the Public Good*, Cambridge MA and London, MIT Press,pp.73-85).

**1972**

Completion of additions to house at Cape Cod, sale of house in New Haven.

**Unpublished texts**

'The Shape of Community Revisited', talk at Yale University, 26 April 1972 (extract in Richard Plunz, ed. (1983) *Design and the Public Good*, Cambridge MA and London, MIT Press, pp.193-8).

**1973**

June: Received Gold Medal from the Royal Canadian Institute of Architects, Montreal; exhibited at one-man show at the Cherrystone Gallery, Wellfleet, Massachusetts.

**Publications**

• *Verses of Anger and Affection, 1957-1973*, Orleans, Massachusetts, Tompson's Printing.

• With Barbara Chermayeff and Sibyl Perry, 'Running Amok in Paradise', Letter to the Editor, *Cape Codder*, 24 May 1973, Sect.2, p.2.

• 'Some Journeys in Search of Questions', Samuel P. Snow, ed. *The Place of Planning*, Auburn, Alabama, Auburn University Graduate School, November 1973, pp.55-64 (extract in Richard Plunz, ed. (1983) *Design and the Public Good*, Cambridge MA and London, MIT Press, pp.87-9).

• 'The Shape of Humanism', Gregory Batcock, ed. (1973) *New Ideas in Art Education*, New York, E.P. Dutton, pp.3-10.

**Other text**

Untitled Gold Medal acceptance speech, Royal Canadian Institute of Architects, Montreal, 1 June 1973 (extract in Richard Plunz, ed. (1983) *Design and the Public Good*, Cambridge MA and London, MIT Press, pp.297-9).

## 1974

Conducted graduate seminar on contemporary issues in architecture at Harvard.

**Publications**

• 'Institutions, Priorities and Revolutions', The Future Role of Professionals in the Built Environment, Cambridge, Harvard University, 1974. Talk at Harvard University, Graduate School of Design, 1 May, 1974 (Gropius Lecture - extract in Richard Plunz, ed., (1983) *Design and the Public Good*, Cambridge MA and London, MIT Press, pp.201-11).

• *'In Search of Questions', The John William Lawrence Memorial Lectures, Serge Chermayeff, 1974*, New Orleans, Tulane University School of Architecture, 1974. Talk and discussion at Tulane University, New Orleans, 19 April 1974.

## 1976

Invited to Cornell University for conference on New Directions for American Architects.

**Unpublished text**

Untitled notes for the conference, 'The Future of Architecture,' Cornell University, October 1976.

## 1977

Exhibited in one-man show at the Wolcott Library in Litchfield, Massachusetts.

## 1978

**Publications**

'Values and Ethics: The Continuity of Change', *Crit*, 4, Association of Student Chapters, AIA, Fall 1978, pp.19-21. Talk given at the State University of New York at Buffalo, School of Architecture and Environmental Design, 7 November 1977. Also published as 'Values and Ethics in Design and Planning Profession:

Questions and Answers', *Spazio e Società*, No.6, June 1979, pp.93-7, 114-16 (extract in Richard Plunz, ed. (1983) *Design and the Public Good*, Cambridge MA and London, MIT Press, pp.301-5).

## 1979

Exhibited in one-man show at Kendall Gallery, Wellfleet, Massachusetts, and at New Art Centre, London.

**Publications**

'An Explosive Revolution', *Architectural Review*, CLXVI, November 1979, p.309 (full original text in Richard Plunz, ed., (1983) *Design and the Public Good*, Cambridge MA and London, MIT Press, pp.213-17).

## 1980

Accepted visiting professorship at Ohio State University. Received American Institute of Architects Association of Collegiate Schools of Architecture Award for Excellence in Architectural Education.

Travelled to London for the last time to recieve Misha Black Award and deliver lecture.

**Publications**

• 'Think before Acting', *AIA Journal*, LXIX, April 1980, pp.58-61. Talk given at Ohio State University, 13 February 1980.

• 'Serge Chermayeff. The Man Who Received This Year's Sir Misha Black Memorial Medal for Distinction in Design Education Reviews His Teaching Career', *Designer*, Society of Industrial Artists and Designers, London, December 1980, pp.7-8.

**Other texts**

• Untitled talk for ASCA Annual Meeting, San Antonio, March 1980.

• 'Continuity and Change. Concern and Commitment', talk to International Design Conference, Aspen, Colorado, 18 June 1980.

• 'Continuities and Changes. Concerns and Commitments', talk to Illinois Council of American Institute of Architects Annual Convention, 12 September 1980.

• Untitled notes for talk to Architectural Student Chapters Annual Meeting, American Institute of Architects, Temple University, 25 November 1980.

• 'Environmental Design is Our Task' tape and slide set, Pidgeon Audio-Visual PAV 5/8017, distributed by World Microfilms, London.

## 1981

'The Third Ecology' (speech on receiving the second Misha Black Memorial Medal of the Society of Industrial Artists and Designers), *DIA Yearbook*, 1981, pp.5-10 (extract in Richard Plunz, ed. (1983) *Design and the Public Good*, Cambridge MA and London, MIT Press, pp.91-100).

**1982**
With Cambridge Seven Associates, alterations to
Cutting House, Truro, Massachusetts for Raymond
Nasher.

**1983**
Publication of *Design and the Public Good*, edited by
Richard Plunz.

**1985**
Interview by Betty Blum for Art Institute of Chicago,
Chicago Architects Oral History Project.

**1990**
*Verses and Prints: Anger and Affection II 1974-1990*,
Cape Cod, Corrected, Connected, Edited, Arranged,
Printed by Ellen Sue Turner, San Antonio, Texas.

**1993-4**
Interviewed by Victoria Milne.

**1996**
8 May: death of Serge Chermayeff at Wellfleet.

# Bibliography and Archive Sources

### Bibliography of general secondary writings

'A London Furnishing Studio – Mr. S. Chermayeff, Director of the Modern Art Studio and Department of Messrs. Waring and Gillow Ltd., Comments on the New Movement', *Cabinet Maker and Complete House Furnisher*, 25 January 1930, pp.158-61.

'The Makers of Broadcasting House', *Country Life*, 28 May 1932, p.603.

'Viewpoint', *House and Garden*, 1959, pp.52-54.

'Chermayeff's Warning to Architects', *Architect and Building News*, 6 May 1964, p.781.

EJK III, 'Images - Serge Chermayeff - Impatience about Idiots', *The Summery*, (Cape Cod) 8 August 1969.

*Architects' Journal*, 22 October 1980 .

Plunz, Richard, ed. *Design and the Public Good. Selected Writings 1930–1980 by Serge Chermayeff*, Cambridge MA and London, MIT Press, 1983.

Tilson, Barbara, 'The Modern Art Department, Waring & Gillow, 1928-1931', *Journal of the Decorative Arts Society*, No.8, 1984, pp.40-49.

Tilson, Barbara, 'Form and Function', Building Design, 4 December 1987, pp.15-17.

Tilson, Barbara, 'Plan Furniture 1932-1938: the German Connection', *Journal of Design History*, III, Nos.2-3, 1990, pp.145-155.

Blake, Peter, *No Place Like Utopia, Modern Architecture and the Company We Kept*, New York, Knopf, 1993.

Powers, Alan, 'Spirit of Modernism', *Architects' Journal*, 19 October 1995, pp.24-26.

MacCarthy, Fiona, Obituary, *Guardian*, 11 May 1996, p.28.

Powers, Alan, Obituary, *Independent* (London), 14 May 1996, p.12.

Obituary, *Daily Telegraph*, Obituary, *The Times*, 16 May 1996.

Obituary, *New York Times*, Powers, Alan, Obituary, *Architects' Journal*, CCIII, 16 May 1996, p.16.

Tilson, Barbara, Obituary, *Building Design*, no.1265, 17 May 1996, p.8.

Obituary, *Architecture* (AIA), LXXXV, June 1996, p.61.

Obituary, *Architectural Record*, CLXXXVII, July 1996, p.29.

'E morto a 96 anni, Serge Chermayeff', *Architettura Cronache e Storia*, XLII, 1996, pp.324-45.

Tzonis, Alexander, 'Serge Chermayeff, umanista/Serge Chermayeff, humanist', *Spazio e Società`*, XIX, July-Sept 1997, pp.12-25.

Vance, Mary, Bibliography of Serge Chermayeff, Benton, Charlotte, 'Buildings in England and the Partnership with Serge Chermayeff 1933-1941', in Regina Stephan, ed. (1998) *Erich Mendelsohn 1887-1953*, New York, Monacelli Press, pp.190-203.

Heinze-Greenberg, Ita, 'The Mediterranean Academy Project and Mendelsohn's Emigration', in Regina Stephan, ed. (1998) *Erich Mendelsohn 1887-1953*, New York, Monacelli Press, pp.182-189.

## Unpublished

Plunz, Richard, 'Chermayeff as Educator', 1980.

'Oral History of Serge Chermayeff, F.A.I.A., interviewed by Betty Blum, compiled under the auspices of the Chicago Architects Oral History Project, Department of Architecture, The Art Institute of Chicago, 1986.

Tilson, Barbara, 'The Architecture and Design of Serge Chermayeff 1928-1939', MA in History of Art and Design, City of Birmingham Polytechnic, School of History of Art and Complementary Studies, May 1984.

Milne, Victoria, 'Never Trivial', typescript based on interviews with Serge Chermayeff and his colleagues, 1996.

## Archive Sources

### Germany

Berlin: Bauhaus Archiv Papers relating to Institute of Design, Chicago, 1947-51.

### Great Britain

Dartington, Devon: Dartington Hall Records Office, High Cross House, Dartington Box File LKE general, 14, Upper Brook Street and additional correspondence with Leonard Elmhirst in 1939.

London: RIBA Library, 66 Portland Place, London W1 Manuscripts collection: letter to Jonathan Glancey, sundry letters in other collections.

Drawings Collection: see printed catalogue volume 'C', Farnborough, Gregg Press, 19xx, with additional items added subsequently.

Norwich: University of East Anglia, Jack Pritchard Papers, catalogue online.

### USA

Cambridge: Harvard University Archives Files relating to Chermayeff's teaching.

Files relating to Chermayeff's involvement in American Society of Architects and Planners.

Cambridge: Harvard Graduate School of Design archives A small number of letters and photographs, one montage picture by Chermayeff.

New Haven: Yale University Archives

New York City: Cooper Union Museum: Designs relating to houses on Cape Cod.

New York City: Columbia University, Avery Library Archives and Drawings Collection. The major Chermayeff archive of letters, photographs and papers, including two videotapes. Drawings, all post 1940.

# Index

# Picture credits and sources

Chapter 1
Frontispiece: Architectural Press
pp.6, 7,8, 14: Chermayeff family
p.14 *Illustrated London News*, 31 October 1925, p.853.
Courtesy of the Illustrated London News Picture
Library;
p.19: (left) *Decorative Art, 1930*, London, The Studio,
1930, p.59
p.19 (right): John C. Rogers, *Modern English Furniture*,
London, 1930, p.30)
p.20 (left): ibid, p.52
p.20 (right) *Decorative Art, 1930*, London, The Studio
Ltd., 1930, p.91
p.21: ibid, p.60; p.22: *Cabinet Maker and Complete
Home Furnisher*, 25 January, 1930, p.158
p.23: *Architectural Review*, February 1932, p.76
p.24: *Architectural Review*, July 1930, p.40
p.25: *Innen Dekoration*, August, 1930, p.32. Courtesy
of *Architektur Innenarchitektur Technischer
Ausbau*/Verlaganstalt Alexander Koch, Leinfelden-
Echterdingen, Germany
p.26: ibid, pp.323, 318, 319; p.27, ibid., p.320
p.29: *Moderne Bauformen*, XXX, May 1931, p.218
p.31: ibid, p.219; p.32, ibid, p.224.

Chapter 2
pp.36 & p.49 (right): *Decorative Art Yearbook, 1934*,
London, The Studio, 1934, p.53
p.37, Architectural Press
p.44: (left) *Architectural Review*, August 1932, p. 55;
(centre) p.56, (right) p.68
p.48: *Architectural Review*, July 1933, p.20
p.49(left): *Design for Today*, February 1934, p.59
p.51, author's collection
p.54: *Design for Today* July 1933, p.94; p.56: *Design for
Today*, January 1934
p.57: *Architectural Review*, September 1934, p.105
p.58: *Design for Today*, October 1933, p.239
p.59: *Architectural Review*, December 1935, p.282.

Chapter 3
p.62, Architectural Press
p.63 (left and right): *Architectural Review*, March 1935,
p.106
p.64, *Architects' Journal* , 10 May, 1934, p.687
p.66 (left) Chermayeff family; (right) reproduced from

Christopher Skelton, *The Engravings of Eric Gill*,
Wellingborough, Skelton's Press, 1983, p.398
p.69: Chermayeff family
p.71: (top and bottom) *Architects' Journal,* 8 February,
1934, p.213
p.72, (top and bottom) ibid, p.213; p.73: (left)
*Architects' Journal*, 12 December 1935, p.882, (right)
p.883
p.74: (left and centre) Chermayeff family; (right)
*Architectural Review*, July 1935, p.27
p.75: (left) Chermayeff family,
(centre) author's collection, (right) *Architectural Review*,
July 1936, p.22
p.76: © English Heritage/NMR
p.77: (left and right) © English Heritage/NMR
p.78: *Architectural Review*, July 1935, pl.iii, facing p.42
p.79: © English Heritage/NMR
p.81: © English Heritage/NMR
p.83: (top left) RIBA Library Drawings Collection; (top
right) F. R. S. Yorke, *The Modern House in England*,
London, Architectural Press, 1937, p.110; ( bottom left
and right) Architectural Press
p.84: (left and right) Architectural Press; p.86:
Architectural Press
p.86: (left) Yorke 1937, p.36, (right) Architectural Press
p.87: Architectural Press; p.88 (top) Architectural Press,
(bottom left) *Architectural Review*, April 1936, p.164;
(bottom right) Ben Nicholson, Naum Gabo and J. L.
Martin, eds., *Circle*, London, Faber & Faber Ltd., 1937,
Architecture pl.11
p.90 Kunstbibliotek, Staatliche Museen Preussicher
Kulturbesitz, Berlin, Mendelsohn collection
p.91 (left and right) Ella Carter, *Seaside Houses and
Bungalows*, London, 1937, p.40.

Chapter 4
pp.97 & 111: © English Heritage/NMR
p.100: *Architects' Journal*, 28 March 1935, p.482;
p.102: *Architects' Journal*, 27 January 1938, p.155
p.104: *Architectural Review*, March 1934, p.80
p.105: Architectural Press
pp.106, 108 109: © English Heritage/NMR
p.110: *Architects' Journal*, 15 July 1937, p.101; p.112:
(left and right) © English Heritage/NMR; p.113:
*Architectural Review*, March 1938, (left) p.117, (right)
p.121; p.114: *Architectural Review*, March 1938, (left)

p.123, (right) p.119.

## Chapter 5

pp.118 & 126: Architectural Press
p.124: *Architects' Journal,* 18 February, 1937, p.293
p.122: Architectural Press
p.123: *Architectural Design and Construction,* August, 1937, p.388
p.129: Architectural Press
p.130: *Architectural Review,* January 1939, p.69
p.130: (top left and two bottom) Architectural Press, (top right) Country Life Picture Library
p.126: (top left) Country Life Picture Library, (top centre and right) Architectural Press, (bottom) *Architectural Review,* January 1939, pp.70-1, image from Richard Plunz, *Design and the Public Good,* Cambridge MA & London, MIT Press, 1983, p.122
p.127 (left and right) Architectural Press; p.129: Architectural Press
p.132: Chermayeff family
p.133 Chermayeff family
p.134: *Architectural Review,* January 1939, p.62
pp.135, 136: Avery Architectural and Fine Arts Library, Columbia University in the City of New York
p.138: Architectural Press

## Chapter 6

pp.142 & 177 (top): Chermayeff family
p.151: Revere Copper/Brooklyn College, *A Children's Center and Nursery School,* 1944
p.154: Museum of Modern Art, New York
p.177 (bottom) *L'Architecture d'Aujourd'hui,* February 1950, p.54; (top) ibid.,
p.178; (top) ibid., p.53; (centre) ibid., p.55; (bottom) ibid., p.59;
p.179: (top) ibid., p.59; (bottom), ibid., p.55
p.180 (left) ibid., p.55, (centre) ibid., p.66, (right) Chermayeff family
p.181: Chermayeff family.

## Chapter 7

pp.188 & 216 (right): Norman McGrath
p.195 Chermayeff family
p.199-200: Chermayeff family
pp.201-205: Chermayeff and Alexander, *Community and Privacy,* New York, Doubleday, 1963
p.208: Chermayeff family
p.211 (all images) Pidgeon Audio-Visual
p.213: (left) Chermayeff family, (right) Chermayeff and Tzonis, *Shape of Community,* Harmondsworth, Penguin Books Ltd., 1971
p.214 ibid., (left) p.152, (centre) p.188, (right) p.79
p.215: ibid., (left) p.103, (right) p.208
p.216: ibid, p.237.

## Chapter 8

pp.220 & 236 (left): Chermayeff family
p.222: *Architectural Review,* July 1947, p.43
p.223: (top left) ibid., p.43, (top right group) p.45; (bottom left and right) p.44;
p.225: (top left and centre) *Architectural Review,* July 1947, p.46, (top right) Marc Treib, (bottom left and centre) Plunz 1983, p.148, (bottom right) *Architectural Review,* July 1947, p.45
p.227: *Architectural Forum,* May 1943
p.228: ibid.
p.230: (top) Chermayeff family, (bottom), Victoria and Albert Museum (Circ.562-1954), V&A Picture Library
p.222: (left) Plunz 1983, p.192; (centre) Ezra Stoller ©Esto, (right) RIBA Library Drawings Collection
p.233: (top left) Ben Schnall, (top right) Plunz 1983, p.170, (bottom three) Norman McGrath
p.234: (left) Chermayeff family, (centre) Norman McGrath, (right) Ben Schnall
p.235 Cooper-Hewitt National Design Museum, Smithsonian Institution/Art Resource, New York
p.236: (left) Chermayeff family, (centre and right) Hans Namuth, p.237: courtesy Professor Aileen Ward
p.238: (left) Hans Namuth, (centre and right) Avery Architectural and Fine Arts Library, Columbia University in the City of New York
pp.239-41: Chermayeff family
p.242: Plunz 1983, p.288
p.243: Norman McGrath
p.245: Norman McGrath.

## Conclusion

pp.248 & 250 (left): Chermayeff family
p.250: (right) Chermayeff family.

## Colour

p.155: (top) *Studio,* XCVII, 1929, p.133, (bottom) Derek Patmore, *Colour Schemes and Modern Furnishing,* London, The Studio, 1945, p.23
p.156: (top) Victoria and Albert Museum (V&A T.157-1978) V&A Picture Library, (bottom) Moderne Bauformen, XXX, May 1931
p.157: (top) *Architectural Review,* August 1932, Pl.V, (bottom) ibid, pl.V
p.158: *Architectural Review,* November 1932, p.215
p.159: (top) *Decorative Art, 1936,* p.89, (bottom) from Serge Chermayeff, *The Application of Colour in Modern Buildings,* 1935, RIBA Library Drawings Collection
p.160: (top) *Decorative Art, 1936,* p.51, (bottom) Chermayeff family
p.161: (top and bottom) Chermayeff family
p.162 Avery Architectural and Fine Arts Library, Columbia University in the City of New York
p.163: (top) author's collection, (bottom) Chermayeff family

p.164 (top and bottom) RIBA Library Drawings
Collection
p.165: (top and bottom) Chermayeff family
p.166: (top and bottom) Norman McGrath
p.167: Norman McGrath
p.168 (top) Chermayeff family, (centre) RIBA Drawings
Collection, (bottom) Chermayeff family
p.169: Norman McGrath
p.170 (top) Norman McGrath, (bottom) *LIFE*
magazine
p.171: (top) Norman McGrath, (bottom) Chermayeff
family
p.172: (top and bottom) Chermayeff family
p.173 (top and bottom) Chermayeff family
p.174: (top and bottom) Norman McGrath.

Back cover: Chermayeff family

All pictures are reproduced with permission of the
copyright holders and their successors, insofar as it has
been possible to trace them.

# ARCHITECTURAL INFLUENCES: 1935-2035

1958  Design for new channel bridge.
Completion of first tower village in rural England (Corb-on-the-Ouse).
Foundation of International Faculty of Structural Art.
First tubo-aerial station in central London zone, connecting aerodrome with city centre.

1959  National Factory of Standard Autogyros built at Tunbridge Wells.
Advisory Panel of Architects appointed to all industries.

1960  Completion of seventh Soviet 5-year Plan.
First use in England of high-explosive for slum demolition.
Urban national distribution system extended throughout England.
Economic manufacture of new light-metal alloy.
Indirect main road and street lighting made compulsory: headlights illegal in urban zones and on main roads.
Fascist dictatorships in Europe.
International standardization of weights and measures.
Five-day week introduced.

1961  Birth of Oswald Benito Benetfink.
The "ergs" controversy.

1962  Discovery of universal "reflectant" (surface insulation), produced from celery.
Legalization of celery-board by National Building Standards Commission: intensive celery cultivation: revival of British agriculture.
Channel Bridge completed, to coincide with Brunel centenary celebrations.
Schools in urban districts compelled by Act to be at over twenty-storey level.
Mass production in U.S.S.R. of "Bassaltoid": (manipulated basalt, stronger than steel block).
Demolition of London University, under National zoning requirements.

1963  First Exhibition in new Permanent Building of Design in Haymarket.
Demolition of Olympia to make way for housing and mono-rail track.
First phantasmic salon at Burlington House.

1964  Round-the-world air race won by Petch and Olf.

### THE DEFENSIVE PERIOD

1965  General election: Fascist majority: first Fascist Government in England.
Period of "fear" architecture: first reconstruction of disused coal mines.
Appointment of National Board for Protective Planning.
First C.R.L. (resin) glazed house.

1966  Defensive architectural design becomes involved in "second battle of the styles"; vertical building versus horizontal-subterranean.
Religious revival: intensive building of churches.
Back to nature movement: "Tarzan Trip" holidays in National Parks.
Picturesque Manchester: Henekey's paper at the R.I.B.A.

1967  First English Air Defence Tower: triumph for vertical strategic building.
Invention of armour board (synthetic sheeting).
Rocket post introduced.

1968  Concrete casing to metal frame no longer compulsory under National Building Regulations.

1969  New Cathedral for the Christ Democrats started in Liverpool.
Anti-fog spray experiments.
C.R.L. (unbreakable) resin glazing becomes compulsory.

1971  A.A. visit to Greenland: beginning of post-pliocene revival.
First subterranean aerodrome.
"Plasto-crete" released for general use: shuttering becomes obsolete.

1972  Research in air-conditioning: opening of first of series of urban-district gas-proof chambers.
Abolition of independent Art Schools.
Art education taken over by the Ministry of Propaganda.
Adolf Halbmuller's lecture on Early Twentieth Century Tramways.

1973  Invention of "down explosives": defeat for vertical strategic building.
"Inso-crete" (insulation concrete) released for general building.

1974  Underground arms factories established.
Institution of a Nobel Prize for Architecture.
Railway termini moved outside central urban zone.
Exodus of British Socialist and Jewish professionals to Germany.
Burlington House Exhibitions taken over by Ministry of Propaganda.
Japan acquires Korea and Manchuckuo by agreement.

1975  International University and Library opened in Jewish State of the U.S.S.R.
Marina Waghorn, first woman president of the R.I.B.A.

1976  Completion of new Central London Elevated Aerodrome at King's Cross.
Seat of English Government moved to Cheltenham.
First Japanese-Continental Bridge.
Death of Joseph Bursting.

1977  First Greek-Orthodox service in the former Palace of the Soviets, now Russian National Cathedral.
Completion of Charing Cross Bridge scheme.
Experiments with the Knot-Hoffman synthetic radium process.

1978  England, allied with European Fascist States, declares war on Far East: second (Lutyens) Liverpool cathedral mistaken, in its unfinished state, for fort and utterly demolished.
R.I.B.A. absorbed by MARS as Royalist wing.
Japanese demolish New Delhi from the air.

1979  Publication of A.A. monograph on The Later Toltec Renaissance.
Charing Cross Bridge demolished in air attack.